Lecture Notes in Computer Science   5355

Commenced Publication in 1973
Founding and Former Series Editors:
Gerhard Goos, Juris Hartmanis, and Jan van Leeuwen

Emile Aarts   James L. Crowley
Boris de Ruyter   Heinz Gerhäuser
Alexander Pflaum   Janina Schmidt
Reiner Wichert (Eds.)

Ambient Intelligence

European Conference, AmI 2008
Nuremberg, Germany, November 19-22, 2008
Proceedings

 Springer

Volume Editors

Emile Aarts
Philips Research Europe, Eindhoven, The Netherlands
E-mail: emile.aarts@philips.com

James L. Crowley
INRIA Rhône-Alpes, Montbonnot, France
E-mail: james.crowley@inrialpes.fr

Boris de Ruyter
Philips Research Europe, Eindhoven, The Netherlands
E-mail: boris.de.ruyter@philips.com

Heinz Gerhäuser
Fraunhofer IIS, Erlangen, Germany
E-mail: heinz.gerhaeuser@iis.fraunhofer.de

Alexander Pflaum
Fraunhofer-ATL, Nürnberg, Germany
E-mail: alexander.pflaum@atl.fraunhofer.de

Janina Schmidt
Fraunhofer IIS, Erlangen, Germany
E-mail: janina.schmidt@iis.fraunhofer.de

Reiner Wichert
Fraunhofer-IGD, Darmstadt, Germany
E-mail: reiner.wichert@igd.fraunhofer.de

Library of Congress Control Number: Applied for

CR Subject Classification (1998): H.4, C.2, D.4.6, H.5, I.2, K.4

LNCS Sublibrary: SL 3 – Information Systems and Application, incl. Internet/Web
and HCI

ISSN   0302-9743
ISBN-10   3-540-89616-3 Springer Berlin Heidelberg New York
ISBN-13   978-3-540-89616-6 Springer Berlin Heidelberg New York

Springer is a part of Springer Science+Business Media

springer.com

© Springer-Verlag Berlin Heidelberg 2008
Printed in Germany

Typesetting: Camera-ready by author, data conversion by Scientific Publishing Services, Chennai, India
Printed on acid-free paper   SPIN: 12570553   06/3180   5 4 3 2 1 0

Preface

This volume contains the proceedings of the Second European Ambient Intelligence (AmI) Conference. The conference took place in Erlangen and Nürnberg, November 19–22, 2008. The concept of ambient intelligence (AmI) was introduced in the late 1990s as a novel paradigm for electronic environments for the years 2010-2020. It builds on the early visions of Weiser describing a novel mobile computing infrastructure integrated into the networked environment of people. According to early definitions, AmI refers to smart electronic surroundings that are sensitive and responsive to the presence of people. The added value for the multi-dimensional society we are living in lies in the fact that the large-scale integration of microelectronics into the environment enables people and objects to interact with this environment in a seamless, trustworthy, and natural manner.

Obviously, AmI solutions deliver a new quality of communication and information exchange, they help people to fulfill their professional tasks with increasing efficiency, enable the older generation to stay much longer in the privacy of their own homes and the younger one to lead a healthy and responsible life. Smart mobile devices navigate in private apartments as well as in complex public or industrial environments in order to support people with a broad variety of services. In logistics employees, smart objects and intelligent surroundings will be able to cooperate and use their communication and negotiation capabilities in order to avoid critical situations or to optimize processes. Today it is obvious that during the last few years Weiser's vision has grown mature in two complementary senses. On the one hand, the technological base is becoming more and more sophisticated. Today AmI solutions are based on electrical engineering, computer science, industrial design, user interfaces, and cognitive sciences. On the other hand, the spectrum of application domains has been extended a lot during the last two years. AmI solutions for private homes, hospitals, for the logistics services industry, for natural environments etc. are addressed in research and development projects financed by the European Union and national governments all over Europe.

AmI 2008 was the third joint conference that perpetuated two events focusing on ambient intelligence. The first event was the Conference on Smart Objects (sOc), which had been organized by France Telecom and by the French National Center for Scientific Research (CNRS) in Grenoble, France in 2001 and 2003. The second event was the European Symposium on Ambient Intelligence (EUSAI), which had been organized by Philips and the University of Eindhoven in Eindhoven, The Netherlands in 2003 and 2004. In 2005 the first joined conference of sOc and EUSAI was organized in Grenoble, France under the name sOc-EUSAI 2005. AmI 2007 in Darmstadt expanded the scope of the series by including three different types of contributions: research contributions, case studies as well as lessons-learned contributions and industry and socio-economic contributions.

During last year's discussion it became quite clear that the overwhelming economic potential of AmI can be realized only provided that technologies and applications perfectly meet people's needs. Solutions have to be embedded into services that deliver real value to the customer. Following that line of thinking, "Services for People" was the key theme of AmI 2008. The call for papers addressed researchers from academia and industry working on hardware and software, on applications and services, as well as on security aspects and ethical issues in order to create integrated and secure AmI solutions based on strong business cases. "Wellbeing and Care" and "Mobility and Logistics" were the two main fields of applications building the setting for technical research contributions, for case studies, for lessons-learned and socio-economic papers. The spectrum of "Wellbeing and Care" spanned from the exciting shopping event in the retail outlets of tomorrow to a service-oriented comfortable private home. "Mobility" addressed the freedom and flexibility of traveling as well as the efficient bridging of distances. In contrast, "Logistics" was connected to the autonomous and self-organized movement of vehicles, goods, and materials in intelligent environments, supply chains, and networks. The two different application or service domains were used to structure the current LNCS volume. Like AmI 2007, this year's conference provided the AmI research community with a venue to discuss in a less formal setting preliminary results and upcoming ideas through a number of workshops. Again we felt that we should not hold back the results obtained in these workshops as they are in many cases quite intriguing and therefore might be stimulating in the development of novel ideas. Therefore, we decided to publish these results in a separate Springer volume under the title *Constructing AmI—AmI 2008 Workshop Proceedings.*

The present volume shows quite clearly that the next steps toward the first implementations of AmI solutions in real life have been taken. The concept is obviously gaining ground. The fact that the "localization and positioning issues" presented in last year's proceedings have been converted into "navigation issues" in the current volume can be taken as a symptom for fundamental change. It seems that today AmI researchers focus much more on problems and services (like navigation) than on technological functions (like position sensing). Thus, research questions concerning social acceptance and security aspects in particular become more and more important and the fact that some of the papers in the current volume address these issues is quite promising. As indicated last year there is a growing awareness of the fact that the success of the AmI paradigm depends on the social acceptance of the newly proposed AmI technology.

The AmI 2008 proceedings can be considered as another important milestone on the scientific roadmap for developing the AmI paradigm. We are confident that they provide a significant contribution to the dissemination of the AmI vision. We would like to thank all those who have contributed – the authors of the research papers as well as the members of the Program Committee. Without their commitment and their enthusiasm neither the conference nor the proceedings would exist. We hope that you as a reader will have many inspiring and fruitful reading hours.

September 2008   Emile Aarts
                                                                                Heinz Gerhäuser

Message from the Program Chairs
"Wellbeing and Care"

At AmI 2008 the spectrum of "wellbeing and care" spanned from the service-oriented comfortable private home to an exciting shopping event in the retail outlets of tomorrow. This track focused on health care issues and measures of achieving wellbeing, exploring its far reaching impact on lifestyles in the ambient intelligence community.

Whereas ambient intelligence research has traditionally been focusing on user experiences in more entertainment-oriented scenarios, there is a recent move toward the deployment of ambient intelligence technologies for wellbeing and care-related application scenarios. Wellbeing and care applications cut across the domains of lifestyle (e.g., persuasive fitness applications) and healthcare (e.g., remote patient monitoring systems for chronic care patients). It should be clear that the development of applications related to our wellbeing and care will demand for some important shifts in the ambient intelligence research paradigm. New requirements for the enabling technologies that relate to ethics, new methodologies for empirical research to better understand the context in which these applications will be positioned, and a shift from system intelligence to social intelligence are just some examples of challenges that call for a paradigm shift in ambient intelligence research.

While technology is miniaturizing and becoming pervasive, ambient intelligence solutions can become actors in wellbeing applications. Rather than being limited to passive monitoring, the ambient intelligence solutions will influence and persuade end users to change their behavior or even modify their lifestyle. The care-focused application scenarios are clearly driven by demographic trends that are signaling the overwhelming need for ICT-based consumer care applications. One of the high potential growth areas is the elderly care domain: according to the World Health Organization, worldwide the proportion of people age 60 and over is growing faster than any other age group. Hence, there will also be a reduction in the number of people that can provide care to seniors. This clearly points to an opportunity for ambient intelligence solutions to support independent living for seniors. Ambient-assisted living refers to electronic environments that are sensitive and responsive to the presence of people and that provide assistive propositions for maintaining an independent lifestyle. The development of these solutions requires a continuous user involvement to ensure a seamless fit with user needs and preferences and to promote care provider endorsement.

The Wellbeing and Care track of AmI 2008 presented some important contributions in the following thematic sessions:

- Service-oriented smart and comfortable homes for better recreation and leisure time

- Intelligent and cooperative domestic devices for smart home and shopping environments
- Context-oriented health monitoring and alerting systems for a carefree life

Boris de Ruyter
Reiner Wichert

Message from the Program Chairs
"Mobility and Logistics"

The real power of ambient intelligence will become increasingly evident as ordinary objects, augmented with computing, communications, sensing and interaction, are increasingly integrated into everyday activities and environments. Thus we organized sessions 4 and 5 around the concept of mobility and interaction within ordinary environments and ordinary tasks.

Session 4 explores the use of mobile ambient intelligence for managing logistics and information. In the paper "Collect&Drop: A Technique for Multi-Tag Interaction with Real World Objects and Information," the authors investigate mobile interaction with multiple mobile objects, using tags to associate information with objects. This paper introduces the technique of collect and drop as a generic technique for multi-tag interaction that supports the collection, storage and management of information from the real world as well as its usage with different services.

In the paper "Tracking Outdoor Sports – User Experience Perspective," the authors examine the potential role for ambient intelligence in tracking outdoor sports. In a user study, the authors provided a mobile tracking tool and related Web services to a group of 28 participants. The system collected and stored workout data such as the route, speed and time, and compiled a training diary that can be viewed during exercise as well as afterwards. The user study illustrates the potential benefits of using mobile telephone technology to provide information both during and after outdoor sports.

The authors of "Rich Tactile Output on Mobile Devices" assess the potential of rich tactile interaction using mobile phones. The results of experiments with up to six actuators within a mobile phone prototype are presented. These experiments explore the user experience that can be created with multi-vibration output in a handheld device. The experiments suggest where vibration motors should optimally be placed and demonstrate that information can be reliably communicated by producing different patterns of vibration output using a small number of actuators.

The paper "Ambient Agent Model Exploiting Workflow-Based Reasoning to Recognize Task Progress" describes the use of a workflow model to allow an ambient agent to discretely recognize and model human activity without interaction.

The last paper of session 4, "An Architecture to Automate Ambient Business System Development," introduces a software architecture that allows the integration of real-world objects into business processes. This architecture decouples architectural concepts from technological solutions. Case studies are explored to illustrate the benefits of such an architecture.

Session 5 addresses the use of ambient intelligence for navigation and guidance in unknown environments and unusual situations. In the first paper, "C-NGINE: A Contextual Navigation Guide for Indoor Environments," the authors present a context-aware navigation guide that draws information from a user profile. The paper focuses on indoor environments and uses an ontology model expressed in OWL to capture and formally model user profiles and context information to provide personalized context-aware navigation services.

In "Creating Design Guidelines for a Navigational Aid for Mild Demented Pedestrians," the authors examine the design options for a GPS-based navigation aid for elderly with early-stage dementia. Lessons learned from a target group were used to design a Wizard-of-Oz experiment to study the effectiveness of landmark based vs left–right navigation instructions. This study shows that landmark-based instructions resulted in fewer errors and less hesitation.

Indoor navigation has the potential to become a popular application for mobile ambient intelligence. In the paper "Context-Aware Indoor Navigation,"the authors focus on path selection. Rather than simply present the shortest path, their system uses contextual information to suggest the most natural path for users. Experiments are described in which the system uses an efficient spatial representation to guide users.

James Crowley
Alexander Pflaum

Organization

General Chairs

Emile Aarts   Philips Research Laboratories Eindhoven
Heinz Gerhäuser   Fraunhofer Institute for Integrated Circuits IIS

Program Co-chairs Wellbeing and Care

Boris de Ruyter   Philips Research Laboratories Eindhoven
Reiner Wichert   Fraunhofer Institute for Computer Graphics IGD

Program Co-chairs Mobility and Logistics

James Crowley   INRIA Rhône-Alpes
Alexander Pflaum   Fraunhofer Center for Applied Research in
     Logistics ATL

Workshop Co-chairs

Christos Efstratiou   Lancaster University, UK
Jürgen Hupp   Fraunhofer Institute for Integrated Circuits IIS

Local Arrangements Chairs

Janina Schmidt   Fraunhofer Institute for Integrated Circuits IIS
Susanne Ruhland   Fraunhofer Institute for Integrated Circuits IIS

Program Committee

Raffaelle de Amicis   GraphiTech, Italy
Hellmuth Broda   Swiss Academy of Engineering Sciences,
     Switzerland
Adrian Cheok   National University of Singapore, Singapore
Joelle Coutaz   Université Joseph Fourier, France
Monica Divitini   Norwegian University of Science and
     Technology, Norway
Berry Eggen   Eindhoven University of Technology,
     The Netherlands

Table of Contents

Mobility and Logistics

Navigation and Guidance in Unknown Environments and Unusual Situations

Context-Oriented Health Monitoring and Alerting Systems for a Carefree Life

Designing Acceptable Assisted Living Services for Elderly Users

Martijn H. Vastenburg[1], Thomas Visser[1],
Marieke Vermaas[2], and David V. Keyson[1]

[1] ID-StudioLab, Faculty of Industrial Design Engineering, Delft University of Technology,
Landbergstraat 15, 2628 CE, Delft, The Netherlands
{M.H.Vastenburg,T.Visser,D.V.Keyson}@tudelft.nl
[2] Isolectra b.v., Department of Care Solutions, Rivium Boulevard 101, 2909 LK,
Capelle aan den IJssel, The Netherlands
Marieke.Vermaas@isolectra.nl

Abstract. With today's technology, elderly users could be supported in living independently in their own homes for a prolonged period of time. Commercially available products enable remote monitoring of the state of the user, enhance social networks, and even support elderly citizens in their everyday routines. Whereas technology seems to be in place to support elderly users, one might question the value of present solutions in terms of solving real user problems such as loneliness and self-efficacy. Furthermore, products tend to be complex in use and do not relate to the reference framework of elderly users. Consequently, acceptability of many present solutions tends to be low. This paper presents a design vision of assisted living solutions that elderly love to use. Based on earlier work, five concrete design goals have been identified that are specific to assisted living services for elderly users. The vision is illustrated by three examples of ongoing work; these cases present the design process of prototypes that are being tested in the field with elderly users. Even though the example cases are limited in terms of number of participants and quantitative data, the qualitative feedback and design experiences can serve as inspiration for designers of assisted living services.

Keywords: design of interactive products, acceptability, assisted living, elderly users.

1 Introduction

Demographic aging is a phenomenon that affects most industrialized countries. According to EuroStat, every 25 senior EU citizens in 2005 were matched with 100 citizens between 15 and 64 years old. This so-called old-age dependency ratio is expected to increase to 40 by 2030 [1]. The traditional elderly care system, which is largely based on human resources and centralized care institutions, has major difficulties in managing the increasing number of care clients. Not only do care companies have problems finding adequate professional caregivers, the societal cost of elderly care is also rising dramatically.

E. Aarts et al. (Eds.): AmI 2008, LNCS 5355, pp. 1–12, 2008.

Many elderly people indicate they would prefer to live independently in their own homes as long as possible [2], which was confirmed in our interview sessions. In many cases, however, support is needed to continue their everyday living routines. Whereas support is nowadays typically given by both professional and informal caregivers, support could in part be taken over and augmented by new technology. This assistive technology is expected to play an increasingly important role in the coming years [3].

When making an inventory of products that support independent living of elderly users, there are plenty of technological solutions available on the market. Typical examples include personal alarms, communication tools, remote monitoring of physical status, and home automation. Current products are generally not aware of the user's context. These products do not take into account the environment, behavior and current activities of the user. A typical solution offers remote access to physical status information such as blood pressure and blood sugar levels, regardless of the current user state. Increasingly, companies are working on products that are context-aware. Such products could help provide support that is tailored to the user's actual situations. Also, context-awareness enables efficient remote monitoring without extensive person-to-person communication. State-of-the-art products range from low-level sensor networks [e.g., 4, 5] to activity-awareness services [e.g., 6].

From a technological perspective, one might conclude that systems are in place to support elderly and improve well-being. When talking to end users, however, acceptability of new assisted living technology appears to be low. Many issues including usability problems, lack of user-perceived benefit, and user-perceived complexity of new technology are reflected in low acceptability scores of existing assisted living solutions [e.g., 7]. Products and services seem to be mostly designed to reduce the costs of professional caregivers, instead of enhancing the quality of life of the elderly user directly. Complexity of assisted living products might even increase due to the increased use of context-aware and pro-active technologies. Furthermore, existing products tend to be standalone rather than inter-connected in a meaningful way. Consequently, end users have to learn new interaction paradigms for each new product, and potential synergies and information-exchange between products are often not exploited. In short, research is needed in order to increase end user acceptability, thereby enabling industry to develop and market acceptable assisted living products.

This paper presents a vision of how to design acceptable and pleasurable assisted living products and services for elderly users. The end user group is primarily defined in terms of user needs, abilities and reference frame rather than age; the focus will be on senior citizens who can profit from assisted living technology towards living independently for a prolonged period of time, who are able to use assisted living technology, and who have similar living routines and a similar reference frame in terms of known metaphors. Acceptability issues of existing products and services were studied, and underlying design challenges were identified. A design approach is proposed in which perceived benefit by the end user and ease-of-use are used as guiding factors.

2 Design Vision

Earlier work [e.g., 7, 8, 9, 10, 11, 12] on acceptability of assisted living technology by elderly users has revealed multiple barriers that keep elderly users from adopting new technology, including:

- **Complexity and learnability.** Elderly often regard technology as to be complex in use, and they consider themselves incapable of mastering new products. This feeling of complexity is reinforced by the lack of standardization; elderly users have to learn operating instructions for each new product they like to use. Consequently, the initial hurdle towards adopting new products tends to be too high.
- **Lack of perceived benefit.** Even though the benefit of new technology can be evident for caregivers, since technology can help improve the efficiency of the care process as well as tailor the care to individual users, perceived benefit for the elderly themselves is often too low. Consequently, elderly often reason that they can just as well do without.
- **Compatibility issues.** Current products are often standalone. Information exchange between products is limited, resulting in suboptimal product behavior. Both product benefit and product use can be affected by compatibility issues.

Due to these issues, elderly users often consider the cost of adopting new technology higher than the expected benefit, resulting in a hesitant attitude towards innovations in general.

Acceptability could be improved by increasing the perceived benefit, as well as by decreasing the perceived cost. In terms of creating benefit, there is a need to make explicit and/or increase the direct benefit of new technology. Whereas for example professional caregivers would like to be able to monitor the presence of their clients using sensor systems, there might not be a direct benefit for the care clients. Care clients tend to be interested in issues such as establishing self-efficacy and countering social isolation. Leveraging benefit by linking a presence monitoring system to –for example- a fall detection system is expected to increase acceptability.

In terms of reducing cost, much effort has been put in improving product usability. For example, products that are potentially very complex to use, can be made easily accessible by designing the right user interface. In the current situation, however, interoperability between products is low. Potential synergies and information-exchange between products, in terms of improved awareness for caregivers and products that better consider the context of use in their adaptive behavior is low. Products are generally not aware of the context of use, and they do not embed in the living routines and context of use of elderly users.

Since perceived cost and benefit change in time, product adoption needs to be considered as a dynamic construct. Rather than focusing on initial product adoption, products should support altering user needs. When a new product is introduced to the users, accessibility and simplicity in terms of learning curve can contribute to acceptability. The same product might be rejected after a few weeks since the perceived benefit does not match the user expectations in time. In other words, the desired level of system complexity can be dynamically linked to the level of user experience.

Towards creating acceptable assisted living technology for elderly users, five concrete design goals have been identified. Even though each of these five goals might be 'common sense' for designers, these goals are considered crucial in view of problems with existing products and in respect to needs and challenges specific to assisted living services for elderly users based on earlier work and design experiences. These goals could therefore serve as inspiration for designers of assisted living services.

Goal 1: Short-term benefit should outweigh short-term cost
Acceptability primarily depends upon short-term benefits. Each product that requires effort from the elderly users needs to give immediate benefit to the elderly in return. External benefit (e.g., benefit for caregivers) needs to be accompanied by internal benefit (i.e., benefit for elderly users). Long-term benefit (e.g., healthy body) needs to be projected on short-term benefits (e.g., being able to visit grand children).

Goal 2: Relate to existing living patterns and known metaphors
Elderly users often have difficulties changing their living patterns and learning new interaction paradigms. New products should therefore fit into existing living patterns, rather than enforce new living patterns. By using metaphors that are already known and that fit into the reference framework of the elderly users, new products can be mastered more easily.

Goal 3: Multiple interfaces, uniform interaction patterns
Assisted living services will be used in different situations and for different purposes. A single central interface will not suffice; for example, a television-based interface when assisting elderly in the bathroom will result in higher cost, since the user has to take more effort using the interface. Alternatively, users might select the optimal interface based on the situation. This could range from a static TV-screen to a mobile tangible device. Uniform interaction styles create a coherent interaction experience, and will enhance the usability of the different devices.

Goal 4: Leverage existing social network
Rather than shifting responsibilities from caregivers and social networks to a techno-logical solution, products and services should respect existing traditions and responsi-bilities. Ideally, technology facilitates the process of human-human social interaction. For example, routine tasks with no social value could be taken over by an automated system, whereas human-human interactions could be encouraged. Likewise, caregiv-ers, family and friends could be involved in complex product operations; hard-to-use functions can then be shielded from elderly users.

Goal 5: Facilitate adaptation in time
User needs and skills change in time. When these changes affect acceptability of assisted living services, these services should be able to dynamically adapt to the changing contextual setting. Furthermore, since the changes in user needs might re-quire a change in services, a service platform should enable dynamic reconfiguration in order to cope with altering user needs.

To achieve these goals, designers need to carefully study the domestic routines, so-cial network, experiences, needs, values, limitations and potentials of the elderly us-ers. Designers can make more use of qualitative instruments such as interviews, diary studies, cultural probes and focus group sessions to elicit the required information. Information is needed not only on how people experience technology, but also on how people interact with products and people. Such insight enables designers to cre-ate interactions that are embedded in the daily lives and routines of people, thereby creating natural experiences. Also, such studies provide a baseline measure that can be used when evaluating the interventions that result from the newly designed products.

In order to understand the acceptability of design concepts, user studies with working prototypes need to be conducted. It is questionable whether or not user-product interaction with assisted living products and services can be studied in a laboratory setting. These products and services are generally linked to living routines, and the validity of studies of living routines in an artificial environment is not clear. Longitudinal field studies are therefore considered an essential part of the design process of assisted living services.

There is no single 'right' procedure for designing acceptable products and services for elderly. A central theme in the design process needs to be the involvement of the end users; the right tools and techniques depend on the problem at hand. The three cases as described in the next section serve as examples of how the design goals can be used to guide the design process.

3 Example Cases

Three example cases of ongoing work are described in the following sections. In these cases, end users have been involved in the early stages of the design process, in order to understand the user needs and reference framework. For each of the cases, the design goals as presented in section 2 have been used to guide the design process. The first example case has resulted in a prototype that has been tested in the field with users; the second and third case represent work-in-progress that yet has to be tested in the field. The findings are generally qualitative in nature; designers tend to be receptive to qualitative input in their design process.

3.1 CASE 1: Interactive Bulletin Board

A first case study focused on creating a message-based interaction platform. The main goal of the case study was to develop an easy-to-use communication product for elderly users [13]. The resulting design concept aims to create direct benefit for the end user (goal 1), is based on a known metaphor (goal 2) and aims to lower the threshold for communicating within the care network (goal 4) and family or friends at home. It was decided to consider multiple interfaces (goal 3) and adaptation in time (goal 5) in a later project.

For the targeted user group of older seniors with little or no prior experience with computers, message-based communication using the Internet could help maintain or improve their social network. Furthermore, a message display could be used to present system-generated messages, such as for example medicine reminders. A field exploration, which aimed to understand the user needs and the context of use, revealed that the user group was reluctant towards adopting new technology; even though they acknowledged the value of communication, they indicated that even though new technology could help, it would surely be too complex to use for them.

In informal interviews, five elderly care clients indicated that they regularly feel lonely, since the number of visits from relatives and friends is low. The feeling of isolation is strengthened by current developments in professional care that leave very little time for social interaction. The interviewees point out that they would like to be actively involved and contribute to the lives of people they know, rather than being dependent and passive. Whereas many of today's care products inflict stigmatization of the latter, they prefer products that do not underline their weaknesses. The care clients indicated a dislike of 'modern' interaction metaphors. Moreover, they were scared off by the complexity of new products in terms of for example functionalities and layered menu structures [9].

Towards finding existing products that could be used for creating an interaction metaphor for messaging systems, the designer visited the homes of the care clients. Participants were asked to describe objects in their homes that were valuable to them. Participants indicated that they most valued objects based on emotional value, in terms of memories and social ties. Souvenirs from abroad, drawings from grandchildren, and pictures of family and friends were also considered valuable. The home visits were also used to get to know the living environment of the participants, and as a source of inspiration for the design phase.

Three messaging metaphors were constructed and evaluated with a panel of three designers. First, a photo frame metaphor was considered. The photo frame represents social contacts; an enhanced photo frame could be used to display status information and to start communications. Second, a convenience chair based interaction metaphor was considered. Each participant had a convenience chair close to the television; since the chair was used a lot, it could be used as a central location for communication. Third, a bulletin board metaphor was considered. The bulletin board is a well-known mechanism to store reminders and notes. These three metaphors could be linked to context-aware technology, in such a way that the technical nature of the systems could be shielded from the users. The three concepts were evaluated based on ease-of-use, functionality, and 'naturalness' of the chosen metaphor. The bulletin board was found to be the most intuitive and would fit best in the homes of the target users.

In designing the electronic bulletin board, the functionalities and affordances of traditional bulletin boards were analyzed and mapped to electronic equivalents. Figure 1 shows the resulting working prototype. A touch screen interface is mounted on top of a secretaire. Using the touch screen, users can view and remove notes. New notes can be added using a scanner built in the secretaire. The number of functions available to the elderly is limited in order to improve system understanding; therefore, notes cannot be archived or re-arranged. In order to be able to save notes, a printer is attached to the system and integrated in the secretaire; a note can be printed by selecting an on-screen menu option on the touch screen.

The bulletin board is linked to an intelligent reminder service. When needed, a medicine reminder can be displayed using multiple levels of intrusiveness. Furthermore, the bulletin board is linked to the Internet. Family members, friends or caregivers can view and modify the contents of the bulletin board via a website. Adding, removing and modifying reminders is only possible using the website; elderly users were not exposed to these management tasks.

To assess the usability and acceptability of the design, the prototype was tested in the field. Field-testing was limited to two participants, four and seven days per participant respectively, due to time constraints. Participants were senior citizens (76 and 84 years old), both living independently in their own houses, taking medicines, and

Fig. 1. The interactive bulletin board provided the user with messaging functionality using a known interaction metaphor

both relying on professional care. Each participant asked a non-professional caregiver to take part in the test; these caregivers were asked to check and update the bulletin board via the website. The bulletin board was placed in the living rooms of the participants; the supervisor then gave an introduction to the bulletin board.

When looking for participants, several potential candidates indicated that they thought they were unable to control an electronic messaging board. Proper presentation of the test was found to be crucial towards recruiting participants. When targeting 'young' seniors rather than 'old' seniors, problems related to technophobia are expected to be of minor relevance. During the introduction of the bulletin board both participants indicated they were afraid of using technology repeatedly, even though they could not indicate why.

Preliminary results indicate that both participants were positive about the way they could interact with the system, and the functionalities the system provided. They considered the system to be a bulletin board rather than a computer system. Since the bulletin board was not experienced as a computer, the fear of using new technology was not found to be a problem during the test. Even though both participants had not used a touch screen before, they were able to control the interface without significant problems. In case the participants did not know how to manage their goals using the bulletin board, a trial and error approach generally led to the desired results. One participant tended to forget the skills right away; he had to re-learn much of the interface time and time again.

The user studies did provide feedback that can be used to improve the design of the bulletin board. First of all, personalization of the content was found to an important facilitator of acceptability. Whereas automated messages were impersonal, content provided by caregivers was personal. The participants explicitly indicated that their enthusiasm in terms of using the prototype was encouraged by personalized content.

Second, the touch screen was found to be a suitable interaction device for this specific application, as the users easily understood the link to the bulletin board metaphor. In order to fit in the user context and environment, some improvements could be made, e.g. regarding day/nighttime differences. One of the participants attempted and succeeded in switching off the system at nighttime because the screen was too bright. A backlit screen device should therefore adjust the brightness to the environment.

In terms of design goals, the bulletin board by nature scored high on short-term benefit (goal 1) and on leveraging the existing social network (goal 4); participants enjoyed the low-threshold communication to their care network that was provided by the system. The interaction metaphor was deliberately chosen based on the interviews and the home visits; the participants considered the system to be a bulletin board rather than a computer system, and intuitively knew how to use the system. This confirms the expected merits of using a known metaphor (goal 2).

3.2 CASE 2: Physical Exercise Coach

A second case study focuses on stimulating the physical activity of elderly people. The amount of physical activity of senior EU citizens tends to be below a healthy level. As a result, their physical condition deteriorates. Assisted living technology could be used to motivate elderly to exercise more. One solution might be to link coaching and motivations directly to the activities done by the elderly user. There are however practical obstacles towards deployment of automated motivational systems. First of all, the long-term benefit of physical exercise (i.e., a healthy body) often does not appeal to the short-term motivation. Secondly, the sensors and user interface that are inherent to automated solutions could scare off end-users. Third, from a technical point of view, it can be hard to measure actual physical activity levels that are needed to link an exercise coach to user activities.

The main goal of this example was to develop a motivational system that appeals to the elderly user group and the naturally fits into their existing living patterns (goal 2). In terms of motivation, the resulting system would have to link to short-term gains rather than long-term goals (goal 1). It was decided to consider the use of multiple interfaces (goal 3), social motivation (goal 4) and adaptation in time (goal 5) in a later project.

Towards selecting an effective motivational mechanism, persuasive principles as described by Fogg [14] were studied. Based on these principles, multiple design goals were defined, including allow self-monitoring of physical activity, induce intrinsic motivation, act at the right time (kairos), and enhance accessibility and simplicity. Three conceptual designs were created and evaluated with a user panel in a focus group session. The first concept was based on goal setting; graphs were used to continuously show progress and goals. The second concept was based on rewards; new family photos would be released when goals were met. The third concept was based on social actorship; a flower that would be happy when the exercise levels were good represented the activity coach.

Five elderly people were invited to join the focus group session. The goal of this session was to discuss the three concepts and to extract key elements of each concept that were or were not appreciated. The participants of the session explained that they would like to have a direct and simplified overview of their current status, so without too much detailed information. They also indicated that they would not like to have their family pictures linked to their activity, as it would seem an illogical link. They much rather would have the clear flower image, but with the possibility to ask for additional information when needed.

Strong elements of each of the three concepts were integrated in a final design: a photo frame sized screen displaying a happy to unhappy flower (figure 2, left), with a second layer of detailed information on activity performance (figure 2, right).

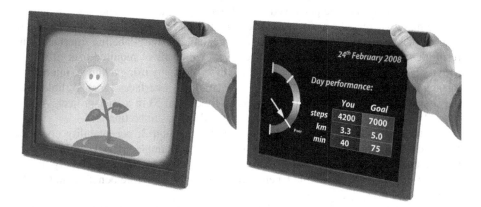

Fig. 2. A photo frame sized touch screen displaying a happy to unhappy flower (left) provides the user with up-to-date information on physical activity. Users can request a detailed overview of the activity levels in respect to preset goals (right).

A working prototype has been developed and will be tested in the homes of three elderly users. Whereas ideally the system would use real-time activity data, the current system is based on a FitSense ActiPed [15] pedometer that streams step-count data to a database on the Internet.

Towards creating a final version of the system, several challenges yet need to be solved. First, the goal setting mechanism needs to be elaborated. Medical doctors are not yet consulted towards setting exercise goals that are balanced with daily activity levels. An understanding of optimal exercise targets in relation to day-to-day activities is needed. Second, an understanding is needed of how automated exercise coaches can be used to actually change user behavior. Third, a non-intrusive mechanism is needed for real-time measurement of physical activity levels.

Even though objective ratings of the design concept cannot be given at this stage of the project, the use of the design goals guided the process towards a concept that supposedly easily fits in the homes and living routines of elderly people. User evaluations are planned to capture actual user experiences of participants for seven days in a row.

3.3 CASE 3: Activity Journal

A third case study focuses on creating a labeling mechanism for user activities. Activity recognition algorithms are increasingly being used not only to remotely monitor living patterns and detect irregular situations [e.g., 16], but also to link routine support to actual activities [17]. As described in section 4.2, one might even link a physical exercise coach to the actual activity levels based on activity recognition.

Activity recognition is based on identification of recurring patterns in sensor data. In order to be able to automatically recognize activities, activity recognition algorithms need to be trained using sensor data with activity labels. Since the sensor layout and user activities differ between people and between locations, algorithms need to be trained for each new setting.

The process of labeling activities might be experienced as interruptive and unacceptable by end users. The perceived cost of interrupted activities and requested effort can be high, whereas the short-term benefit might not be clear to the users. The main goal of the case study was to develop an acceptable activity-labeling interface. The resulting design concept aims to lower the cost (in terms of required user effort) of activity labeling (goal 1), and to improve the ease-of-use by using a known interaction metaphor (goal 2). It was decided to consider multiple interfaces (goal 3), linking to the social network (goal 4) and adaptation in time (goal 5) in a later project. A conceptual design is currently under development and yet has to be finalized.

In line with the first design goal, as stated in section 3, acceptability could be improved by increasing the immediate benefit, for example by developing a new service that uses activity information to support the user. In the present study, it was however decided to focus on the labeling interface only; therefore benefit could not be improved.

Instead, the cost of labeling could be decreased. One option would be to delegate the labeling effort to a third party. For example, all labeling questions could be sent to a family member, thereby shielding the labeling process from the elderly users. This would be in line with goal 4, but a problem would be that a delegate has no clear overview of the situation at hand, resulting in false labels. For the present study, it was therefore decided to involve the elderly users in the labeling process.

As the choice of interaction metaphor can affect the learnability and understandability of the final design, the first stage of the design process involved an exploration of suitable metaphors. First, a calendar metaphor was studied. Because activities are linked to time frames, a calendar seemed a logical way to present activities. A calendar-based concept was sketched and evaluated in a focus group session with five elderly users. The participants however indicated that a calendar metaphor led to false expectations and misunderstandings. They also stated that that they never write day-to-day activities in their home calendar, since they do not consider these activities as appointments. Therefore, the calendar metaphor was rejected.

A second concept is based on an activity journal metaphor, as a journal seems to be a logical place to write down activities. A journal-based interface could be used to present system suggestions and ask for user feedback. Furthermore, since the journal concept can easily be manifested in a mobile book-size device, technology does not seem to be a limitation for implementation. The journal could be placed on any location where elderly have the time and willingness to use it, for example on a coffee table.

This design process has so far resulted in a design concept (figure 3) that is focused on accessibility, understandability and direct feedback. This way, the design links to the design goals as described in section 3 in terms of relating to existing patterns and known metaphors (goal 2). As a next step, the concept is now being implemented in a working prototype, in order to collect user experiences in a realistic setting, and to iteratively improve the design.

Fig. 3. An activity journal enables elderly users to label activities while hiding system complexity

4   Discussion and Future Work

While assisted living technology is gaining attention of researchers and companies, an integrated user centered design vision in which the focus of user-product interaction is developed around end-user acceptability is lacking. Acceptability of current care products targeted at elderly users tends to be low.

The case studies as described in the present paper show how acceptability of assisted living products and services can be improved by a design vision targeted at creating short-term benefit, leveraging known interaction metaphors, and leveraging existing social networks. The design goals guide the design process, thereby making sure that the designer focuses on issues relevant to the domain and end user group. Even though the user studies so far were limited in duration and number of participants, the studies do suggest that the design concepts were acceptable; the elderly participants were willing to adopt the new technology, even though they were skeptical at first.

Only three of the five design goals were covered in the example cases; *multiple interfaces, uniform interaction patterns* (goal 3) and *facilitate adaptation in time* (goal 5) were not studied. Since none of the example cases resulted in a system with multiple user interfaces, uniform interaction was not an issue. Adaptation in time could not be covered by the case studies presented here; this goal will be studied as soon as a stable platform for longitudinal tests in the field is available.

Whereas the case studies were based on dedicated sensor systems and communication platforms, creating a generic activity-aware service platform could enhance the design process. A generic service platform is now being developed and will be deployed in a series of houses towards facilitating the iterative design of future prototypes. Furthermore, by linking multiple prototypes to a single platform, researchers will be able to study the use of multiple interfaces to a single system more easily, and they can better embed interactions in domestic routines of elderly users.

Acknowledgments. The work presented in this paper was part of the Independent at Home project, funded by SenterNovem through the IOP-MMI program. The authors like to thank Erwin van Veldhoven, Niels Bovendeur and Iñaki Merino Albaina for their contributions to the example cases. Thanks to the participants and the ID-StudioLab for their support throughout the product design and user studies.

References

1. Eurostat: Projected Old-Age Dependency Ratio,
   `http://epp.eurostat.ec.europa.eu/tgm/`
   `table.do?language=en&pcode=tsdde511`
2. Vermeulen, J.: Langer zelfstandig wonen en hoe ICT daarbij kan helpen. PhD Thesis, University of Tilburg, The Netherlands (2006)
3. Schuurman, J., Moelaert El-Hadidy, F., Krom, A., Walhout, B.: Ambient Intelligence. Toekomst van de zorg of zorg van de toekomst? Rathenau Instituut, Den Haag (2007)
4. Pervasa, `http://www.pervasa.com`
5. RF Monolithics, `http://www.rfm.com`
6. Innoviting, `http://www.innoviting.nl`
7. Melenhorst, A.S.: Adopting Communication Technology in Later Life. The Decisive Role of Benefits. PhD Thesis, Eindhoven University of Technology, The Netherlands (2002)
8. Czaja, S., Charness, N., et al.: Factors Predicting the Use of Technology: Findings from the Center for Research and Education on Aging and Technology Enhancement (CREATE). Psychology and Aging 21(2), 333–352 (2006)
9. Docampo Rama, M.: Technology Generations Handling Complex User Interfaces. PhD Thesis, Eindhoven University of Technology, The Netherlands (2001)
10. McCreadie, C., Tinker, A.: The Acceptability of Assistive Technology to Older People. Ageing & Society 25, 91–110 (2005)
11. Rogers, E.M.: Diffusion of Innovations, 4th edn. The Free Press, New York (1995)
12. Selwyn, N.: The Information Aged: A Qualitative Study of Older Adults' Use of Information and Communications Technology. J. of Aging Studies 18, 369–384 (2004)
13. van Veldhoven, E.R., Vastenburg, M.H., Keyson, D.V.: Designing an Interactive Messaging and Reminder Display for Elderly. In: European Conference on Ambient Intelligence 2008, Nürnberg, Germany (2008)
14. Fogg, B.J., Grudin, J., Nielsen, J., Card, S.: Persuasive Technology: Using Computers to Change What We Think and Do. Science & Technology Books (2002)
15. FitSense ActiPed, `http://www.fitsense.com/ActiPed.aspx`
16. Kaushik, P., Intille, S., Larson, K.: Observations from a Case Study on User Adaptive Reminders for Medication Adherence. In: PervasiveHealth 2008. IEEE Press, New York (2008)
17. Tran, Q.T., Calcaterra, G., Mynatt, E.D.: Cook's Collage: Deja Vu Display for a Home Kitchen. In: Home Oriented Informatics and Telematics 2005, York, UK (2005)

Dynamic vs. Static Recognition of Facial Expressions

Bogdan Raducanu[1] and Fadi Dornaika[2]

[1] Computer Vision Center, Edifici O - Campus UAB
08193 Bellaterra (Barcelona), Spain
bogdan@cvc.uab.es
[2] Institut Géographique National
2 avenue Pasteur
94165 Saint Mandé (Paris), France
fadi.dornaika@ign.fr

Abstract. In this paper, we address the dynamic recognition of basic facial expressions. We introduce a view- and texture independent schemes that exploits facial action parameters estimated by an appearance-based 3D face tracker. We represent the learned facial actions associated with different facial expressions by time series. Furthermore, we compare this dynamic scheme with a static one and show that the former performs better than the latter. We provide evaluations of performance using several classification schemes. With the proposed scheme, we developed an application for social robotics, in which an AIBO is mirroring the facial expression recognized.

1 Introduction

Facial expression plays an important role in recognition of human emotions. Psychologists postulate that facial expressions have a consistent and meaningful structure that can be backprojected in order to infer people inner affective state [7,8]. Basic facial expressions typically recognized by psychologists are: happiness, sadness, fear, anger, disgust and surprise [9]. In the beginning, facial expression analysis was essentially a research topic for psychologists. However, recent progresses in image processing and pattern recognition have motivated significantly research works on automatic facial expression recognition [10,11,12]. In the past, a lot of effort was dedicated to recognize facial expression in still images. For this purpose, many techniques have been applied: neural networks [16], Gabor wavelets [17] and active appearance models [19]. A very important limitation to this strategy is the fact that still images usually capture the apex of the expression, i.e., the instant at which the indicators of emotion are most marked. In their daily life, people seldom show apex of their facial expression during normal communication with their counterparts, unless for very specific cases and for very brief periods of time.

More recently, attention has been shifted particularly towards modelling dynamical facial expressions. This is because that the differences between expressions are more powerfully modelled by dynamic transitions between different

E. Aarts et al. (Eds.): AmI 2008, LNCS 5355, pp. 13–25, 2008.

stages of an expression rather than their corresponding static key frames. This is a very relevant observation, since for most of the communication act, people rather use 'subtle' facial expressions than showing deliberately exaggerated poses in order to convey their message. In [3], the authors found that subtle expressions that were not identifiable in individual images suddenly became apparent when viewed in a video sequence.

Dynamical classifiers try to capture the temporal pattern in the sequence of feature vectors related to each frame such as the Hidden Markov Models (HMMs) and Dynamic Bayesian Networks [20]. In [21], parametric 2D flow models associated with the whole face as well as with the mouth, eyebrows, and eyes are first estimated. Then, mid-level predicates are inferred from these parameters. Finally, universal facial expressions are detected and recognized using the estimated predicates. In [12], a two-stage approach is used. Initially, a linear classification bank was applied and its output was fused to produce a characteristic signature for each universal facial expression. The signatures thus computed from the training data set were used to train discrete Hidden Markov Models to learn the underlying model for each facial expression. A Bayesian approach to modelling temporal transitions of facial expressions represented in a manifold has been proposed in [18]. However, the fact that the method relies heavily on the gray level of the image can be a serious limitation.

As can be seen, most proposed expression recognition schemes require a frontal view of the face. Moreover, most of them rely on the use of image raw brightness changes. The recognition of facial expressions in image sequences with significant head motion is a challenging problem. It is required by many applications such as human computer interaction and computer graphics animation [13,14,15] as well as training of social robots [5,6].

In this paper we propose a novel scheme for dynamic facial expression recognition that is based on an appearance-based 3D face tracker [4]. Compared to existing dynamical facial expression methods our proposed approach has several advantages. First, unlike most expression recognition systems that require a frontal view of the face, our system is view independent since the used tracker simultaneously provides the 3D head pose and the facial actions. Second, it is texture independent since the recognition scheme relies only on the estimated facial actions—invariant geometrical parameters. Third, its learning phase is simple compared to other techniques (e.g., the HMM). As a result, even when the imaging conditions change, the learned expression dynamics need not to be recomputed. The proposed approach for dynamic facial expression recognition has been compared afterwards against static frame-based recognition methods, showing a clear superiority in terms of recognition rates and robustness.

The rest of the paper is organized as follows. Section 2 briefly presents the proposed 3D face and facial action tracking. Section 3 describes the proposed recognition scheme. In section 4 we report some experimental results and method comparisons. Section 5 describes a human robot interaction application that is based on the developed facial expression recognition scheme. Finally, in section 6 we present our conclusions and some guidelines for future work.

2   3D Facial Dynamics Extraction

2.1   A Deformable 3D Face Model

In our work, we use the 3D face model *Candide* [2]. This 3D deformable wireframe model was first developed for the purpose of model-based image coding and computer animation. The 3D shape of this wireframe model is directly recorded in coordinate form. It is given by the coordinates of the 3D vertices $\mathbf{P}_i, i = 1, \ldots, n$ where n is the number of vertices. Thus, the shape up to a global scale can be fully described by the $3n$-vector $\mathbf{g}$; the concatenation of the 3D coordinates of all vertices $\mathbf{P}_i$. The vector $\mathbf{g}$ is written as:

$$\mathbf{g} = \mathbf{g}_s + \mathbf{A}\,\boldsymbol{\tau}_\mathbf{a} \tag{1}$$

where $\mathbf{g}_s$ is the static shape of the model, $\boldsymbol{\tau}_\mathbf{a}$ the animation control vector, and the columns of $\mathbf{A}$ are the Animation Units. The static shape is constant for a given person. In this study, we use six modes for the facial Animation Units (AUs) matrix $\mathbf{A}$. We have chosen the following AUs: lower lip depressor, lip stretcher, lip corner depressor, upper lip raiser, eyebrow lowerer, and outer eyebrow raiser. These AUs are enough to cover most common facial animations. Moreover, they are essential for conveying emotions. Thus, for every frame in the video, the state of the 3D wireframe model is given by the 3D head pose parameters (three rotations and three translations) and the internal face animation control vector $\boldsymbol{\tau}_\mathbf{a}$. This is given by the 12-dimensional vector $\mathbf{b}$:

$$\mathbf{b} = [\theta_x, \theta_y, \theta_z, t_x, t_y, t_z, \boldsymbol{\tau}_\mathbf{a}^T]^T \tag{2}$$

where:

- θ_x, θ_y, and θ_z represent the three angles associated with the 3D rotation between the 3D face model coordinate system and the camera coordinate system.
- t_x, t_y, and t_z represent the three components of the 3D translation vector between the 3D face model coordinate system and the camera coordinate system.
- Each component of the vector $\boldsymbol{\tau}_\mathbf{a}$ represents the intensity of one facial action. This belongs to the interval $[0, 1]$ where the zero value corresponds to the neutral configuration (no deformation) and the one value corresponds to the maximum deformation. In the sequel, the word "facial action" will refer to the facial action intensity.

2.2   Simultaneous Face and Facial Action Tracking

In order to recover the facial expression one has to compute the facial actions encoded by the vector $\boldsymbol{\tau}_\mathbf{a}$ which encapsulates the facial deformation. Since our recognition scheme is view-independent these facial actions together with the 3D head pose should be simultaneously estimated. In other words, the objective is to compute the state vector $\mathbf{b}$ for every video frame.

For this purpose, we use the tracker based on Online Appearance Models—described in [4]. This appearance-based tracker aims at computing the 3D head pose and the facial actions, i.e. the vector **b**, by minimizing a distance between the incoming warped frame and the current *shape-free* appearance of the face. This minimization is carried out using a gradient descent method. The statistics of the *shape-free* appearance as well as the gradient matrix are updated every frame. This scheme leads to a fast and robust tracking algorithm.

3   Facial Expression Recognition

Learning. In order to learn the spatio-temporal structures of the actions associated with facial expressions, we have used a simple supervised learning scheme that consists in two stages. In the first stage, continuous videos depicting different facial expressions are tracked and the retrieved facial actions $\tau_\mathbf{a}$ are represented by time series. In the second stage, the time series representation of all training videos are registered in the time domain using the Dynamic Time Warping technique. Thus, a given example (expression) is represented by a feature vector obtained by concatenating the registered $\tau_\mathbf{a}$.

Video sequences have been picked up from the CMU database [1]. These sequences depict five frontal view universal expressions (surprise, sadness, joy, disgust and anger). Each expression is performed by 7 different subjects, starting from the neutral one. Altogether we select 35 video sequences composed of around 15 to 20 frames each, that is, the average duration of each sequence is about half a second. The learning phase consists of estimating the facial action parameters $\tau_\mathbf{a}$ (a 6-element vector) associated with each training sequence, that is, the temporal trajectories of the action parameters. Figure 1 shows the retrieved facial action parameters associated with three sequences: surprise, anger, and joy. The training video sequences have an interesting property: all performed expressions go from the neutral expression to a high magnitude expression by going through a moderate magnitude around the middle of the sequence. Therefore, using the same training set we get two kinds of trajectories: (i) an entire trajectory which models transitions from the neutral expression to a high magnitude expression, and (ii) a truncated trajectory (the second half part of a given trajectory) which models the transition from small/moderate magnitudes (half apex of the expression) to high magnitudes (apex of the expression). Figure 2 show the half apex and apex facial configurations for three expressions: surprise, anger, and joy. In the final stage of the learning all training trajectories are aligned using the Dynamic Time Warping technique by fixing a nominal duration for a facial expression. In our experiments, this nominal duration is set to 18 frames.

Recognition. In the recognition phase, the 3D head pose and facial actions are recovered from the video sequence using the appearance-based face and facial action tracker. We infer the facial expression associated with the current frame t by considering the estimated trajectory, i.e. the sequence of vectors $\tau_{\mathbf{a}(t)}$ within a temporal window of size 18 centered at the current frame t. This trajectory (feature vector) is then classified using classical classification techniques that rely

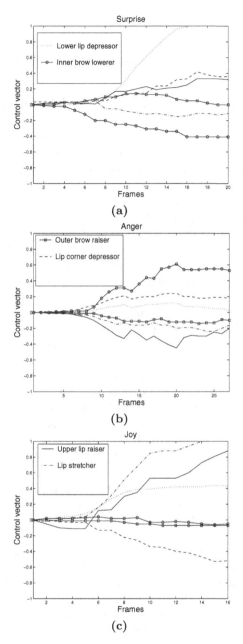

Fig. 1. Three examples (sequences) of learned facial action parameters as a function of time. **(a)** Surprise expression. **(b)** Anger expression. **(c)** Joy expression.

on the learned examples. We have used three different classification schemes: i) Linear Discriminant Analysis, ii) Non-parametric Discriminant Analysis, and iii) Support Vector Machines with a Radial Basis Function.

It is worth noting that the static recognition scheme will use the facial actions associated with only one single frame. In this case, the training examples correspond to the apex of the expression or to its half apex.

4   Experimental Results and Method Comparisons

In our experiments, we used a subset from the CMU facial expression database, containing 7 persons who are displaying 5 expressions: surprise, sadness, joy, disgust and anger. For dynamical facial expression recognition evaluation, we used the truncated trajectories, that is, the temporal sequence containing 9 frames, with the first frame representing a "subtle" facial expression (corresponding more or less with a "half apex" state, see the left column of Figure 2) and the last one corresponding to the apex state of the facial expression (see the right column of Figure 2). We decided to remove in our analysis the first few frames (from initial, "neutral" state to "half-apex") since we found them irrelevant for the purposes of the current study. The results reported in this section are based on the "leave-one-out" cross-validation strategy. Several classification methods have been tested: Linear Discriminant Analysis (LDA), Non-parametric Discriminant Analysis (NDA) and Support Vector Machines (SVM). For LDA and NDA, the classification was based on the K Nearest Neighbor rule (KNN). We considered the following cases: K=1, 3 and 5. In order to assess the benefit of using temporal information, we performed also the "static" facial expression recognition, by comparing frame-wise the instances corresponding to half-apex and apex states respectively. The results for LDA and NDA classifiers are reported in tables 1 and 3, respectively. The SVM results for the dynamic classifier are reported in table 5. The kernel was a radial basis function. Thus, the SVM used has two parameters to tune 'c' and 'g' (gamma). In this case we wanted to see how the variation of parameters 'c' (cost) and 'g' (gamma) affect the recognition performance. We considered 7 values for 'c' and 3 for 'gamma'. Table 8 shows the confusion matrix associated with a given "leave-one-out" for the dynamic classifier using SVM. Since we noticed that 'gamma' doesn't have a significant impact on the classification results, for the study of frame-wise case we set this parameter to its default value $(1/dim(vector) = 1/54)$ and considered only different values for the 'c' parameter. The results for the static classifier based on SVM are presented in table 6. To conclude this part of the experimental results, we could say that, in general, the dynamic recognition scheme has outperformed all static recognition schemes. Moreover, we found out that the SVM clearly outperforms LDA and NDA in classification accuracy.

Besides the experiments described above, we performed also a cross-check validation. In the first experiment, we trained the static classifier with the frames corresponding to half-apex expression and use the apex frames for test. We refer to this case as 'minor' static classifier. In a second experiment, we trained the classifier with the apex frames and test it using the half-apex frames ('major' static classifier). The results for LDA, NDA and SVM are presented in the tables 2, 4 and 7, respectively. By analyzing the obtained results, we could observe that

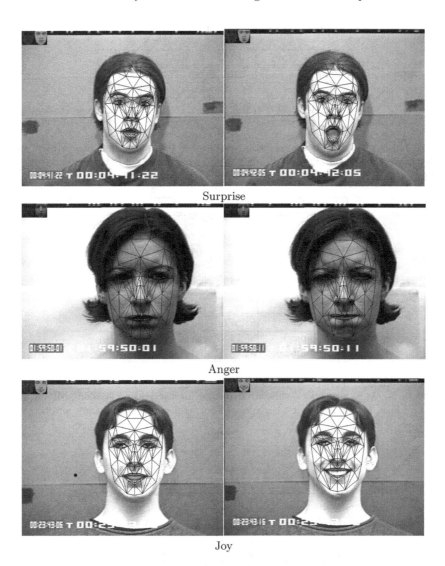

Fig. 2. Three video examples associated with the CMU database depicting surprise, anger, and joy expressions. The left frames illustrate the half apex of the expression. The right frames illustrate the apex of the expression.

the 'minor' static classifier has comparable results to the static half apex classifier. This was confirmed by the three classification methods: LDA, NDA, and SVM. This means that a learning based on data featuring half apex expressions will have very good generalization capabilities since the tests with both kinds of data (half-apex and apex expressions) have a high recognition rate. Also, one can notice that the recognition rate of the minor static classifier is higher than that of the major static classifier.

Table 1. LDA - Overall classification results

Classifier type	K=1	K=3	K=5
Dynamic	94.2857%	88.5714%	82.8571%
Static (apex)	91.4286%	91.4286%	88.5714%
Static (half-apex)	85.7143%	82.8571%	80.0000%

Table 2. LDA - Cross-check validation results for the static classifier. Minor: train with half-apex frames and test with apex. Major: train with apex frames and test with half-apex.

Static classifier	K=1	K=3	K=5
Minor	82.8571%	85.7143%	85.7143%
Major	57.1429%	65.7143%	62.8571%

Table 3. NDA - Overall classification results

Classifier type	K=1	K=3	K=5
Dynamic	88.5714%	88.5714%	85.7143%
Static (apex)	85.7143%	88.5714%	91.4286%
Static (half-apex)	82.8571%	80.0000%	80.0000%

Table 4. NDA - Cross-check validation results for the static classifier. Minor: train with half-apex frames and test with apex. Major: train with apex frames and test with half-apex.

Static classifier	K=1	K=3	K=5
Minor	94.2857%	88.5714%	85.7143%
Major	65.7143%	62.6571%	60.0000%

Table 5. SVM - Overall recognition rate for the dynamic classifier

c (g=1/54)	g/2	g	2 g
1	91.4285%	91.4285%	91.4285%
5	91.4285%	94.2857%	97.1428%
10	97.1428%	97.1428%	97.1428%
50	97.1428%	100.0000%	97.1428%
100	100.0000%	97.1428%	97.1428%
500	97.1428%	97.1428%	97.1428%
1000	97.1428%	97.1428%	97.1428%

This result may have very practical implications assuming that training data contain non-apex expressions, specially for real-world applications. In human-computer interaction scenarios, for instance, we are interested in quantifying

Table 6. SVM - Overall recognition rate for the static classifier

Static type	c=1	c=5	c=10	c=50	c=100	c=500	c=1000
Apex	82.8571%	97.1428%	100.0000%	94.2857%	94.2857%	94.2857%	94.2857%
Half-apex	82.8571%	82.8571%	85.7142%	94.2857%	94.2857%	94.2857%	91.4285%

Table 7. SVM - Cross-check validation results for the static classifier. Minor: train with half-apex frames and test with apex. Major: train with apex frames and test with half-apex.

Static type	c=1	c=5	c=10	c=50	c=100	c=500	c=1000
Minor	80.0000%	80.0000%	85.7142%	85.7142%	82.8571%	80.0000%	82.8571%
Major	48.5714%	60.0000%	51.4285%	45.7142%	48.5714%	48.5714%	48.5714%

Table 8. Confusion matrix for the dynamic classifier. The results correspond to the case when c=1 and g=0.0185.

	Surprise	Sadness	Joy	Disgust	Anger
Surprise (7)	7	0	0	0	0
Sadness (7)	0	6	0	1	0
Joy (7)	0	0	7	0	0
Disgust (7)	0	0	0	7	0
Anger (7)	0	1	1	1	4

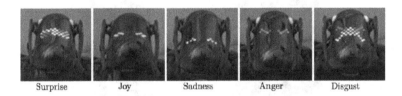

Surprise   Joy   Sadness   Anger   Disgust

Fig. 3. AIBO showing facial expressions

human reaction based on its natural behavior. For this reason, we have to acquire and process data online without any external intervention. In this context, it is highly unlikely to capture automatically a persons apex of the facial expression. Most of the time we are tempted to show more subtle versions of our expressions and when we indeed show apex, this is in very specific situations and for very brief periods of time.

5 Application for AIBO: Mirroring Human Facial Expression

With the dynamic facial expression recognition scheme proposed in this paper, we developed an application for human-robot interaction. For this purpose, we

Fig. 4. Left column: Some detected keyframes associated with the 1600-frame original video. **Middle column:** The recognized expression. **Right column:** The corresponding robot's response.

have used an AIBO robot which has the advantage of being specifically designed for interaction with people. Among its communication mechanisms, it is endowed with the ability of displaying 'facial expressions' (according to its inner state) through a set of colored LEDs located in the frontal part of the head (see figure 3).

From its concept design, AIBO's affective states are triggered by an emotion generator engine. This occurs as a response to its internal state representation, captured through a multi-sensorial mechanism (vision, audio, and touch). For instance, it can display the happiness feeling when it detects a face or it hears a voice. But it does not possess a built-in system for vision-based automatic facial-expression recognition. For this reason, the current developed application can be considered as a natural extension of its pre-built behaviors. This application is a very simple one, in which the robot is just imitating the expression of a human subject. In other words, we wanted to see its reaction according to the emotional state displayed by a person. Some extracted frames are depicted in figure 4.

6   Conclusions and Future Work

In this paper, we addressed the dynamic facial expression recognition in videos. We introduced a view and texture independent scheme that exploits facial action parameters estimated by an appearance-based 3D face tracker. We represented the corresponding learned facial actions associated with different facial expressions by time series. In order to show even better the benefits of employing a dynamic classifier, we compared it with static classifiers, built on the half-apex and apex frames of the corresponding facial expressions. We also showed that only by using half-apex frames to train the static classifiers, we still get very reliable predictions about the real facial expression (test were done with apex frames). With the proposed scheme, we developed an application for social robotics, in which an AIBO is mirroring the facial expression recognized.

In the future, we want to further explore the results obtained in this paper by focusing on two directions: using facial actions as a hint to assess persons' level of interest during an event and trying to discriminate between a fake and a genuine facial expression.

Acknowledgements

This work is supported by MEC Grant TIN2006-15308-C02 and CONSOLIDER-INGENIO 2010 (CSD2007-00018), Ministerio de Educacin y Ciencia, Spain. Bogdan Raducanu is supported by the Ramon y Cajal research program, Ministerio de Educación y Ciencia, Spain. The authors thank Dr. Franck Davoine from CNRS Compiegne France for providing some test videos.

References

1. Kanade, T., Cohn, J., Tian, Y.L.: Comprehensive database for facial expression analysis. In: Proc. of IEEE International Conference on Automatic Face and Gesture Recognition (2000)
2. Ahlberg, J.: Model-based coding: extraction, coding and evaluation of face model parameters. Ph.D. Thesis, Dept. of Elec. Eng., Linköping Univ., Sweden (September 2002)
3. Ambadar, Z., Schooler, J., Cohn, J.: Deciphering the enigmatic face: the importance of facial dynamics to interpreting subtle facial expressions. Psychological Science 16(5), 403–410 (2005)
4. Dornaika, F., Davoine, F.: On appearance based face and facial action tracking. IEEE Trans. on Circuits and Systems for Video Technology 16(9), 1107–1124 (2006)
5. Breazeal, C.: Robot in society: friend or appliance? In: Proc. of Wksp. on Emotion-Based Agent Architectures, pp. N/A (1999)
6. Breazeal, C.: Sociable machines: Expressive social exchange between humans and robots. Ph.D. dissertation, Dept. Elect. Eng. & Comput. Sci. MIT, Cambridge (2000)
7. Ekman, P.: Facial expression and emotion. American Psychologist 48(4), 384–392 (1993)
8. Ekman, P., Davidson, R.: The nature of emotion: fundamental questions. Oxford Univ. Press, New York (1994)
9. Ekman, P.: Facial expressions of emotions: an old controversy and new findings. Philos. Trans. of the Royal Society of London B 335, 63–69 (1992)
10. Fasel, B., Luettin, J.: Automatic facial expression analysis: a survey. Pattern Recognition 36(1), 259–275 (2003)
11. Kim, Y., Lee, S., Kim, S., Park, G.: A fully automatic system recognizing human facial expressions. In: Negoita, M.G., Howlett, R.J., Jain, L.C. (eds.) KES 2004. LNCS (LNAI), vol. 3215, pp. 203–209. Springer, Heidelberg (2004)
12. Yeasin, M., Bullot, B., Sharma, R.: Recognition of facial expressions and measurement of levels of interest from video. IEEE Trans. on Multimedia 8(3), 500–508 (2006)
13. Cañamero, L., Gaussier, P.: Emotion understanding: robots as tools and models. In: Nadel, J., Muir, D. (eds.) Emotional Development: Recent Research Advances, pp. 235–258. Oxford Univesity Press, Oxford (2005)
14. Pantic, M.: Affective Computing. In: Pagani, M. (ed.) Encyclopedia of Multimedia Technology and Networking, vol. I, pp. 8–14. Idea Group Publishing (2005)
15. Picard, R.W., Vyzas, E., Healy, J.: Toward machine emotional intelligence: analysis of affective physiological state. IEEE Trans. on Patt. Anal. and Machine Intell. 23(10), 1175–1191 (2001)
16. Tian, Y., Kanade, T., Cohn, J.F.: Recognizing action units for facial expression analysis. IEEE Trans. on Patt. Anal. and Machine Intell. 23, 97–115 (2001)
17. Bartlett, M., Littlewort, G., Lainscsek, C., Fasel, I., Movellan, J.: Machine learning methods for fully automatic recognition of facial expressions and facial actions. In: Proc. of IEEE Intl. Conf. on SMC, vol. I, pp. 592–597. The Hague, The Netherlands (2004)
18. Dynamic facial expression recognition using a bayesian temporal manifold model. In: Proc. of British Machine Vision Conference, Edinburgh, UK, vol. I, pp. 297–306 (2006)

19. Sung, J., Lee, S., Kim, D.: A real-time facial expression recognition using the STAAM. In: Proc. of Intl. Conf. on Pattern Recognition, Hong Kong, PR China, vol. I, pp. 275–278 (2006)
20. Zhang, Y., Ji, Q.: Active and dynamic information fusion for facial expression understanding from image sequences. IEEE Trans. on Patt. Anal. and Machine Intell. 27(5), 699–714 (2005)
21. Black, M.J., Yacoob, Y.: Recognizing facial expressions in image sequences using local parameterized models of image motion. Intl. Journal of Comp. Vision 25(1), 23–48 (1997)

Towards Human Centered Ambient Intelligence

Thomas Plötz, Christian Kleine-Cosack, and Gernot A. Fink

Intelligent Systems Group, Robotics Research Institute,
Technische Universität Dortmund, Dortmund, Germany
{Thomas.Ploetz,Christian.Kleine-Cosack,Gernot.Fink}@udo.edu

Abstract. In this paper we present a novel approach to the integration of humans into AmI environments. The key aspect of the concept which we call human centered Ami is a dynamic and active user model which creates a virtual doppelganger of the user on software level. This agent not only complies to the specific characteristics of humans but directly affects and triggers environmental activities. In fact the user's persona and behavior is mapped to system level. Utilizing this doppelganger we introduce the integration of the users' capabilities and skills into the functionality of the environment. Human services enrich intelligent environments and allow to overcome the "all-or-nothing" dilemma which we identified in conventional approaches. The concept of human centered AmI is put into effect within the perception-oriented intelligent environment FINCA. Results of a Wizard-of-Oz experiment with real users show the benefits of the presented approach.

1 Introduction

With the availability of more and more powerful and cheap computing facilities together with their substantially and continuously shrinking size one of the most fascinating visions of computer scientists today appear to be truly realizable: Ubiquitous computing systems integrated into and designed to permanently support the users' everyday life. The principle goal is the "disappearing computer" [1,2] which silently serves humans whereby they are (most of the time) not even aware of it. Consequently, it is the humans' environment which becomes more "intelligent" – the advent of Ambient Intelligence (AmI).

In the last few years tremendous progress in AmI research allowed for the realization of impressive applications utilizing ubicomp techniques. Prominent examples are so-called Smart Rooms and Smart Houses (cf. e.g. [3,4]). Here, various sensors and actuators are integrated into the installations of buildings aiming at the support of humans in their private home, or for elderly care, just to mention two examples.

Compared to, e.g., standard desktop applications the key issue in all AmI techniques is the permanent system awareness w.r.t. the global environmental context which is necessary for generating appropriate system reactions. These reactions often depend on hardly predictable actions performed by the very humans to be served. In fact, permanent and reliable context awareness is the main feature of the central AmI paradigm [5,6,7].

E. Aarts et al. (Eds.): AmI 2008, LNCS 5355, pp. 26–43, 2008.

Reconsidering the aforementioned Smart Houses, a principle problem of current AmI applications becomes manifest. For successfully realizing the necessary context awareness at a global scale plus, in this case, the required physical feedback of the system, significant effort for soft- and hardware deployment is mandatory. Numerous sensors (e.g. microphones, cameras, tactile sensors etc.) and, probably more importantly, actuators (automatic door openers, light dimmers, servos for diverse installation equipment like sun-blinds etc.) need to be deployed and in collectivity provide intelligent functionality. If only certain parts of this hardware "zoo" are missing or malfunctioning the overall Ambient Intelligence will fail and the particular Smart House becomes useless. Furthermore and probably more important, a transfer of certain AmI solutions to different but related scenarios requires exactly the same high effort in hard- and software installation. We call this the "all-or-nothing" dilemma which is, in our mind, very obstructive for the generalization of AmI.

In our research we try to overcome the aforementioned "all-or-nothing" dilemma. The motivation for this is the development of AmI techniques which, among others, should easily be transferable between related scenarios putatively exhibiting different hardware settings. More specifically our work is directed to the development of techniques for Smart Houses with special focus on the deployment of perception-oriented approaches analyzing, e.g., visual and acoustic data. Exemplarily integrated into a conference room equipped with, more or less, standard hardware components, thereby explicitly avoiding special solutions like automatic door openers etc., we target our vision of AmI "for the masses".

In contrast to existing approaches for Smart Houses and as the key innovation presented in this paper we propose the explicit integration of human users and their physical abilities into the overall AmI system. Humans are an decisive part of the context and capable of doing numerous things which – for the sake of keeping a system running instead of complete malfunction (see above) – should be used for the design and practical operation of AmI systems. As an example windows or doors can easily be opened or closed by humans if they are – at the right time – asked to do so. The common alternative in standard AmI settings is to integrate some kind of artificial actuator allowing for the automation of the process – the "all-or-nothing" dilemma. Basically, this kind of paradigm shift opens up ways out of the dilemma. Clearly, the user of an AmI system must not be bothered by the system to do anything which would contradict the general vision of AmI. We propose to explicitly integrate humans into the architecture of AmI systems and to make use of their physical capabilities whenever it is appropriate and necessary. Consequently, our approach is directed towards human centered AmI.

The technical realization of Ambient Intelligence environments is in practice based on a Service Oriented Architecture (SOA) [8] which allows for easy modularization and to handle the complexity and dynamics of the system. Related software frameworks like OSGi (cf., e.g., [9]) or Microsoft's .NET currently represent the state-of-the-art and enable transparent communication between certain (software) services dedicated to specific tasks. In this paper we describe a technical realization of the proposed human centered AmI integrated into a Smart

House management system which is based on OSGi. As a key contribution for the technical integration of humans into the framework virtual doppelgangers are created, which – at the software level – transparently represent users of an AmI system as any other device. The specific (physical) abilities of humans are modeled by a new class of software services – human services. It is important to mention, that the roles of humans in an AmI scenario might change dynamically. Thus, certain human services principally offered by this person might be disabled (or enabled again). As an example, related to our smart conference room, a person, who is principally able to open the door for a mobile service robot trying to enter the room, should not be asked to do so when he is presenting a talk. Once the person is back in the audience he clearly can be asked to open the door, though. By means of the proposed technique of human services dynamic changes of a person's available capabilities are realized via design patterns allowing for flexible reconfiguration of objects at run time.

In reality the user plays an active, central and determining role in every intelligent environment. However, the analysis of state-of-the-art projects in this field as, e.g., the GatorTech Smart House [10], or the AMIGO platform [11] reveal the fact, that user modeling takes place only within a passive and integral context model. Contrary, in our approach we separate this modeling process and create a user model which adapts to the specific characteristics of humans. In consequence user centered design also at system level is achieved.

In this paper we develop the concept of human services as a tool for the realization of human centered Ambient Intelligence. Human services are designed as a general concept for at least partially overcoming the identified "all-or-nothing" dilemma in AmI scenarios. As a first concrete implementation of human centered AmI we integrated human services in our smart environment – the FINCA which is briefly described in section 2. Following this in section 3 human services are presented in detail. For a qualitative evaluation of the effectiveness of the proposed human services we conducted a practical case-study in the FINCA. Therefore, Wizard-of-Oz experiments with real users of the FINCA's smart conference room were performed and the cognitive load of the users was measured. It is shown, that the application of human services lowers the cognitive load of AmI users which makes the particular systems easier and more intuitive to use (section 4). As a side effect this study shows the acceptance and the intuitive understanding of the concept of human services by the user. The paper concludes with a discussion.

2   A Perception-Oriented Smart Environment: The FINCA

The work described in this paper was conducted within the greater context of a research project aiming at the development of techniques for sophisticated and natural human-computer interaction. Therefore, especially sensor data related to human perception (visual or acoustic signals) are processed using statistical pattern recognition techniques. Serving as an integration scenario for Ambient

Fig. 1. Overview of the FINCA (left) and inside view of the smart conference room. Ceiling mounted microphones are marked with red circles whereas the active cameras (also mounted at the ceiling) are marked with blue, dashed circles.

Intelligence applications a Smart House has been created – the FINCA, a Flexible, Intelligent eNvironment with Computational Augmentation [12].

Basically, the FINCA subsumes two areas under one roof: a smart conference room and, connected to this, an open and flexible lab-space. Within both areas various sensors, namely cameras, microphones, infra-red sensors etc. are integrated. Electro-mechanical sensors (e.g. light switches) and actors (e.g. light or sunblind control units) are integrated and connected via an EIB (European Installation Bus) installation. All sensors and actuators are standard, off-the-shelf components. The reason for this is, that we – for better transferability of developed solutions – explicitly aim to avoid special solutions which are only available for the FINCA. Furthermore, a mobile service robot is integrated into the FINCA. According to its capabilities the robot is used as an "external sensor" and actuator, e.g., for concierge services within the smart environment. For general system integration an OSGi based middleware framework is used.

Ultimately an intelligent, cooperative house environment, which supports human users during various activities (conferences, information retrieval, communication, entertainment etc.) is created. For natural and thus intuitive interaction with the environment special teaching of human users will not be required. Therefore, the FINCA detects, locates and tracks communication partners by analyzing visual and acoustic data. The results are combined allowing for multimodal scene analysis aiming at a successful automatic interpretation of user's intentions.

In figure 1 an overview of the FINCA (left hand side) is given plus an inside view of the smart conference room. The FINCA is integrated into a larger laboratory including numerous machines and working places. Thus, a (realistic) rendering of the actual smart house gives a better overview rather than an actual photo of the Smart House.

3   User Modeling and Human Services

In everyday life humans are confronted with numerous different computer based systems. It is the central aspect of AmI to combine their functions into intelligent environments whose emergent characteristics should generate substantial benefits for the human thereby improving his experience. However, without an integration concept this combination process results in a tangled mass of user interfaces and usage concepts each demanding for specialized knowledge. Eventually, human computer interaction looses all its originally intended intuitiveness and the central concept of assistance is doomed.

In the last few years various approaches addressing this integration challenge have been developed where the focus is, basically, on the creation of context aware AmI environments. The strong dependency on sensors and actuators, however, results in the "all-or-nothing" dilemma as discussed in section 1. The representation of humans at system level, i.e. within the particular middleware frameworks integrating the different software services and hardware control, is realized within in a passive context model. This traditional concept of context awareness, basically, does not cope with the special characteristics of humans.

In this paper we present a new approach aiming at the integration of humans as active components into intelligent environments. The motivation for this is to open up ways out of the "all-or-nothing" dilemma. We target on a user representation within an intelligent environment's middleware framework which explicitly respects the characteristics and specific role of the user in the real world. Thus, it allows for the dynamic integration of human capabilities into the functionality of the environment.

As a concrete technical realization of the proposed concept we create a virtual doppelganger of the user at software level. Separated from the standard passive context model this concept allows for user integration at the service level – human services which represent the key aspect to overcome the "all-or-nothing" dilemma. The functional gap of most intelligent environments substantially depending on the existence of all required hardware devices is closed. The key idea here is to transfer the approach for resolving software dependencies as known from service oriented architectures (SOA) to hardware related dependencies. The central aspect for filling the gap of missing sensors or actuators in an intelligent environment is the dynamic assistance by humans.

In the following the concept of human centered AmI, namely the explicit modeling of users, modeling the users' behavior, and human services are discussed in detail.

3.1 Explicit Modeling of Users

In the research field of ubiquitous computing and AmI the user context model primarily consists of the user's location and his social context. Recent studies, however, argue that modeling only the external context does not comply with the characteristics of humans in reality [13]. Accordingly, an explicit modeling of the user separated from a general context model is discussed in the related literature [14,15].

In fact a close relation between the user model and the environment model exists which constitutes the specific context at system level as illustrated in figure 2. The environmental context (right hand side of the figure) influences the

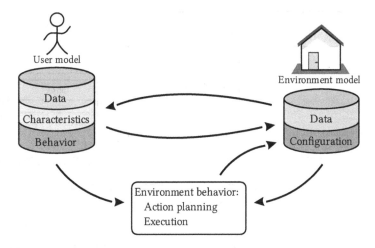

Fig. 2. There is a close relation between user and context model. The state of the environment directly influences the role of the user and vice versa the user implicitly determines the current state of the environment.

user model (left) and, vice versa, the state of the user model directly affects the general context of the environment. In particular the role of the user within an intelligent environment might change due to changes within the general context model. Therefore, specific user activity is not necessarily to be observed. Similarly, user actions might change the environmental context. In consequence the user model and the context model have to be linked according to interference and integrity rules.

In our approach human users are represented by software objects at system level. This object oriented technique allows for modeling human characteristics and their activities in detail as well as for providing methods for direct communication between the virtual doppelgangers and software modules. Furthermore, intelligent user oriented system behavior becomes possible which accounts for the user's individual characteristics.

3.2 Modeling the User's Behavior

The conceptual goal of virtual doppelgangers is to represent the active and dynamic character of the user within the software framework of an AmI environment. Integral part of this concept is the mapping of user activities to system actions. Consequently, the user model not only consists of passive information about the user and his present state – which corresponds to conventional AmI designs – but, instead, is an active part of the system, able to trigger actions. Changes of local user data as well as system activities are controlled by this virtual doppelganger. As an example a single observed user action can lead to a continuous sequence of system actions controlled by the user model. According

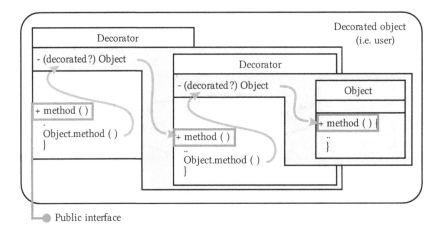

Fig. 3. The decoration of objects, i.e. the representation of the human user, allows for dynamic changes of their methods at runtime. Due to the use of abstract interfaces even multiple decorations and different properties can be combined.

to its equivalent in the real world the virtual doppelganger becomes a system component which actively and continuously determines the system behavior.

The implementation of the user model at the software level is based on different design patterns [16] to achieve a highly dynamic and flexible virtual doppelganger. The user's attributes and methods can be decorated at runtime allowing to adapt the model constantly (cf. figure 3). Based on abstract interfaces new decorations can be provided by external modules and they can be applied to already existing instances of the user model. By decoration not only static data of the model can be changed but, additionally, the specific implementation of methods. As an example methods which are responsible for the communication between the real human user and his virtual doppelganger can change dynamically allowing to adopt to context information or user characteristics (e.g. to change the modality or language of communication). Consequently, a user centered intelligence emerges.

Utilizing the state pattern the active and continuous role of the user is modeled. Each thread based state is able to use the framework's functionality to control the environmental conditions in accordance to the users activity. For example, the virtual doppelganger could continuously adapt the lighting conditions according to the current activity thus avoiding disturbances of the user.

3.3 Human Services

Generally, hardware devices and software modules propagate their functionality as services within the middleware of an intelligent environment. According to this paradigm of service orientation the idea behind the proposed concept of human services is to analogously propagate the capabilities of humans dynamically and dependent on the global context. Consequently, while holding all the user data the

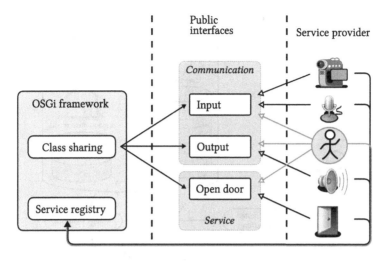

Fig. 4. Abstract service interfaces can be implemented by conventional modules and the user model. The service itself is completely described by the interface and no special knowledge about a (human) service in needed. In consequence human services in usage do not differ from conventional services.

user model itself represents the instance to decide which human service to offer or to withdraw. Depending on the information about the human user, the environmental context, and the current activities these decisions about dynamic offering of human services are taken by the user model. In consequence the dynamics of the model affects this process directly and determines the service offering.

The typical SOA of an intelligent environment (as implemented in our own Smart House – the FINCA, see section 2) combined with the explicit user model represent a perfect base for the realization of human services. In our case we use the OSGi framework functions for propagating human services of the user model which, in this case, are implementations of defined abstract Java interfaces. Note that the proposed concept of human centered AmI incl. human services does not rely on utilizing an OSGi framework.

In general those interfaces can be sorted by function in two groups which is illustrated in figure 4. On the one hand there are service interfaces describing skills and capabilities of humans. As an example for the case study presented in this paper (see next section) a service interface describing a door-opening service was defined and implemented. On the other hand there are so called communication interfaces which account for the lack of a direct communication channel between the system and the user. These interfaces provide abstract input and output methods for software modules to contact the user. Dependent on the user's actual state these methods are mapped within the user model to sensor and actuator based environmental functions. Examples of communication services are speech- and handwriting-recognition, visual terminals and speech synthesis. The communication interfaces provide context adaptive communication channels encapsulated by the user model.

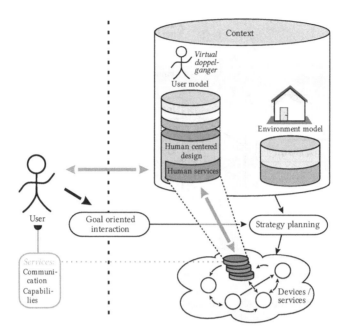

Fig. 5. Human services allow for the integration of the user's capabilities into the action planning of intelligent environments and are the key feature of the approach developed in this paper. On the left hand side the real user is shown, on the right his virtual doppelganger. The integration of the user model into the system is accomplished at service level. The role of the user shifts from being the trigger of system activities to an active component within the overall system. The user model thereby controls the intelligent communication between the user and his virtual doppelganger.

Human services extend the role of humans in AmI environments and lead to the proposed user integration at service level which is illustrated in figure 5. In consequence the user is no longer considered to be only the trigger of system activities but, instead, the functionality of the environment is enhanced by the user's skills. Functional dependencies at hardware level as discussed above are dramatically reduced by human services. The intelligence of the environment extends beyond the boundary of physical sensor and actuator installations.

4   Human Services in Action: A Case-Study

Traditionally, AmI systems are evaluated by means of usability studies. Due to the complexity of such systems the evaluation with (naive) users in the loop in practice turns out to be a challenging task with numerous issues to be respected. In particular methods used in HCI studies are not likely to be feasible in situations with disappearing computing. As an example, the communication interfaces are invisible and – at least partially – unknown to the user. Furthermore, often input methods tend to be error prone.

In addition improving the usability in fact corresponds to a multidisciplinary task and, unfortunately, no general solutions exist [17]. The evaluation of a general concept like the one presented in this work raises further questions regarding the methodology of experiments to be conducted. The goal of the evaluation is to measure the overall influence of a system's design on it's usability rather than limiting to some isolated functionality of certain components.

The hypothesis to be verified in the experiments are the following:

1. The concept of human services accompanied by intelligent user interaction lowers the cognitive load of AmI users. In consequence the overall system usability increases and the system becomes easier and more intuitive without the need of precise user instructions.
2. The concept of human services is naturally understood by the untaught user and specific user instructions are superfluous.

4.1   Experiment Design

In these premises we performed a case-study with human services integrated into the FINCA. Therefore, real users were asked to interact with the smart conference room of the FINCA. More specifically they should check and rate environmental functions like speech and gesture recognition, localization and control of lighting conditions. As an example while pointing to a specific light source the user had to give a voice command to turn on the light. A reference sheet explaining the available functionality was given to the subjects before the experiment started. The underlying goal of these experiments was to encourage human users to perform realistic (and unconstrained) interaction with the intelligent environment.

In addition to this rather simple task, in order to evaluate the usability in a cognitively demanding situation, the subjects were given a more complex interaction task. This advanced interaction task is triggered and defined by the following occurrences and accordant solutions. Note that only the goals of this task were pre-defined, the interaction between users and the FINCA remained unconstrained.

- The mobile service robot, which at some point tries to enter the conference room, must be assisted. Therefore, the door needs to be opened by the subject.
- A software module occasionally malfunctioning during the experiment is required to be restarted.

In order to minimize functional influences of (putatively error prone) input methods and to concentrate on the evaluation of the new concept of human services this study was designed as an *Wizard-of-Oz* experiment [18]. Thus, speech and gesture recognition were simulated by an (invisible) operator whereby the particular subject was in belief of using real intelligent functionality of the conference room.

Operator Mobile   Cameras   Speech   System   Subject   AmI envi-
          service   recognition console   ronment
          robot   module

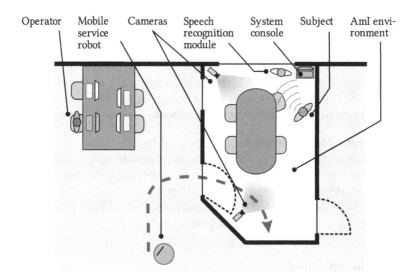

Fig. 6. During the experiment the subject is interacting with the intelligent environment (it's active components are marked blue). Interaction is accomplished via the speech recognition and synthesis module based on an artificial head equipped with stereo microphones and speakers. The operator remains in background out of view of the subject.

Using installed cameras and microphones the operator monitored the subject and coordinated system activities following a specified and detailed protocol. Speech commands and gestures given by the subject were treated by the operator, outputs to the subject were entered in textform and processed by a speech synthesis module. In order to handle unpredicted incidences the mobile service robot was at some point during the experiment manually navigated into the FINCA. The experimental setup is illustrated in figure 6.

After completion the experiment was evaluated by means of a questionnaire survey. This survey was targeted on the subject's role in the environment, the complexity of the tasks and, finally, examined whether the concept of (offering) human services (e.g. manually opening the door for the robot) were naturally accepted or perceived to be distracting. Answers had to be given based on the 5-point Likert scale [19].

4.2   Dual-Task Interference

Although the role of the user in the environment as examined by the questionnaire survey is important concerning the goal of user integration, this survey does not provide a measure of neither the usability of the system nor, in this context, the advantages over conventional AmI concepts. In consequence some additional examination of how the subjects managed to fulfill the advanced interaction task is needed. Unfortunately, standard evaluation methods from HCI applications are often inappropriate (see introduction of section 4).

In order to measure the usability of the smart conference room we additionally performed an evaluation following the dual-task paradigm which evolved from psychological research (cf. e.g. [20]). It addresses the analysis of the cognitive load of humans while fulfilling given tasks. In fact, the cognitive load corresponds to a direct measure of the usability: The lower the cognitive load the more intuitive and, thus, higher is the usability of the smart environment. The basis of this assumption is the fact that people tend to have problems when processing multiple cognitively demanding activities in parallel. The reason for which lies in the limited capacity of certain cognitive resources and the competition of parallel activities for such. This mutual interference of activities is called dual-task interference and is utilized in this study by giving the subjects a second, cognitively demanding and *measurable* task – the control task – in parallel to the advanced interaction task.

The memorization of unassociated information has been proved to be appropriate as control task [21]. In our experiments a multi-digit random number was presented to the subjects and the memorization performance was measured at the end of the experiment. Preliminary tests have identified a nine-digit number, presented in three blocks with 3 digits each, as reasonable. To assure for equal conditions w.r.t. cognitive elaboration the number is not visually presented but read to the subject by the investigator until it was correctly repeated. For quantifying the results the Levenshtein distance [22] is used which conforms to typical errors made in such tasks.

This control task provides a simple yet effective measure for the cognitive load of a subject during the experiment. By design these results correlate with the complexity of the intelligent environment, which is directly connected to the usability.

4.3   Test Procedure

We conducted experiments with 15 different participants (namely undergraduate students), all of them being naive users w.r.t. AmI related research. Three disjoint sub-groups were created by (randomly) splitting the cohort and assigned to one of the following experimental conditions:

1. Subjects contained by the first group are not confronted with extended and cognitively demanding interaction task. The results of the control task are expected to be optimal as no cognitive interference will occur. The results of the memorization task of this control group will serve as reference value.
2. Prior to the experiment the subjects of this group are given detailed instructions on how to solve the advanced interaction task (cf. section 4.1) but at the time of occurrence no interactive help is given. Instead, the subjects must recall the required information. The condition in this group complies with conventional AmI design: The user does not offer a human service which can be dynamically requested by the environment. In order to be able to handle

certain situations – i.e. the door needs to be opened, a software module is malfunctioning – the user needs specific and detailed knowledge.

3. The subjects of the last group do not have any detailed pre-instructions on how to handle the advanced interaction task. At the time of occurrence, however, the user is given interactive help by the intelligent conference room. Utilizing human services the environment is able to involve the user's capabilities in action planning, i.e. for opening the door for the robot a service is used which is offered by the user – an instance of a human service. In consequence the handling of the proposed advanced task – a task which exceed the possibilities of conventional AmI – is managed by the environment itself to disburden the user. This is what we call human centered AmI.

As already mentioned, at the beginning of an experiment the subjects received short introductions about the functionality of the smart conference room. Depending on the sub-group the subject belongs to, the particular task description was given to the user. During the experiment the subject was left alone within the FINCA ensuring the completion of the task with as little disturbances as possible. At the end of the experiment the performance in the memorization task was measured and the questionnaire was filled out.

Reconsidering the initial assumptions w.r.t. the practical evaluation the effectiveness of human services can be evaluated. The results of the memorization task measure the cognitive load of the subject during experiment and, in consequence, the complexity of the specific experimental condition. The acceptance of the concept of human services is implicitly examined and further information regarding the perception of the particular subject's role is gathered by questionnaire.

4.4   Results

For the quantitative evaluation of the experimental results we utilized the well-established ANOVA (analysis of variances) method (cf. e.g. [23]), a statistical procedure which evaluates the differences of certain measurements in dependency of the condition of the particular experiment. Basically, different experimental conditions are compared aiming for the analysis of the effectiveness of the proposed human services. By means of the analysis of certain statistical measures differences between the experiments performed by the three sub-groups are investigated. In this case-study the group conditions differ in presence or absence of the proposed human centered AmI (see previous section). Thus, results are analyzed by means of one-factor ANOVA.

In the following the results for the evaluation of both the complexity of the task itself and for the control task results are given.

Task Complexity. Although the complexity of both the standard interaction task (see definition of the control group in section 4.3) and the advanced interaction task (second and third sub-group assigned to the actual evaluation of human centered AmI) are comparable, different subjects might differently perceive its complexity. Since it is the general goal to evaluate the memorization results such putative biases need to be eliminated.

Table 1. ANOVA table of general task complexity – no significant changes are caused by the introduction of the proposed human services which allows for direct comparison of the memorization results to those obtained from the control group.

source of variance	S^2	df	MS	F	p
human centered AmI	0.93	2	0.47	0.64	0.5462
random error		8.8	12	0.73	
total	9.73	14	0.7		

Table 2. Descriptive statistics of general task complexity. The results show no significant differences between either groups.

group	N	mean	standard error	standard deviation
1	5	4.6	0.24	0.54
2	5	4.2	0.58	1.3
3	5	4.8	0.2	0.44
total	5	4.53	0.22	0.83

In order to measure the complexity of the task to fulfill, a questionnaire – completed by the test persons after conducting the experiment – was evaluated thereby offering standardized numerical answers from the 5-point Likert scale. In table 1 and 2, respectively, the results of this survey are summarized. Table 1 contains the ANOVA measures squared sum S^2, degree of freedom df, mean sum MS, F-test statistics F, and statistical significance p – each w.r.t. the Likert based answers given in the questionnaires. The results of the first row (human centered AmI) are averaged over the three sub-groups with different experimental conditions. According to standard ANOVA presentations and for completeness also figures for random error and total are given. In the second table the descriptive statistics are given separately for the three sub-groups.

The influence of the experimental condition is given by statistical significance of $p = 0.5462$ which is close to random and the mean differs only marginally.[1] It can be seen that the introduction of human services does not change the perceived complexity of the task – which justifies the overall evaluation approach. The results obtained from control group experiments and those obtained when human services are activated are, thus, directly comparable.

Control Task Results. In the previous section the general evaluation methodology was justified by verifying the comparability of the general task complexities. Consequently, we can now focus on the main evaluation of the effectiveness

---

[1] According to ANOVA the statistics of significance is the probability that the difference in variance between groups is caused by random and not by experimental conditions. The level of significance is defined as $\alpha = 0.05$ and a difference of significance is given by $p \leq \alpha$. [23]

Table 3. ANOVA table of error rates in control task (memorization of nine-digit numbers during the experiments). The results show a trend towards a significant difference between the particular sub-groups of the case-study which gives evidence for the effectiveness of human services.

source of variance	S^2	df	MS	F	p
human centered AmI	22.8	2	11.4	2.9	0.0940
random error		47.2	12	3.93	
total		70	14	5	

Table 4. Descriptive statistics of control task results. The results show a substantial improvement in memorization performance by human centered AmI (group 3) compared to conventional AmI conditions (group 2).

group	N	mean	standard error	standard deviation
1	5	1.8	0.66	1.48
2	5	3.6	1.33	2.96
3	5	0.6	0.4	0.89
total	15	2	0.58	2.23

of human services. This means the measurement of the cognitive loads of the test persons while conducting the particular experiments either using human services or not. Therefore, the memorization performances of the subjects assigned to the particular sub-groups are compared.

The ANOVA analysis of the mismatches, i.e. the Levenshtein distances between the nine-digit numbers to be memorized and those numbers which actually were reproduced by the subjects, shows a trend towards a significant difference ($p = 0.094$) between the sub-groups of the case-study. In table 3 the particular measures are summarized accordingly. It can be seen that the proposed approach of human centred AmI (group 3) reduces the error rate to a level similar to the control group (group 1) where no cognitive interference was inducted (table 4). Contrary to a conventional AmI system (group 2) the error rate is halved – which gives strong evidence for the effectiveness of human services in related AmI domains.

4.5   Conclusion

By means of an user-oriented case-study where naive users interacted without constraints in a Wizard-of-Oz setup with an intelligent environment which was designed according to the proposed approach, the effectiveness of human services has been demonstrated. The results of the experimental evaluation show that the new concept of human centered AmI not only enriches the environmental functionality as described in section 3. Furthermore, the usability of the intelligent environment has become more intuitive. Evidence for these improvements is given by means of the results of dual-task interference experiments. The quantitative analysis of the memorization performance of test persons interacting with the FINCA shows that their cognitive load is decreased when human services are enabled – the AmI has become easier to use. To summarize, intelligent interaction, user guidance, and the integration of human services in action planning processes allow for intuitive interaction with a complex intelligent environment without the need for detailed pre-instructions.

Furthermore, this case-study shows a natural understanding for the proposed concept by the user. None of the test persons responded irritated when he was asked to help the robot or to restart a software module, i.e. when the subject was asked for a human service. A qualitative analysis of the questionnaire survey unveiled the stronger integration of the user into the environment by the presented approach: The role of the user shifts from a trigger of actions to an integral component of the environment which in fact is the main goal of human centered AmI on system level.

5 Discussion

The key to successful applications within the field of Ambient Intelligence is the permanent system awareness w.r.t. the particular environmental context. In contrast to, e.g., desktop applications, AmI scenarios are based on the integration of various software services running in parallel on different computers.

In this paper we proposed a new concept for direct user integration into Ambient Intelligence environments resulting in human centered AmI. The motivation for this is to overcome the "all-or-nothing" dilemma which we identified for conventional AmI applications: If a certain application relies on specific soft- or hardware services the overall application is hardly transferable to related scenarios where the setup just slightly differs. As an example, AmI solutions developed for Smart Houses substantially depend on the existence of the same hardware "zoo". Otherwise, i.e. if some device is missing or malfunctioning the application will fail completely. We used the example of automatic door-openers allowing a mobile robot to enter a room. If such a device is not available or malfunctioning the robot cannot be used at all and the AmI probably becomes, at least partially, useless.

In order to open up ways out of the "all-or-nothing" dilemma we explicitly integrate human users and their physical abilities into the overall AmI system. Within the software framework of AmI architectures human users are explicitly represented by virtual doppelgangers. These objects are transparently integrated as any other devices (i.e. sensors and actuators) thereby also offering services – human services. Via software patterns dynamic role changes of the human users – depending on their, now explicitly modeled, context and the state of the environment – are realized at runtime. By means of an experimental evaluation within a practical case-study in our own Smart House the effectiveness of the proposed approach has been shown. For a quantitative evaluation we utilized the dual-task interference paradigm. Due to the integration of human services the cognitive load of the users is lowered which indicates a more intuitive usability.

In this paper we presented the general framework for human centered AmI. In order to concentrate on the new concept and to avoid getting stuck in certain practical implementation issues its general effectiveness was evaluated by means of Wizard-of-Oz experiments. Clearly, when entering the real-world such practical details have to be solved. Probably the most important module required is the one which decides whether a human service or some (original) technical service shall be used. In a worst-case scenario the proposed concept would degenerate and human users offering human services are doing all the work – which is far from the original AmI vision. Such decisions, however, can be solved very effectively when integrating global reasoning modules (e.g. based on onthologies). By design such functionalities can easily be integrated into the framework of human centered Ambient Intelligence.

References

1. Weiser, M.: The computer for the 21st century. Scientific American 265 (1991)
2. Streitz, N., Kameas, A., Mavrommati, I. (eds.): The Disappearing Computer – Interaction Design, System Infrastructures and Applications for Smart Environments. LNCS. Springer, Heidelberg (2007)
3. Brooks, R.A.: The Intelligent Room project. In: CT 1997: Proceedings of the 2nd International Conference on Cognitive Technology (CT 1997), Washington, DC, USA, p. 271. IEEE Computer Society, Los Alamitos (1997)
4. Hirsh, H., Coen, M., Mozer, M., Hasha, R., Flanagan, J.: Room Service, AI-Style. IEEE Intelligent Systems 14(2), 8–19 (1999)
5. Coen, M.H.: Design principles for intelligent environments. In: AAAI 1998/IAAI 1998: Proceedings of the fifteenth national/tenth conference on Artificial intelligence/Innovative applications of artificial intelligence, Menlo Park, CA, USA, American Association for Artificial Intelligence, pp. 547–554 (1998)
6. Coen, M., Phillips, B., Warshawsky, N., Weisman, L., Peters, S., Finin, P.: Meeting the computational needs of intelligent environments: The metaglue system. In: Proceedings of MANSE 1999, Dublin, Ireland (1999)
7. IST Advisory Group (ISTAG): Ambient intelligence: from vision to reality. Technical report, Brussels, Belgium, ISTAG draft consolidated report (2003)
8. Natis, Y.V.: Service-oriented architecture scenario, Research Note, Gartner Research (2003)
9. Lee, C., Nordstedt, D., Helal, S.: Enabling smart spaces with osgi. Pervasive Computing 2(3), 89–94 (2003)
10. Helal, S., Mann, W., El-Zabadani, H., King, J., Kaddoura, Y., Jansen, E.: The gator tech smart house: A programmable pervasive space. Computer 38(3), 50–60 (2005)
11. Danielsen, T., Pankoke-Babatz, U., Prinz, W., Patel, A., Pays, P.A., Smaaland, K., Speth, R.: The amigo project: advanced group communication model for computer-based communications environment. In: CSCW 1986: Proceedings of the 1986 ACM conference on Computer-supported cooperative work, pp. 115–142. ACM, New York (1986)

12. Plötz, T.: The FINCA: A Flexible, Intelligent eNvironment with Computational Augmentation (2007), http://finca.irf.de
13. Jameson, A., Kruger, A.: Preface to the special issue on user modeling in ubiquitous computing. User Modeling and User-Adapted Interaction 15(3-4), 193–195 (2005)
14. Bravo, J., Alamán, X., Riesgo, T.: Ubiquitous computing and ambient intelligence: New challenges for computing. Journal of Universal Computer Science 12(3), 233–235 (2007)
15. Heckmann, D.: Ubiquitous User Modeling. PhD thesis, Department of Computer Science, Saarland University, Germany (November 2005)
16. Gamma, E., Helm, R., Johnson, R., Vlissides, J.: Design Patterns. Addison-Wesley Professional, Reading (January 1995)
17. Kray, C., Larsen, L.B., Olivier, P., Biemans, M., van Bunningen, A., Fetter, M., Jay, T., Khan, V.J., Leitner, G., Mulder, I., Müller, J., Plötz, T., de Vallejo, I.L.: Evaluating ubiquitous systems with users. In: AmI 2007: Workshop Proceedings of the European Conference on Ambient Intelligence, Darmstadt, Germany (2007)
18. Preece, J., Rogers, Y., Sharp, H., Benyon, D., Holland, S., Carey, T.: Human-Computer Interaction. Addison-Wesley, Reading (1994)
19. Likert, R.: A technique for the measurement of attitudes. Archives of Psychology 22(140), 1–55 (1932)
20. Pashler, H.: Dual-task interference in simple tasks: data and theory. Psychological Bulletin 116(2), 220–244 (1994)
21. Olive, T.: Working memory in writing: Empirical evidence from the dual-task technique. European Psychologist 9(1), 32–42 (2004)
22. Levenshtein, V.I.: Binary codes capable of correcting deletions, insertions, and reversals. Soviet Physics Doklady 10(8), 707–710 (1966)
23. Minium, E.W.: Statistical reasoning in psychology and education, 2nd edn. Wiley, New York (1978)

HOMEinTOUCH
Designing Two-Way Ambient Communication

Marianne Graves Petersen[1], Aviaja Borup Hansen[2], Kaspar Rosengreen Nielsen[3],
and Rasmus Gude[1]

[1] Computer Science Department, University of Aarhus, Aabogade 34,
DK- 8200 Aarhus N, Denmark
{mgraves,gude}@daimi.au.dk
[2] Bang & Olufsen
Peter Bangs vej 15, DK- 7600 Struer, Denmark
ABH@bang-olufsen.dk
[3] Alexandra Institute
Aabogade 34,
DK- 8200 Aarhus N, Denmark
kaspar@daimi.au.dk

Abstract. Digital Picture Frames has received attention both research wise and by consumers, who are increasingly buying existing solutions. In this paper we investigate how to design improved picture frames through providing means for two-way communication and through exploring the potential in providing automatically generated context information. We report on the design and trial use of a HOMEinTOUCH, an experience prototype of a picture frame for domestic environment, supporting two-way communication and context-information around pictures. We tested this prototype, as well as two other commercial products during a journey and interviewed both the people traveling and the ones at home after the completion of the journey. Based on this material we provide design indications for future generation of such products.

Keywords: Digital Picture Frames, Extended family members, context-information, two-way ambient communication, and interaction design.

1 Introduction

"joy which we cannot share with others is only half enjoyed"
- *The Old Street Lamp by H.C. Andersen*

The potential for Digital Picture Frames in connecting people who are apart has been pointed out in a number of designs and studies [6][14]. In addition, digital picture frames have become a commercial success over the past years, and are expected to become even more in the years to come. In this paper we investigate the potential in supporting sharing of experiences between extended family members with HOMEin TOUCH a new type of digital picture frame, which explores the potential in

E. Aarts et al. (Eds.): AmI 2008, LNCS 5355, pp. 44–57, 2008.

- Supporting better two-way communication than are offered in most commercial picture frames
- Integrating the communication mechanism in the physical home and in everyday life
- Exploring the role of context-data for supporting the communication

Thus while these aspects have been investigated separately, in this study we explore them in conjunction. Our investigation consists of the design of a prototype of a new type of picture frame HOMEinTOUCH, an experience prototype we have developed to explore the above themes. We set up a field trial where three different means of communication were explored on the same trip. One of the communication channels was HOMEinTOUCH. In addition an iGoogle site and a commercial Picture frame (Seeframe) were used. These three communication mechanisms were set up in three different households. After the trip all the parties involved were interviewed to investigate the strengths and weaknesses of existing solutions and to point towards potential future solutions.

This paper outlines the rationale and experiences from designing the frame and report on the experiences from the use of this frame and other related communication means during a travel.

The experiences from the design and trial use lead to reflections about the experience prototype. This paper is a roundup on some of the outcome and discussions concerning two-way ambient awareness. One theme is concerning the two-way communication in this specific case with one part being away and the other part being home, another theme is the obligations that the infected have towards each other when communicating and a last theme is the connectedness through this prototype. This paper outlines related work and puts the work in the context of a larger project investigating new means for people to make home where they are. It describes and motivated the designed experience prototype and outlines experiences from a trial use. Finally design indications are synthesized from the experiment.

2   Related Work

A range of research has investigated how to support connections between people who are apart.

Various devices supporting one-way communication have been suggested for the home. Examples include picture frames such as the Digital Family Portrait [14], which connects elderly people to their extended family members. Both the digital family portrait [ibid] and Tollmar and Persson's 6th sense [16] conveys activity awareness from one home to another home and thus allows for the awareness between people in different homes. Both these concepts support one-way communication. These concepts concentrate primarily on the ambient awareness and not on the sharing of experiences and contents.

Examples of two-way communication systems include InTouch, which allows for synchronous and tangible connections between individuals. This is an early concept, which is not developed in particular for a home and does not hold considerations on how such a concept would fit into a home and everyday life.

Virtual intimate objects [7] also explore two-way communication between closely related people. This study investigates how extremely simple information and interaction can support intimacy between couples in long-distance relationships. The concept explored consists of a small circle in the menu-bar on a desktop, which changes color as it is clicked. This research focuses on the desktop environment and is not particularly focused on the specific context of use.

A number of studies have explored the potential of situated displays, such as the HomeNote [13] and Whereabouts clock [3], which are both people-to-place communication displays. HomeNote supports communication between family members in the same household allowing text messaging or scribbling to a shared display in a kitchen. This device supports the daily contact and connections between people who live in the same house. Communication here is one way, from people to the display.

The Whereabouts clock [3] conveys coarse-grained position information of household members on a situated display in the home, typically placed in the kitchen. This device has successfully used position information solely to support rich awareness about family members activities.

Context photography [10] explores the potential in conveying context-information through modifying the pictures themselves in response to e.g. the sound level. This work uses the mobile phone as the platform for both capture and experience, where we are more interested in how this context information contributes meaning in the context of a remote household.

In line with others, [1], we are concerned about the communication demands new devices can impose, but at the same time, several of the above cases point out how rich and complex interpretations are done over seemingly simple information [7][3] [11] and indeed provide value to the people using these systems. In particular, people who are closely connected interpret the data in the context of the knowledge they have about each other. We are intrigued by these findings and seek additional ways of supporting this.

3 Connected While Apart

HOMEinTOUCH has been developed as part of a larger project which seeks to investigate new means for supporting people in living a mobile and global life, through devising means for people to *make home* where they are. This perspective is inspired by the research of ethnographer Ida Winther [15] who is also interested in how people increasingly live a mobile life. She emphasizes that this does not mean that people are place-less nomads [ibid] but rather that our ability to make home in these changing circumstances is key to be in the world. Inspired by this perspective, the challenge of the increasing mobilization and globalization is to develop strategies for making home as a way of being in the world. To understand better the conditions, practices, everyday life and advanced strategies developed by people who travel, we have conducted an ethnographic study of different kinds of people who are frequently on the move and have strong connections with people and places throughout the world.

One of the people we followed as part of this study works as a steward, Paul who has a flat and a wife in London, a son in Copenhagen, Denmark, He was born in New Zeeland where his parents and brother still live, and as part of his job he flies regularly between London, Los Angeles and Singapore. Figure 1 illustrates Paul's desktop in his hotel room in Los Angeles, where he is waiting to take a flight back to London. He has carefully organized the desk in the room with his computer. On his desktop, he continuously has his messenger contacts as well as the current weather conditions in places where people he cares about live or in places where he is often traveling.

Fig. 1. Paul pointing at his desktop where he monitors the weather in different places around the world. These are places where his loved ones are and where he is traveling often.

4   Designing the Frame

The aim was to create an artifact to support sharing of experiences between extended family members and friends. We were interested in designing an artifact for a home as "in homes, people are concerned first and foremost with other household members, followed by family members outside of the household and then, less importantly, friends and other relationships such as those of shared interest groups" [6]. We were interested in supporting the communication between close relatives. Further, as pointed out by Hindus et al [ibid], these new communication resources also potentially impose new communication obligations. Thus we were interested in carefully designing the communication mechanism in the home in a way, which fits into the daily routines in this context. The intention was to support awareness of the relatives while they are traveling and to give the travelers a medium to communicate their experiences with their family and friends and for the receivers' to communicate back to the travelers in a way that fits in with their everyday life in the home.

We constructed an experience prototype [4] to explore the potential qualities of supporting better two-way communication than are offered in most commercial picture frames, of integrating the communication mechanism in the physical home and in everyday life, and finally of exploring the role of context-data for supporting the communication. Our experience prototype consists of two artifacts. One is an augmented digital picture frame and one is a mobile phone, which communicates with the picture frame. The experience prototype can be seen in figures 2 and 3.

Fig. 2. HOMEinTOUCH picture frame during the field trial

The prototype realizes the above qualities in the following way. The largest picture in the picture frame displays the picture sent by the relative. In this case the picture of a cruise ship. Above this to the right, there are three small pictures, a portrait of the person who sent the picture, a clock showing the current local time where the picture is taken, as well as the current weather. Below this is the position indicated on a globe. The black round spots on the sides of the frame are squeezable zones where the recipient of the photo can squeeze to indicate that she or he has seen the picture. As these are squeezed, the sender gets a small round icon on the mobile phone with the picture seen at the time of the squeeze.

The intention with the squeezable sides on the frame is to allow for a way to acknowledge that the picture has been seen, in a way that integrated with the situation of viewing the picture and in a way that did not impose a burden in terms of complex interaction on the viewer of the picture. The intention with the context-information was to support the ambient awareness about the distant locality of the relatives. In particular, we were also inspired by the steward Paul, discussed in section two, who

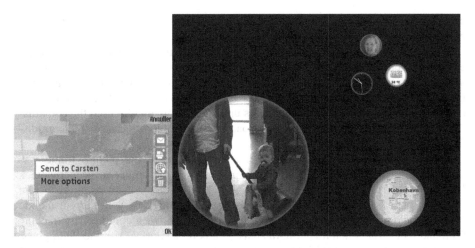

Fig. 3. Sending an image from the mobile phone in the left picture to the frame with the contents depicted on the right side

finds that the weather information is a useful way of establishing awareness on relatives who are far away.

5   Implementing the Experience Prototype

Focusing on the potential qualities of the experience, we chose to implement an experience prototype using a combination of existing technologies and services. The prototype consists of the picture frame and a mobile device for taking and uploading pictures.

The picture frame is a custom built case containing a tablet pc displaying a full screen .Net/Flash application (see Fig. 2 and 3). The application displays a picture slideshow fetched from PicasaWeb using the Google PicasaWeb API. Photos are refreshed at a given time interval and if new images have been uploaded the frame will give audio feedback.

In addition to the picture slideshow the application also displays various contextual information related to the pictures. This includes the current location of the sender on a map, the current weather conditions fetched from Yahoo! Weather and the current, local time at the position where the picture is send from. For the purpose of the experiment, some of this information was prepared and not truly updated real time. The clock was set to Philippine time and the weather was shown for the Capital Manila while Aviaja and her family was traveling around the Philippines. The location of the sender was basically a series of Google Maps screenshots displayed at a given time.

Another feature of the picture frame is the possibility for the viewer to squeeze the frame to reply to the sender. We incorporated a Phidget pressure sensor to detect squeezing of the frame. An e-mail was then sent to the traveler when the pressure on the Phidget pressure sensor was above a certain threshold in the application.

The other part of the setup was the mobile device. We decided to use a Nokia N95 8GB smart phone. The only explicit hardware requirements to the phone are built-in camera and Internet access, which are more or less standard equipment in today's cell phones.

For the purpose of taking pictures we decided to use the built-in camera (and camera application) on the phone. In addition to this we used Shozu. Shozu is a photo sharing software program for mobile devices; it connects to social photo sharing sites on the Internet (like PicasaWeb, Flickr and Facebook) and it's able to upload pictures taken with the camera and receive pictures uploaded by others. We used the combination of Shozu and build-in camera to upload the pictures to a PicasaWeb album displayed on the picture frame.

An e-mail account was set up to give notifications if the picture frame was squeezed. An improvement of the prototype could be the ability to properly track location of the sender using the phone. This is part of giving the viewers of the picture frame an opportunity to follow the journey. Implementing this with current mobile phones would be a challenge due to poor battery lifetime when continuously tracking GPS and moreover, when traveling in areas with poor network as e.g. the Philippines. A solution could be to display the location of the current image being displayed on HOMEinTOUCH. But that would also mean losing the awareness of the current location and conditions of the traveler.

6 The Journey Experiment

We conducted a qualitative experiment where we set up different means of communication between Aviaja and different members of her extended family. Figure 4 illustrates the communication mechanisms, which were set up before the travel. All participants got introduced to the communication types immediately before Aviaja and her family went on their trip. Aviaja. Anders and Anton went on a holiday to the Phililppines for two weeks.

6.1 Participants

Aviaja lives with her husband, Anders and their one-year old son in a flat in a medium sized city in Denmark. They frequently see and communicate with their extended family on a weekly basis either face to face or via phone calls. Aviaja also communicates via text messages with her father and more often her mother.

Aviaja's father and his younger daughter live in the same city. They were equipped with the HOMEinTOUCH prototype. Aviaja's mother lives in the capital and she received a commercial digital picture frame (eStarling seeframe) in the airport where she came to send off the family. Aviaja's mother in law got introduced to an igoogle website set up for the journey and her father in law was not introduced to any communication means by Aviaja and her family, but discovered some of them during the travel. The four parents all live in each their household. Table 1 provides an overview of the qualities of the different communication types.

Immediately after the journey was completed interviews were conducted with Aviaja, her father, her mother, her father in law, and mother in law. In the following we analyze these interviews to understand the strengths and weaknesses of these different communication mechanisms.

Mapping of setup

Fig. 4. The communication ecology set up before the travel

Table 1. The communication mechanisms explored in the field trial and the qualities represented by the different solutions

	Physical artifact	Displaying pictures	Displaying metadata	Two-way communication
HOMEinTOUCH (**Carsten**)	X	X	X	X
iGoogle website (**Jane and later Bent**)		X	X	
SeeFrame (**Kisser**)	X	X		

7   The Journey Experiences

One of the immediate findings was that that in the course of the travel, the communication mechanisms introduced only formed part of an ecology of communication devices, which were exploited by the participants. Figure 5 provides a map of the communications during the trip and key statements from the interviews with the participants.

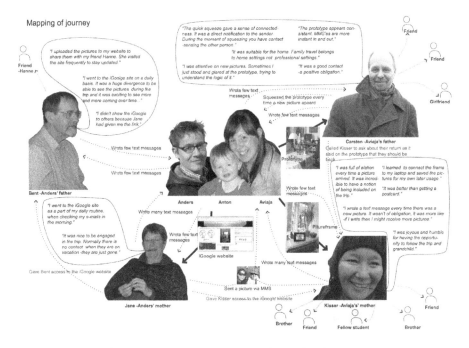

Fig. 5. Mapping of the communication during the travel

All the relatives were pleased to be involved in the trip:

"It was nice to be engaged in the trip. Normally there is no contact when they are on vacation -they are just gone." (Jane, testing the iGoogle version).

Even though Bent, Anders' father had not been introduced to the experiment, he engaged in the material as he learnt about the iGoogle site from Anders' mother. Both Bent and Kisser engaged very actively with the contents send by Aviaja. E.g. both Bent and Kisser uploaded some of the pictures to their own website / laptop and Kisser got motivated to further research the area where Aviaja and her family were travelling: *"The pictures inspired me to do some background research about different things: When I saw a picture of the beach I looked up coco beach on the Internet to learn more about the place. When I saw that they were diving, I searched for diving in the specific area. It was a way of indirectly following the trip." (Kisser, testing the commercial picture frame).*

The introduction of the communication channel imposed some expectations from the participants. Both Kisser and Carsten touched upon this during the interview. Carsten argued that he found that there were slightly too few pictures being sent to the frame. He speculated on the need to make an agreement beforehand regarding the frequency of pictures, but he also found that this could introduce unneeded concerns if this frequency for various reasons were not obeyed. Carsten argued that the communication on his side (the touch on the frame) was not a burden. It was like a positive obligation. Kisser sent an SMS with her mobile phone each time she received a picture in this way trying to encourage Aviaja and her family to send more pictures. It is interesting that the two people having the physical artefact were the ones who expressed the biggest expectations regarding new content. This suggests that centrally placed physical artefact is a powerful means for supporting continuous awareness, but on the other hand also potentially impose greater expectations.

Aviaja, at the Philippines, found that all the SMS messages sent by Kisser was to some extend a burden in that they introduced expectations on her to communicate back.

The attraction clearly was when new contents arrived. *"I was joyous and humble for having the opportunity to follow the trip and the grandchild"* and *"I was full of elation every time a picture arrived" (Kisser, testing the commercial picture frame).* But none of the solutions tried out offered good notification mechanisms when new contents had arrived. Carsten (HOMEinTOUCH) regularly gleaned through the whole sequence to see if new materials had arrived, and felt quite awkward having to do this. Kisser (commercial picture frame) adjusted the speed of the shifting of pictures on her frame. She set it to shift every 10 seconds when she expected new material to come and after the travel was completed, and she did not expect new contents she adjusted it to shift every 3 minutes. Kisser checked the frame several times every day. This clearly points to the need for investigating graceful notification mechanisms for this kind of material in the home. Jane (iGoogle website) established a routine where she visited the site one time every day.

The context information seemed to support awareness well, but it was slightly hard to investigate the specific role it played through the interview. It did though seem to provide the context for the pictures explored and the idea about where Aviaja and her family were. For instance, Carsten was surprised to see when, according to the HOMEinTOUCH picture frame, Aviaja and her family had arrived back in Copenhagen prior to his expectations. He called Kisser to ask whether she knew about their position, and it turned out that they were not there yet, it was the frame, which had displayed it at a wrong time (it was pre-programmed). When asking directly about it, both Carsten, Jane and Bent, who had the weather conditions available had all noticed how great the weather had been though at times a bit cloudy.

Kisser and Carsten with the physical frames were pleased with the way they integrated in the home. Carsten argued: *"This belongs to the home. It is a home-thing. It is good that it belongs here in the home. I did not think about it while in Copenhagen".* (Carsten was away from the home 2 days during the time of the trip) Kisser found it a luxury to have the frame. When showing it, one of her friends spontaneously pointed out, that is a real grandmother thing.

8   Design Indications

The experiment is an example of research-through-design [11] as we tested the potential in

- Supporting better two-way communication than are offered in most commercial picture frames
- Integrating the communication mechanism in the physical home and in everyday life
- Exploring the role of context-data for supporting the communication

This was done through the experience prototypes to understand the potentials of the design and to learn about the imprints it made in the family. Our findings lead in various directions where some of our assumptions were supported and others could be further developed in the next generation of prototypes. The following is a discussion about different design indications we find from the experience. In this way we can improve our design to make a product that improve the various communication strategies.

8.1 Two-Way Communication

The first strategy was our setup for two-way communication. All the receivers responded to new content (pictures) with a message to the senders. Using a separate media (text message) was not convenient in this setup, as it was a start of a conversation that obligated the travelers to respond again. The squeeze on the other hand was very straightforward and gave the sense of connection without further obligations. It can be discussed whether the feedback should be attached with a comment on the photo or the notification is enough. Another issue for further design investigation is the squeeze action – is it the right way to interact with the frame? Carsten said that it "gave a sense of connection" and that is interesting to follow. How can we support the semantics about the feeling of connection? There is an indication that we can embody this notion [8] without doing it in a 1:1 translation. A way to support it better may be to have both squeeze areas activated simultaneously as an electrical system, where you have to establish the connection, thereby establishing both the physical and the conceptual connection. It could also be further enhanced through haptic feedback as you push the frame and then you can physically feel the connection. One thing is clear and that is the potentials in supporting the connected feeling.

The obligation theme came up several times and the participants expressed that it was a positive obligation to give feedback or not an obligation at all. The travelers on the other hand felt too obligated to answer all the text messages, which they were not interested in as they were on vacation. It is therefore an indication towards an open communication where neither of the participants should feel obligated to respond.

8.2 Person-to-Place Communication

Researchers from related fields have implied that there's potential in designing for communication from person-to-place [12] specifically in a home context with several family members. HOMEinTOUCH is a home artefact and we have therefore decided to put it in the field of slow-design and slow technology [5] that doesn't call for speed nor efficiency. HOMEinTOUCH is a way of making slow messaging [8] from person-to-place that sometimes is instant, when traveler or the ones at home explore new content/feedback as it comes in.

The experience prototype HOMEinTOUCH was integrated in a home setting as was the SeeFrame but not the iGoogle site. The biggest difference was that the pictures were seen by others in the homes and became center for conversation, The frames were also checked for new content several times daily in the homes, but only once daily in iGoogle, as it was facilitated by the computer which was only used once daily. This made it more ambiently integrated through the physical object and the people in the home were reminded about the ones being away in a peripheral sense. Carsten said that HOMEinTOUCH was best to have in a specific place, being in the home as it was "not a work thing". He didn't give it any thoughts while being away from it but stared at it often when being home. This supports our anticipation of it being integrated in the home settings. This then brings us to another issue concerning trust. The HOMEinTOUCH is a window to the world, but at the same time a part of the decoration of the home juxtaposed to picture frames. The sender/traveler can expose pictures that the receiver might not want to look at in their homes. This might not become a problem as it is made for people in close relationships, but it is an issue that we have to consider for future development.

8.3 Visual Communication

HOMEinTOUCH is a rapid way of communicating through pictures that is seamless and convenient while on the move. We experienced that the travelers started to think in new ways of picture taking –telling a story through the picture. In this way they didn't have to write to tell where they were or what they did. They began to take pictures that were self-explanatory e.g. in front of a sign (Figure 6) or illustrating more of an atmosphere. (Figure 7).

Fig. 6.   **Fig. 7.**

Other research indicates that this kind of photosharing between family members and close friends is a culture itself (Kodak Culture) that have a need for more private sharing tool than for instance Flickr.com [12]. The Kodak Culture people use pictures to tell stories, stay connected with others and show different activities and experiences. We suggest that HOMEinTOUCH is an answer to this need as it is direct from person-to-place and it provides a stage for the stories. It represents some kind of an enriched interactive postcard with several pictures telling the stories. This is further supported with the context for data shown. In that way it is possible to send a picture, just to show where in the world you are and what time it is at this longitude or showing what the weather is like. We see HOMEinTOUCH as stage for several users. Perhaps the parents have several children traveling or living around the world. They can then keep in contact/track of them via HOMEinTOUCH. That is why the picture of the sender is also being displayed. We would like to test this use in a future setup, letting it stay in the home for a longer period because it would be interesting to see how the receivers would like to be able to edit the content over time. This leads to another issue concerning ownership of the content. When a picture has been displayed for a while the receiver may either want to delete it or save it to another media. Both was actually seen in our testing of SeeFrame as Kisser deleted some pictures from testing the setup and saved some pictures to her computer as it then came under her ownership. We have to decide if we want to support this hacking of the digital content or try to avoid it. Most indications draw towards supporting it as it has already been edited and given as a gift/message from the traveler. It can then transform into a more persistent picture.

9 Conclusion

We have investigated design indications for HOMEinTOUCH and found that it should support two-way communication in a seamless way giving a notion of connectedness. We also found it relevant to design for slow messaging from person-to-place having a physical object in the home as a stage for storytelling. In that way HOMEinTOUCH is an enriched interactive postcard with context aware metadata displayed.

Acknowledgments

We thank Aviaja and her close as well as extended family for participating in the study. In addition we thank our colleagues at center for interactivespaces and our partners at Bang & Olufsen. We thank the Danish High Technology Foundation for sponsoring this research.

References

1. Bergstrom, T., Karahalios, K.: Communicating more than nothing. In: CHI 2006 Extended Abstracts on Human Factors in Computing Systems, Montréal, Québec, Canada, April 22 - 27. CHI 2006, pp. 532–537. ACM, New York (2006)
2. Brave, S., Dahley, A.: Intouch: a medium for haptic interpersonal communication. In: CHI 1997 Extended Abstracts on Human Factors in Computing Systems: Looking To the Future, pp. 363–364. ACM Press, New York (1997)
3. Brown, B., Taylor, A., Izadi, S., Sellen, A., Kaye, J.: Locating family values: A field trial of the Whereabouts Clock. In: Krumm, J., Abowd, G.D., Seneviratne, A., Strang, T. (eds.) UbiComp 2007. LNCS, vol. 4717, pp. 354–371. Springer, Heidelberg (2007)
4. Buchenau, M., Suri, J.F.: Experience prototyping. In: Boyarski, D., Kellogg, W.A. (eds.) Proceedings of the 3rd Conference on Designing interactive Systems: Processes, Practices, Methods, and Techniques, New York City, New York, United States, August 17 - 19. DIS 2000, pp. 424–433. ACM, New York (2000)

5. Hallnäs, L., Redström, J.: Slow Technology – Designing for Reflection. Personal and Ubiquitous Computing 5(3), 201–212 (2001)

6. Hindus, D., Mainwaring, S.D., Ledc, N., Hagström, A.E., Bayley, O.: Casablanca: Designing Social Communication Devices for the Home (2001)

7. Kaye, J.: I just clicked to say I love you: rich evaluations of minimal communication. In: CHI 2006 Extended Abstracts on Human Factors in Computing Systems, Montréal, Québec, Canada, April 22 - 27. CHI 2006, pp. 363–368. ACM, New York (2006)

8. King, S., Forlizzi, J.: Slow messaging: Intimate communication for couples living at a distance. In: DPPI 2007, pp. 451–454. ACM Press, New York (2007)

9. Lakoff, G., Johnson, M.: Philosophy in the Flesh: The embodied mind and its challenge to Western thought, ch. 1. Basic Books, New York (1999)

10. Ljungblad, S., Hakansson, M., Gaye, L., Holmquist, L.E.: Context photography: modifying the digital camera into a new creative tool. In: CHI 2004 Extended Abstracts on Human Factors in Computing Systems, Vienna, Austria, April 24 - 29. CHI 2004, pp. 1191–1194. ACM, New York (2004)

11. Ludvigsen, M.: Social Interaction. PhD dissertation, Aarhus School of Architecture 2007 (2007)

12. Miller, A., Edwards, K.W.: Give and Take: A study of Consumer Photo-Sharing Culture and Practice. In: CHI 2007, pp. 347–356. ACM Press, New York (2007)

13. Sellen, A., Harper, R., Eardley, R., Izadi, S., Regan, T., Taylor, A.S., Wood, K.R.: HomeNote: supporting situated messaging in the home. In: Proceedings of the 2006 20th Anniversary Conference on Computer Supported Cooperative Work, Banff, Alberta, Canada, November 04 - 08. CSCW 2006, pp. 383–392. ACM, New York (2006)

14. Rowan, J., Mynatt, E.D.: Digital Family Portrait Field Trial: Support for Aging in Place. In: Proceedings of CHI 2005, pp. 521–530. ACM Press, New York (2005)

15. Winther, I.: Hjemlighed, Homeliness. Danish Paedagogical University Press (2006)

16. Tollmar, K., Persson, J.: Understanding Remote Presence. In: Proceedings of NordiCHI 2002, pp. 41–50. ACM, New York (2002)

17. Truong, K.N., Richter, H., Hayes, G.R., Abowd, G.D.: Devices for sharing thoughts and affection at a distance. In: CHI 2004 Extended Abstracts on Human Factors in Computing Systems, Vienna, Austria, April 24 - 29. CHI 2004, pp. 1203–1206. ACM, New York (2004)

The Influence of Control on the Acceptance of Ambient Intelligence by Elderly People: An Explorative Study

Lambert Zaad[1,2] and Somaya Ben Allouch[1]

[1] University of Twente, Drienerlolaan 5, 7522 NB Enschede, The Netherlands
s.benallouch@utwente.nl
[2] HAN University of Applied Sciences, Information Technology, Media and
Communication, Ruitenberglaan 26, 6826 CC Arnhem, The Netherlands
lambert.zaad@han.nl

Abstract. This paper presents the results of a study on how elderly people perceive an intelligent system, embedded in their home, which should enable them to live independently longer. Users of a motion sensor system were interviewed about their experiences. A sensor system that autonomously works as well as a manipulated version was studied. The manipulation contained a touch screen that informed the users if the gathered information was correct before sending it to caregivers, so more control over personal information was provided. To test the use intention of the motion sensor system Spiekermann's Ubiquitous Computing Acceptance Model of was used. This study shows that people, who perceive more control over their wellbeing, show more use intention. And that the subjective norm influences their acceptance. This study shows that acceptance models for Ambient Intelligence application in care situations need to be developed.

Keywords: ambient intelligence, user experiences, elderly, telecare.

1 Introduction

The vision of Ambient Intelligence (AmI) proclaims a future life filled with small computers embedded in environments of everyday life. The aim of AmI is that people in a particular environment will be assisted by the ubiquitous distribution of small computers in this environment [1]. Due to the context awareness of AmI, the environment should adapt itself to its present users and their needs. The users should interact with their environment in a natural way [1, 2]. The smart environment so provides more comfort and saves time and money, empowering the user and providing more entertainment [3]. The Institute for Prospective Technological Studies (IPTS) describes it as: "...'human centred computing' where the emphasis is on user-friendliness, efficient and distributed service support, user-empowerment, and support for human interactions [2]. Thus, AmI should strengthen humans in their own environments.

Together with these positive sides, some major concerns are frequently voiced as well. Loss of privacy, autonomy and control are often cited as downsides of the vision of AmI [2, 3, 4, 5].

E. Aarts et al. (Eds.): AmI 2008, LNCS 5355, pp. 58–74, 2008.

Up to this moment it is unclear whether these enrichments or threats will actually occur, since this has not been studied often and because the technology has not been presented yet. This study investigates whether the level of control influences the use intention of AmI.

As the IST Advisory Group (ISTAG) forecasted, many intelligent systems will surround humans in their daily lives and activities in 2010 [6]. These forecasts have been criticized on their sense of reality and optimistic vision [7], but this does not mean that the realization of the vision has been compromised. At present many major research centres focus on the development of AmI, such as Philips, Microsoft and MIT. Also the European Commission and the Dutch government see many possibilities of AmI, for society and economy. Their policy focuses strongly on investing in ICT as an important part of, for example, health care and transport.

Despite the ongoing development of AmI, user centredness and use intention have not been researched much. At the Ubicomp 2007 conference, only five of the twenty-nine surveys focus partly on user experiences and expectations in their studies [8]. This is understandable, as the technology to realize the vision has not yet been fully developed. There are not many applications or settings that contain all the five key features of AmI [9]. To develop and test a technology that contains *embedded* network devices and is *context aware, personalized, adaptive* and *anticipates* towards the users' needs, is, at this moment, practically impossible. To be user centred, you must test how people perceive intelligent and assistive technology. Especially the equilibrium between personalized and assistive possibilities versus perceived invasion of privacy and threat to autonomy needs more attention and research.

The first AmI-like environments are gradually appearing in daily life. Intelligent vehicles and home equipment trickle through to the consumer market. One example is the safety features to assist the driver in automobiles. Examples of intelligence at home are sensor technology to automatically adjust light or energy use, robot vacuum cleaners and remote controls for managing lighting. Especially the care for elderly people makes use of information and communication technology to help the elderly live more independently. The technology should improve their way of live.

In spite of these technological improvements, the question remains how people react to this integration of 'smart' technology in their daily life. How do they cope with the possible threats and new opportunities elicited by AmI? This study tries to gain insight in the attitude of elderly people who could live in an 'assistive' environment and how this influences their intention to use and accept such an environment. The goal of this study is to investigate whether the level of perceived control over well-being influences the use intention of such an intelligent environment. A sub goal of the study is to look for indications of differences in use intention between Potential Users (PU), the ones that participated in the study, and Actual Users (AU).

The next section highlights some of the methods of user studies within the field of AmI or Ubiquitous Computing[1] (Ubicomp), followed by the introduction of the Ubiquitous Computing Services Acceptance Model (UC AM), introduced by Spiekermann [10].

---

[1] The two concepts are closely related [1, 2] and for the readability of the text only the term AmI will be used in the remainder of this paper.

2 Previous Research on AmI and Related Technologies

The user studies in the field of AmI are mainly executed by using films or scenarios of a future with smart devices [11, 12] or by the use of single prototypes of systems that could be used in an AmI environment [13, 14]. These studies mainly focused on perceived effects of 'smart' devices on humans; in particular perceived control and perceived privacy were measured. They also show effects of the experiences people have with suggested scenarios or used prototypes. However, none of these studies used technology that is actually deployed in real life or that fits two or more key features of AmI as stated by Aarts [1]. This could mean that the perception of the participants will not correspond with the perception of actual users of AmI-like technology. The perception of privacy and the level of control can be perceived differently by actual users than by potential users. Another way to study the perceptions of users in AmI-like settings is by the use of a living laboratory or a Smart Home. Such laboratory studies create real-time interaction with AmI technology and can provide in results of actual use experiences.

The next paragraphs describe the research methods and results of other user studies of AmI-like technologies.

Spiekermann [11] used a film showing the future of shopping, in which Radio Frequency Identification (RFID) is used to provide personalized services. RFID is considered one of the important building blocks of Ubicomp [7], and therefore also of AmI. The results showed that people prefer to destroy the RFID tag, despite the perceived value of after sales services which it could provide. It seems that people put the protection of their privacy above the possible benefits of the use of RFID technology. There was also an indication that people did not prefer to manually activate the RFID tag (User scheme) over automatically determine the privacy settings of the user through a "watchdog" (Agent scheme). There was no difference in perceived control between the two settings, so an autonomous system was not seen as less preferable than the system with more user control. However, the results suggested that the level of information control provided by the User scheme does influence its appreciation. Perceived control appeared to influence the appreciation of automated personalized services.

Another study by Niemelä, et al [12] used three scenarios of AmI environments to test the attitude of elderly people towards AmI applications that support the elderly in living independently. One scenario introduced a smart pillbox. A second scenario drew a *sleep quality logger* to check for sleep apnoea. The third scenario described a home equipped with several interlinked ambient sensors. Overall some privacy concerns arose, as did questions about usability: The first two scenarios transferred personal data to someone else, which led to some worries. In two scenarios, it was required to interact with the system by using a mobile phone. Several participants considered this to be difficult and preferred an easier interface. But mainly the participants did accept services and applications that improved their living and facilitated a more independent way of living.

A study that also surveyed perceived privacy and presence was conducted by Brown et al [13]. They used a Whereabouts Clock (WAC) to investigate the experiences of using a family locating system. The clock could, coarse-grained, track the whereabouts of relatives. The researchers investigated whether the WAC was perceived as a helpful smart tool to enhance family values. This study showed that the technology can also help families to "be a family": it can enhance social cohesion. The participants perceived the WAC as supporting their reassurance, connectedness, expression of identity and social touch.

Janse et al [14] also studied perceived privacy and presence and looked at the preferences for manual or automatic operation of the system. One result was that perception of privacy and level of control is a personal experience. This study also showed that people prefer to share their information with only a small group of closely related people, with whom sharing location information does have some benefits. So privacy concerns did influence their attitudes towards the system.

Besides user studies that used scenarios or single service prototypes, there are also studies that used a simulated environment like the Philips HomeLab [15] or the Aware Home [16]. The aim of these smart homes is to discover the subtle characteristics of human behaviour and experiences when interacting with technology in a home situation. The use of technology in a home setting is different than in a working environment [16]. Creating realistic prototypes in a controlled but realistic environment [15] could gain insight into how people interact with and perceive a smart environment.

The papers cited above contain good ways to study user behaviour in AmI, but despite the high fidelity of the settings, they are still laboratory situations. To gain more insight into the role of smart technology, more field study is necessary [15] because "both the impact of the environment and the impact of time on the behaviour of the users of these applications must be considered." [17]. Due to the laboratory setting of these methods the social environment of the user is mainly left out, and as the Unified Theory of Acceptance and Use of Technology [18] states: social environment does influence the intention of technology use.

The user studies of AmI technologies described above showed that privacy does indeed somehow concern the users, especially the control over personal information and over who receives this information. Automatic situations were preferred in one situation, but not in others. Perceptual presence reassured people. Stimuli were used to invoke user perceptions. Live laboratory studies used actual stimuli, but lacked the social environment of the users. However, these studies did not apply to natural settings. This study tries to avoid this pitfall with the use of a real time system that meets most AmI characteristics.

3 Home Automation

As the previous section shows, using scenarios, films, single prototypes or laboratory settings are helpful ways to gain insight in the perception and experience of users of AmI-like environments. But all these methods use unreal settings, so actual experiences that form real intentions are not revealed. To avoid this, this study uses an environment that is actually deployed with technology strongly related to AmI: home automation.

Home automation can be seen as a precursor of AmI. The aim of home automation is the same as the aim of AmI: both should strengthen the users in their own environment. The Rathanau Institute describes the comparison between AmI and home automation as follows: home automation is the integration of technology and services within the home, emphasizing the improvement of the quality of life by enhancing safety, comfort and better communication. With home automation as well as with AmI, the technology ought to be 'intelligent' and disappear into the background [24]. The system used in this study consists of motion detecting sensors. This motion sensor system (MSS) approaches the five key elements of AmI. It is embedded in the environment, it is adjusted to the settings of the user, the monitoring makes it possible to detect differences in the context, and it informs care givers and relatives when differences are observed. Only the pro-active element is not yet deployed in the MSS.

As stated before, AmI is seen as a worthwhile supplement in health care. It could provide personalized care and surveillance at home, especially for the care of elderly people. Home automation is seen as a way to maintain a good level of care for the elderly. The use of ICT is seen as one way to meet the rising demand for elderly care [16, 24]. This study used one of the latest forms of home automation. This consisted of monitoring devices that unobtrusively keep an eye on the behaviour of the elderly by using motion sensors. The MMS was installed in the home of the user. These sensors registered daily habits, such as the pattern of taking medicine, eating, the sleep/wake pattern and the room temperature. By means of these patterns of behaviour a personalized care program could be facilitated. After about two weeks a lifestyle pattern could be determined. When the MSS detected differences in this lifestyle pattern a signal was automatically given to a central care giving organization and to designated relatives. Detected differences in lifestyle patterns might indicate that the person's abilities have started to degenerate or that some problem has occurred. The MSS used informed the care giving centre whether differences in sleeping pattern, kitchen use or room temperature had taken place. The MSS could generate an immediate alert when a serious problem would take place, such as a fall in the bathroom. This MSS worked automatically and did not inform the elderly user whether an alert was transferred.

In December 2007 a home care organization in the Netherlands started a field study to determine whether the MSS would be suitable for their clients. This created the opportunity to investigate the difference in use intention if the MSS would be less autonomous and to ask the user whether registered differences in lifestyle patterns are correct or not. As the previous studies [11, 12] indicated, control over information flow influenced the appreciation of a smart system.

The model and the method used to measure the experiences in this setting are described in the following sections.

4 Measuring Use Intention and Acceptance

To avoid the pitfall mentioned in section two, this research aims to study the influence of the level of control on use intention of an actually deployed home automation system. In this way the real experiences of living in an assistive environment can be measured. These results can be compared with the expected experiences of potential users of the same system. The setting was described in the previous section.

To measure the experiences with this technology, we used a new model: the Ubiquitous Computing services Acceptance Model (UCAM) of Spiekermann [10].

Spiekermann developed a model that predicts the acceptance and use intention of Ubicomp applications. As stated before, AmI is closely related to Ubicomp. Ben Allouch [19] described the differences and similarities between the two in her dissertation. Spiekermann's model could therefore be used for investigating the experience and acceptance of AmI.

As AmI focuses on the empowerment of people in their everyday life, one needs to measure the elements that influence the experience of everyday life. Spiekermann tried to capture these elements in the following variables: *usefulness, cognitive attitude, affective attitude, privacy, control* and *risk*. The model is shown below and the variables are explained in the following paragraphs.

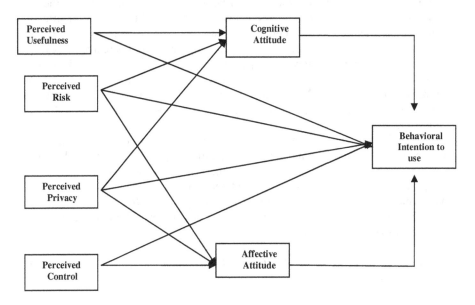

Fig. 1. Ubiquitous Computing-service Acceptance Model, Spiekermann (2007)

The UCAM is based on the Technology Acceptance Model (TAM) [20]. The TAM was developed to test the adoption of information systems in organizations. It was not designed for measuring the adoption of Ambient Intelligence. The variable *usefulness* is one of two used in the TAM. Spiekermann follows the TAM by treating it as a variable that influences the acceptance of UC, even though it is not in a professional environment. She leaves the second variable, *ease of use*, out of the model, because the vision of Ubicomp, and of AmI as well, describes an intuitive interaction with the system. This makes *ease of use* part of the system. Usefulness influences the cognitive attitude as well as the affective attitude. These attitudes are the centre of the acceptance model of UC. Spiekermann here follows Yang and Yoo [21], who have expanded the TAM with cognitive attitude and affective attitude. The cognitive attitude describes the expected performance of the system and the affective attitude is closely related to the appeal and usability of the system. Both attitudes have their own effect on the use intention of the technology.

Spiekermann states that the dimension "compatibility" is an important missing variable in the TAM. Compatibility has been defined by Spiekermann as the degree to which an innovation is perceived as consistent with existing values, past experience, and needs of potential adopters. According to Spiekermann, the UC characteristics that potentially undermine privacy and control fall into this category. *Perceived privacy concerns* (privacy) influences both the cognitive attitude and the affective attitude because privacy is formed through a cost-benefit rationale. Moreover, she states that privacy could influence the intention to use a system. *Perceived control* (control) is another part of the compatibility dimension and also closely related to privacy [6, 5]. Although the vision of AmI states that people will have more control over their environment, an intelligent environment can be a threat to the autonomy of the user [3]. That is why Spiekermann estimates that perceived control influences the affective attitude and the intention to use intelligent technology. The last variable of the model is *perceived risk*. Spiekermann has chosen to measure an overall perceived risk (risk). She follows Featherman and Pavlou [22] who state that several types of risk, as identified by Kaplan, Szybillo and Jacoby [23], share a common core. That is why a unified risk perception is measured by the risk variable. Perceived risk influences the attitudes towards the technology and the intention to use the technology, as well as the cognitive and affective attitude.

The main focus of this study was on the intention of elderly people to use a 'smart' environment. In this study we mean by 'use intention' the same as the variable *intention to use* in Spiekermann's UCAM. The other variables of the UCAM were also taken into account to find out how they stand out in the care for the elderly.

We wanted to study the use intentions of elderly people for a smart device and whether the level of control influences this use intention for an AmI application. This led to the following research question.

RQ: How does the level of control influence the use intention of Ambient Intelligence technology by elderly?

5 Methodology

To study the use intention of the MSS, three groups were formed. One group consisted of Actual Users (AU) of the MSS. These were participants in the field study of the home automation experiment. The two other groups both consisted of Potential Users (PU), and were named PU1 and PU2. The PU1 group received a description of an existing system, which works autonomously. The PU2 group received a description of an adjusted system, which means that it had a touch screen that could ask the participant a question about the registration. This adjustment is explained further below table 1, which shows the design of the research experiment.

For this study a description of the MSS was used. The description was reviewed by two home automation specialists and a Dutch language specialist for accuracy and neutral tone of voice.

A description of an existing home automation system was presented to the participants. It described the features of the system neutrally. The participants received a questionnaire with questions about perceived privacy concerns, perceived control,

Table 1. Research design

	Actual Users	**Potential Users 1**	**Potential Users 2**
Autonomous system	X	X	-
User control	X	-	X

perceived usefulness, perceived risk and attitude towards such a system. This questionnaire was based on Spiekermann [6] and the text was translated into Dutch and adjusted to the home automation system used. The context of the question changed from a smart refrigerator and smart car to living safely and independently. The questions to measure the variables of the model could be taken over from the questionnaire. Only the question to measure the variable *perceived control* was changed from *"I think that <with the system> I can decide any time on <the task> myself"* and *"this system leaves me sufficient control over my <task>"* to *"with the <name> I can do my daily tasks more safely"* and *"with the <name> I can do my daily tasks more independent"*. And the question *"the <name> gives sufficient control over my wellbeing"* was added in this study to test the difference between the actual used system and the adjusted version.

The readability and comprehensibility of the questionnaire was tested by a test group (n=12, mean age=68.8). Only small textual adjustments had to be made.

For the AU group the description of the system and text of the questionnaire were adjusted to the fact that they were familiar with the system and had actual use experience. For both PU groups the description as well as the questionnaire was formulated with the focus on potential use.

The AU (n=18) were approached by people of the home care organization which conducted the field test with the system used. This test lasted five months. Fifteen persons agreed to participate. The participants of the PU groups (n=208) were over sixty and lived independently, but could move to a supported environment in the near future. All the participants were visitors of a Day Activity Centre (DAC) that helps them to be socially active. They all have an indication, which means that a low level of care is necessary and that the health insurance pays for the cost of the DAC.

These PU were split into two equal groups. The PU1 group received the description of the MMS as it was deployed. The PU2 received an adjusted version of the description. This adjustment consisted of a user control function. If the system registered an irregularity in the patterns, it asked a question by means of a little touch screen monitor, mounted on the home central. For example if the system detected an irregularity in medicine use, it asked the user whether this detection was correct. See figure 2.

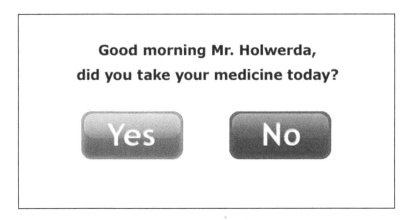

Fig. 2. Example question from the PU2 experiment

Earlier work has indicated that autonomous systems were preferred above manual systems [12, 13, 14], but that the transfer of personal data led to privacy concerns [8, 14]. That is why this extra level of control for the user was inserted in the scenario.

After the results of the questionnaire were collected and analyzed, a focus group meeting was organized. The goal of the focus group meeting was to elaborate on the results of the questionnaire. The groups consisted of five to seven people who had participated in the study. This was smaller than suggested [25], but followed the recommendations of Zajicek [26] to minimize the number of participants in focus groups if they consist of elderly people. By using smaller groups, the participants could contribute more easily and focus more on the discussion.

6   Results

The results of this study are divided into two sections. First we will present the results of the questionnaires, followed by the qualitative results of the focus group meetings.

6.1   Quantitative Results

This section presents the results of the questionnaires. First the variables used will be explained briefly, followed by the results of the study.

Usefulness measured the perceived benefits of the system. The variable *control* checked the perceived control over well-being. The variable *risk* measured the perceived risks of using such a system. The variable *privacy* measured perceived privacy concerns. The variables *cognitive attitude* and *affective attitude* measured the personal attitudes towards the presented or used system. The variable *use intention* measured the level of willingness to use or reject the system.

The three research groups consisted of 15 (AU), 43 (PU1) and 40 (PU2) persons. To test the results of the questionnaire, a reliability check was done for variables of UCAM. Cronbach's alpha (α) was used as an indication of how well a set of items measures a latent construct. A scale is regarded as reliable when Cronbach's alpha is at least between .60 and .70. Therefore all variables with $\alpha < 0.60$ were not taken into further analysis.

The variables that were usable for further processing were: *usefulness* ($\alpha = 0.76$), *affective attitude* ($\alpha = 0.88$), *cognitive attitude* ($\alpha = 0.95$) and *privacy* ($\alpha = 0.87$). For the Touch Screen setting, the variable *privacy* ($\alpha = 0.81$) was the only reliable one. The variable *use intention* was formed by three questions, but these had a low alpha. That is why only one question was used to represent the variable *use intention*. The question *I would naturally adopt the system, without any advice of others* was used because its high face validity for measuring use intention.

In the two other groups (PU 1 and PU2), all variables had an alpha between 0.64 (*affective attitude*, PU1) and 0.87 (*control* in PU2).

Table 2. Cronbach's Alpha in groups PU1 and PU2

Variable	Cronbach's alpha (α) PU1	Cronbach's alpha (α) PU2
Usefulness	0.82	0.74
Affective Attitude	0.77	0.64
Cognitive Attitude	0.86	0.74
Control	0.87	0.87
Risk	0.76	0.78
Privacy	0.73	0.69

To test the correlation between use intention and the other variables of the UCAM, we used Spearman´s Rho. The results are shown in table 3 below. Only the significant correlations between the variables of the model are shown in the table.

The results for the AU group show a positive association between *cognitive attitude* and *use intention* ($\rho = 0.62$; $p < 0.05$). The association between *usefulness* and use intention was also positive ($\rho = 0.62$; $p < 0.05$).

For the potential users who were offered a description of the actual, non-control, version of the system (PU1), the following results appeared after the Spearman's Rho test. Only two variables of the UCAM had a significant association with use intention. *Usefulness* had a positive association with *use intention* ($\rho = 0.34$; $p < 0.052$) and *control* had a positive association with use intention ($\rho = 0.38$; $p < 0.05$).

The results of the Potential Users who received a description of the system, containing an extra control function, the Touch Screen (PU2), showed three significant associations between *use intention* and other variables of the UCAM. *Usefulness* had a positive association with use intention ($\rho = 0.38$; $p < 0.05$). Also *risk* had a positive association with *use intention* ($\rho = 0.36$; $p < 0.05$). But the most interesting result was the positive association between *control* and *use intention* ($\rho = 0.54$; $p < 0.01$).

The results show that the association between *control* and *use intention* in the situation with the user control function was stronger than the association between *control* and *use intention* in the existing system. In table 3 below, all significant results of the correlations between the variables and use intention are presented. These results also clearly show that many relations, as predicted by the UCAM, were not found in this study.

Table 3. Correlations between the variables of the UCAM* p < 0.05, ** p < .0.01

	Use intention Actual Users	Use intention Potential Users 1	Use intention Potential Users 2
Cognitive Attitude	0.62*		
Usefulness	0.62*	0.34*	0.38*
Control		0.38*	0.56**

The *subjective norm* was also tested and it showed that this was positively corre-lated with four variables of the UCAM within the AU group, namely *use intention* (ρ = 0.64; p < 0.05), *cognitive attitude* (ρ = 0.55; p < 0.05) *affective attitude* (ρ = 0.58; p < 0.05) and *usefulness* (ρ = 0.65; p < 0.05). For the PU1 group also four posi-tive associations were found between the subjective norm and variables of the model. These were *cognitive attitude* (ρ = 0.53; p < 0.01), *usefulness* (ρ = 0.33; p < 0.05), *privacy* (ρ = -0.32; p < 0.05) and *control* (ρ = 0.63; p < 0.01). The negative correla-tion between *subjective norm* and *privacy* indicates that people who have low con-cerns about their privacy rate high on the *subjective norm*.

For the PU2 group five positive associations occurred between *subjective norm* and variables of the model. These were *use intention* (ρ = 0.60; p < 0.01), *cognitive atti-tude* (ρ = 0.57; p < 0.01), *usefulness* (ρ = 0.58; p < 0.01), *risk* (ρ = 0.57; p < 0.01), and *control* (ρ = 0.83; p < 0.01).

This shows that people in the social environment of the elderly influence their per-ception, attitude and use intention towards such a system. Fulk et al [27] already pos-tulated that the social environment influences the attitude towards communication technology.

The Mann-Whitney U was used to test whether the differences between the control setting by the added touch screen and the system as it was actually deployed were significant. For the AU group this test could not be performed. Due to the low reli-ability of the variables they could not be compared.

For the PU groups the results show that there were significant differences in *use-fulness* and *control* between both groups. There was a significant difference for *per-ceived usefulness* (U = 618.000; p < 0.05) between PU1 (mean rank = 36.21) and PU2 (mean rank = 47.05). The potential users with touch screen system (mean rank = 47.08) also differed significantly (U = 621.000; p < 0.05) with regard to the *perceived control* of the system from the potential users who did not have the touch screen sys-tem (mean rank = 36.44). These results indicate that the potential user group with the adjusted system perceived the system as more useful and that they perceived having more control over their well-being than the potential user group that had experienced the autonomously working system.

6.2 Qualitative Results

To get more insight into the results of the questionnaires, three focus group meetings were scheduled with the user groups. Since the actual users lived dispersed and lack the mobility to come to a central place for a focus group meeting. That is why open interviews were conducted with them. For both PU groups a focus group meeting was held.

First we will describe the results of the open interviews with the AU, followed by the results of the focus group meetings of PU1 en PU2.

Five participants of the AU were randomly selected to answer some open questions about their experience with the system. Four of the five persons thought the system was useful as a precautionary system for living safely. One person had fallen during the research period and the system did not respond immediately. Thanks to her personal alarm trigger she could alert the care givers. None of the participants were bothered by the fact that the home care organization could monitor their life pattern. As one person said "I rely on them to be careful with it". All participants also used a personal alarm trigger and stated that they preferred the direct action that occurs when the alarm button is pushed. Direct control over an alarm was appreciated over the sensor technology by the actual users. The personal alarm gave a greater sense of security to the elderly than the sensor system did. If the system would have a direct interaction possibility with care givers, or if the presented touch screen could facilitate mediated contact to check up on them, they would appreciate the sensor system more. All the interviewed persons said that they relied more on their personal alarm than they did on the sensor system. The tested system was seen as secondary by the interviewed participants.

These results correspond with the results of the questionnaires of the PU groups; the more control people perceived over their well-being, the more useful the system seemed to them. A higher level of personal control, for instance the possibility to contact a caregiver directly, increased their perception of the usefulness of the system. Communication via a screen or an alarm button could fill this need.

The results of a focus group meeting with 5 participants of the PU1 group show that they perceived the presented system as useful. The system gave them the feeling of being less lonely and of being looked after. Three of them stated that the system is better than the personal alarm trigger that has to be worn around your neck. "People forget to wear those", was their comment.

Privacy was considered important by the elderly, but they stated that when you need help it becomes less important. The home care organization was trusted to deal carefully and discretely with the collected data. The participants stated that good agreements between the user and the organization are necessary. The cost of such a system was an important variable for them. If they live alone and if they can afford it, they would like to use and buy such a system. Relatives or other closely related persons were another main variable. If those people would say that the system is useful, they would use it. So the subjective norm of family and others seemed to have a positive and strong effect on the intention of the elderly to use the system.

The target group of the system would be elderly people who live alone, according to most of them. Three persons also stated that it would be preferable if the system would also work outside their house. Control over their well-being provided by their social environment was preferred by most of the participants. But the system could also support their children in combining their own lives with taking care of their parents. Two persons saw this as a positive aspect of the system. If the care givers would visit them in case of a false alarm, it would not be a problem. It was important, though, that the care giver should be a person known to the care receiver.

During the focus group meeting of 7 participants of the PU2 group the following results could be derived. The adjusted system was especially useful for people who live alone. It provided a secure feeling for the elderly. However, 5 participants stated that they preferred to be watched over by their social environment instead of being watched by 'technical surveillance'. The fact that the system was able to check on medicine intake, mainly as a reminder, was appreciated by three persons. As someone said "everybody forgets something sometimes". Two persons preferred the data being sent to the care giver automatically, without a control check.

According to the elderly, the cost of such a system was an important variable in deciding whether they were going to use it or not. However, one person stated that security was more important than cost. Furthermore, privacy was also a concern for two persons in this group, but the care giver or volunteer aids were allowed to know 'everything' in case of health situations. The other persons did not care much about their privacy. As someone said: "What does privacy matters at our age".

All of the participants were clear with respect to the fact that if a relative or closely related person would think that the system would be useful for them, they all would use the system. Within this group the subjective norm was also a strong variable for use intention. The system would be more useful if it were expanded with more alarm functions, as was the case in the bathroom, or with a personal alarm trigger. The elderly thought that this would increase their level of control over their well-being in case of an emergency.

The results of the focus group meetings and interviews show that, for most of the elderly, control over their well-being and contact with caregivers was considered important and the elderly's social environment strongly influenced their intention to use the system. This corresponds with the findings of the questionnaires for PU1 and PU2, in which more control was preferred. The qualitative results also show that privacy for the elderly in a care situation was considered to be not very important. The results were similar with regard to the *subjective norm*: The results of the questionnaires and the interviews and focus groups show that the *subjective norm* played an important role for the elderly in their intention to use such systems. Summarized, elderly people perceived the subjective norm of family and other closely related persons and the perceived control over their well-being as important variables for their intention to use intelligent systems in a care setting. Privacy seemed to play a less important role for the elderly. The results of the questionnaires already indicated this. However, the relevance of these results became clearer in the interviews and focus group meetings.

In the next section we will present the overall conclusions, which will then be discussed further.

7 Conclusions and Discussion

The aim of this study was to investigate how the level of control influences the use intention of an intelligent system for elderly people who might need it to live independently. The main conclusion of this study is that the more control someone perceives, the greater the use intention is. Another important result is that the subjective norm also has a strong influence on use intention. These results appeared in the questionnaire as well as in the focus group meetings. The next paragraph elaborates on the overall conclusions of this study.

The subjective norm is found to play an important role in the use intention of the system by the elderly. This is shown by the results of the questionnaires and this was also clearly reflected by the elderly in the interviews. Based on these findings, it is clear that the attitude of closely related people and contact with care givers influence the use intention of the elderly with regard to an intelligent care system. To increase the acceptance of AmI in the care setting by elderly people, it is very important to involve the social environment of the elderly in the acceptance process.

This study shows that the acceptance of ambient intelligence in a care setting is not completely comparable with the acceptance process of intelligent devices that are not meant directly for care settings. In the explorative interviews the Actual Users stated that if the system would integrate an alarm trigger, such as they were all using at the time, it would be more useful. The participants missed the direct control over their well-being. This indicates that actual users, as well as potential users, prefer more control over when to call for help or to contact care givers. This finding does not correspond with some earlier work [13, 14] in which 'intelligent' applications that worked automatically were preferred over a manual working system. This could be caused by the target group of this study and the goals of the used system. Maybe elderly people prefer more control because their well-being is at stake. For example, in the work of Janse et al [14] families participate in the study, and not elderly people.

Furthermore, more research into the role of control is needed to get a better understanding of its part in the acceptance process of ambient intelligence. The UCAM provides an ambiguous picture of the control variable. Sometimes the variable is used to measure personal autonomy and sometimes it is used to measure control over personal information. This study shows that more control, such as control over one's well-being, leads to a higher use intention. Privacy, which is regarded to be an important factor of success for the acceptance of ambient intelligence, can also be seen as the lack of control over personal information. In this study, privacy is not regarded as very important for elderly people in a setting in which they depend on care. By definition, when you come to depend on the care of someone else, you lose a bit of control over your well-being and also some privacy. Apparently, privacy seems less important for the use intention of AmI-like systems by the elderly, if they need it for living independently. In the study of the after sale services provided by RFID [11], manual control was preferred over autonomous services. The study of Niemelä et al [12] also showed that automatically transferred personal information led to privacy concerns. However, the studies of the whereabouts clock [14] and the presence detecting lamp [14] show that an automatic system is preferred over a manual one. These differences between the results of different studies towards perception of control and privacy in different settings need more attention. Especially because AmI wants to empower people in their own environment, control and privacy can play a vital role in that process.

An explanation for the contradictory findings with regard to control in the different studies could be that the user in a care setting is not the care taker, but the care giver. So the actual user of the system is not always clear on first sight. Besides this, in a care setting you do not always want a user to have control over a system that should support them. If a person lacks the insight that he or she needs care, or just ignores it, then they could overrule the system. So it could be that AmI in elderly care could be a part of some kind of compassionate interference,

This creates a thin dividing line between user in control and user centeredness. Especially in care for the elderly, more attention should be given to this issue.

One of the limitations of this study is that the small group of actual users who participated in this study all used a personal alarm trigger beside the sensor system. They did not completely have to rely on the system. This could influence their perception of the system. Future research should try to include more elderly persons, although their inclusion in research projects can prove to be very difficult.

This study showed that financial risks also seem to influence the use intention of an intelligent system but this variable was only significant within the PU2 group. The interviews showed that costs are an important issue for the users, but the other types of risks, as identified by Kaplan, et al [23] were not frequently mentioned by the participants of all the groups.

Furthermore, the results of this study show that most relations, as predicted by the UCAM, did not appear in this study. In all three research groups, only a few correlations were significant. This could indicate that the UCAM is not suited to predict the use intention of AmI applications that should enable assistive living for elderly people. A possible explanation for this finding could be that the UCAM stems from the TAM. The TAM was designed for acceptance of technology in organizations and not for a domestic setting or a health care setting. The UCAM was originally used in a retail setting and not tested in a care setting. The specific target group of elderly people could also have played a role in the outcome of this study. More research is needed to explore this finding in more depth. However, this study shows that we have to be careful with using general acceptance models of AmI which may not be suitable for specific contexts and specific target groups. Furthermore, more research is needed to investigate the relationship between use intention and actual use of specific ambient intelligent applications such as domestic health care applications or intelligent retail systems.

References

1. Aarts, E.: Ambient intelligence: A multimedia perspective. IEEE Trans. Multimedia 11(1), 12–19 (2004)
2. Punie, Y. (ed.): Institute for Prospective Technological Studies: A social and technological view of Ambient Intelligence in Everyday Life. What bends the trend? (2003)
3. Brey, P.: Freedom and privacy in Ambient Intelligence. Ethics and Information Technology 7(3), 157–166 (2005)

4. Bohn, J., Coroama, V., Langheinrich, M., Mattern, M., Rohs, M.: Social, economic, and ethical implications of ambient intelligence and ubiquitous computing. In: Aarts, E., Weber, W., Rabaey, J. (eds.) Ambient Intelligence. Springer, Heidelberg (2004)
5. Spiekerman, S.: Perceived control: Scales for privacy in ubiquitous computing environments. In: Proceedings of the 10th International Conference on User Modeling, Edinburgh (2005)
6. ISTAG: Scenarios for ambient intelligence in 2010, Institute for Prospective Technological Studies (IPTS), Seville (2001)
7. Friedewald, M., Gutwirth, S., Punie, Y., Wright, D., Vildjiounaite, E.: Safeguards in a World of Ambient Intelligence. In: Security in Pervasive Computing. Springer, Heidelberg (2007)
8. UbiComp 2007: Proceedings Ubiquitous Computing 9th International Conference (2007)
9. Ben Allouch, S., Van Dijk, J.A.G.M., Peters, O.: Our future home: A content analysis of ambient intelligence promotional material. In: The annual meeting of the International Communication Association, Dresden, Germany (2006)
10. Spiekermann, S.: User Control in Ubiquitous Computing: Design Alternatives and User Acceptance (2007)
11. Spiekermann, S.: Privacy Enhancing Technologies for RFID in Retail- An Empirical Investigation. In: Krumm, J., Abowd, G.D., Seneviratne, A., Strang, T. (eds.) UbiComp 2007. LNCS, vol. 4717, pp. 56–72. Springer, Heidelberg (2007)
12. Niemelä, M., Fuentetaja, R.G., Kaasinen, E., Gallardo, J.L.: Supporting Independent Living of the Elderly with Mobile-Centric Ambient Intelligence: User Evaluation of Three Scenarios. In: Schiele, B., Dey, A.K., Gellersen, H., de Ruyter, B., Tscheligi, M., Wichert, R., Aarts, E., Buchmann, A. (eds.) AmI 2007. LNCS, vol. 4794, pp. 91–107. Springer, Heidelberg (2007)
13. Brown, B., Taylor, A.S., Izadi, S., Sellen, A., Kaye, A.A., Eardley, R.: Locating Family Values: A Field Trial of the Whereabouts Clock. In: Krumm, J., Abowd, G.D., Seneviratne, A., Strang, T. (eds.) UbiComp 2007. LNCS, vol. 4717, pp. 354–371. Springer, Heidelberg (2007)
14. Janse, M., Vink, P., Soute, I., Boland, H.: Perceived Privacy in Ambient Intelligent Environments. In: Proceedings of Context Awareness and Trust 2007 (CAT 2007), First International Workshop on Combining Context with Trust, Security and Privacy, New Brunswick (2007)
15. de Ruyter, B., Aarts, E., Markopoulos, P., Ijsselsteijn, W.: Ambient Intelligence Research in HomeLab: Engineering the User Experience Ambient Intelligence. In: Weber, W., Rabbaey, J., Aarts, E. (eds.) Ambient Intelligence. Springer, Berlin (2005)
16. Kidd, C., Abowd, G., Atkeson, C., Essa, I., MacIntyre, B., Mynatt, E., Starner, T.: The Aware Home: A living laboratory for ubiquitous computing research. In: Streitz, N.A., Hartkopf, V. (eds.) CoBuild 1999. LNCS, vol. 1670. Springer, Heidelberg (1999)
17. Intille, S.S., Munguia Tapia, E., Rondoni, J., Beaudin, J., Kukla, C., Agarwal, S., Bao, L., Larson, K.: Tools for studying behavior and technology in natural settings. In: Dey, A.K., Schmidt, A., McCarthy, J.F. (eds.) UbiComp 2003. LNCS, vol. 2864, pp. 157–174. Springer, Heidelberg (2003)
18. Venkatesh, V., Morris, M., Davis, G., Davis, F.: User acceptance of information technology: toward a unified view. MIS Quarterly 27(3), 425–478
19. Ben Allouch, S.: The design and anticipated adoption of ambient intelligence in the home. Dissertation (2008)
20. Davis, F.: Perceived usefulness, perceived ease of use, and user acceptance of information technology. MIS Quarterly 13(3), 319–340 (1989)

21. Yang, H., Yoo, Y.: It's all about attitude: revisiting the technology acceptance model. Decision Support Systems 38(1), 19–31 (2004)
22. Featherman, M.S., Pavlou, P.A.: Predicting e-service adoption: a perceived risk facets perspective. In: Proceedings of the Eighth Americas Conference on Information Systems (2002)
23. Kaplan, L.B., Syzbillo, G.J., Jacoby, J.: Components of perceived risk in product purchase: A cross-validation. Journal of Applied Psychology 59, 287–291 (1974)
24. Het Rathenau Instituut (eds.): Ambient intelligence: toekomst van de zorg, of zorg van de toekomst? (2007)
25. Patton, M.Q.: Qualitative Research and Evaluation Methods. Sage, Thousand Oaks (2002)
26. Zajicek, M.: Successful and available: interface design exemplars for older users. Interacting with Computers 16(3), 411–430 (2004)
27. Fulk, J., Steinfield, C.W., Schmitz, J., Power, J.G.: A Social Information Processing Model of Media Use in Organizations. Communication Research 14(5), 529–552 (1987)

JXTA-SOAP: Implementing Service-Oriented Ubiquitous Computing Platforms for Ambient Assisted Living

Michele Amoretti, Maria Chiara Laghi, Francesco Zanichelli, and Gianni Conte

Dipartimento di Ingegneria dell'Informazione, University of Parma,
Via Usberti 181/a, 43039 Parma, Italy

Abstract. The challenging context of Ambient Assisted Living (AAL) demands for a service-oriented technological shift in the field of ubiquitous computing. Recently, novel paradigms have been proposed, most of them envisioning arbitrary pairs of peer application entities communicating and providing services directly with each other and to users. In order to enforce these paradigms even to systems which include devices with limited processing and storage resources, lightweight middleware components are required. JXTA-SOAP, a portable software component supporting peer-to-peer sharing of Web Services, is a suitable solution. We illustrate its features and a possible deployment to enable AAL services.

Keywords: ubiquitous computing, ambient assisted living, services, peer-to-peer.

1 Introduction

The concept of ambient intelligence (AmI), which refers to a digital environment that proactively supports people in their daily lives, was introduced by the information Society Technologies Advisory Group (ISTAG) of the European Commission [11]. AmI overlaps with other concepts, such as ubiquitous computing, pervasive computing, context awareness, embedded systems and artificial intelligence [21].

In the AmI context, the European Commission recently started the Ambient Assisted Living (AAL) technology and innovation funding programme, aiming at extending the time older people can live in their home environment by increasing their autonomy and assisting them in carrying out activities of daily living, feeling included, secure, protected and supported. AAL spaces are physical places featured with AmI enabling technologies, including the intelligence which supports the services. Examples of AAL spaces are the home where the user lives, the neighborhood, the town, but also the body of the user itself. The technical challenge is to develop an integrated technological platform that allows the practical implementation of the AAL concept for the seamless and natural access to those services indicated above, to empower the citizen to adopt ambient intelligence as a natural environment in which to live.

E. Aarts et al. (Eds.): AmI 2008, LNCS 5355, pp. 75–90, 2008.

In this paper we mainly focus on AAL exploitation based on the concept of *ubiquitous computing*, whose main objective is to provide globally available services and resources in a network by giving users the ability to access them anytime and anywhere. In particular, we consider novel paradigms for regulating the interactions among the software entities of AAL-oriented AmI systems.

Recently, Gaber [7] has proposed two alternatives to the traditional client/server paradigm (CSP) to design and implement ubiquitous and pervasive applications: the Adaptive Services/Client Paradigm (SCP) and the Spontaneous Service Emergence Paradigm (SEP). In other words, the peer-to-peer paradigm is completed respectively by the self-organization and the self-adaptation principles. In SCP a decentralized and self-organizing middleware that implements an intelligent network should be able to provide services to users according to their availability and the network status. In SEP, spontaneous services can be created on the fly and be provided by mobile devices that interact through ad hoc connections without any prior planning.

In order to enforce these paradigms to systems which include devices with limited processing and storage resources, lightweight middleware components are strongly required. In [5], Bodhuin *et al.* compare some traditional solutions for net-centric computing middleware, such as Jini, OSGi and CORBA, listing their pros and cons. Not surprisingly, the survey does not include Sun MicroSystem's JXTA [25], probably due to the fact that in year 2005 an implementation for mobile devices was not completed. JXTA is mainly the specification of a set of open protocols for building overlay networks, independent from platforms and languages. Currently there are three official implementation of JXTA protocols: J2SE-based, J2ME-based and C/C++/C♯-based. In particular, an almost complete version of the JXTA Java Micro Edition (JXTA-J2ME, a.k.a. JXME) has been recently released. It provides a JXTA compatible platform on resource constrained devices using the Connected Limited Device Configuration (CLDC) with Mobile Information Device Profile 2.0 (MIDP), or Connected Device Configuration (CDC). Supported devices range from smartphones to PDAs.

How does JXTA cope with the service concepts characterizing the previously summarized paradigms for ubiquitous computing? The Web Service community considers services as *the only mean* for accessing resources (this concept has been explicitly formalized in the WSRF specification [31]), yet centralized registries, themselves exposed as services (like UDDI), are still deemed the primary tool to support the publication and the discovery phases.

Unfortunately, a peer-to-peer network of Web Service providers with a publication/discovery infrastructure implemented as a set of interacting Web Services would be absolutely unefficient due to the heaviness of the SOAP messaging protocol. On the other side, in JXTA each peer's service is just an example of resource which can be exploited by the user which owns the peer, or shared in the network, *i.e.* advertised by the user and exploited by other users. Resource descriptions have the shape of XML documents, namely advertisements. A JXTA advertisement can be filled with any document, *e.g.* a WSDL interface if the shared resource is a Web Service. In summary, JXTA provides a lot of flexibility by separating basic infrastructural services, mandatory for all peers, from specialized services, with different levels of description and efficiency.

Within the context of JXTA and Web Service integration, we are responsible for the development and maintenance of the JXTA-SOAP component [12], enabling Web Service deployment in JXTA peers, as well as distributed WSDL publication and discovery, and SOAP message transport over JXTA pipes (*i.e.* virtual communication channels which may connect peers that do not have a direct physical link, resulting in a logical connection bound to peer endpoints corresponding to available peer network interfaces with an example being a TCP port and associated IP address). JXTA-SOAP is currently implemented in two versions: J2SE-based (fully featured, extending JXTA-J2SE) and J2ME-based (partially featured, extending JXME).

The remainder of the paper is organized as follows. Section 2 illustrates User Activity Monitoring as emblematic example of complex AAL service, which requires the cooperation of several components providing diversified information and/or specific services. Section 3 describes related work on AmI (and in particular AAL) systems, middleware for peer-to-peer service-oriented ubiquitous computing, and Web Services on resource-constrained devices. Section 4 illustrates the internal design of the JXTA-SOAP component. Some interesting details of the implementation, referring to both J2SE and J2ME versions of JXTA-SOAP, are given in section 5. Section 6 describes how the component has been tested, with several different settings. Finally, section 7 provides a conclusive discussion and describes future work.

2   AAL Service Example: User Activity Monitoring

One of the most challenging AAL services is *User Activity Monitoring*, which is transversal to every AAL scenario. The SCP and SEP paradigms illustrated in section 1 are able to provide the flexibility required to deal with highly dynamic environments where devices continuously change their availability and (or) physical location (*e.g.* those which are carried or worn by the user). This complex problem of composing and decomposing connections among nodes is abstracted in an overlay network where the Activity Monitor (AM) component subscribes for raw context events coming from other distributed components (sensors, specialized data filters, etc.), searches for remote services which may provide useful information for its reasoning function, and publishes context events which describe indoor and outdoor activity of the user, taking into account different contour information such as medical prescriptions, planned agenda, etc (figure 1).

A distinction between *static* and *dynamic* activities is necessary. Static activities like "standing" or "sitting" can be inferred directly from the low-level data at a particular time instant (such as the pose of the person at a certain time using some kind of thresholding mechanism on the pose estimate). By contrast dynamic activities, such as "moving around", are usually composite activities requiring a monitoring of a full sequence of low-level data (*e.g.* context events

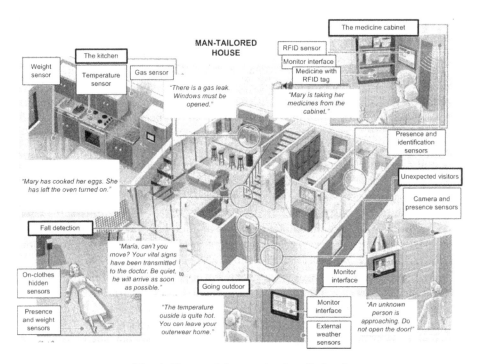

Fig. 1. User activity monitoring (indoor)

describing ongoing sub-activities). Low-level data needs to be stored for several time frames (in a context buffer), as the whole sequence is needed to infer that activity from an evolution of the low level data. For example: "cooking" may be composed of several low-level data at different time instances: "opening the fridge", "closing the fridge", "standing in front of the oven", etc.

Outdoor user activities are even more challenging to detect. The user may wear a personal mobile device (PMD) and sensors that monitor the level of its activity. The PMD should have a mechanism to be called from an external entity to deliver the activity level. Thus, the mobile device would be both service provider and service consumer. Collected information, which is analyzed in deferred time, may be useful for several other AAL services, *e.g.* planning the weekly menu (the less activity, the less amount of calories to ingest).

3   Related Work

In the first part of this section we discuss four recent AmI projects that in our opinion are the most advanced (one of them is clearly AAL-oriented). Then we revise the state of the art of technologies for ubiquitous peer-to-peer sharing of services. Finally, we discuss current middleware solutions for deploying and consuming Web Services on resource-constrained devices.

3.1   State-of-Art AmI Projects

The Agent-based Intelligent Reactive Environments (AIRE) project [1] is dedicated to examining how to design pervasive computing systems and applications for people. To this purpose, AIRE designs and constructs Intelligent Environments (IEs), which are spaces augmented with basic perceptual sensing, speech recognition, and distributed agent logic. AIRE's IEs have encompassed a large range of form factors and sizes, from a pocket-sized computer up to networks of conference rooms. Each of these serves as individual platform, or AIRE-space on which pervasive computing applications can be layered. Examples of AIRE applications currently under development include a meeting manager and capture application, contextual and natural language information retrieval, and a sketch interpretation system [19].

The Reconfigurable Ubiquitous Networked Embedded Systems (RUNES) project [22], funded by the EU Commission, envisions to enable the creation of large-scale, widely distributed, heterogeneous networked embedded systems that interoperate and adapt to their environments. The inherent complexity of such systems requires a standardised architecture allowing self-organisation to suit a changeable environment. To this purpose, RUNES aims to realize an adaptive middleware platform providing a common language that simplifies the application creation process. This should allow for a dramatic cut in the cost of new application development and a much faster time to market, transforming applications which are already technically possible into forms that are easy and straightforward for designers to use, and enabling applications which were previously unattainable. The project also examines the potential uses and implications of the technology, develop demonstrator systems and design training courses to aid in dissemination of RUNES technology. At this time, the theoretical framework proposed by RUNES is really convincing, but the middleware is almost uncomplete and has the strong limitation of being tailored for MANETs.

Another EU-funded AmI project is AMIGO [26], developing middleware that dynamically integrates heterogeneous systems to achieve interoperability between services and devices. For example, home appliances (heating systems, lighting systems, washing machines, refrigerators), multimedia players and renderers (that communicate by means of UPnP) and personal devices (mobile phones, PDAs) are connected in the home network to work in an interoperable way. This interoperability across different application domains can also be extended across different homes and locations. The project develops applications in different domains to show the potential for end-users and the benefits of the service oriented-middleware architecture for application developers. These applications are: "Home Care and Safety", "Home Information and Entertainment", and the "Extended Home Environment" in which multiple homes are connected. The enhanced service discovery and the semantic service composition methods addressed in Amigo are interesting and fall inline with requirements for composability and interoperability of services in an AmI environment. One drawback is the integration of input and output processing components into the middleware (UI service), while support for pluggability whould have been a better strategy.

Clearly AAL-oriented, the ASK-IT project [6] is driven by the vision of developing services that allow mobility impaired people to live more independently. By means of a mobile phone or PDA, users should have access to relevant and real-time information primarily for travelling but also whilst home, for work and leisure services. ASK-IT has not the objective to develop a standard ambient intelligence architecture. The emphasis is on a seamless service provision and a device that is intelligent enough to address the personal needs and preferences of the user. For example, information for a visually impaired person should be given orally, while for an illiterate person mostly in graphics.

Finally, project PERSONA [3], funded by the European Commission, aims at advancing the paradigm of Ambient Intelligence through the harmonisation of Ambient Assisted Living technologies and concepts for the development of sustainable and affordable solutions for the social inclusion and independent living of Senior Citizen, integrated in a common semantic framework. Project PERSONA seeks to develop a scalable open standard technological platform to build a broad range of AAL services, which are the services that the end user perceives as the final services and what he pays for. Each AAL service is composed by a hardware infrastructure and software components together with a user interface to communicate with the user. All accessible operations of software components provided with a usable interface are atomic services. Atomic services provided by the same component or by different components may be composed according to one or more patterns, resulting in composite services.

In conclusion, the lesson we learned is that AmI systems require a light and flexible middleware layer, providing facilities for building both client/server and peer-to-peer applications, supporting standard data and service descriptions, and allowing run-time component pluggability.

3.2 Ubiquitous Peer-to-Peer Sharing of Services

OSGi [18] is a Java-based technology which provides a service-oriented plug-in-based platform for application development. The core component of the OSGi Specifications is the OSGi Framework, which provides a standardized environment to applications (called bundles). On top of the Framework, services are specified by a Java interface. Bundles can implement this interface and register the service with the Service Registry. Clients of the service can find it in the registry, or react to it when it appears or disappears. Advanced networking features, such as *e.g.* peer-to-peer connectivity, are not provided by OSGi and must be implemented on top of it. For example, in the PERSONA platform [3] a middleware layer has been implemented (as a set of OSGi bundles), which hides the distribution and enables collaboration and communication, whether using a central registry or not.

To the best of our knowledge JXTA-SOAP is the sole open source project for P2P sharing of Web services being actively maintained and updated. WSPeer [10] is a J2SE toolkit for deploying and invoking Web Services in peer-to-peer Grid environments, which wraps Globus Toolkit core libraries to support the WS Resource Framework (WSRF) [31]. More interesting for ubiquitous computing environments is the Mobile Web Services Mediation Framework (MWSMF) [23,24], an adaptation of Apache ServiceMix, which is an open source ESB (Enterprise Service Bus). It provides an hybrid solution, since it must be configured as JXTA-J2SE peer and established as an intermediary between Web Service clients and mobile hosts, the latter being configured as JXME peers. Web Service clients can invoke the services deployed on mobile hosts via the MWSMF, which compresses SOAP messages (to BinXML format) and sends them through JXTA pipes. The MWSMF also manages message persistence, guaranteed delivery, failure handling and transaction support. Unfortunately, the source code is not publicly availble and few details are given about the realization of lightweight Web Service providers running on mobile hosts.

3.3   Web Services on Resource-Constrained Devices

Besides hardware constraints, mobile devices introduce many other specific challenges which make difficult the deployment of Web Services on top of them [4]. Unlike dedicated servers, mobile devices will typically have intermittent connectivity to the network. As a result, the services offered on a mobile device may not be accessible all the time. An application that uses or composes such Web Services needs to operate in an opportunistic manner, leveraging such services when they become available. On the server side, Web Services on mobile devices should also attempt to keep messages as short as possible. Another issue to be addressed is the change of IP address which may arise when a mobile device moves between different locations, and from one administrative domain to another. However, with the P2P in place, the need for the Public IP can be eliminated and the mobiles can be addressed with unique peer ID. Each device in the P2P network is associated with the same peer ID, even though the peers can communicate with each other using the best of the many network interfaces supported by the devices like Ethernet, WiFi, etc. [23].

Since the WS message protocol, namely SOAP, introduces some significant overhead, few toolkits support the deployment of Web Services on limited devices, such as PDAs, smart phones, etc. One is gSoap [27], which provides a WS engine with run-time call de-serialization. Unfortunately, gSoap is written in C/C++, thus requiring a priori stub/skeleton generation by means of a specific compiler, which also means lack of portability.

.NET Compact Framework [17] is a subset of the .NET platform, targeting mobile devices. Its class library enables the development of Web Service clients, but does not allow to host Web Services.

Looking at the Java Micro Edition (J2ME) platform, most libraries are only for client side functionality. The Java Wireless Toolkit (WTK) provides J2ME Web Services API (WSA) [29], based on JSR 172 [13], which specifies runtime ServiceProvider interface to allow the generation of portable stubs from WSDL files. The specification contains some notable limitations, most of them due to the requirement for WS-I Basic Profile compliance. Conforming to the profile ensures interoperability, but also prevents using alternative methods. Another widely used solution is the kSoap2 [15] open source component, which is a parser for SOAP messages (with RPC/literal or document/literal style encoding), not supporting the generation of client side stubs. kSoap2 is compliant with devices lacking JSR 172 support, and allows to access non WS-I conformant services.

To the best of our knowledge, the unique solution enabling J2ME applications (CLDC, CDC) as service endpoints is the Micro Application Server (mAS) [16]. It can be considered a lightweight version of Axis, by which it is inspired. For this reason we have chosen it to implement the J2ME version of JXTA-SOAP.

4   Internal Architecture of the JXTA-SOAP Component

The JXTA-SOAP component extends JXTA which is a set of open, generalized peer-to-peer protocols that allow a vast class of networked devices (smartphones, PDAs, PCs and servers) to communicate and collaborate seamlessly in a highly decentralized fashion. JXTA-SOAP has been designed having in mind ubiquitous computing needs, such as those defined by the SCP and SEP paradigms [3]. JXTA-SOAP completes the JXTA framework (which defines a naming scheme, advertisements, peergroups, pipes, and a number of core policies) with service supporting mechanisms based on state-of-art software design patterns, with the purpose to reduce the complexity otherwise required to build and deploy peer-to-peer service-oriented applications.

In this section we shortly describe the internal architecture of JXTA-SOAP, with the purpose of conceptualizing its main features at a high abstraction level. Technical details are out of the scope of this paper, but the interested reader may refer to [2].

4.1   Service Deployment

In order to deploy its services, a JXTA-SOAP based peer has to instantiate and configure the related service objects (one for each hosted service), and to advertise the service interfaces in the network. The diagram in figure 2 illustrates the relationships among objects which are involved in this tasks. The Peer class represents the generic peer application implemented by the developer, and relies on JXTA-SOAP's API which provides all the other classes illustrated in the diagram.

At start-up, each peer bootstraps the JXTA platform, configuring basic connectivity settings, such as TCP/IP and HTTP ports. Bridges to existing common membership and access technologies allow the peer to establish its identity within peergroups (the main one, *i.e.* JXTA public peergroup, and its subgroups). These tasks are illustrated by the sequence diagram in figure 3, and detailed in the following of this section.

For each service to be deployed, a service descriptor must be istantiated and filled with service-specific information, such as the service name, a brief description of the functionalities the service provides, the implementation class name, the peergroup ID, the security tag. Moreover, the service descriptor accepts a *Context Object* [14] (constructed by the user application) to the Web Service class.

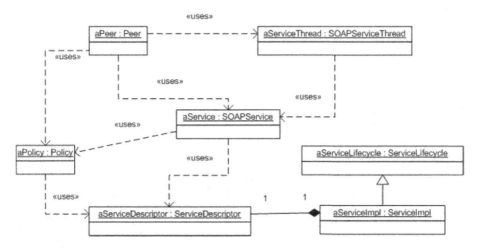

Fig. 2. Objects involved in service deployment

Then, the service advertisement (*i.e.* a XML document describing a resource, in JXTA jargon) must be filled with the service WSDL. Next step is to create the context object, whose parameters are stored in a hashmap, and to pass it to the service instance, along with the associated security policy.

Moreover, the initialization of the service triggers the creation and publication of the advertisement of a public pipe for the invocation of the service itself. For each service implementation, the peer spawns a thread which waits for consumers' connections to that service, on the service public pipe, and creates a pool of invocation threads to serve requests concurrently, according to the *Threadpool* pattern [20]).

4.2 Service Publication and Lookup

The main enhancement of JXTA-SOAP with respect to traditional Web Service frameworks is the adopted distributed approach for service advertising and lookup. JXTA-SOAP allows to encapsulate WSDL interfaces in specific JXTA advertisements, which can be spread into the network using one of the routing policies which can be inserted in JXTA protocol stack.

Service publication is a distributed process, which uses network nodes as a distributed repository (on the contrary, traditional UDDI registries are centralized interface description repositories). As for publication, service lookup is a distributed process, which can be conceptualized as message exchange between low-level JXTA modules.

JXTA's default message routing protocol for advertisement sharing and discovery is called SRDI. Its description is out of the scope of this paper, thus we suggest the interested reader to read the paper of Traversat *et al.* [25] for details.

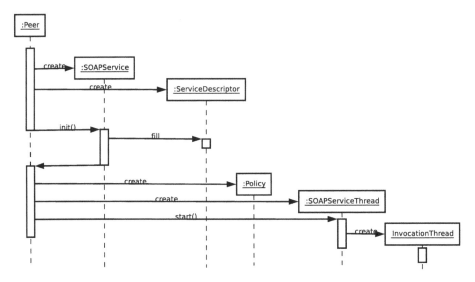

Fig. 3. The service deployment process represented with a sequence diagram

4.3   Service Invocation

Figure 4 illustrates associations among objects which are involved in the service invocation task, performed by a generic peer. The latter, once it has discovered the service advertisement and the WSDL interface of the Web Service, creates a SOAP transport deployer, which manages the transmission of SOAP messages to and from the service using its pipe. Moreover, the peer creates a service descriptor which is used by the call factory to instantiate a call (the adopted strategy is the *Factory Method* [9]). Each call implements the *Requestor* pattern [28],

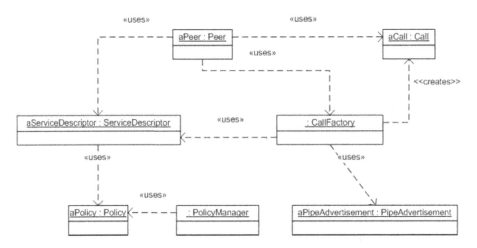

Fig. 4. Objects involved in service invocation

which constructs a message from the absolute reference of the remote service, the operation name, its arguments and return type.

5   Implementation of the JXTA-SOAP Component

We implemented two (interoperable) versions of JXTA-SOAP: J2SE-based, extending JXTA-J2SE, and J2ME-based, extending JXTA-J2ME. In the following we describe their features and the different technological solutions they rely on.

5.1   JXTA-SOAP for Java Standard Edition (J2SE)

The J2SE version of the JXTA-SOAP component supports service deployment, discovery, and invocation, with optional use of standard mechanisms to secure communications among peers. The core of the component is the Apache Axis engine (v1.4), which is a producer/consumer of SOAP messages. Usually Axis is deployed in a Web application server, such as Apache Tomcat, together with the implementions of the Web Services to be deployed, while client applications use the Axis Java API to create request instances. The Axis engine provides the processing logic, either client or server. When running, it invokes a series of Handlers according to a specific order which is determined by two factors - deployment configuration, and whether the engine is a client or a server. The object which is passed to each Handler invocation is a MessageContext, *i.e.* is a structure which contains several important parts: 1) a "request" message, 2) a "response" message, and 3) a bag of properties.

At runtime, for a service provider its service objects are deployed in the Axis engine, which implements the JAX-RPC API, one of the standard ways to program Java services, also supporting the lifecycle of service endpoint instances. After being loaded and instantiated, the JAX-RPC runtime system is required to initialize the service instance before any requests can be serviced. A context parameter is pssed to the initialization function, enabling the service instance to access the context provided by the underlying JXTA-SOAP based runtime system. The context parameter is typecasted to an appropriate Java type. For services deployed in a JXTA-SOAP based runtime system, the Java type of the context parameter is defined by the developer that is using the JXTA-SOAP API, and passed to the service object. The latter instantiates the Service Descriptor, creates and publishes the public pipe and the service advertisement, and notifies itself to the Axis engine. Services can be deployed anytime, without the need to restart the peer.

Once a service instance has been initialized, the Axis engine may dispatch multiple remote invocations to it. After that, when the Axis engine determines that the service instance needs to be removed from service of handling remote invocations, it destroys it. In the implementation of the destruction functionality, the service object releases its resources.

For remote service invocation, a consumer peer needs to intantiate a Call object. JXTA-SOAP's Call class extends Axis' default one, overloading the use of service URLs with the use of the Service Descriptor and the public pipe advertisement of the service. To create Call instances, the peer uses the implementation of the Call Factory class provided by Axis.

We previously described the tasks which are performed when a Web Service is deployed by a peer, and we mentioned that some parameters are put in the Service Descriptor for further use by the Axis engine. In particular, one of these parameters is the Web Service Deployment Descriptor (WSDD). When the WSDD is sent to the Axis engine running in the peer, an *Invoker* [28] is informed that it supports the new Web Service. Thus, when an invocation reaches the peer, the Invoker looks up the class which implements the service, and lets the instance handle the request message. In details, the Invoker reads incoming messages and demarshals the parameters inserted by the consumer peer's Requestor (absolute reference of the service, operation name, arguments, return value) and dispatches the message to the targeted service.

5.2   JXTA-SOAP for Java Micro Edition (J2ME)

The J2ME version of the architecture illustrated in section 4 supports Connected Device Configuration (CDC) and Personal Profile. We implemented the API which enables the development of peers that are able to deploy, provide, discover and consume Web Services in a JXTA-SOAP network. Since Axis is not available for the CDC platform, we adopted kSoap2 [15] as SOAP parser (for consumer functionalities) and, for service provision, we integrated the mAS [16] lightweight engine.

Service invocation is allowed by a kSoap2 based implementation of the Call Factory class. The latter instantiates a kSoap2's Soap Object, and sets all the properties for message exchanging through JXTA pipes. Soap Object is a highly generic class which allows to build SOAP calls, by setting up a SOAP envelope. We have maintained the same structure of J2SE-based version for Call Factory, to allow portability of service consumer applications from desktop PCs or laptops to PDAs. Internally, the Call Factory class creates a Soap Object passing references to the Service Descriptor, the public pipe advertisement of the service and the peergroup as parameters for the creation of the Call object.

The Call Factory class also allows to create an instance of kSoap Pipe Transport, the class we implemented to manage the transmission of SOAP messages using service pipes. The kSoap2 API provides a Transport class that encapsulates the serialization and deserialization of SOAP messages, but does not manage communication with the service; the HTTP Transport subclass, both in CDC and CLDC version, allows service invocation over HTTP, setting up the required properties, but it uses URLs as absolute references of remote services, and it is not suitable for usage in JXTA-SOAP, where services (as every resource) are identified by JXTA-IDs and must be invoked through JXTA pipes. Thus, we extended the Transport class with the implementation of a call functionality that configures a JXTA pipe and creates the messages to be sent over it.

After instantiating the transport using the Call Factory class, the consumer peer creates the request object, indicating the name of the remote method to invoke and setting the input parameters as additional properties. This object is assigned to a Soap Serialization Envelope, as the outbound message for the soap call; Soap Serialization Envelope is a kSoap2 class that extends the basic Soap Envelope, providing support for the SOAP Serialization format specification and simple object serialization. The same class provides a getResponse method that extracts the parsed response from the wrapper object and returns it.

Referring to service provision, we integrated the Server class of the Micro Application Server (mAS) into the basic service class of the JXTA-SOAP API.

mAS implements the Chain of Responsibility pattern [9], the same used in Axis. It avoids coupling the sender of a request to its receiver by giving more than one object a chance to handle the request; receiving objects are chained and the request passed along the chain until an object handles it. Moreover, mAS allows service invocation by users and service deployment by administrator; it also supplies browser management of requests, distinguishing if the HTTP message contains a Web page request or a SOAP envelope.

6   Experimental Evaluation

Using a simple, ping-pong like Web Service, we tested several point-to-point configurations, combining different settings for each participant. JXTA-J2SE peers have been deployed on laptops and desktop computers running either Windows XP, Linux or Mac OS X, equipped with 1GB RAM and 1.6GHz processors. A JXTA-J2ME peer has been hosted on an I-Mate JASJAR Pocket PC PDA, equipped with 64MB RAM and 520MHz processor.

The memory footprint of a Java program is predominantly due to objects, classes, and threads that the users create directly, and native data structures (like the constant-pool, the string-table, etc.), native code, and the virtual machine (JVM) itself that are loaded indirectly by the user. For JXTA-SOAP peers running on laptops and desktop conputers with J2SE v1.5, we measured a 22.5MB

Table 1. JXTA-SOAP test configurations

overlay peers	data link	multicast	t_r (s)	t_s (s)	t_i (s)
edge J2SE c, rdv J2SE p	Ethernet	off	2.5	0.5	0.1
edge J2SE c, rdv J2SE p	Ethernet	on	n.n.	2.0	0.1
edge J2SE c, edge J2SE p	Ethernet	on	n.n.	0.5	0.1
edge J2SE c, edge J2SE p, rdv J2SE b	Ethernet	off	2.5	0.5	0.1
edge J2SE c, rdv J2SE p	WiFi	off	2.0	0.5	0.7
edge J2SE c, rdv J2SE p	WiFi	on	n.n.	2.0	0.7
edge J2SE c, edge J2SE p	WiFi	on	n.n.	1.0	0.4
edge J2ME c, rdv J2SE p	WiFi	on	n.n.	3.1	2.0
edge J2ME c, edge J2ME p	WiFi	on	n.n.	2.5	2.0
adhoc J2SE c, adhoc J2SE p	adhoc	on	n.n.	1.0	0.4
edge J2ME c, rdv J2SE p	adhoc	on	n.n.	1.0	4.4
adhoc J2ME c, adhoc J2SE p	adhoc	on	n.n.	1.0	0.4
adhoc J2ME c, adhoc J2ME p	adhoc	on	n.n.	1.0	0.5

footprint (at least 10MB are needed by the sole JVM). On the other side, the peer installed on the Pocket PC with J2ME (personal profile v1.1) had a 7MB RAM footprint (with 3MB for the JVM).

All tested configurations are listed in table 1. At the overlay network level, *i.e.* JXTA level, a peer may be configured in one of the following modes:

- rendezvous supernode (shortly, rdv) - routes messages using the JXTA-SRDI strategy [25]
- relay supernode (relay) - provides message relaying services, enabling cross firewall traversal
- ad-hoc node (adhoc) - such peer will not use any infrastructure peers (rendezvous or relay), but rely on ad-hoc multicast to discover other peers to connect with
- edge node (edge) - in addition to supporting the Ad-Hoc behavior, an Edge node can attach to an infrastructure peer (a Rendezvous, Relay, or both)

In our testbed, we did not use relays and we configured peers as service providers (p), consumers (c), or bridge nodes (b) which store advertisments and route messages but do not provide or consume Web Services. At the data link layer we considered Ethernet, WiFi and ad-hoc mode.

Experimental results refer to the following sequential actions performed by the consumer peer:

- elapsed time for rendezvous peer discovery (t_r)
- elapsed time for service discovery (t_s)
- elapsed time for service invocation (t_i)

Rendezvous peer discovery is not necessary (n.n.) when multicast is active (on), but service discovery requires much time with respect to the multicast off case. Without multicast, a list of rendezvous hosts must be used to allow peers join the network at bootstrap. Once an edge peer is connected to its rendezvous, if the service has been advertised (and replicated among rendezvous peers) the discovery process is very fast.

Test results are encouraging, being performance significant in almost all examined cases. It appears that, when hosts are connected in ad-hoc mode, best performance is achieved if also at the application level peers are configured in ad-hoc mode.

7   Conclusions and Future Work

To design ubiquitous and pervasive applications, the traditional client/server approach is being superseded by new emerging paradigms, such as the Adaptive Services/Client Paradigm (SCP) and the Spontaneous Service Emergence Paradigm (SEP), based on a peer-to-peer approach. JXTA middleware is a viable solution to implement such architectures. In this paper we presented the JXTA-SOAP component, which enables Web Service deployment in JXTA peers, as well as distributed WSDL publication and discovery, and SOAP message transport over JXTA. Particularly, the JXTA-J2ME implementation enables Web Service invocation from mobile platforms in a JXTA P2P Network.

We proposed JXTA-SOAP as a powerful solution for building service-oriented, peer-to-peer ubiquitous platforms, for which Ambient Intelligence is a natural application field.

Future work on JXTA-SOAP will mainly focus on supporting the Web Service Resource Framework [31], in order to provide peers the ability to access and manipulate state, *i.e.* data values that persist across, and evolve as a result of, Web Service interactions. This is particularly important for AAL services like User Activity Monitoring, which requires to collect contextual data but also historical information from services dispersed over the network.

References

1. MIT Computer Science and Artificial Intelligence Laboratory, AIRE Group, http://aire.csail.mit.edu/index.shtml
2. Amoretti, M., Bisi, M., Zanichelli, F., Conte, G.: Enabling Peer-to-Peer Web Service Architectures with JXTA-SOAP. In: IADIS International Conference e-Society 2008, Algarve, Portugal (April 2008)
3. Avatangelou, E., Dommarco, R.F., Klein, M., Muller, S., Nielsen, C.F., Soriano, M.P.S., Schmidt, A., Tazari, M.-R., Vichert, R.: Conjoint PERSONA-SOPRANO Workshop. In: Proc. of the first European Conference on Ambient Intelligence (AmI 2007), Darmstadt, Germany (November 2007)
4. Berger, S., McFaddin, S., Narayaswami, C., Raghunath, M.: Web Services on Mobile Devices - Implementation and Experience. In: Proc. of the Fifth IEEE Workshop on Mobile Computing Systems & Applications, Monterey, CA, USA (October 2003)
5. Bodhuin, T., Canfora, G., Preziosi, R., Tortorella, M.: Open Challenges in Ubiquitous and Net-Centric Computing Middleware. In: 13th IEEE International Workshop on Software Technology and Engineering Practice (September 2005)
6. Edwards, S.: User Driven and Seamless Mobility Services for Disabled and Older People: the ASK-IT Project. In: Proc. of the 5th Annual Moving On Conference, Glasgow (March 2006)
7. Gaber, J.: Spontaneous Emergence Model for Pervasive Environments. In: IEEE Globecom Workshop 2007, Washington DC (November 2007)
8. Granville, L.Z., Panisson, A.: GigaMAN P2P project, http://gigamanp2p.inf.ufrgs.br
9. Gamma, E., Helm, R., Johnson, R., Vlissides, J.: Design Patterns. Addison-Wesley, Reading (1995)
10. Harrison, A., Taylor, I.: WSPeer - An Interface to Web Service Hosting and Invocation. In: Proc. of the 19th IEEE International Parallel and Distributed Processing Symposium (IPDPS 2005), Denver, Colorado, USA (May 2005)
11. IST Advisory Group, Scenarios for Ambient Intelligence in 2010, European Commission (2001)
12. Distributed Systems Group and Sun MicroSystems, JXTA-SOAP project, https://soap.dev.java.net
13. Sun MicroSystems, JSR 172: J2ME Web Services Specification, http://jcp.org/en/jsr/detail?id=172

14. Krishna, A., Schmidt, D.C., Stal, M.: Context Object: A Design Pattern for Efficient Middleware Request Processing. In: Proc. of the 12th Pattern Language of Programming Conference, Allerton Park, Illinois (September 2005)
15. Haustein, S., Seigel, J.: kSoap2 project, http://ksoap2.sourceforge.net
16. Plebani, P.: mAS project, https://sourceforge.net/projects/masproject
17. Microsoft, .NET Compact Framework,
    http://msdn.microsoft.com/en-us/netframework/aa497273.aspx
18. OSGi Alliance, OSGi: the Dynamic Module System for Java, http://www.osgi.org
19. Peters, S., Shrobe, H.: Using Semantic Networks for Knowledge Representation in an Intelligent Environment. In: Proc. of 1st Annual IEEE International Conference on Pervasive Computing and Communications (PerCom 2003), Ft. Worth, TX, USA (March 2003)
20. Pyarali, I., Spivak, M., Cytron, R., Schmidt, D.C.: Evaluating and Optimizing Thread Pool Strategies for Real-Time CORBA. In: Proc. of the ACM SIGPLAN Workshop on Optimization of Middleware and Distributed Systems (OM 2001), Snowbird, Utah, USA (June 2001)
21. Ramos, C., Augusto, J.C., Shapiro, D.: Ambient Intelligence - the Next Step for Artificial Intelligence. IEEE Intelligent Systems 23(2) (March/April 2008)
22. Costa, P., Coulson, G., Mascolo, C., Motolla, L., Picco, G.P., Zachariadis, S.: A Reconfigurable Component-Based Middleware for Networked Embedded Systems. International Journal of Wireless Information Networks (2006)
23. Srirama, S.N., Jarke, M., Prinz, W.: A Mediation Framework for Mobile Web Service Provisioning. In: Proc. of the 10th IEEE International Enterprise Distributed Object Computing Conference Workshops (EDOCW 2006), Hong Kong, China (October 2006)
24. Srirama, S.N., Jarke, M., Prinz, W.: MWSMF: a Mediation Framework Realizing Scalable Mobile Web Service. In: Proc. of Mobilware 2008, Innsbruck, Austria (February 2008)
25. Traversat, B., Arora, A., Abdelaziz, M., Duigou, M., Haywood, C., Hugly, J.-C., Poyoul, E., Yeager, B.: Project JXTA 2.0 Super-Peer Virtual Network, Technical Report, Sun Microsystems (2003)
26. Vallee, M., Ramparany, F., Vercouter, L.: A multi-agent system for dynamic service composition in ambient intelligence environments. In: Proc. of the Third International Conference on Pervasive Computing (Pervasive 2005), Munich, Germany, May 8-11 (2005)
27. van Engelen, R.A., Gallivan, K.: The gSOAP Toolkit for Web Services and Peer-To-Peer Computing Networks. In: Proc. of the 2nd IEEE International Symposium on Cluster Computing and the Grid (CCGrid 2002), Berlin, Germany, pp. 128–135 (May 2002)
28. Volter, M., Kircher, M., Zdun, U.: Remoting Patterns. Wiley, Chichester (2005)
29. Sun MicroSystems, J2ME Web Services APIs (WSA),
    http://java.sun.com/products/wsa/
30. Banaei-Kashani, F., Chen, C., Shahabi, C.: WSPDS Web Services Peer-to-peer Discovery Service. In: The 2004 International Symposium on Web Services and Applications, Las Vegas, Nevada, USA (June 2004)
31. OASIS, Web Services Resource Framework (WSRF) v1.2 (April 2006)

The PERSONA Framework for Supporting Context-Awareness in Open Distributed Systems

Álvaro Fides-Valero[3], Matteo Freddi[4],
Francesco Furfari[1], and Mohammad-Reza Tazari[2]

[1] CNR-ISTI, Pisa, Italy
francesco.furfari@isti.cnr.it
[2] Fraunhofer-IGD, Darmstadt, Germany
saied.tazari@igd.fraunhofer.de
[3] ITACA-TSB, Valencia, Spain
alfiva@itaca.upv.es
[4] Vodafone Omnitel, Milan, Italy
matteo.freddi@consultant.vodafoneomnitel.it

Abstract. Although several context-aware systems have been developed within the past 15 years that use contextual info captured from the physical environment in combination with system usage context and personalization data, it seems that a breakthrough has not been achieved yet, because still more and more research projects work on adequate solutions for supporting context-awareness. It seems that the major difficulties have to do with a hurdle called context modeling and its extensibility as well as the open nature of such systems that must allow for dynamic pluggability of components distributed over several physical nodes. This paper presents the related work results from the EU project PERSONA that feature remarkable conceptual solutions for the above issues. It consists of a middleware solution for open distributed systems dealing with seamless connectivity and adequate support for interoperability that makes use of ontological technologies and defines appropriate protocols along with an upper ontology for sharing context. A set of standard platform components together with a general conceptual solution for binding ultra-thin nodes top off the presented approach.

1 Introduction

An open distributed system is a system with several communicating physical nodes, each possibly hosting several logical (software) units, that allows to dynamically add and remove components – physical as well as logical – and nevertheless guarantees a certain level of operation without having to recompile, reinstall or restart any part of the existing and running system. The components of an open distributed system may be "redundant", competing with other, existing components or bring new functionality with them. To join to such a system, a component must follow the provided specifications and be somehow authorized. The WWW is the largest known open distributed system constantly in dynamic evolution. As components are removed and added, WWW continues to work

E. Aarts et al. (Eds.): AmI 2008, LNCS 5355, pp. 91–108, 2008.

without essential affection even if some end-points and users may experience difficulties with certain changes.

AmI environments can be realized using the paradigm of open distributed systems, because a typical AmI environment is inherently comprised of several physical nodes and logical components, on one hand, and, on the other hand, an open solution in the above sense would perfectly meet the requirements of dynamic configurability and system evolution.

As context-awareness is considered a major feature of AmI environments, the question that arises when realizing an AmI environment as an open distributed system is how to arrange for context-awareness within the system so that the independence of the pluggable components from each other remains untouched. In this paper, we describe our answer to this question. The solution is called "a framework for supporting context-awareness", because it consists of not only architectural building blocks but also communication protocols and ontologies that altogether guarantee the expected reactivity and configurability of open distributed systems.

Considering the definition of *context* as "any information that can be used to characterize the situation of an entity" [7], where an entity may be "a person, place, or object that is considered relevant to the interaction between a user and an application, including the user and applications themselves" [ditto], support for context-awareness should particularly include the acquisition and publishing of context data from physical "things", such as human beings, locations, and devices. The second important aspect is the provision of mechanisms for interpreting context and triggering appropriate actions on the side of the system when context changes. These two features altogether account for the "intelligence" of the surrounding space, the "ambient intelligence".

The presented solution and the related concepts has been developed within the EU project PERSONA (PERceptive Spaces prOmoting iNdependent Aging), which has started in January 2007 under IST-FP6-Call6 "AAL[1] in the Aging Society". PERSONA follows an open source philosophy and aims at developing an AmI-based scalable open platform for building AAL Services on top of it. Example services under development within the time frame of the project range from support in daily life activities to early risk detection, through personal protection from health-related and environmental risks and support in mobility and moving within the town, among others.

In the following, after a short survey of related work in the past, we first outline our solution for supporting context-awareness in the context of the general architectural design in PERSONA and then try to deal more deeply with specific building blocks in this framework. Section 3.4 focuses on the underlying ontological approach for modeling and exchanging context. The last major part finalizing this discussion is the introduction of the general-purpose solution used in PERSONA for binding extremely thin sensors and actuators that are not directly programmable due to resource limitations.

---

[1] Ambient Assisted Living: a European technology and innovation program to support older people still living in their home environment. [http://www.aal169.org/]

2   Related Work

Since the PARCTAB project [18] in the beginning of 1990s there have been many research activities in the field of context- and situation-aware computing for "breaking out of the virtual realm and extending into the physical world" [4]. Thus, we consider a comprehensive survey of all related research results within this paper as unrealistic and discuss here only those solutions that have influenced our work more directly. The interested reader may refer to existing surveys in the field of context-awareness, such as [3], [5], [6], [16], [19], and [21].

One of the solutions with considerable impact on PERSONA was provided within the German national project EMBASSI (1999-2003), even if this influence relates more to the general architectural design than the specific support for context-awareness. The EMBASSI architecture described in [11] foresees several instances of a context manager storing the environmental data and the profiles of users, applications, and resources and three different communication buses with (1) a sensor protocol for obtaining biometrics and environmental information, (2) a resource protocol for keeping resource profiles up-to-date, and (3) a context protocol supporting both pull (queries) and push (notifications) interfaces for providing consumers with contextual info. The push interface supported subscriptions based on the so-called event-condition-action (ECA) rules, which served as the means for context aggregation and reasoning, as well. In addition to guaranteeing a certain level of persistence, each context manager instance was supposed to act as a specialist in translating some of the low-level events on the sensor and / or resource buses into the high-level representation appropriate for the exchange on the context bus. In practice, because the "normalized" data exchange on the sensor and resource buses made the "transformation specialists" unnecessary, EMBASSI provided just one centralized context manager as to guarantee persistence of sensory and profile data and allow to easily aggregate using logical combinations over all available data, .

The Amigo project[2] supports context-awareness using a set of "Intelligent User Services" built upon the Amigo base middleware [17]. Among these services, there are two that provide most of the context-awareness functionalities: the Context Management Service (CMS), and the Awareness and Notification System (ANS). In the CMS, which uses ontologies for context modeling, components that provide context information are abstracted as Context Sources with three concrete component types: Context Wrappers that wrap low-level sensory data, Context Reasoners that use low-level context and infer high-level contextual info (there is only one rule-based implementation of it called the Context Interpreter), and Context Stores that provide persistence and long-life histories of the data produced by the two other component types (also here only one specific component called the Context History was provided). Once context sources are connected, they have to present themselves to the Context Broker, which maintains a registry of them. Context clients may ask the broker for a

---

[2] Amigo: Ambient intelligence for the networked home environment, an EU-funded integrated project (2004-2008), www.hitech-projects.com/euprojects/amigo/

specific source using an RDF[3] description of the required capabilities; in return, they receive references to matching context sources, which they can query using SPARQL[4] or subscribe to. The clients always receive SPARQL results both in reply to queries and when receiving notifications. The ANS works as a permanent client for all context sources and lets the subscribers create ECA rules for context triggering. A client can subscribe a rule to the ANS that will fire an event to the client whenever the context conditions expressed in the rule are met. The language used for defining these rules is specific to AMIGO[5].

MobiLife[6] defines its Context Management Framework (CMF) based on a thorough understanding of context providers (CPs) and augments it with specific functions, namely reasoning and personal and group contexts, to form the whole context-awareness function (CAF) within MobiLife (cf. [13]).CMF deals with context data modeling, representation, and reasoning and provides a registry-based discovery mechanism that facilitates the exchange of context between context providers and consumers (CCs). A CP encapsulates some context sources that may be out of the control of MobiLife – i.e. accessible only over a specific protocol with an arbitrary data representation. CPs may be a CC at the same time. That is, a generic consumer / producer model is used that facilitates different levels of context usage so that CPs from different domains and of different types can co-exist and even depend on each other. Other components are: *Context Representation* modeling CP advertisements and interfaces and specifying the format of context subscriptions, notifications, queries and query results, *Context Interpretation* covering the expression of context in terms of the underlying ontology, and a *Context Broker* that takes care of registration of CPs and provides a single point of entry for CCs.

SOCAM (Service Oriented Context Aware Middleware) [10] defines a formal context model using Semantic Web technologies and provides support for acquiring, discovering, interpreting and accessing context. By taking a service-oriented approach, the SOCAM architecture is composed of a set of independent services that can be easily added to augment the system capabilities. They are organized in three levels, namely the *Context Sensing Layer*, the *Context Middleware Layer* and the *Context Application Layer*. The middleware layer consists of *Context Providers* offering OWL-based abstraction over the sensing layer that are categorized in external context providers (e.g. weather forecast Web services) and internal context providers acquiring context directly from local sensors, a *Service Locating Service* to which the context providers register, and a *Context Interpreter* responsible for logical reasoning, detecting inconsistencies, and resolving conflicts. The middleware layer uses the SOCAM ontology divided

---

[3] Resource Description Framework, www.w3.org/RDF.

[4] SPARQL Protocol and RDF Query Language, www.w3.org/2001/sw/DataAccess/

[5] It seems that apart from the different rule languages, the difference between ANS and the singleton Context Interpreter described in D4.7 as part of the CMS is that the CI handles only a predefined set of rules, whereas the ANS allows for dynamic registration of rules to be provided directly by the context clients.

[6] MobiLife: Life goes mobile! – wireless world initiative, an EU-funded integrated project (2004-2006), www.ist-mobilife.org

into a common upper ontology for general concepts of smart environments, and domain-specific ontologies (i.e. Home-Domain, Vehicle). Service Locating allows users and applications to discover and locate providers – no matter if the context interpreter or normal context providers – based on RDF statement templates. The advertisement of capabilities by context providers can be based on OSGi service templates, Java/Jini objects or OWL expressions.

Based on an analysis of the common concepts and specific strengths of the above solutions, the following statements could be concluded:

- The major operational needs of context-aware components (context consumers – CCs) are twofold: (1) they may want to be notified promptly when the state of a context element of interest changes, and (2) they may want to query contextual data not only for the most up-to-date states but probably also for "historical" data.
- In order to facilitate the extensibility of context-awareness and the free plug-and-play of context providers (CPs) and CCs, the interdependencies at the development time should be reduced to using a shared understanding of context data, a unique language for the exchange of such data, and a brokering service. All of the above solutions chose ontological approaches, mostly using the Semantic Web technologies RDF and OWL. With the exception of EMBASSI buses that broker messages, all the other chose an object brokering approach which additionally necessitates to standardize the interface of context providers.
- The above abstractions imply that most of the sensors or components that controll the state of some context elements must be wrapped in order to be bound into a system, unless the component was originally developed using the above abstractions.
- The context model may suggest context elements whose states neither are under the control of any components nor can be sensed or measured directly. Then, special CPs may be needed as to derive the state of such context elements using aggregations, statistical analysis, and / or logical rules, to name the most common methods. Such CPs are normally called context reasoners or interpreters. They are the major use case for playing both of the CP and CC roles simultaneously.

3 The PERSONA Framework for Supporting Context-Awareness

The PERSONA framework for supporting context-awareness (CASF) can be understood best when we start with an overview of the PERSONA middleware as the main building block in the general architectural design of PERSONA.

3.1 The PERSONA Middleware

From the point of view of the PERSONA architecture, open distributed systems are physically equivalent to a dynamic ensemble of networked physical nodes.

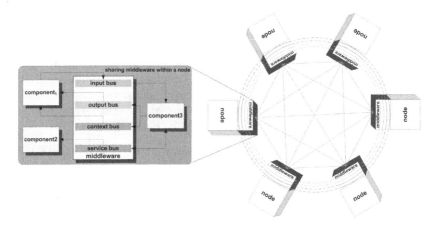

Fig. 1. The four global buses provided by the middleware hide the distribution of functionality through cooperation of instances in the whole ensemble

Each physical node may host several logical components that share a piece of software called the PERSONA middleware, which is responsible for seamless connectivity among the nodes and the interoperability of the components distributed on these nodes. In order to solve the problem of interoperability, PERSONA chose a *message brokering* approach using virtual communication buses, quite similar to the EMBASSI architectural style [11]. As shown in figure 1, the middleware provides four "buses" called the *input*, *output*, *context*, and *service* buses[7]. Instances of the middleware start single instances of each bus type according to specific configuration parameters. As middleware instances discover each other, the bus instances of the same type cooperate with each other, and provide a view of the system as being composed of four global buses, thus hiding the distribution of the system. When the software components on the nodes register with these buses as sender or receiver of messages, they provide a description of their capabilities to the corresponding buses. The distributed dispatch strategies of the buses use these descriptions in the course of ontological matchmaking to find the appropriate receivers and dispatch received messages directly to them.

The middleware is currently implemented as a set of bundles (pluggable software components packaged as JAR files) on the OSGi platform [www.osgi.org]. It is organized in three logical layers (cf. figure 2):

– The lowest layer, the abstract connection layer (ACL), is responsible for the peer-to-peer connectivity between instances of the middleware. It is populated by several bundles implementing the P2PConnector interface. This interface provides uniform access to different discovery and message transfer

---

[7] The input and output buses are responsible for interoperability in regard to capturing user input and presenting output to the user. All other inter-component communication needs should go over the context bus (for event-based communication) and the service bus (for call-based communication). See also [1] and [8].

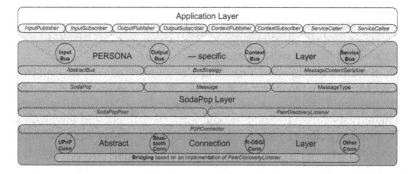

Fig. 2. The internal architecture of the PERSONA middleware

protocols, such as UPnP, R-OSGi or Bluetooth, that can be used to provide competing solutions for network connectivity. A bridging solution is also available to guarantee interoperability among the different connectors.

– The Sodapop[8] Layer is the core of a middleware instance (*peer*). It uses the P2PConnector interface to discover all the connectors available on the platform and to communicate with the remote peers. It introduces the concepts of *bus* (either event-based or call-based), *bus strategy* and *message* along with an interface for message serialization.
– The topmost layer implements the PERSONA specific approach to modeling the AAL spaces. Using an RDF serializer for the exchange of messages among peers, it extends the abstract bus concept from the Sodapop layer to provide the PERSONA application layer with the input, output, context, and service buses, each with its specific distributed bus strategy.

The PERSONA middleware and its four communication buses aim at the provision of mechanisms that facilitate the independent development of components that nonetheless are able to collaborate in a self-organized way as they come together and build up an ensemble. Therefore, the buses act as brokers that resolve the dependencies at runtime using the registration parameters of their members and semantic match-making algorithms.

3.2   Basic Concepts Underlying the PERSONA CASF

At an abstract level, we understand context as a characteristics / features space, in which there are resources that can be perceived or recognized based on their properties. The types of these resources and their properties must be modeled in an ontology containing also the conceptual relationships between them, probably along with some significant instances shared widely in the underlying domain. Based on this elementary assumption, we define here a set of basic concepts serving as the mainstay of the PERSONA CASF:

---

[8] Self-Organizing Data-flow Architectures suPporting Ontology-based problem decomPosition, a middleware model proposed by Thomas Kirste, see [11] and [12].

Context Element. A distinct characteristic or feature of a distinct resource. Using the RDF representation techniques, a context element in this sense can be identified uniquely by a pair of URIs, namely the URI of the resource and the URI of the corresponding property.

Context Event. A statement reporting the state of a context element at a specific time where the state was changed into the reported value. In terms of RDF, this could be as simple as an RDF statement – the two URIs identifying the underlying context element would form the subject and predicate of the RDF statement and the state value would be the object of the statement – however, as a reporting statement bound to a specific time, a context event should be treated as a reified statement in order to be able to specify the associated time, too. Additionally, listeners to such events may need to also know who is reporting this value with which level of confidence and / or temporal validity. If the reported value is the result of a measurement, its accuracy could also be of importance.

Context Publisher. The functional role of a software component that publishes context events to the context bus.

Context Provider. The functional role of a software component that provides info about the state of context elements by publishing context events onto the context bus and / or answering context queries on the service bus. Major subgroups of context providers are (cf. figure 3): (1) *Controllers* that have the states of some context elements under their control, like a component controlling the lights in a place that can also provide info about the state of the controlled light sources, (2) *Gauges* that wrap a sensing or measurement device, and (3) *Reasoners* that estimate the state of some context elements by combining different known information and applying certain methods of aggregation, statistical analysis and / or logical deduction. The values reported by gauges could be measured dimensions. If so, the concepts *DimensionMeasure* or *MultiDimensionMeasure* from figure 3, or subclasses of them, can be used for building the object part of the reified statements.

Context Consumer. The functional role of a software component that uses info about the state of context elements by subscribing to the context bus

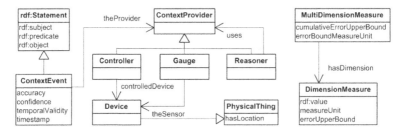

Fig. 3. Summary of major concepts related to the provision of context

for context events and / or querying context on the service bus. A component
playing this role is considered to be context-aware.

3.3   The Role of the Middleware in PERSONA CASF

The middleware is the cornerstone of the PERSONA CASF, which in turn goes
beyond the inherent capabilities of the middleware and provides additional capabilities to be discussed later. The push interface of CASF provides a publisher/
subscriber mechanism using the broadcasting strategy of the context bus. The
CASF pull interface, however, uses the service bus, which is a caller/ callee bus
allowing for direct utilization of (remote) services.

The context bus provides a lightweight communication channel which can be
used for publishing context events to local and remote end-points. In order to
act as a context publisher, a component must find the OSGi service realizing
the context bus and register with it. Components acting as context subscribers
must additionally specify a filter for context events they are interested in as their
registration parameters. The context bus strategy is as simple as broadcasting
a received event to all peers, then each peer does a local match-making with
limited ontological inference capabilities to find interested subscribers. Therefore,
the registration parameters of the subscribers are stored only locally by each
instance of the context bus. Alternatively, one single node could play the role
of a permanent coordinator that gathers all registration parameters from all
subscribers to all peers, where a peer that has received an event from a locally
registered context publisher, would forward the event only to the coordinator
which in turn would forward the message only to those peers that had at least
one local subscriber interested in that event. Of course, other strategies are also
possible, but in the first version we chose the broadcasting strategy to avoid a
single point of failure, accepting the relatively increased messaging traffic.

On the service bus, callees provide service profiles in OWL-S[9] at the registration time. The callers request services using "service queries". The service
bus finds the appropriate callee(s) by examining its repository of service profiles
using the same limited ontological inference as in case of the context bus, calls it
(them) by providing the required input extracted from the original query, gets
the output and prepares it as the response to be returned to the caller. The
details of the service bus strategy, however, go beyond the scope of this paper.
Interested readers are invited to read the project deliverable mentioned above.
The pull interface provides the following functionalities:

- context query with limited ontological inference, whether recent or older
  data, from one source or involving several sources, using simple wildcards or
  complex SPARQL queries (see the sections 3.4 and 3.5)
- adding new reasoning rules to CASF for short term or long term storage (see
  section 3.5)
- checking for availability of context elements with request to switch on event
  publishing onto the context bus (not discussed further in this paper)

---

[9] An OWL-based ontology for describing services. See www.daml.org/services/owl-s/.

3.4   Some Insights into the Ontological Approach

The context elements of interest for PERSONA components, services and applications cover a wide range. Among these are the information directly related to the user (e.g. identity, location, activity or health status), information about the surrounding area (like weather, light level and available resources) and information regarding the system (e.g running dialogs). They originate from different sources with no strict limitation or division posed. Parts of such information must be gathered from the real world and made available to the framework. Obviously, this can be achieved by sensors of many different types; example sensors relevant for the PERSONA applications are heart rate monitors and pulsioximeters for health-care, accelerometers assisting activity and fall detection, cameras helping location and posture recognition, scales, light sensors, and flooding detectors.

In order to overcome the resulting complexity and enable extensible interoperability, the PERSONA CASF has adopted / provided three elementary tools: (1) the knowledge representation technologies of the Semantic Web consisting of RDF and OWL, (2) an upper ontology with appropriate programming support consisting of those concepts that all users of the middleware must know, and (3) a general conceptual solution described in section 4 with certain shared tools for integrating thin devices and embedded sensors and transforming the tapped data into an appropriate ontological representation. Using this framework, providers and consumers that share the same ontological concepts can achieve the needed level of interoperability without the need for the middleware to know those concrete concepts. Still, the middleware is able to adopt ontological reasoning, to some extent, in its brokerage function.

Figure 4 summarizes the Java class hierarchy used by the middleware for handling ontological resources. The class ManagedIndividual is the root of all ontology classes that register with the middleware. This way, each instance of the middleware will have a repository of ontological classes that are relevant for the local members of its buses. The repository provides a mapping between class URIs and their Java representation and enables the middleware to infer hierarchical relationships between the registered classes and check class memberships at Java level. This reveals the previously mentioned limitations of the ontological reasoning within the middleware: the limited knowledge stored about the underlying ontologies and match-making to the extent supported by Java. The reason for this way of realizing the first version of the middleware is to be spare of the resources needed by the middleware, in order to reach the widest portability by keeping it as small as possible, even at the level of Java 1.3. As a trade-off for these limitations, the middleware supports not only the whole capacity of the OWL class expressions but also enhances it by supporting more specific restrictions that can be posed on the properties of classes.

The context upper ontology consists of two major concepts, namely ContextEvent, already discussed in section 3.2, and ContextEventPattern, which is basically an OWL class expression (see figure 4 for the powerfulness of class expressions) that specifies a subset of context events by restricting certain properties of them. Context consumers may use such patterns both to specify the

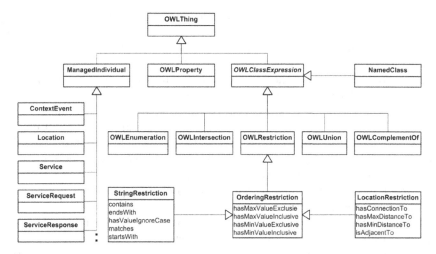

Fig. 4. The Java class hierarchy used and exported by the PERSONA middleware for handling ontological resources

set of context events for which they subscribe to the context bus and to query context on the service bus. Context providers may use them for specifying the set of context events they have in their repositories when they register as a context query handler with the service bus. In case of the context bus, whenever a concrete context event is published onto it, each instance of the bus checks which locally registered context patterns match the event. This way, the bus can determine the set of local subscribers that should receive the context event at hand. In case of the service bus, the match-making is done between two context event patterns: the "query pattern" provided by the context consumer and each of the patterns provided by the context query handlers for describing their capabilities. If the compared patterns are compatible, the corresponding context provider is selected to answer the query. Obviously, both match-making methods benefit from the inference capabilities described in the previous paragraph.

3.5   Special Components Enhancing the PERSONA CASF

The PERSONA platform provides three concrete components that share a central repository of ontological facts and rules and enhance the capabilities of the PERSONA CASF. These are the Context History Entrepôt (CHE), the Situation Reasoner (SR), and the profiling component.

CHE gathers the history of all context events in the central repository not only to fill the gap caused by context publishers that provide no query interface, but also to provide a fallback solution for those context providers that cannot maintain the whole history of data provided by them. Additionally, it guarantees the essential support to reasoners that perform statistical analysis and need context stored over time[10]. As a singleton component, CHE takes care of logging every context event that is published in the context bus by specifying a "pass-all" filter (an empty context event pattern) when subscribing to the bus. In order to have the growth of the repository under control, CHE also implements a deletion policy based on the likeliness of the data to be needed further on; the policies consider a time-based threshold as well as the abstraction level of the data[11]. For making the context history available to context consumers, CHE registers with the service bus as a callee supporting two kinds of context queries by accepting both context event patterns and full-fledged SPARQL queries. The latter is possible just because CHE relies on such a repository containing data from all possible sources. It is worth repeating that the existence of CHE with its central DB does not negate the possibility for context providers to keep their own repositories of specific context data if they have enough resources for storing and managing the data or even for acting as a concurrent context query handler. Context consumers may also keep their own histories of needed context data in a purposeful way that is more appropriate for them and guarantees a better performance.

As already discussed, different reasoners may adopt different methods for deriving the states of context elements that are not readily controlled or measured. Due to the variety of inputs (and their sources), on which the reasoners may depend, as well as the variety of logical methods (and their complexities) that could be used for deriving new context elements, it won't be possible to cover all possible context reasoning needs with just one universal reasoner. Therefore, PERSONA classifies the reasoners in two major categories: the general-purpose reasoners and the special-purpose reasoners. According to this categorization, a special-purpose reasoner has a topical focus in which it is specialized. The PERSONA project is developing some of such reasoners, like a location reasoner that uses different sources – e.g. the position of personal and wearable devices, the location of a microphone that has caught the user voice, computer-vision based location estimation, and still user appointments from his / her personal calendar – for reasoning about the user location and an activity detector that combines computer-vision based info with the system usage context and the info from personal agenda to estimate the current activity of the user. A general-purpose reasoner, however, is a configurable reasoner without any topical focus that covers a relatively large class of high-level context elements by applying specific logical methods to data from specific sources. The configurability of general-purpose reasoners is a major characteristic of them, because they do not hard-code the topic-specific logic so that the set of the concrete context elements, whose values they derive, can be decided over configuration parameters; especially, such reasoners should be able to derive the states of new context elements by just adding new rules / instructions without needing any re-compilation.

---

[10] Many of reasoners that predict context need even long term histories that pluggable context providers may not be able to maintain, as discussed in [15].

[11] The latter is based on the assumption that the time-based threshold for more detailed data already aggregated into more abstract data could be reached sooner.

The PERSONA Situation Reasoner (SR) is a general-purpose reasoner that uses the database of CHE and infers new contextual info using the logical power of the RDF query language SPARQL. It stores "situation queries" persistently and indexes them based on context events that must trigger its evaluation – as they are not meant as a one-time query that are answered and then forgotten, but they must generate related situational events whenever appropriate, depending on changes in the context. It provides two services on the service bus, one for accepting new situation queries and the other for dropping them. These services are also used by a graphically interactive tool for administrators in order to facilitate the introduction of new relevant situations for human users. It provides an overview of existing context providers, allows drag-and-drop interaction based on widgets representing context elements, catches logical errors made by the user, and generates the appropriate SPARQL query string, to name a few of its features. The SR takes its name from a modeling theory for situations introduced in [20]. The power of the SR for recognizing situations is limited by the two following restrictions: (1) the source of data that can be used in the declaration of a situation is limited to the history of reported context events and (2) only situations that can be derived by a single SPARQL query can be recognized.

The profiling component uses an OWL-based user model for handling user identity, capabilities, constraints and preferences. It provides specific interfaces on the service bus and may publish certain context events onto the context bus. But, apart from this, sharing its data with the two other components, CHE and the SR, empowers them to combine context and personalization data to respectively answer complex queries and infer the state of more high level context elements. The other way around, the profiling component can let the SR to derive conditional preference values when a user preference value was not specified directly but by a rule leading to different values in different situations.

A fourth component called the Dialog Manager (not shown in the above figure) that is responsible for the system-wide dialogs with the user – such as provision

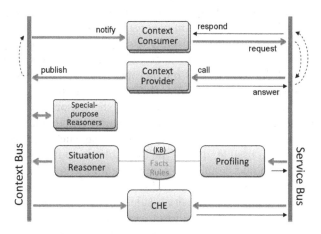

Fig. 5. Summary of the PERSONA framework supporting context-awareness

of the user with possibilities to navigate through the available services – complements the picture drawn so far by caring about the overall system reactivity. It manages a configurable repository of rules that associate service calls with situations. For each added rule, the Dialog Manager subscribes to the context bus for the corresponding situational event and calls the associated service as soon as it is notified by the context bus that the situation holds. Also here a graphically interactive tool should help the administrators to configure the system behavior.

4 Binding Thin Context Sources

The PERSONA middleware targets small but reasonably powerful devices, therefore not all the components can be integrated by using an instance of the PERSONA middleware. Typically, wearable components as well as nodes of wireless sensor networks (WSN) or Home Automation Systems (HAS) require a special approach because of their limited computational resources. In such cases a gateway solution can be adopted. It allows the PERSONA application layer to share information by communicating with other application layers residing on different network infrastructures (e.g. ZigBee [1] or Bluetooth applications).

4.1 Integrating WSN Nodes

Wireless Sensor Networks [2] are an important technological support for smart environments and ambient assisted applications. Up to now most applications are based on ad hoc solutions for WSN, and efforts to provide uniform and reusable applications are still in their youth. General requirements for the use of WSN include (1) integration of different sensor network technologies, such as ZigBee or IEEE 802.15.4 standard, and Bluetooth, (2) sharing communication medium by concurrent sensor applications, (3) management of different applications on the same WSN, (4) management of multiple instances of the same application, (5) dynamic discovery of sensor applications, (6) management of logical sensors, and (7) Configuration and calibration of sensor applications.

The first requirement above is usually faced by enabling the dynamic deployment of ad hoc network drivers in the system, while we can assume that requirements 2 to 5 largely depend on the operating systems and middleware used for the sensor nodes programming. However, the addressing of the requirement 6 is still an open issue because, on one side, the sensor nodes should locally pre-process and transmit aggregated data as much as possible in order to reduce the power consumption. On the other side, to arrange such a processing on the network is not always possible, due to the available computational power. Then an integration layer should enable the combining and aggregation of the sensed data before to pass them to the application layer, namely a part of the sensor network application resides on the server side.

In a first attempt to provide a uniform model for sensor applications, we designed the SAIL architecture [9] based on three layers, namely the Access, Abstraction, and Integration layers. This architecture aimed at defining a shared sensor model at Abstraction level for different WSN solutions integrated with SAIL. As a result, client applications could ignore the effective sensor model provided by the network drivers at access layer. SAIL adopted also a data-centric approach using query-oriented TinyDB [14]. Data-centric approaches assume almost an arbitrary number of sensors with homogeneous features and capabilities. However, smart environments are generally indoor and limited, hence the size of the WSN hardly scales up to hundreds of sensors, and the network often has a small diameter (in some cases it may even be a star). For this reason and because of the general tendency in PERSONA towards the ZigBee industry standard, we decided to design an optimized version of SAIL tailored on ZigBee.

4.2   Integrating ZigBee Networks

Maintaining the same three-layered architecture introduced in [9], we developed a ZigBee Base Driver for the SAIL access layer that uses native libraries implementing the ZigBee Application Layer. In fact, while Bluetooth drivers are usually integrated with different operating systems and platforms, the standardization process of the network interfaces for ZigBee is still in progress. Therefore, we chose to adopt USB ZigBee dongles available on the market which come either with a simple AT command-like interface or a more elaborated API (the native driver).

Interestingly, the ZigBee Alliance publishes application profiles that allow multiple manufacturers to create interoperable products. The current list of application profiles, either published or in progress, are: Home Automation, ZigBee Smart Energy, Telecommunication Applications, and Personal Home and Hospital Care. In general, those profiles use a combination of clusters defined in the ZigBee Cluster Library. Vendors can define their custom library for devices not defined by the ZigBee Alliance. According to this, the PERSONA project is now working on the definition of a PERSONA Cluster Library and Profile in order to integrate most of the existing profiles and special devices like the smart glove or the smart carpet that will be developed by the consortium partners.

A diagram of the current SAIL architecture is depicted in figure 6. The ZigBee Base Driver is a network driver in charge of executing the scan of the network, getting the description of the various nodes and registering a proxy service for accessing the discovered remote services. This proxy is a generic ZigBee service, registered with the OSGi Platform that exposes the properties retrieved during the network inquiry. It allows to access the remote service by means of simple primitives that have to be filled by the proper clusters. Thus, in contrast to the more generic model used by the previous version of SAIL, we have defined a specialized model tailored on an extension of ZigBee profiles, namely the PERSONA profiles. The components on the upper layers may act as Refinement Drivers (in OSGi terms). Thus, the second layer is specialized to represent the service according to a specific profile, e.g. the Home Automation profile. The topmost layer is the final step for integrating the ZigBee services within PERSONA. It is composed of Sensor Technology Exporters (STE) that discover the services implementing standard or extended profiles and register proxies that are

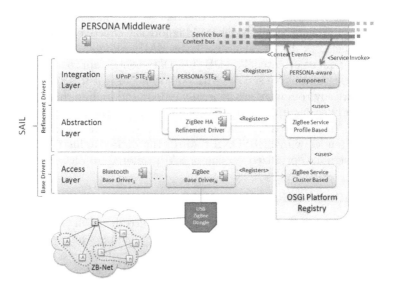

Fig. 6. The SAIL layered architecture

PERSONA-aware components. At this level, the mapping between the services compliant with the ZigBee model and PERSONA OSGi services is realized by sending events through the context bus and by registering service bus members according to the PERSONA protocols. In a nutshell, the abstract layer is populated by custom drivers that may combine and process the sensed data to instantiate logical sensor services (e.g. a sensor providing the user's position by elaborating RSSI measurements – Received Signal Strength Indication – coming from different stationary sensors), as well as refine the cluster-based services. Finally, we believe that with this solution we can easily realize, at PERSONA application level, the user interfaces addressing the last requirement from the previous section, namely the provision of a uniform way of configuring sensor applications.

5   Conclusions

Referring to the conclusions on the related work in section 2, we can argument that the solution provided within PERSONA (1) satisfies the operational needs regarding push and pull interfaces, (2) handles the interdependencies between the pluggable components in a way that enables development teams to work independently from each other and focus on the business behavior of their components, while keeping the ability to seamlessly integrate them on an extensible base using well-defined protocols, (3) provides a concrete mechanism for wrapping legacy and resource-limited nodes, and (4) establishes the needed base for realizing special-purpose reasoners that complement the standard rule-based reasoner provided by the PERSONA platform as a configurable general-purpose reasoner.

A remarkable feature of this solution is that even the platform components follow the same interoperability framework as the pluggable components so that the provided platform components may actually be challenged by competing components that can be plugged into the system at any point in time. Even the middleware is built in such a modular way, that different parts of it, such as the distributed bus strategies, can be replaced by new modules without affecting its function. The neutrality of the middleware regarding concrete domain ontologies and its portability onto a wide range of devices are other essential characteristics of the provided framework.

The PERSONA CASF is still under development so that selective parts of the framework may be improved. A still open challenge is the completion of the domain- and application-specific ontologies. The difficulty consists in the lack of well-established (sub)ontologies that causes us to work them out from scratch, with additional latency for them to get mature enough. A possible improvement concerns the situation reasoner that may use additional data sources other than the context history in order to enhance its coverage of recognizable situations. A second area for future work is the benchmarking of the provided solution regarding scalability and performance. The general configurability of the situation reasoner and the dialog manger altogether opens a door towards meaningful end user programming. The administrative tools to be provided within PERSONA can be seen as a preliminary milestone in this direction.

References

1. Avatangelou, E., Dommarco, R.F., Klein, M., Müller, S., Nielsen, C.F., Soriano, M.P.S., Schmidt, A., Tazari, M.R., Wichert, R.: Conjoint persona – soprano workshop. In: Constructing Ambient Intelligence – AmI 2007 Workshops. Springer CCIS Series, Darmstadt, Germany, pp. 448–464 (2007)
2. Baronti, P., Pillai, P., Chook, V.W.C., Chessa, S., Gotta, A., Hu, Y.F.: Wireless sensor networks: A survey on the state of the art and the 802.15.4 and zigbee standards. Computer Communications 30(7), 1655–1695 (2007)
3. Barrett, K., Power, R.: State of the art: Context management. Tech. rep., M-Zones Research Programme, Deliverable 1.1: State of the Art Review, Release 2 (2003), www.m-zones.org
4. Berners-Lee, T., Hendler, J., Lassila, O.: The Semantic Web. Scientific American 284(5), 34–43 (2001)
5. Brown, P., Burleston, W., Lamming, M., Rahlff, O., Romano, G., Scholtz, J., Snowdon, D.: Context- awareness: Some compelling applications (2000), http://www.dcs.ex.ac.uk/~pjbrown/papers/acm.html
6. Chen, G., Kotz, D.: A survey of context-aware mobile computing research. Tech. Rep. TR2000-381, Dept. of Computer Science, Dartmouth College (2000), citeseer.ist.psu.edu/chen00survey.html
7. Dey, A.K.: Understanding and using context. Personal Ubiquitous Computing 5(1), 4–7 (2001)
8. Furfari, F., Tazari, M.R.: Realizing ambient assisted living spaces with the persona platform. ERCIM News (74), 47–48 (2008)

9. Girolami, M., Lenzi, S., Furfari, F., Chessa, S.: SAIL: a Sensor Abstraction and Integration Layer for Context Aware Architectures. In: Proceedings of the 34th EUROMICRO Conference on Software Engineering and Advanced Applications (SEAA 2008), pp. 374–381. IEEE, Parma (2008)
10. Gu, T., Pung, H.K., Zhang, D.Q.: A service-oriented middleware for building context-aware services. Journal of Network and Computer Applications 28(1), 1–18 (2005)
11. Heider, T., Kirste, T.: Architecture considerations for interoperable multi-modal assistant systems. In: Proceedings of the 9th International Workshop on Design, Specification, and Verification of Interactive Systems, Rostock, Germany, pp. 403–417 (2002)
12. Hellenschmidt, M., Kirste, T.: Sodapop: A software infrastructure supporting self-organization in intelligent environments. In: Proceedings of INDIN 2004: the 2nd IEEE International Conference on Industrial Informatics, pp. 479–486. IEEE, Berlin (2004)
13. Kernchen, R., Bonnefoy, D., Battestini, A., Mrohs, B., Wagner, M., Klemettinen, M.: Context-Awareness in MobiLife. In: Proceedings of IST Mobile Summit 2006, Mykonos, Greece (2006)
14. Madden, S.R., Franklin, M.J., Hellerstein, J.M., Hong, W.: Tinydb: an acquisitional query processing system for sensor networks. ACM Trans. Database Syst. 30(1), 122–173 (2005)
15. Mayrhofer, R.: Context prediction based on context histories: Expected benefits, issues and current state-of-the-art. In: Proceedings of ECHISE 2005: 1st International Workshop on Exploiting Context Histories in Smart Environments, Munich, Germany (2005)
16. Mitchell, K.: A survey of context-awareness. Tech. rep., Lancaster University (England), Internal Technical Report (2002)
17. Ramparany, F., Euzenat, J., Broens, T., Pierson, J., Bottaro, A., Poortinga, R.: Context management and semantic modeling for ambient intelligence. In: First Workshop on Future Research Challenges for Software and Services, Vienna, Austria (2006)
18. Schilit, B.N., Adams, N., Gold, R., Tso, M.M., Want, R.: The PARCTAB mobile computing system. In: Workshop on Workstation Operating Systems, pp. 34–39 (1993), citeseer.ist.psu.edu/schilit93parctab.html
19. Strang, T., Linnhoff-Popien, C.: A context modeling survey. In: Workshop on Advanced Context Modelling, Reasoning and Management as part of UbiComp 2004, Nottingham, England (2004)
20. Tazari, M.R., Grimm, M.: D11 – report on context-awareness and knowledge representation. Public deliverable, MUMMY, IST-2001-37365 (2004), http://www.mummy-project.org/downloads.html
21. Winograd, T.: Architectures for context. Human-Computer Interaction 16(2), 401–419 (2001)

Enabling NFC Technology for Supporting Chronic Diseases: A Proposal for Alzheimer Caregivers

Jose Bravo[1], Diego López-de-Ipiña[2], Carmen Fuentes[1,3], Ramón Hervás[1], Rocío Peña[1], Marcos Vergara[1], and Gregorio Casero[1]

[1] MAmI Research Lab-Universidad de Castilla La Mancha, Ciudad Real, Spain
[2] Facultad de Ingeniería (ESIDE), Universidad de Deusto, Bilbao, Spain
[3] General Hospital of Ciudad Real, Spain
Jose.Bravo@uclm.es, dipina@eside.deusto.es

Abstract. Alzheimer's disease makes great demands on care by caregivers, since they cannot distract their attention from patients while they are managing records at the same time. For this reason, technologies to complement this process need to be considered. In this work we propose to adapt Near Field Communications (NFC), applying it to an Alzheimer's day centre. With a simple interaction, which involves touching tags with mobile phones, it is possible to manage the information easily. In addition, a complement for Alzheimer care visualization activities at home and monitoring is presented.

Keywords: NFC, Ambient Assisted Living, Context-Ontology, DTT.

1 Introduction

AmI promotes environments where humans will be surrounded by intelligent interfaces, supported by computing and networking technology that is embedded in everyday objects. These environments will adapt to the needs of users and will be capable of responding intelligently to any human form of communication. [1]. This is an evolution from Ubiquitous Computing, a vision originating in Mark Weiser [2], where computers disappear, being embedded into the background. Weiser's vision has to do with Ubiquitous Communication, which takes place between objects and users and whose main goal is to get the information at the time and place that users need it. This vision is also related to Natural Interfaces, which make the interaction friendlier and closer to the user. Basically, users are focused on the task and not on the tool, so that the technology should disappear. Using a computer to support daily activities is not yet a reality nowadays. The reason for that may be related to the interaction required. In healthcare contexts, workers do not have time to manage daily routines. Moreover, they complain about the difficulties of using healthcare applications [3]. Another important aspect is the great percentage of time that workers in a care-giving environment consume in managing patients' information [4]. This time should be invested in care activities rather than in using computers.

E. Aarts et al. (Eds.): AmI 2008, LNCS 5355, pp. 109–125, 2008.
© Springer-Verlag Berlin Heidelberg 2008

Care of elderly people and the increasing occurrence of chronic conditions among the ageing population are major social and economic challenges for the European society and its healthcare systems. Thus, the AAL Joint Programme [5] aims to find out innovative Information and Communication technologies for elderly people with identified risk factors and/or chronic conditions. The economic aspect for caring elderly people in Europe also has to be considered. For example, one year's stay of an Alzheimer patient in a nursing home costs $64,000, while staying at home costs only $20,000. This fact, added to the estimation that the number of elderly people will double by 2050, is a basic one in finding appropriate AAL solutions.

This work presents a solution which aims to improve and complement Alzheimer's care based on the use of two technologies NFC (Near Field Communications) [13] and DTT (Digital Terrestrial Television). The main idea behind it is that care givers interact trough NFC enabled mobile phones by touching tags attached to equipment or patients with their mobile phones, i.e. through a very natural and easy to use touch computing paradigm [14]. Additionally, Alzheimer's therapy through the use of DTT is also suggested.

The structure of the paper is as follows. Section 2 gives an introduction to two application scenarios; a day centre environment and a home-based setting is given. Besides, a description of the technology used in each case is offered. Section 3 describes an ontology which allows us to model the context gathered on the Alzheimer scenarios considered upon which aiding services are offered. Section 4 presents the actual prototypes we have carried out applying NFC technologies in day-care centres and DTT for home-based monitoring and therapy. Finally, section 5 draws some conclusions and suggests further work.

2   The Context

The technological contributions proposed by this work address issues on Alzheimer care in two kinds of environments: day centres and homes. In the former one, patients go to a day centre every day from 9 am to 4 pm in order to receive some therapy that reinforces their memory. The aid received in the day centre is often complemented by other in-house based therapy exercises. Besides, it is important to be in contact, during the whole caring process, with family members in order to have better knowledge about the patients' behaviour in both places. In the next section we describe these activities and the related exchange of information.

2.1 Day Centre

These care environments relieve families from the continuous daily care of an Alzheimer patient. In the care centre we have studied for this work, namely Alzheimer Day Centre of Ciudad Real (Centre II), patients are divided into several groups, of about seven people, where they develop their activities in different rooms. Once the patients arrive to the centre, by using the daily transport service, they eat breakfast together. Then, the different therapy activities are started:

- *Rehabilitation / Physiotherapy.* The objective of this therapy is to observe patients behavior and to promote activities which will delay their loss of movement and agility. For that, patients have several exercises for their hands, arms, legs, feet and torso. In this activity, caregivers need to know about recent injuries caused by falls or domestic accidents. In addition, information about patient profiles and the physician's recommendations are also relevant.

- *Therapy*. This is the main activity that seeks to reinforce the patient's memory through the recognition of relatives and objects. Patients are asked details about their families, e.g. names of children, wife or husband, parents they have and so on. In the object recognition exercises, patients are asked to recognize pictures with the aid of their assistants. Also, a few games to reinforce memory are included in this activity.
- *Handwork (Occupational Therapy)*. Here patients do some handwork, cutting out drawings painted on cardboard, sticking different parts together and finally creating figures. In this activity, the place where each patient sits down is particularly important, as well as whom they are sitting next to, because affinities are crucial for proper development.
- *Visual*. Once a week, patients watch films and documentaries in the projection room. Meanwhile, the staff manages the weekly information in order to draw recommendations for the families in their weekend care. This can be done because this activity does not require great deal of attention. Two people are enough to monitor about twenty patients.
- *Lunch*. Finally, lunch is considered another important activity as it includes the patient's behaviour when eating. Patient attitudes and reactions at lunch time, such as rejection of food, have to be monitored by care-assistants. Facts such as menu acceptance, refusal to eat, affinities with other patients or fights are important aspects in the centre's daily life.

The information collected from these activities and the occurring incidents are currently written in a patient notebook. In addition, assistants record the corresponding recommendations in that very book, which is handed to the patient's family at the weekend. Noticeably, many incidents are also transmitted informally just by speaking. This means that some things are often forgotten since there is no corresponding annotation in the notebook.

2.2 Home

At the moment, therapy activities are managed by relatives or home care staff in collaboration with the day centre's caregivers. Daily, relatives provide care assistants with information concerning the behaviour of the patient at home, receiving, at the same time, information of the patient's activities in the day centre. In addition, families provide information concerning the patients' memory in order to build personalized exercises to reinforce their minds. Finally, families receive recommendations from the caregivers towards safety for patients at home or with suggestions regarding possible therapies to apply at home.

2.3 Technologies for Alzheimer Care Support

In our work we have experimented with four core technologies which we deem can aid in the Alzheimer care giving process. Taking into account the two contexts of

Alzheimer care considered: a) day centre and b) home, the technologies regarded are as follows. As far as the home is concerned the only realistic approach is to consider a minimal introduction of new technologies. In this regard, we think that the adoption of DTT-based interactive services through which therapy to Alzheimer patients can be provided are a good option. Additionally, both at home and in a day centre the adoption of patient wandering systems with lowering prices such as the Agotek's Gerotek [15] product with which we have experimented is a very good option. However, the work described in this paper has focused on two key technologies:

- **Context Modelling through Ontology.** As it has been described in the previous two sections in order to provide a personalised and valuable service to Alzheimer patients it is paramount to know as much information as possible about their current status and daily therapy exercises and reactions to them. A common current approach is to adopt semantic technologies to model such knowledge given the flexibility such technologies offer in terms of new knowledge inference and reasoning.
- **Context Sensing and Phone-mediated natural interaction with NFC.** If there is a truly pervasive device, this is the mobile phone. Therefore, if there is a device that a care giver is ready to use is a mobile phone. The integration of NFC technology into the latest mobile phones eases the pairing between users and surrounding tagged devices. Based on this promise we have carried out some experiments for improving the care given in a day centre, which are described in the following sections. However, before concluding this section we offer a brief overview of this technology and its capabilities.

In order to create applications for supporting daily activities in an assisted environment, it is necessary to adapt sensorial capabilities. Our approach on this regard has always considered identification technologies. Initially, we used Radio Frequency Identification technology (RFID). By placing readers and antennas appropriately in the environment, it is possible to be closer to Weiser's vision, as this system offers an easy method for interacting with the environment [6], establishing bindings between users and tagged objects. By just wearing tags, people can obtain services relevant to the context in which they are living. However, some disadvantages have to be considered. Firstly, even a single interaction requires the patient to pass near an antenna. The fixed nature of such antennas and readers carries associated infrastructure costs. On the other hand, the NFC technology changes the model (see Fig. 1). While in the first case both readers and antennas are fixed, in the second one, they are mobile. In addition, in the first case, tags are mobile, while in the second one, they are either mobile or fixed [7]. Thus, we deem that a key technology to support Alzheimer caregiver's work in day centres is NFC.

NFC [13] is a short-range technology using a frequency of 13.56 MHz. The system consists of two elements: the Initiator, which controls the information exchange (called reader in RFID); and the Target, which responds to the promptings of the Initiator (called tag in RFID). Furthermore, two operation modes are available: Active and Passive. In the Active one, both devices generate their own field of radio frequency to transmit data (peer to peer). In the Passive one, only one of these devices generates the radiofrequency field, while the other is used to load modulation for data

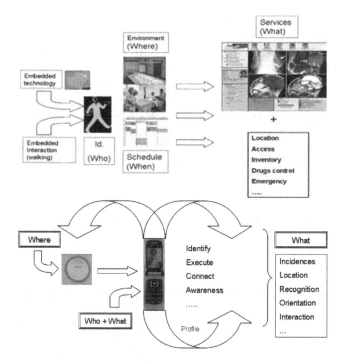

Fig. 1. RFID vs. NFC models

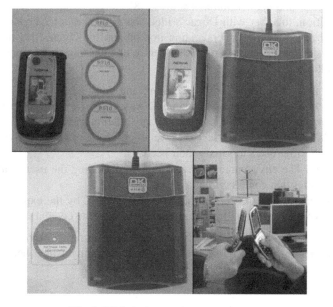

Fig. 2. NFC devices and operation modes

transfers. Fig. 2 shows the three types of NFC devices: mobile phone, tag and reader. It also shows the Active and Passive interaction modes.

A very interesting feature of NFC in Java ME devices is that by just bringing a mobile phone near a tag, the information contained in the tag can activate the execution of the corresponding mobile phone application automatically. This is due to the PushRegistry of the JSR 257 API of NFC. Registration for mobile application or service enacting start-up is based on the record type name and format of the NFC Data Exchange Format (NDEF) record. There can be one application for each record type name and format pair registered for start-up at a time. If the data on the target contain more than one NDEF record, the start-up is based on the record type name and format of the first matching record in the data. When a target is discovered, the application management software checks the PushRegistry entries. If there is an entry for the NDEF record type name and format in the target, the application having that entry is started. An example NDEF record would be the following: `MIDlet-Push-1:ndef:mime?name=App/Therapy,Presentation.VisualMIDlet_IN CIDENCES,*`.

3   Ontology-Based Context Modelling for Alzheimer Care

As mentioned in the previous section a key requirement to offer a better Alzheimer care support is to gather, model and process patient related information, i.e. their current and past context. According to A. Dey, context is "*any information that can be used to characterize the situation of an entity. An entity is a person, place, or object that is considered relevant to the interaction between a user and an application, including the user and application themselves*" [8].

This definition, together with Dogac's idea about the creation of context ontology to achieve a better scenario understanding in Ambient Intelligence [9] made us consider the division of a caring setting (day centre or home) in four important aspects defined as follows:

- *User.* The user is an active entity requiring and consuming services that interact implicitly with an intelligent environment, which is aware of the user's identity, profile, schedule, location, preferences, social situation and activity.
- *Services.* When we talk about services, we are referring to all the activities that the system might offer users to satisfy their needs.
- *Environment.* The environment is everything surrounding the user; that is, all the physical entities that could be found.
- *Device.* Mechanisms capable of modifying the context, by the explicit or implicit interaction of the user, or collecting information about the context or users.

Each and every one of these aspects or concepts is, in turn, composed of a set of entities or instances that depend on the scenario, thus distinguishing between the day centre and home.

3.1   User

The number of users taking part in a day centre is considerably higher than that in a home and, what is more, there are some entities in the day centre ontology that are not considered in the home ontology. We will start by defining the entities shared by both scenarios.

- *Dependant person.* A user with a degree of dependency who requires special care. These will be those favoured by the services available.
- *Visitor.* A user who gets in contact with the system temporarily.

Now we indicate the entities bound, specifically, to the day centre ontology.

- *Assistant.* A user who helps in particular tasks related to patient care.
- *Physician.* A doctor entrusted with the monitoring of the dependant person's state of health.
- *Nurse.* A user with enough professional training to take specialized care of the dependant person.
- *Relative.* A user who belongs to the family or caring circle of the dependant person. This user receives specific information from the incidence service.
- *System administrator.* A user who maintains and operates a computer system.

The entities described above are not included in the home ontology; however, the home ontology has its own two entities:

- *Primary physician.* Refers to someone with a medical degree who visits the dependant person daily.
- *Caregiver.* A user who takes care of the dependant person. This person related to the patient or not, is in charge of carrying out the exchange of information with the day centre staff (when the dependant person arrives or leaves the centre).

3.2 Services

At first glance, the two scenarios present the same classification on the service ontology. All the services defined can be included in one of the following three general services:

- *Information management.* This means processing and filtering context information so that it can be visualized and understood for later decision making. Most of the users would benefit from this service. Services of this type offered in the day centre differ from the ones offered at home. In the day centre there is more information to manipulate and some of the activities do not exist at home. The *activity support* service is especially important, as it tries to avoid the advance of the disease. *Incidence management* is also a key term. Both concepts will be explained in depth further on in this document.
- *Monitoring.* To understand what is happening in the environment, it is necessary to know the origin of the information, using sensors. Users, as well as the environment, need to be monitored, and this is done by taking their life signals (*patient tele-monitorization* service) and by controlling their location.
- *Decision making.* Reactive care in AAL environments implies that actions should be taken based on the information available at the exact moment an incident happens.

3.3 Environment

In the environment ontology, there are slight differences between both scenarios, at least at first sight. The main entities that take part in this ontology are now listed.

- *Door.* In a place like a day centre, it is necessary to control doors to avoid the possibility of patients escaping (or intruders entering).
- *Outside area.* Places outside the building.
- *Room.* The day centre is composed of a group of rooms. Each of them would have certain attributes to differentiate them from each other.

The room types we can find in a day centre differ from the ones found at home. As shown in Fig. 3, at the day centre there are specific rooms for the activities carried out (emphasized with a green square), while at home, the rooms correspond to the common places of a simple house. Another difference is the orientation panel used to facilitate the movement of the dependant person between the different rooms (see home diagram in Fig. 3).

3.4 Devices

The types of devices used to modify the home context are more than those deployed in the day centre. This is due to the fact that not only NFC technology has been introduced, but also RFID, so as to know where the dependant person is at every single moment so that incidents related to the person can be avoided. Once the differences have been explained, we can begin defining the devices found in both scenarios:

- *Tag.* It is a near field RFID tag that contains information about the place, object or person it is attached to. Depending on the kind of tag (for place, object or person) the information stored in it and its structure will vary.
- *NFC Mobile Phone.* Device capable of reading near RFID tags. It is a special type of mobile phone that contains an NFC reader and allows information exchange between two mobile phones, as well as reading and writing of information stored in RFID tags.
- *Sensor.* Bluetooth-enabled devices recording the dependent person's state of health.
- *Visualization system.* System used to show the information needed by the user. In the home ontology there is a specialization of this entity used to visualize exercises that slow down the Alzheimer's disease.
- *Door actuator.* Its function is related to the *Door control* service. This service will send an opening signal to the device, so that it executes the order.

An additional entity is defined in the day centre ontology: the *server*, which is similar to the *computer* entity defined in the home ontology with the only difference being its central role as information gatherer. Further entities only included in the home ontology are listed below:

- *Reader.* Device capable of reading RFID tags. It is useful for finding where the dependant person is. This device is used in the orientation and location services.
- *RFID tag.* It is a device similar to the one called *tags*. They differ in their reading distance range.

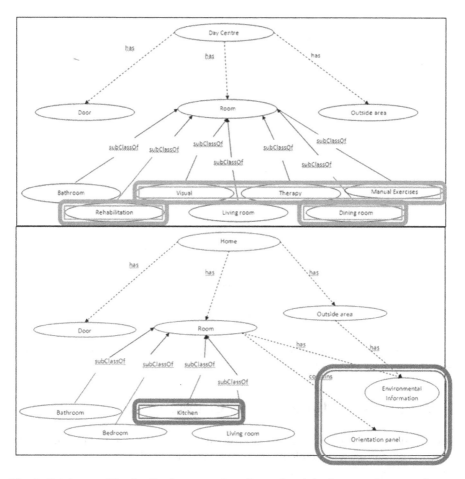

Fig. 3. Ontology entities for the day centre (top diagram) and the home environment (bottom diagram). The differences between both diagrams are marked with green boxes in the day centre ontology and with red boxes in the home ontology.

- *Tele-Alarm.* Mechanism used for help requests. It is associated with the telephone and works by pressing a button that immediately contacts with an emergency service.
- *Alarm.* It is a composition of an alarm and an RFID tag. The alarm starts ringing when a danger is detected.

3.5 Context Ontology

Our context ontology results from merging the four types of concepts mentioned. The *User* (physician, dependent person, assistant, etc.) is in the *Day centre*, being able to use the active *Devices* and, at the same time, to benefit from the *Services* offered. The most significant part of the resulted context ontology is shown in Fig. 4. The figure shows where the activities take place (*Activity Support* is developed in a *Room)* and

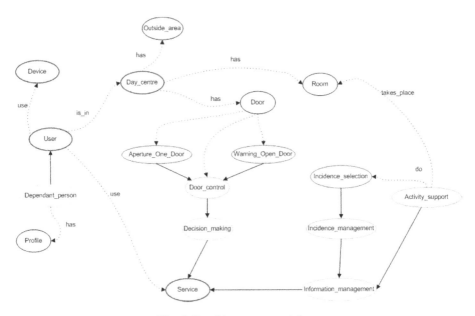

Fig. 4. Resulting context ontology

how the incidences are linked with the activity being done. In addition, we can observe that the door is linked with the services containing the name.

4   An Approach to Home and Day Centre Services

Next, we detail some of the main services defined which make use of the knowledge modelled by our context ontology. Prototype versions of all these services for Alzheimer care support have been developed.

4.1 Simple Interaction

Elderly people are not familiar with new technology. Thus, interaction methods as simple and natural as possible are highly desirable. This is also applicable to caregivers or relatives, whose hard work taking care of the patient does not allow them to waste their time with annoying common interactions. Stopping their work to write records in a PC is not an option. They (both patients and caregivers) must interact with the system in a transparent way, with the simplest possible actions. Technology should be at the service of the users and not the other way around.

We can achieve this objective by using a Bluetooth-enabled NFC mobile phone. The interaction is as simple as bringing the mobile phone close to the device or person that will take part in the action: life signal monitoring devices, displays, computers to store data or, even, the patients. Examples will be detailed in next sections.

In order to use a device or to get the information of a patient, a person has to touch the corresponding NFC tag with the phone in order to launch the needed mobile phone application, as it was explained in §2.3.

4.2 Incident Management

The management of patient incidents is a key service to be offered by an Alzheimer care support system, because it facilitates the inherently difficult job of the caregivers.

At present, when a patient incident is noticed, caregivers have to stop doing their job, leaving their patients with another caregiver and writing the incidence in a notebook manually. There are many clinics and centres that follow this protocol, which causes numerous problems, such as the interruption of daily work, lack of formalism and the impossibility of searching for the information and generating accurate reports for physicians at a later date.

This problem has to be addressed in a way that will help caregivers with the simplest possible interaction, without making their job even harder. Reaching this objective is discussed in the following three stages.

The first step in accomplishing our task successfully is to formalize the type of incidence a patient may have. It is not a good idea for each member of the staff to record the same incident in a different way. Therefore, a long list of all possible incidents and issues has been devised. In this list, we have separated each area of the day centre into a separate category (see Fig. 5). In addition, each centre could add its own incidents through a common server interface or even a website. This is a concept that we have called *meta-incidents*.

With the incidents already formalized, a form is offered to the user to fill in a consistent way. NFC technology is used to simplify this task. In combination with a mobile phone, NFC technology allows a user to "insert" the incidence about the patient via the NFC tag. This can be then accessed easily by others caregivers, assistants or relatives.

On the other hand, users should receive the personalized data needed to avoid the extra effort of reading incidents that may not be related to their job. Physicians would

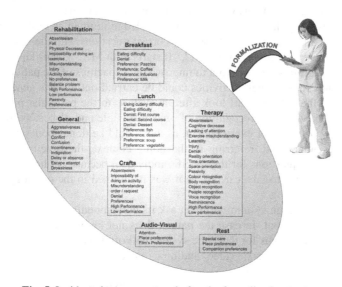

Fig. 5. Incidents by area captured after the formalization process

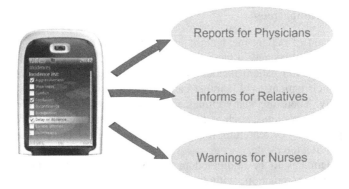

Fig. 6. Different information is displayed depending on the interest of each person

receive clinical information, while assistants and caregivers would obtain just the behavioural incidents. Moreover, this information should be shown as clearly as possible, trying to summarize all related incidences and put them together. In a further step, these summaries should be mixed with the patient's clinical information and previous reports, so that professionals could receive valuable recommendations. Fig. 6 describes the proposed idea.

4.3 Therapy Activity Support

Day centres use different services to help their patients. One of the most important services is occupational therapy. Therapy activities are focused on stimulating the patient's memory, orientation, calculation, language, and so forth.

Normally, there are general games that help the dependant person without the interaction of a caregiver. However, if we want to make personalized games or activities, we need to keep the patient's personal knowledge in mind as well as an assistant who knows all this data, in order to ask the correct questions with their corresponding clues (e.g., "What is your wife's name?", "It starts with M…"). This knowledge is, in fact, the most helpful when we want to improve the capacities of the patient.

At day centres, all of these activities could be carried out under a general concept; referring to all the patients staff look after, as well as to the particular patients themselves. In other words, the recognition of objects, people and places, as well as other activities, may be valid for every patient, as they could be done about general knowledge. On the other hand, referring to the home context, these activities would be mostly centred on questions for the specific individual because, at home, there would be just a few patients to take care of, as it was mentioned in the ontology previously presented.

For each activity, the system will then ask its corresponding question and wait for the answer of the patient. In case the patient does not know the answer (the patient may become a bit nervous for that), the system will offer the possibility of visualizing some clues composed of text, video, audio or images, or even, the correct answer to stimulate the patient's learning.

Therefore, caregivers or relatives should be able to define different kinds of activities from their work places or homes, through a Web environment. They could make it through predefined formularies or by building their own ones. To achieve this, server applications used to get data for therapy activities must provide enough mechanisms to allow the introduction of different kinds of information, whether it is personal or general.

As an example, they could introduce into the system information related to some patient's relatives, along with some clues to help the patient's memory when remembering them. Here is where an activity plan could be taken into consideration, avoiding the patient's disconnection from their closest environment. This will stimulate their identity as well as their self-esteem.

They can also create general questions that will be useful for every patient; for instance, information about celebrities, books, TV series, etc. A patient could thus watch a piece of a film or listen to an animal sound to recognize it. In case the predefined activities may not be enough for caregivers, they could use an open form to enter any question they want, defining the question itself, its answer, and its clues.

Moreover, assistants could build their own activity through meta-forms, defining tags and contents, which correspond to the custom activities considered by each centre. These meta-forms will help them to create forms that could be filled in by anyone with the personal data of each patient.

In accordance with the rest of services, we propose a simple interaction to get activities displayed in any screen from the server. It is possible to visualize an exercise on any public display knowing just the activity and the patient tag. The exercise, contained within the server, is sent to a display, thanks to a wireless video sender. Those taking part in the exercise wear some tags, which makes the interaction possible. This device can show different data, such as video, voice, text, etc. In addition, the corresponding navigation through an exercise structure is given by just touching tags.

Regarding the home case, this device could be a common television with DTT enabled. This complement to therapy could be managed at the patient's own home too. For this reason we have implemented some applications through DTT. These have been developed with the MHP [11][12] language and their content is automatically generated from the information provided by the day centre server using the XML markup language. Hence, relatives wishing to help patients only have to interact with a television set, using the remote control.

The device used to send the application to the DTT television is a DVB-T (Digital Video Broadcasting – Terrestrial) decoder with MHP technology. This device will decode the interactive application distributed in a television channel and will offer the interactivity demanded by our activity plan. This technology provides the possibility of developing applications in which the user could interact using a simple remote control. The system, of course, allows us to show multimedia content (video, audio or images) to the user. As an example, Fig. 7 shows an object recognition activity, where a user can watch clues, answer or, even the user's own experiences with this object, just by touching the colour buttons on the remote control.

The MHP application reads from the served XML file and, through an MHP decoder, shows on the television screen an interactive activity played by the patient or his/her companion via a remote control. They can navigate across the therapy activities, while the patient will be practicing with the corresponding exercises. This kind of system offers us a technological environment at minimum cost, just a DVB-T decoder

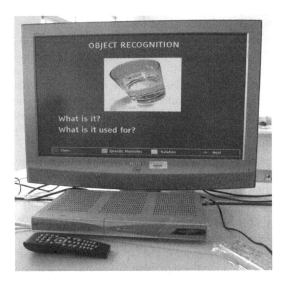

Fig. 7. Object recognition activity through DTT

ready to understand MHP code, and a display or television, which joins multimedia content with an easy interaction.

4.4 Patient Tele-monitoring

In order to keep control the patients' health when they are at home or at the day centres, it is necessary to monitor their vital signs, which are measurements of the basic functions of the body.

There are several available Bluetooth enabled devices that support monitoring of vital signs in the market. For instance, the electrical activity of the heart can be controlled with a Bluetooth ECG device. To monitor the Peak Expiratory Flow Rate (PEFR) and for diagnosing lung conditions like asthma, a Bluetooth Spirometer can be used. The oxygen saturation in the blood (SpO2) can be measured with a Bluetooth Pulse Oximeter, in the same way that blood pressure can be measured with a Bluetooth Blood Pressure Monitor. People with diabetes can check their blood sugar with a Bluetooth Glucose Meter. The weight can also be daily controlled with a Bluetooth Weight Meter.

Communicating with these devices should not involve a complex interaction with common personal computers. To use a monitoring device, a person (the patient or assistant) should be able of just touching its NFC tag with the phone, in order to launch the mobile phone application. As a result, the monitoring device should be activated and the measurement sent to the mobile phone through a Bluetooth connection. When the mobile phone obtained the measurements, it could make recommendations and send the corresponding alert messages, if necessary. Hopefully, this king of Bluetooth- and NFC-enabled vital sign devices will emerge soon.

According to the patient medical records and other data, like age or measurement limits are set. When the mobile phone gets a measure from a monitoring device, it checks the limits and performs an action. When the measurements are inside the patient's predefined thresholds, the mobile phone will play a voice message telling the patient that everything is all right. However, when the measurements are over the limits it means that something is going wrong and, therefore, it is very important to calm the patient, mainly when he or she is alone at home. When this happens, the mobile phone tells the patient what to do. The patient will hear a voice message with the recommendation of the mobile phone. This recommendation will depend on the patient's medical record. A recommendation example would be "your pulse rate is very high, you must rest" or "your glucose levels have increased, you should go for a walk for about 30 minutes". However, the most common scenario when dealing with Alzheimer's patients is the one in which their companion (a relative or a caregiver) is near them, so that they will receive such recommendations as well. In addition, since they can understand our offered data better, these recommendations could be more complete than those provided to the patient alone.

When the measurements are dangerous, the mobile phone will send a message to the primary doctor. The doctor will see in her computer the patient's medical record and the dangerous measurement, assessing the incident and deciding what treatment of special care the patient should receive. Moreover, the doctor can give a simple recommendation to the patient via the mobile phone. The physician can also prescribe some pills to the patient and the prescription will be saved on the mobile phone. If needed, the doctor can also send an ambulance. Fig. 8 summarizes this process.

Finally, all the information is always included in the patient medical record and saved into the mobile phone. This is very important because in this way patients (or their caregivers) will always carry medical records updated in the mobile phone. When the patient (or caregiver) goes to the chemist or to the doctor, the authorized

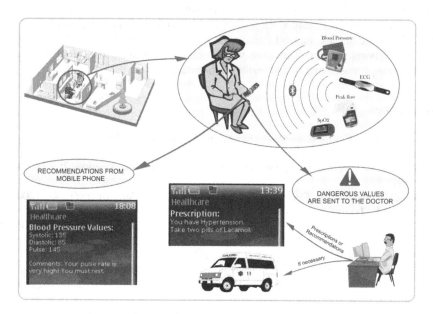

Fig. 8. Patient Tele-monitoring Process

professionals can see the patient's medical information just by touching a NFC reader with the patient's mobile phone.

Hence, in our proposal, the only devices needed are the mobile phone and monitoring devices. Home computers are not necessary because the mobile phone can manage all the data and communicate with the health assistance centre when required. However, in the day centre case, an additional server is very convenient since it could store every patient measurement in order to make logs and statistics for future consulting.

5 Conclusions and Future Work

This work has described how the application of NFC technology to Alzheimer care can significantly improve both the caring services received by patients and the daily activities of caregivers, both at day centres (nurses, doctors and so on) and homes (relatives or home caregivers). Only the adoption of natural interaction mechanisms can encourage the use of technology by the very busy caregivers. The services suggested by this work are a clear sample of the capabilities of NFC technology to improve Alzheimer patient care. In addition, all the information gathered both from caregivers' mobile devices and vital sign devices has to be modelled and analyzed to offer even better services to patients. Thus, the use of data modelling instruments such as the context ontology describe are required. The application of semantic modelling techniques enables a very flexible and evolutionary knowledge repository upon which incident management, patient tele-monitoring or therapy support services can be provided. Referring to this last type of services, we have described our experiences applying DTT technology to transfer and continue part of the therapy process from day centres to homes. Future work will assemble our current prototypes into an NFC-enabled chronic disease support framework which we aim to deploy for evaluation in local care giving centres. Thus, we will be able of assessing the suitability of the mechanisms proposed and to add further improvements.

References

1. ISTAG, Scenarios for Ambient Intelligence in 2010 (Febuary 2001),
   http://www.cordis.lu/ist/istag.htm
2. Weiser, M.: The Computer for the 21st Century. Scientific American 265(3), 94–104 (1991)
3. Want, R.: People First, Computers Second. IEEE Pervasive Computing 6(1), 4–6 (2007)
4. Favela, J., Tentori, M., Castro, L., Gonzalez, V., Moran, E., Martinez, A.I.: Estimating Hospital Workers' Activities and its use in Context-Aware Hospital Applications, Pervasive Healthcare, Innsbruck, Austria (2006)
5. Ambient Assisted Living, http://www.aal169.org/
6. Bravo, J., Hervás, R., Sánchez, I., Chavira, G., Nava, S.: Visualization Services in a Conference Context: An approach by RFID Technology. Journal of Universal Computer Science 12(3), 270–283 (2006)
7. Bravo, J., Hervás, R., Chavira, G., Nava, S., Villarreal, V.: From Implicit to Touching Interaction: RFID and NFC Approaches. In: Human System Interaction Conference (HSI 2008), Krakow, Poland (2008)

8. Dey, A.: Understanding and Using Context. Personal and Ubiquitous Computing 5(1), 4–7 (2001)
9. Dogac, A., Laleci, G., Kabak, Y.: Context Frameworks for Ambient Intelligence. In: eChallenges 2003, Bologna, Italy (October 2003)
10. Fridman, N., Musen, M.: An Algorithm for Merging and Aligning Ontologies: Automation and Tool Support, Stanford (1999)
11. DVB Multimedia Home Platform tutorials and information for interactive TV developers, http://www.tvwithoutborders.com/
12. MHProject v.2.0. Universidad Pública de Navarra, http://www.mhproject.org/
13. NFC Forum (2008), http://www.nfc-forum.org/aboutnfc/
14. The Touch Computing Project (2008), http://www.nearfield.org/about/
15. http://www.agotek.com/web/PDF/triptico%20Gerotek%20web.pdf

Designing an Interactive Messaging and Reminder Display for Elderly

Erwin R. van Veldhoven, Martijn H. Vastenburg, and David V. Keyson

ID-StudioLab
http://studiolab.io.tudelft.nl
Faculty of Industrial Design Engineering, Delft University of Technology
Landbergstraat 15, 2628 CE, Delft, The Netherlands
{E.R.vanVeldhoven,M.H.Vastenburg,D.V.Keyson}@tudelft.nl

Abstract. Despite the wealth of information and communication technology in society today, there appears to be a lack of acceptable information services for the growing elderly population in need of care. Acceptability is not only related to human factors such as button size and legibility, but rather relates to perceived value and harmony in relation to existing living patterns. This paper describes the design of an asynchronous interactive communication system based upon a bulletin board metaphor. A panel of end-users was involved in various stages of the design process. To improve ease of use, functionality exposed to elderly users is limited, while caregivers are given extended control. A pilot field study with a working prototype showed a high degree of user acceptance. The user centered approach resulted in a design concept that was acceptable for the elderly participants.

Keywords: Product design, asynchronous communication, interactive message display, elderly users, acceptability.

1 Introduction

In most industrialized countries, the number of elderly people is steadily growing. According to EuroStat, for every 100 EU citizens between 15 and 64 years old in 2005, there were 24.7 persons aged 65 and older. The old-age dependency ratio is expected to increase to 39.8 by 2030[1]. Many elderly people indicate they prefer to live independently in their own homes as long as possible, which was confirmed in interview sessions held by the researchers involved in this study. In many cases, however, support is needed to continue their everyday living routines. Whereas support is nowadays typically given by both formal and informal caregivers, support could also be given by technology. This assistive technology is expected to play an increasingly important role in the coming years.

Various kinds of technological solutions can already be deployed to support elderly, in which communication has been recognized as a central theme [6, 17, 19, 21, 23]. Existing communication means available to elderly include traditional telephones,

---

[1] http://epp.eurostat.ec.europa.eu/tgm/table.do?tab=table&init=1&language=en&pcode=tsdde511

E. Aarts et al. (Eds.): AmI 2008, LNCS 5355, pp. 126–140, 2008.

mobile phones, and video communication. In recent years, services have been developed for monitoring behavior and for providing automated feedback to users, e.g., giving medicine reminders. Even though these solutions might eventually contribute to the quality of life of elderly clients, elderly users still seem to have a hard time using modern technology.

Low acceptability of new technology might be partially caused by usability problems. Most ICT-based products require a basic understanding of computer applications, whereas many elderly have little experience with this type of systems. The very fact that functionality is hidden in menus and layers, for example, can be hard to grasp for elderly users. Furthermore, devices such as mobile phones require fine motor skills, whereas these abilities tend to be limited for elderly users. Such usability issues form a practical barrier towards acceptance by the elderly target group.

Apart from usability issues, other reasons can be found for elderly users having difficulties adopting new technology. For example, it can be difficult to change existing living patterns, thereby making it hard to introduce new procedures and products. Even though the added value of new technology appears to be obvious to the caregivers, elderly users tend to be skeptical and hesitant. Product designers therefore face the challenge of creating products that support the elderly user that make use of the possibilities offered by new technology, while maintaining appropriate acceptability levels.

2   Related Work

The design of assistive technology to support elderly users in living independently has been studied before. In the next section, existing work in the area of acceptability, cognition, perceived control, implementation and design in relation to designing assistive technology will be described.

2.1   Acceptability

Most existing projects in the area of assistive living share a common goal in terms of increasing the independence of elderly people [1, 4, 15, 19]. Supposedly, an increase in independence results in a decrease in professional care per client, which in turn would result in a cost reduction. From an economic perspective, the need for technological solutions seems obvious.

A major obstacle towards deployment of assistive living technology, however, appears to be acceptability [10, 15, 23, 25]. As will be discussed in the following paragraphs, existing studies revealed multiple issues that were found to be crucial towards creating acceptability.

Acceptability is a subjective construct that varies between users and in time. For example, personal circumstances, such as education and income, could influence the attitude towards new technology [10]. Absolute age, on the other hand, is expected to be of minor relevance.

Acceptability has also been found to be related to perceived benefit [23]. Supposedly, when elderly users experience little added value, acceptability is low. When new products would better link to everyday problems, the perceived benefit is expected to be higher, and consequently acceptability is expected to improve. Guiliani et al. [10] studied the attitude of elderly towards technology, and found that technological innovations are likely to be accepted when the practical benefits are clear. Similarly, Czaja and Lee [6] studied the use of e-mail amongst elderly women, and concluded that perceived usefulness was an important factor with respect to usage.

Next to perceived benefit, reliability has been found to be important by McCreadie and Sanchez et al. [15, 22]. In a study on the acceptability of assistive technology, 67 people aged over 70 were interviewed. No participants were found to be technophobic. However, reliability of technology was judged to be an important condition for product adoption. In line with the studies above, elderly were found to be willing to use assistive technology, despite opposite expectations, if only the system would address their needs correctly.

Finally, to increase acceptability, technology might also have to be pleasurable in use. Interview data collected by Selwyn [23] showed that elderly are less involved in the pleasures of ICT than younger users, which makes it hard to fit ICT solutions into their everyday lives.

2.2 Cognitive Aspects

Several cognitive issues might underlie the control problems that elderly users encounter when using new technology. For example, the ability to learn new skills relies on fluid intelligence, which is the capacity to associate, independent of previous specific practice or instructions [9]. Since the capacity to learn new skills to operate technology decreases when people get older, elderly people can have difficulty using new products [6]. Furthermore, the spatial memory capacity of elderly users tends to be reduced. It is therefore suggested that designers should aim to reduce demand on the spatial memory resources of elderly [6, 11]; this could be achieved by using simple and flat interface structures. Thirdly, elderly users were found to be sensible for failures and inconsistencies; young users tend to be less affected by usability problems than elderly users [6, 11, 22]. The learning process should be simple. Inconsistencies in the interface may slow down the learning process, especially for elderly users, and should therefore be avoided.

2.3 Interaction Issues

Whereas humans are capable of interpreting contextual information and providing feedback, computer based systems tend to offer limited data, often lacking desired qualitative information. Combining human input with raw data collected by sensors, is a complex issue [3]. In the CareNet study of Consolvo et al., the suggestion to enrich data with background information (adding a "human touch") made potential users anxious, because they were suspicious of being given extra responsibility. Implementation of 'common sense', which appeals most to the perception of inexperienced users, into autonomous products is still complex [8].

When designing pro-active systems, controllability could be a challenge. Even though people tend to accept a large degree of system autonomy [2], the sense of being in control has great value to elderly users [3]. Perceived control is, amongst others, related to the predictability of a product behavior.

2.4   Role of Designer

The difficulties elderly experience accessing modern technology could partly be caused by the fact that product designers are not aware of the special characteristics of the target group, or do not know how to implement the needs of elderly in the design process [6]. Sanchez et al. introduced the expression 'imperfect automation', which represents the design of 'perfect' products, not performing according to the criterion of the task, and, consequently, not satisfying its users [22]. Elderly users form a user group with special needs and desires, which need to be addressed by designers.

Research by Irizarry on promoting the use of modern technology and Internet access for Australian people over 55 indicated that elderly preferred to use technologies that are recognizable in everyday use [12], which could be a motivation to use existing interaction principles. However, recent ambitions to provide elderly with ICT technology are often based on the assumption that ICT is useful and desirable for everyone, while in reality, seniors are often not served by these technologies [23]. When designing assistive technology for elderly users, designers should consider the specific needs of the target group in terms of, for example, understandability, controllability and perceived benefit, in order to create acceptable products.

2.5   Social Network

Interaction with modern ICT solutions could be stimulated by members of the social network of an elderly person. Involvement in a social network is also beneficial in terms of well-being [17]. In a user and concept study on the acceptability of mobile communication services for elderly, future services where perceived as beneficial when social relationships were maintained, as well as health and the ability to live at home. Besides this benefit, engagement and connectedness could have "powerful health benefits" [5, 18], which is another motivation to stimulate social commitment.

Several applications of communication services for elderly have been studied. An example of a communication device involving distant relatives can be found in the study of Mynatt et al., in which a Digital Family Portrait was tested in household environments [19]. This picture frame, which is an augmented domestic object, provides back-story information about geographically distant people. They found that the target group of elderly users demands the complexity to be restricted. The study results also emphasize the importance of supporting ageing adults, in terms of peace of mind for all members of the care network.

2.6   Medicine Reminders

An interesting application of assistive technology is providing care clients with medicine reminders [7, 14]. Reminders could be dynamically linked to user activities, which can be monitored using various sensors. An example is the iCabiNet [14], which is designed to select the most appropriate communication device for each reminder. Whereas iCabiNet creates a flexible mechanism for reaching users, the system has so far only been tested using a mobile phone.

2.7 User Experiences

User experiences with interactive technology are often studied inartificial settings [13, 14]. User experiences in a home situation can be quite different [24]. If target group users participate in user studies in a lab setting, they are often requested to reproduce every-day activities, which is hardly realistic. Bringing the prototype to the user is likely to initiate more natural behavior, which contributes to the validity of the findings.

2.8 Project Goal

Even though new technologies might support elderly in their everyday lives, accept-ability of existing systems tends to be low. The goal of the present case study is to find out how existing technology can be made accessible to elderly users in an ac-ceptable way. In the case study, the focus is on the design of an interactive product that enables communication between elderly people and their care network, which can be applied to present medicine reminders as well.

3 Design Steps

3.1 Field Exploration

To get insight in the application domain and user needs, technology suppliers, poten-tial users and caregivers were interviewed. Ten experts in hard- and software for technological care solutions, promoting their products on a Care&ICT fair, were asked about the problems and challenges in their domain. They indicated that many companies are guided by the availability of modern technology in developing their products. Involvement of elderly end users in the design process tends to be very limited; requirements are generally set by care companies. In the near future, the main focus seems to be on developing integrated support systems, rather than developing new products for each single need. However, the vast number of "standard" commu-nication protocols slows down the development of integrated support systems.

To explore how new technology can be implemented in the life of elderly care cli-ents in an acceptable way, a care giver was observed in her morning round, and the target sample group (n=5) was interviewed. The informal interviews were held with elderly care clients living at home or in a protected housing environment. In terms of user needs, all elderly participants indicated a desire to remain living independently as long as possible. This desire is complicated by the understanding that they are starting to, or may soon start degenerating mentally and physically. The interviewees also complained about people in their surroundings who slowly but surely change their attitude towards them. Relatives and friends tend to visit the elderly less frequently, which leads to an increase in loneliness. Loneliness could contribute to the mental degeneration of elderly individuals. Having influence on their social environment and being involved in every-day activities was preferred over being a passive client of care.

The interviewed care clients stated that being confronted with inevitable degenera-tion creates a despondent feeling, in spite of the fact that one has much time to pre-pare for this. The elderly complained that many available care solutions stress their weaknesses, because usage is similar to admitting one's degeneration. This is alleged to be a difficult psychological coping process, which is hard to imagine for younger adults. The interviews showed that elderly prefer to use products that do not directly confirm their limitations and carry a negative connotation for them. New support technology could thus best be based on familiar interaction principles, preventing stigmatization.

During the field exploration, care clients as well as caregivers underlined an unwanted development in the care context. Due to efficiency improvements, there is less time available for social interaction between caregivers and clients; this consequence is supported by neither caregivers nor clients.

In general, the elderly expressed their appreciation for contact with family members and friends, as well as caregivers. Elderly enjoyed the interaction, and the attention made them feel safe and respected. The effort of the other party to establish contact is highly appreciated. Communication features can contribute to the acceptability of new devices, since elderly seem willing to communicate.

An interesting example of modern ICT in the context of elderly users is the mobile phone. A large part of the elderly participants recognize the added value of being reachable, and having the possibility to call someone in case of emergency. However, few actually use the mobile phone. One older individual, who owns a mobile phone and recognizes its advantages, did not know how to use the device. This attitude towards modern technology is representative for the acceptability problems that need to be challenged.

3.2   Concept Development

In the interviews, the elderly participants indicated their dislike of 'modern' interaction metaphors, such as Windows-like layout details. These are tempting to be exploited by a younger group, but would almost certainly not appeal to elder users. Even worse, they tend to be scared off by the complexity of new products, even though the benefit of these products is recognized. In designing new products for elderly, one should therefore conceive interaction principles that are already familiar to the target group. The interaction should have an intuitive character, which needs only short introduction.

3.2.1   The Interaction Metaphor

To provide the elderly users with communication possibilities, an asynchronous messaging product is being developed. Since product designs based on familiar metaphors are expected to lower the threshold to start using new technology, an appropriate metaphor had to be found to present information, specifically for in a domestic environment. First, a photo frame metaphor was considered (similar to the Digital Family Portrait of Mynatt et al.), since the interviewed elderly had many pictures of relatives and friends in their homes. Although each frame could symbolize contact with the person in the picture, the mental step required to perceive it as an interactive device was expected to be too abstract. As a second step, a bulletin board metaphor was considered. A bulletin board is a central place for physical notes and reminders, which are somehow interesting for passers-by (figure 1). A bulletin board display could

Fig. 1. The interactive bulletin board resembles a traditional bulletin board

easily be linked to context-aware technology and does not stress the technical nature of context-aware systems.

3.2.2 Functionalities
The usability of a bulletin board with (too) many functions would probably be low. In designing the product functionality, complexity and usability need to be balanced.

In developing the electronic bulletin board, the affordances [20] of a traditional bulletin board were mapped to functions of the interactive bulletin board. Affordances can be described as a product's properties defining how it could possibly be used, to a reasonable extent. Table 1 shows the affordances of a bulletin board. Re-arranging items and pinning/removing thumbtacks have not been mapped to the interactive bulletin board, in order to improve the ease-of-use of the system.

To create an interactive bulletin board, an LCD monitor could be linked to a keyboard and a mouse. However, these modern devices could nullify the perception of the bulletin board metaphor. Therefore, a touch screen was used as the interaction

Table 1. Affordances of a bulletin board

Affordances	Traditional Bulletin Board	Electronic Bulletin Board
Read	√	√
Pin (=add) items	√	√
Remove items	√	√
Re-arrange items	√	-
Pin/remove thumb-tacks	√	-

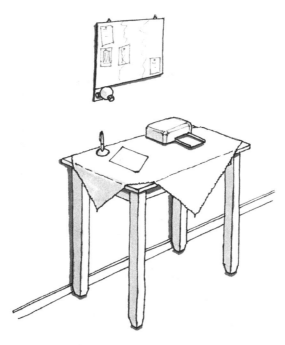

Fig. 2. The basic components of the electronic bulletin board, all controlled by a personal computer

Fig. 3. The context menu enables the user to delete and print items. The last option is hiding this menu.

medium to make sure users have to touch the items on the bulletin board physically (figure 2). A webcam is used for adding messages to the bulletin board. The snapshots from the webcam automatically appear on the board as new items. Electronic items can be stored by sending it to a printer; items can not be stored electronically, since

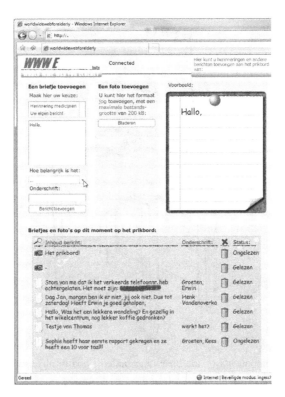

Fig. 4. The web site enables family and friends to inspect the bulletin board (bottom half), and to add messages and pictures (top half)

this would unnecessarily increase the system's complexity. Figure 3 shows the options that are displayed when an item is selected by the user.

3.2.3 Development of the Prototype

The monitor, webcam and printer have a distinct modern and technologic appearance, which could have a negative impact on the user. A secretaire, selected for its traditional appearance, was used to shield the technical parts. The main interaction device of the prototype, the touch screen, was placed on top of the secretaire (figure 5). The webcam, the printer and speakers, were visible to the user. A laptop, adapters, (extension) leads and hubs were hidden behind the doors of the secretaire. The visible side of the secretaire was free of redundant wiring and other electronic connections.

The software runs on the laptop, and all data is centrally stored on a web server; communication with the bulletin board is via the Internet.

To keep the elderly user socially involved in the everyday lives of others, connectivity to the Internet offers possibilities. To realize social contact, family and friends, as well as caregivers, can consult and adjust the contents of the bulletin board by using a website (figure 4).

Compared to the bulletin board, located in the homes of the elderly user, the web site offers more complex functionalities. The system offers the possibility to enter and display reminders, of which the presentation can be adapted to the urgency of the reminders.

Fig. 5. The final prototype. New messages could be added using a webcam (with the yellow button). Messages could be printed using a printer.

4 Pilot Study

4.1 Services

To create a 'live' prototype, two realistic messaging services have been linked to the bulletin board. The first service enables family and friends to add messages using the Internet. Since the elderly interviewees enjoyed displaying personal knickknacks of relatives and friends around the house, reminding them of valuable people and experiences, photographs could be added to the messages as well.

Secondly, a context-aware reminder service is linked to the prototype. Reminders are automatically generated whenever the user forgets to take medication, in reference to a predefined medicine schedule. A micro-switch sensor was linked to the medicine-box in order to monitor the intake of medication. Each reminder gradually asks for more attention, until the user touches the reminder of the bulletin board, or medication is taken. Eventually, an alarm message could be sent to a caregiver. This alarm-function has not been implemented in the prototype.

4.2 Goal and Procedure

A small-scale pilot study was conducted to collect user experiences with the prototype in a realistic setting. Given the time constraints on the project, the study was limited to two participants.

Participants for the pilot study were selected on the basis of being older adults, living at home, receiving professional care, and taking medication on a regular basis. Two subjects were recruited (76 and 84 years of age). The first subject had to take medication twice a day, and was slightly forgetful. The second subject had to take eye-drops twice a day. Both participants were asked to indicate which person they were most involved with. The first participant selected her daughter as the most important person in her daily life. The domestic helper was chosen as the most important helper for the second participant. These persons were involved in the test.

Before starting the field test, the prototype and procedure were demonstrated in the homes of the participants. The participants were shown how to add, print and remove items. During the test, interaction with the bulletin board was monitored through an online log-file. In the course of the field test, the supervisor contacted the participants every other day to check if everything was in order. After the test, an evaluation interview was held, in which the experiences of the elderly users and their problems concerning usability and perception were discussed.

In both tests (which lasted for four and seven days, respectively), the bulletin board was placed on a central position in the living room. When awake, both subjects spent most time of the day in the living room, and thus in viewing distance of the bulletin board.

5   Results and Discussion

Both participants perceived the usability of the prototype as being clear and uncomplicated, which made their general opinion positive. The participants understood the applied metaphor; they literally indicated to be using a bulletin board, and did not label the prototype with a technology-oriented name.

5.1 The Metaphor

The affordances of a traditional bulletin board that were mapped to the interactive bulletin board were easily accepted; the participants understood its functions without explanation. An example of adopting an original affordance can be given by explaining an automatic action of the second subject. To select an item, he touched the thumbtack rather than the message. Physical interaction with notes on a bulletin board starts by pulling out the thumbtack, which could be an origin of this behavior. This shows that the affordances of a traditional bulletin board create certain expectations. This link between physical and virtual interaction has added value for the elderly user, since it relies less on their fluid intelligence.

During the second test, a pop-up window appeared for a software update. The test subject chose to add a question about this event to the bulletin board, in which he claimed that the pop-up window was just another item on his bulletin board. The subject was found to be completely unacquainted with the concept of Windows-based computer interfaces. In this case, the bulletin board metaphor was fully accepted.

5.2 User Expectations

A general hesitation towards technology was found to be a recurring theme through-out the study. During the introduction of the study, both subjects stressed their fear of technology repeatedly. Afterwards, both participants claimed that this attitude had not changed. However, they both had to admit that their hesitation towards the bulletin board in particular was low. At this moment, it is difficult to grasp what influenced their hesitation most.

5.3 Perceived Control

The test subjects were offered continuous control over the content of the bulletin board. However, lack of control was displayed during the first night of the first test. A medicine reminder was displayed in combination with a subtle sound, but the test subject did not dare to stop the reminder, being afraid that something might break. Consequently, the bulletin board continued playing the sound. The test subject complained about this to her neighbor and daughter, who simply stressed that touching the relevant item would solve the problem. In this situation, absence of interaction with the user interface resulted in lack of user control.

The feeling of being in control was found to be related to how smooth an interaction was experienced. Just before the end of the second study, a server-side problem caused the bulletin board to stop functioning. The screen got a static appearance and all functionality was lost. The failure made the participant doubt his own skills to control the bulletin board, while it was totally due to external parties.

5.4 Usability

A touch screen was used for display and manipulation of the items on the bulletin board. Barriers for actually touching the screen were found to be anxiety and forget-fulness. Although both subjects had not used a touch screen before (even though the

Fig. 6. A participant using the prototype

second subject knew the term), this interaction skill was easily mastered. Moreover, the participants indicated that the bulletin board offered sufficient usability clues (figure 6), which improved their skillfulness with the prototype in general. The test showed that even a trial-and-error process led to desired results, since the first subject tended to forget the instructions.

5.5 Social Network

The role of friends and family was found to be decisive when looking at the hesitant attitude towards technology of the elderly subjects. The personal items provided by members of the social network and the subsequent enthusiasm were found to be a catalyst for using the prototype.

Finding suitable participants for this study appeared to be difficult. Several potential test subjects eventually decided not to participate, since they were scared of new technology. The communication between the elderly participants and their social network gave problems grasping each other's frame of reference. Caregivers, family and friends often assigned computer characteristics to the prototype, in the presence of the elderly user. These subconscious contributions might have caused confusion. In introducing the prototype to potential participants, it therefore seems important to use plain language.

5.6 Test Setting

An event during the second night of the first study illustrated the unpredictable nature of a realistic environment. In the belief that the subject's wishes were met, the neighbor of the elderly user dropped by to put off the bulletin board. The neighbor did not realize that she was not able to turn the bulletin board on again (it was expected to be impossible to turn it off as well), as she had planned to do the next day. The neighbor applied her basic computer knowledge to reason how the prototype should function. This event is a clear example of the structural difference between a lab environment and the field; it would probably not have happened in a lab.

5.7 Design Process

Based on the results of the pilot study, one might conclude that designers should get to know the reference framework of the target group, by exploring the user's earlier experience, in order to design acceptable solutions. Even though a wide range of technologic possibilities are available, and tempting for designers to implement in the context of elderly users, the early involvement of elderly care clients catalyzed a process in which modern technology was cut down to a basic and accessible concept, while at the same time avoiding stigmatization.

6 Conclusions and Future Work

This pilot study shows that new technology can be presented to elderly individuals in an accessible manner, by understanding the context of use, user needs and experiences, and by leveraging existing interaction metaphors.

The technology used in current ICT applications might well be used for applications for elderly users. When these applications are designed without considering the user group appropriately, acceptability problems might occur. These acceptability problems are partly caused by poorly chosen interaction principles of applications for the elderly. Familiar interaction principles can contribute to usability.

The case study showed that by involving the target group early in the design process, the interaction principles applied could be better linked to user needs. As a result, the complexity of the prototype could be limited to a basic level, thereby improving the usability. Where 'upgrading' products seems to be the tendency for modern electronic devices, in terms of user needs and system functionality, 'downgrading' would be more appropriate designing products for elderly users.

The bulletin board might be a future solution to allow elderly to live independently at home longer. It is explicitly not designed to replace personal contact, but rather to encourage social involvement of elderly users.

The question remains how far designers should go in providing the oldest old with new technology, considering the fact that coming generations of elderly users may be more capable of handling computers. However, problems related to reduced fine motor skills and limited cognitive resources shall always be an issue. For the current elderly, designers should be looking for solutions that fit the experience and perception of this group of users.

Acknowledgements

The work presented in this paper was part of the Independent at Home project, funded by SenterNovem through the IOP-MMI program. The authors would like to thank the participants, all persons who provided necessary assistance and the ID-StudioLab for their support throughout the design process and user studies.

References

1. Arcelus, A., Jones, M.H., Goubran, F., Knoefel, F.: Integration of Smart Home Technologies in a Health Monitoring System for the Elderly. In: AINAW 2007, pp. 820–825 (2007)
2. Barkhuus, L., Dey, A.: Is Context-Aware Computing Taking Control Away from the User? Three Levels of Interactivity Examined. In: Dey, A.K., Schmidt, A., McCarthy, J.F. (eds.) UbiComp 2003. LNCS, vol. 2864, pp. 149–156. Springer, Heidelberg (2003)
3. Consolvo, S., Roessler, P., Shelton, B.E.: The CareNet Display, Lessons Learned from an In Home Evaluation of an Ambient Display. In: Davies, N., Mynatt, E.D., Siio, I. (eds.) UbiComp 2004. LNCS, vol. 3205, pp. 1–17. Springer, Heidelberg (2004)
4. Consolvo, S., Roessler, P., Shelton, B.E., LaMarca, A., Schilit, B.: Technology for Care Networks of Elderly. In: Pervasive Computing, April-June 2004, pp. 22–29 (2004)
5. Coughlin, J.F.: Technology and the Future of Aging – Technologies for Successful Aging. Journal of Rehabilitation Research and Development 28(1), 40–42 (2001)
6. Czaja, S.J., Lee, C.C.: The Impact of Aging on Access to Technology. Universal Access in the Information Society 5, 341–349 (2007)

7. Dey, A.K., Abowd, G.D.: Cybreminder: A Context-Aware System for supporting Reminders. In: Proceedings of the 2nd International Symposium on Handheld and Ubiquitous Computing, pp. 172–181 (2000)
8. Erickson, T.: Some Problems with the Notion of Context-Aware Computing. Technical Opinion, Communication of the ACM 45(2) (2002)
9. Gray, P.: Psychology, 4th edn. (2002)
10. Guilliani, V., Scopeletti, M., Fornara, F.: Elderly People at Home: Technological Help in Everyday Activities. In: IEEE, International Workshop on Robots and Human Interactive Communication (2005)
11. IJsselsteijn, W., Nap, H.H., de Kort, Y., Poels, K.: Digital Game Design for Elderly Users. Social and Behavioral Sciences (2007)
12. Irizarry, C., Downing, A., West, D.: Promoting Modern Technology and Internet Access for Under-Represented Older Populations. Journal of Technology in Human Services 19(4), 13–30 (2002)
13. Kaushik, P., Intlle, S.S., Larson, K.: Observations From a Case Study on User Adaptive Reminders for Medication Adherence. Pervasive Health (2008)
14. López-Nores, M., Pazos-Arias, J.J., García Duque, J.: Blanco-Fernández. Monitoring Medicine Intake in the Networked Home: The iCabiNET Solution. Pervasive Health (2008)
15. McCreadie, C., Tinker, A.: The Acceptabiliy of Assistive Technology to Older People. Aging & Society 25, 91–110 (2005)
16. Meyer, S., Schulze, E.: Smart Homes and the Aging User, Trends and Analyses of Consumer Behavior. In: Berlin Institute for Social Research Symposium Domotics and Networking, Miami (2006)
17. Mikkonen, M., Väyrynen, S., Ikonnen, V., Heikkilä, O.: User and Concept Studies as Tools in Developing Mobile Communications Services for the Elderly. Personal and Ubiquitous Computing (2002)
18. Morris, M., Lundell, J., Dishman, E., Needham, B.: New Perspectives on Ubiquitous Computing from Ethnographic Study of Elders with Cognitive Decline. In: Dey, A.K., Schmidt, A., McCarthy, J.F. (eds.) UbiComp 2003. LNCS, vol. 2864, pp. 227–242. Springer, Heidelberg (2003)
19. Mynatt, E.D., Rowan, J., Jacobs, A., Craighill, S.: Digital Family Portraits: Supporting Peace of Mind for Extended Family Members. SIGCHI 2001 3(1), 333–340 (2001)
20. Norman, D.: The Design of Everyday Things. MIT Press, Cambridge (1988)
21. Romero, N., Markopoulos, P., van Baren, J., de Ruyter, B., IJsselsteijn, W., Farshchian, B.: Connecting the Family with Awareness Systems. Personal Ubiquitous Computing 11, 299–312 (2007)
22. Sanchez, J., Calcaterra, G., Tran, Q.T.: Automation in the Home: the Development of an Appropriate System and its Effects on Reliance. In: Proceedings of HFES: Human Factors Engineering Society (2005)
23. Selwyn, N.: The Information Aged: A Qualitative Study of Older Adults' Use of Information and Communications Technology. Journal of Aging Studies 18, 369–384 (2004)
24. Tolmie, P., Pycock, J., Diggins, T., MacLean, A., Karsenty, A.: Unremarkable Computing. In: CHI 2002, April 20-25 (2002)
25. Vastenburg, M.H., Visser, T., Vermaas, M., Keyson, D.: Designing acceptable assisted living services for elderly users. In: European Conference on Ambient Intelligence, Nuremberg, Germany (2008)

Adaptive Estimation of Emotion Generation for an Ambient Agent Model

Tibor Bosse, Zulfiqar A. Memon, and Jan Treur

Vrije Universiteit Amsterdam, Department of Artificial Intelligence,
de Boelelaan 1081a, 1081 HV Amsterdam, The Netherlands
{tbosse,zamemon,treur}@few.vu.nl
http://www.few.vu.nl/~{tbosse,zamemon,treur}

Abstract. To improve the performance and wellbeing of humans in complex human-computer interaction settings, an interesting challenge for an ambient (or pervasive) agent system is to recognise the emotions of humans. To this end, this paper introduces a computational model to estimate the process of emotion generation based on certain triggers. The model has been implemented and tested using the modelling language LEADSTO. A first evaluation indicates that the model is successful in estimating a person's emotions, and is robust to different parameter settings.

1 Introduction

Ambient Intelligence [1], [2] represents a vision of the future where we will be surrounded by pervasive and unobtrusive electronic environments, which are sensitive, and responsive to humans. Such an environment has a certain degree of awareness of the presence and states of living creatures in it, and supports their activities. It analyses their behaviour, and may anticipate on it. Ambient Intelligence (AmI) integrates concepts from ubiquitous computing and Artificial Intelligence (AI) with the vision that technology will become invisible, embedded in our natural surroundings, present whenever we need it, attuned to the humans' senses, and adaptive to them. In an ambient intelligent environment, people are surrounded by networks of embedded intelligent devices that can sense their state, anticipate, and when relevant adapt to their needs. Therefore, the environment should be able to determine which actions have to be undertaken in order to keep this state optimal. For this purpose, it has to be equipped with knowledge about the relevant physiological and/or psychological aspects of human functioning.

In Cognitive Science and many other human-directed scientific areas (such as psychology, neurosciences, and biomedical sciences), models have been and are being developed for a variety of aspects of human functioning, among which visual attention, emotional processes, stress and workload. If such models of human processes are represented in a formal and computational format, and incorporated in the human environment in devices that monitor the physical and mental state of the human (cf. [19]) then such devices are able to perform a more in-depth analysis of the human's functioning. This can result in an environment that may more effectively affect

E. Aarts et al. (Eds.): AmI 2008, LNCS 5355, pp. 141–156, 2008.

the state of humans by undertaking - in a knowledgeable manner - certain actions that improve their wellbeing and performance. For example, the workspaces of naval officers may include systems that, among others, track their eye movements and characteristics of incoming stimuli (e.g., airplanes on a radar screen), and use this information in a computational model that is able to estimate where their attention is focused at; see [8]. When it turns out that an officer neglects parts of a radar screen, such a system can either indicate this to the person or arrange on the background that another person or computer system takes care of this neglected part. In these types of applications, an ambience is created that has a better awareness and understanding of humans, based on computationally formalised knowledge from the human-directed disciplines.

Within the last decade, the literature in Cognitive Science and Artificial Intelligence shows an increasing amount of attempts to develop (computational) models of processes related to emotion [3]. In general, two classes of approaches can be distinguished: those that focus on *emotion elicitation* processes e.g., [5], [13], and those that focus on *emotion regulation* (or coping) processes e.g., [10], [20]. The first process addresses the way how human beings develop emotions, based on stimuli from the environment e.g., [14] whereas the second process addresses the way how humans control their emotions in case they do not correspond with the emotions they desire to have e.g., [17].

The current paper focuses on the former, i.e., on emotion generation processes. Its main aim is to present a generic model of emotion generation, which can be used by ambient systems to get insight in the emotion generation processes of a human.

Moreover, the model should be *adaptive*, i.e., it should be able to learn individual characteristics of a person, based on experiences with this person. The idea is that the ambient system observes the *environment* (e.g., which positive and negative events happen?) and the *behaviour* (e.g., which emotional expressions and actions does the human show, and for how long?) of a human in a certain scenario for a certain period, and uses this information to determine the characteristics of this person with respect to emotion generation. Examples of conclusions that the system may draw are "this person is in the process of becoming angry", or "this person is so angry that (s)he must be calmed down immediately". This information will allow the system to continuously estimate the emotional state of the human, but also to *predict* its emotional state in future situations. When necessary, it will then use this information for adaptive support. For example, in settings where humans and machines have to cooperate in complex and dynamic environments (e.g., the naval warfare case described above), the system could encourage the human when it predicts he will become sad, or take over some of his tasks when he is becoming angry.

In Section 2, the model for emotion generation is described at a conceptual level, using the modelling language LEADSTO [6]. The idea is that the model is so generic that it can be applied to any arbitrary domain. Section 3 described the model to estimate emotion generation, based on the concept of *Theory of Mind*. In Section 4, a number of simulation results are shown that were generated based on this model. Finally, in Section 5, the model is evaluated and conclusions are drawn.

2 A Model for Emotion Generation

In this section, the model for emotion generation will be described at an intuitive, conceptual level, using the agent-based modelling language LEADSTO [6]. This language allows the modeller to integrate both qualitative, logical aspects and quantitative, numerical aspects. In LEADSTO, direct temporal dependencies between two state properties in successive states are modelled by executable dynamic properties. The format is defined as follows: let α and β be state properties of the form 'conjunction of ground atoms or negations of ground atoms'. In LEADSTO the notation $\alpha \rightarrow\!\!\!\rightarrow_{e, f, g, h} \beta$ means:

If   state property α holds for a certain time interval with duration g,
then   after some delay (between e and f) state property β will hold
*   for a certain time interval of length h.*

Here atomic state properties can have a qualitative, logical format, such as an expression desire(d), expressing that desire d occurs, or a quantitative, numerical format such as an expression has_value(x, v) which expresses that variable x has value v. For more details, see [6].

In Section 2.1, first a global overview of the model will be provided. Next, Section 2.2 will present the formalisation of the model in LEADSTO.

2.1 Emotion Generation Based on a Body Loop

In this and the next section the model to generate emotional states for a given stimulus is introduced. It adopts from [13] the idea of a 'body loop' and 'as if body loop', but extends this by making these loops recursive. According to the original idea, emotion generation via a body loop roughly proceeds according to the following causal chain; see [7], [13]:

sensing a stimulus → sensory representation of stimulus →
(preparation for) bodily response → sensing the bodily response →
sensory representation of the bodily response → feeling the emotion

As a variation, an 'as if body loop' uses a causal relation

preparation for bodily response →
sensory representation of the bodily response

as a shortcut in the causal chain. In the model used here an essential addition is that the body loop (or as if body loop) is extended to a recursive body loop (or recursive as if body loop) by assuming that the preparation of the bodily response is also affected by the state of feeling the emotion (also called emotional feeling):

feeling the emotion → preparation for bodily response

as an additional causal relation. Thus the obtained model is based on reciprocal causation relations between emotional feeling and body states, as roughly shown in Figure 1.

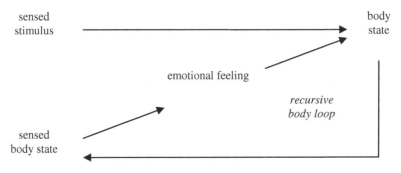

Fig. 1. Recursive body loop

Both the bodily response and the emotional feeling are assigned a level or grada-
tion, expressed by a number, which is assumed dynamic. The causal cycle is modelled
as a positive feedback loop, triggered by the stimulus and converging to a certain
level of emotional feeling and body state. Here in each round of the cycle the next
body state has a level that is affected by both the level of the stimulus and of the emotional feeling state, and the next level of the emotional feeling is based on the level of
the body state. In the more detailed model described below, the combined effect of
the levels of the stimulus and the emotional state on the body state is modelled as a
weighted sum (with equal weights 0.5 in this case). This implies that the pattern of
generation (and extinction) of an emotion upon a stimulus is as shown in Figure 2
(where the horizontal axis denotes time and the vertical axis denotes the level of experienced emotion).

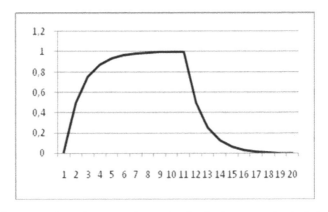

Fig. 2. Pattern of emotion generation and extinction by a recursive body loop

2.2 Formalisation of the Emotion Generation Model

The specification (both informally and formally) of the model for emotion generation
based on a recursive body loop is as follows. This model is based on dynamic Local
Properties (LP), expressing the basic mechanisms of the process.

LP1 Sensing a stimulus
If a negative stimulus occurs, then a sensor state for the negative stimulus will occur.

neg_stimulus → has_state(human, sensor_state(neg_stimulus))

LP2 Generating a sensory representation of a stimulus
If a sensor state for a negative stimulus occurs,
then a sensory representation for the negative stimulus will occur.

has_state(human, sensor_state(neg_stimulus)) → has_state(human, srs(neg_stimulus))

LP3 From sensory representation and emotion to preparation
If a sensory representation for a negative stimulus occurs and emotion e has level v,
then a preparation state for facial expression f will occur with level $\alpha * v + (1-\alpha) * 1$

has_state(human, srs(neg_stimulus)) & has_state(human, emotion(e, v)) →
has_state(human, preparation_state(f, $\alpha * v + (1-\alpha) * 1$))

If no sensory representation for a negative stimulus occurs and emotion e has level v,
then a preparation state for facial expression f will occur with level v/2.

not has_state(human, srs(neg_stimulus)) & has_state(human, emotion(e, v)) →
has_state(human, preparation_state(f, v/2))

LP4 From preparation to body modification
If a preparation state for facial expression f occurs with level v,
then the face is modified to express f with level v.

has_state(human, preparation_state(f, v)) → has_state(human, effector_state(f, v))

LP5 From body modification to modified body
If the face is modified to express f with level v,
then the face will have expression f with level v.

has_state(human, effector_state(f, v)) → has_state(human, own_face(f, v))

LP6 Sensing a body state
If facial expression f with level v occurs,
then this facial expression is sensed.

has_state(human, own_face(f, v)) → has_state(human, sensor_state(f, v))

LP7 Generating a sensory representation of a body state
If facial expression f of level v is sensed,
then a sensory representation for facial expression f with level v will occur.

has_state(human, sensor_state(f, v)) → has_state(human, srs(f, v))

LP8 From sensory representation of body state to emotion
If a sensory representation for facial expression f with level v occurs,
then emotion e is felt with level v.

has_state(human, srs(f, v)) → has_state(human, emotion(e, v))

3 A Theory of Mind Model to Estimate Emotion Generation

So far, a model was presented that describes a person's mental states and the relations
between them at a global level. However, to be able to provide some intelligent support,
an ambient system somehow needs the capability to attribute instances of these mental

states to a human, and to reason about these. In psychology, this capability is often referred to as *Theory of Mind* (or ToM, see, e.g., [4]). According to [9], (human and software) agents can exploit a ToM for two purposes: to *anticipate* the behaviour of other agents (e.g., preparing for certain actions that the other will perform), and to *manipulate* it (e.g., trying to bring the other in a certain state in which he will perform certain desired actions, or not perform certain unwanted actions).

A number of approaches in the literature address the development of formal models for ToM, e.g., [9], [21]. Usually, such models focus on the epistemic (e.g., beliefs) and/or motivational states (e.g., desires, intentions) of other agents. However, since the concept of emotions nowadays is receiving more and more attention, such models ideally also address emotions. This idea is in line with the theories of many Cognitive Scientists like Gärdenfors [15], who claims that humans have a ToM that is not only about beliefs, desires, and intentions, but also about other mental states like emotional and attentional states [15]. Based on these ideas, this paper proposes to apply a ToM to a model for emotion generation as described in the previous section.

3.1 Formalisation of a Theory of Mind Model to Estimate Emotion Generation

In order to obtain a Theory of Mind model for generated emotions, the idea of *recursive modelling* is used [21]. This means that the beliefs that agents have about each other are represented in a nested manner. To this end, each mental state is parameterised with the name of the agent that is considered, creating concepts like has_state(human, emotion(e, 0.5)) and has_state(AA, performed(remove_neg_stimulus)). In addition, a number of meta-representations, expressed by meta-predicates are introduced. For example, has_state(AA, belief(has_state(human, emotion(e, 0.7)))) states that the Ambient Agent (AA) believes that the human has an emotion level of 0.7. The agent AA has also beliefs about relationships between mental states of the human. This is represented in the format:

> has_state(AA, belief(leads_to_after(I, J, D)))

which expresses that when state property I occurs, then after time duration D state property J will occur. An example of a specific case of this is when it is taken:

> I   has_state(human, srs(f, v))
> J   has_state(human, emotion(e, v))
> D   1

With these instances for the variables the representation becomes

> has_state(AA, belief(leads_to_after(has_state(human, srs(f, v)),
>   has_state(human, emotion(e, v)), 1)))

This expresses that agent AA believes that when for the human state property srs(f, v) occurs, then after one time unit state property emotion(e, v) will occur. In such a way it is expressed that agent AA believes that the emotion generation model presented in Section 2 holds. Temporal reasoning based on this model is performed by agent AA using the general reasoning rule

> has_state(AA, belief(at(I, T))) ∧ has_state(AA, belief(leads_to_after(I, J, D))) →
> has_state(AA, belief(at(J, T+D)))

This rule can be considered a temporal forward simulation rule.

3.2 Adaptive Aspects in the Model

The model for emotion generation discussed in Section 2 includes a parameter α for the persistence of an emotional state. The value of such a parameter may not be easy to determine, and may differ between different individuals. Therefore a more realistic approach should include capabilities to adapt and fine tune the value of this parameter. Such a capability has been incorporated in the model. To this end, first the emotion generation model was rewritten to a differential equation model, as follows.

$$emotionlevel(t+1) = \alpha \, emotionlevel(t) + (1 - \alpha) \, s(t)$$
$$emotionlevel(t+1) - emotionlevel(t) = - (1 - \alpha) \, emotionlevel(t) + (1 - \alpha) \, s(t)$$
$$= (1 - \alpha) \, (s(t) - emotionlevel(t))$$
$$d/dt \, (s(t) - emotionlevel(t)) = - (1 - \alpha) \, (s(t) - emotionlevel(t))$$

Here $s(t)$ is the level of the stimulus over time. Note that the time unit here covers exactly one cycle of update of the emotion level (that is 6 time steps in the simulation). This differential equation has the following solution:

$$s(t) - emotionlevel(t) = (s(0) - emotionlevel(0)) \, e^{-(1 - \alpha)t}$$
$$emotionlevel(t) = s(t) - (s(0) - emotionlevel(0)) \, e^{-(1 - \alpha)t}$$

The next step is to identify the sensitivity of the emotion level with respect to a change of α. To this end the partial derivative with respect to α is:

$$\partial/\partial\alpha \, emotionlevel(t) = \partial/\partial\alpha \, (s(t) - (s(0) - emotionlevel(0)) \, e^{-(1 - \alpha)t})$$
$$= - (s(0) - emotionlevel(0)) \, \partial /\partial\alpha \, (e^{-(1 - \alpha)t})$$
$$= - (s(0) - emotionlevel(0)). \, t \, . \, e^{-(1 - \alpha)t}$$

When at time point t a difference $d(t) = \Delta \, emotionlevel(t)$ in observed emotion level[1] and calculated emotion level is detected, then based on the derivative w.r.t α this $\Delta \, emotionlevel(t)$ can be related to a difference $\Delta\alpha$ in α, as follows:

$$d(t) = \Delta \, emotionlevel(t) = \partial/\partial\alpha \, emotionlevel(t) \, . \, \Delta\alpha$$
$$= - (s(0) - emotionlevel(0)). \, t \, . \, e^{-(1 - \alpha)t}. \, \Delta\alpha$$

So

$$\Delta\alpha = - d(t) / (s(0) - emotionlevel(0)). \, t \, . \, e^{-(1 - \alpha)t}.$$

This is used in the adaptation process of α with adaptation speed factor γ as follows:

$$new \, \alpha = \alpha + \gamma \, \Delta\alpha = \alpha - \gamma \, . \, d(t) / (s(0) - emotionlevel(0)). \, t \, . \, e^{-(1 - \alpha)t}$$

When at time 0 the stimulus is 1 and the emotion is 0, this becomes:

$$new \, \alpha = \alpha + \gamma \, \Delta\alpha = \alpha - \gamma \, . \, d(t) / t \, . \, e^{-(1 - \alpha)t}$$

Here, for example, γ can be taken 0.9. If t and $d(t)$ are given, the new α can be calculated using this formula. Within LEADSTO, this mechanism is modelled via the following rules:

LP9 Adapt estimated alpha

Adapt the estimation of α based on the difference in observed and calculated emotion level.

```
real_emotion_available & estimated_alpha(a) & current_time(t) & has_state(human, emo-
tion(e, v1)) & has_state(AA, belief(has_state(human, emotion(e, v)))) →
estimated_alpha(a - gamma * (v1-v2) / (t * 2.71828 ^ (-1 * (1-a) * t)))
```

---

[1] Hence, this approach assumes that every now and then the real emotion level can be observed.

LP10 Take over observed emotion level
If the real emotion level can be observed, use that level in the model (instead of the calculated level).

real_emotion_available & has_state(human, emotion(e, v)) →
has_state(AA, belief(has_state(human, emotion(e, v))))

4 Simulation Results

To test the behaviour of the model to estimate emotion generation, it has been used to perform a number of simulation runs within the LEADSTO simulation environment [6]. The model was tested in a small scenario, involving an ambient agent and a human (indicated by AA and human, respectively). The agent AA was equipped with the model to estimate emotion generation. The central emotion used in the scenario is anger. In order to simulate this, every now and then certain events take place, which influence the level of anger of the human either positively (e.g., a request for an annoying task) or negatively (e.g., the removal of an annoying task from the todo list). The main goal of the agent is to estimate the level of anger of the human. To this end, it starts with some default model of the human's emotion generation dynamics, and then keeps on updating this using the strategies explained earlier. When the human becomes too angry, the ambient agent can take measures to calm him down (e.g., removing an annoying task from the todo list, or taking away an annoying stimulus). In Section 3.1 it was explained how in the model representations of the form

has_state(AA, belief(leads_to_after(I, J, D)))

together with one forward simulation rule were used. For the sake of simplicity within the simulation the general rule was replaced by instantiated versions, some of which are shown below (i.e., LP12-LP19; note that the explicit temporal dependencies have been left out as well). The first property specifies how the agent AA observes that the human senses a stimulus.

LP11 Observing human's sensing negative stimulus
If the human senses a negative stimulus then the ambient agent AA will observe this.

has_state(human, sensor_state(neg_stimulus)) →
has_state(AA, observed(has_state(human, sensor_state(neg_stimulus))))

LP12 Belief generation of human's sensing negative stimulus
If the ambient agent observes that the human senses a negative stimulus, then it will generate a belief on it.

has_state(AA, observed(has_state(human, sensor_state(neg_stimulus)))) →
has_state(AA, belief(has_state(human, sensor_state(neg_stimulus))))

LP13 Generating a sensory representation of human sensing negative stimulus
If AA believes that the human senses a negative stimulus, then it will generate a belief that the human will have a sensory representation for this stimulus.

has_state(AA, belief(has_state(human, sensor_state(neg_stimulus)))) →
has_state(AA, belief(has_state(human, srs(neg_stimulus))))

LP14 From sensory representation and emotion to preparation

If AA believes that the human has a sensory representation for a negative stimulus and AA believes that the human has emotion e with level v, then it will generate the belief that the human's preparation state for facial expression f will occur with level $\alpha * v + (1-\alpha) * 1$.

    has_state(AA, belief(has_state(human, srs(neg_stimulus)))) &
    has_state(AA, belief(has_state(human, emotion(e, v)))) →
    has_state(AA, belief(has_state(human, preparation_state(f, α * v + (1-α) * 1))))

If AA believes that the human has NO sensory representation for a negative stimulus and AA believes that the human has emotion e with level v, then it will generate the belief that the human's preparation state for facial expression f will occur with level v/2.

    not(has_state(AA, belief(has_state(human, srs(neg_stimulus))))) &
    has_state(AA, belief(has_state(human, emotion(e, v)))) →
    has_state(AA, belief(has_state(human, preparation_state(f, v/2))))

LP15 From preparation to body modification

If AA believes that the human's preparation state for facial expression f with level v occurred, then it will believe that the humans' face is modified to express f with level v.

    has_state(AA, belief(has_state(human, preparation_state(f, v)))) →
    has_state(AA, belief(has_state(human, effector_state(f, v))))

LP16 From body modification to modified body

If AA believes that the human's face is modified to express f with level v, then it will believe that the human's face will have expression f with level v.

    has_state(AA, belief(has_state(human, effector_state(f, v)))) →
    has_state(AA, belief(has_state(human, own_face(f, v))))

LP17 Sensing a body state

If AA believes that the human's face has expression f with level v, then it will believe that the human will sense this facial expression.

    has_state(AA, belief(has_state(human, own_face(f, v)))) →
    has_state(AA, belief(has_state(human, sensor_state(f, v))))

LP18 Generating a sensory representation of a body state

If AA believes that the human has sensed facial expression f with level v, then it will believe that the human has a sensory representation for facial expression f with level v.

    has_state(AA, belief(has_state(human, sensor_state(f, v)))) →
    has_state(AA, belief(has_state(human, srs(f, v))))

LP19 From sensory representation of body state to emotion

If AA believes that the human has a sensory representation for facial expression f with level v, then it will believe that the human has emotion e with level v.

    has_state(AA, belief(has_state(human, srs(f, v)))) →
    has_state(AA, belief(has_state(human, emotion(e, v))))

In addition, a number of other rules have been established to model the behaviour of the human and the ambient agent, and its effect on the world:

LP20 Intervention by the Ambient Agent
If AA believes that the human has emotion e with level v which is higher than a certain threshold th1, then it will remove a negative stimulus.
   has_state(AA, belief(has_state(human, emotion(e, v)))) & v ≥ th1 →
   has_state(AA, performed(remove_neg_stimulus))

LP21 Effect of intervention in the world
As long as AA does not remove a negative stimulus, it persists in the world.
   not has_state(AA, performed(remove_neg_stimulus)) → neg_stimulus

LP22 Performance of human
If the human has emotion e with level v which is higher than a certain threshold th2, then (s)he will show bad performance.
   has_state(human, emotion(e, v)) & v ≥ th2 → has_state(human, performed(bad_performance))

If the human has emotion e with level v which is lower than threshold th2, then (s)he will show good performance.
   has_state(human, emotion(e, v)) & v < th2 → has_state(human, performed(good_performance))

Based on the model, a number of simulations (under different parameter settings) have been performed, and some of the simulation traces are included in this section for analysis; see Figure 3 to Figure 6. In all of these figures, where time is on the horizontal axis, the upper part shows the time periods, in which the binary logical

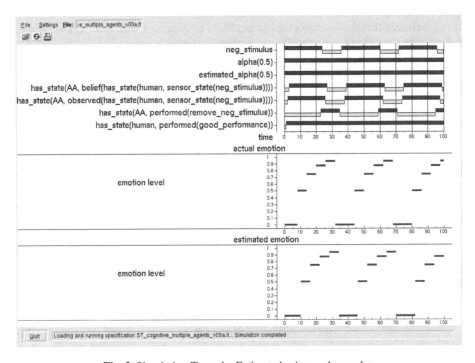

Fig. 3. Simulation Trace 1 - Estimated α is equal to real α

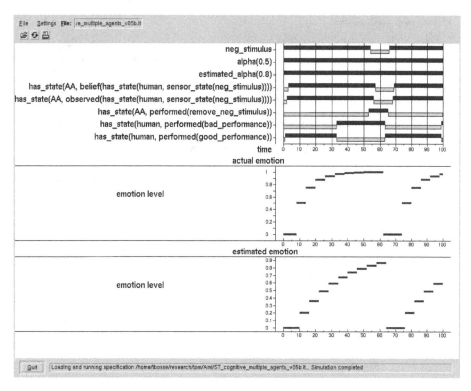

Fig. 4. Simulation Trace 2 - Estimated α is higher than real α

state properties hold (indicated by the dark lines); for example; neg_stimulus, esti-mated_alpha(X), and has_state(AA, belief(has_state(human, sensor_state(neg_stimulus)))). Below this part, quantitative information is provided about the human's actual emo-tion level, and the Ambient Agent's estimation of this emotion level, respectively. Values for these levels for the different time periods are shown by the dark lines. For example, in Figure 3, at time point 10 AA estimates that the human's emotion level is 0.5, but this increases to 0.75 at time point 15 and further. The graphs show how the recursive body loop approximates a state for emotion with value 1. Note that only a selection of relevant state properties is shown.

Trace 1
This trace (see Figure 3), shows a normal situation, in which the estimated α is equal to the real α indicated in the upper part of the Figure 3, by state properties esti-mated_alpha(0.5) and alpha(0.5) respectively. As shown in the figure, the Ambient Agent removes the negative stimulus exactly at the right moments (i.e., at time point 22, 59, and 95). As a result, the human never shows bad performance. Note that, in this trace (as well as the next two), threshold th1 for intervention (see LP15) was set to 0.8, and threshold th2 for negative performance (see LP17) was set to 0.95.

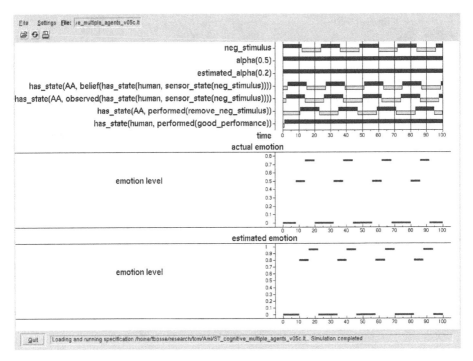

Fig. 5. Simulation Trace 3 - Estimated α is lower than real α

Trace 2

This trace (see Figure 4), shows a situation in which the estimated α (0.8) is higher than the real α (0.5), as indicated in the upper part of the Figure 4. As shown in the figure, the Ambient Agent estimates the level of emotion of the human much too low, so that it is too late in removing the negative stimulus, indicated in the upper part by state property has_state(AA, performed(remove_neg_stimulus)) at time point 52. This is too late, because, as shown in the "actual emotion" graph below, the human's emotion level has gone too high already at time point 32. As a result, the human shows bad performance at time point 33 (as indicated by the state property has_state(human, performed(bad_performance)) in the upper part of Figure 4).

Trace 3

This trace (see Figure 5) shows a situation in which the estimated α (0.2) is lower than the real α (0.5), as indicated in the upper part of the Figure 5. As shown in the figure, the Ambient Agent estimates the level of emotion of the human too high, so that it is a bit too early in removing the negative stimulus, as indicated in the upper part by property has_state(AA, performed(remove_neg_stimulus)) at time point 11. This is not a crucial error (the human does not show bad performance), but it is a waste of energy.

Trace 4

This trace (see Figure 6) shows a situation in which the estimated α is learned. In this trace, speed factor γ (see LP9) was set to 0.9, threshold th1 was set to 0.5, and th2 was

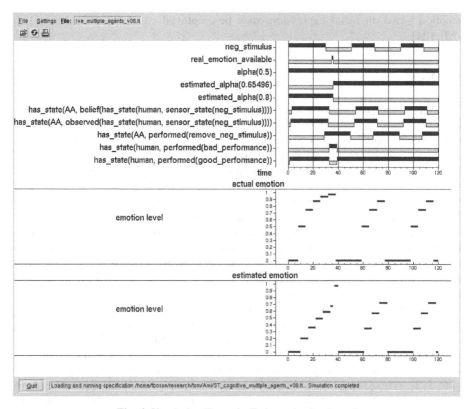

Fig. 6. Simulation Trace 4 - Estimated α is adapted

set to 0.95. As shown in the figure, the Ambient Agent initially estimates the level of emotion of the human much too low, indicated in the upper part by the state property estimated_alpha(0.8). As a result, at time point 32, the human's emotion level has gone too high (shown in the "actual emotion" graph below), so that AA is too late in removing the negative stimulus. However, after information about the real emotion became available (at time point 35) (shown by state property real_emotion_available), AA changes its estimation of α (from 0.8 to 0.65). As a result, from then on the agent estimates the emotion much better, and removes the stimulus at the right moments (at time points 67 and 93), so that the human does not show bad performance anymore.

All in all, the model has been used to generate a large number of simulation traces, using different parameter settings for the real and estimated parameter α. Due to space limitations, not all of these results are shown here. However, the simulation experiments pointed out that the model in general is successful in estimating a (simulated) person's emotion generation dynamics, and is robust to different parameter settings.

The obvious next step is to test the model in a real world setting. This can be done, for example, in a laboratory experiment where a person is asked to perform a computer task during which certain emotion-eliciting events occur. To measure the person's emotional reactions to these events, recent methods to recognise levels of emotion based on facial expressions may be employed e.g., [11], [12], [16], [18], [22], [24].

5   Discussion

To improve the performance and wellbeing of humans in complex human-computer interaction settings, ambient systems need to assess many aspects of the human's state. In addition to its state of awareness, stress, and motivation, the system needs to assess the human's emotional state, and more specifically, its emotion generation capabilities. One step further, the system requires the ability to reason about these emotion generation capabilities, and to make predictions based on them. For example, if the system knows that the human is very quick in developing a state of anger, this will be useful to determine how to communicate with the user for the next hours.

As a first step in this direction, the current paper introduces an adaptive computational model to estimate emotion generation processes. The model combines two main components, namely a model for emotion generation (inspired by [13]) and a model for Theory of Mind cf. [21]. The model has been implemented using the modelling language LEADSTO, and has been tested under different parameter settings.

The model is based on several important assumptions. For one, it is assumed that it is possible to measure a person's emotional reactions to certain events. The simulation runs, abstract from a specific technique that may be used for this, but in real world experiments, obviously this cannot be done anymore. For future research the plan is to test the model in laboratory experiments; here emotion recognition approaches like [11], [12], [16], [18], [22], [24] may be used. In recent years, such approaches have proven to be very adequate in recognising emotion *elicitation* processes in humans. Future work should point out how different types of approaches can be compared. One of these differences may be the possibility to reason over time about the emotion generation process, for example, to predict future emotions, or to predict effects of a certain intervention on the emotion level.

Another interesting direction for further research is to explore the possibilities to apply the model to computer-computer interaction instead of human-computer interaction settings. For example, a recent trend in the development of *intelligent virtual agents* (IVAs, see [23]) is to equip them with emotions and emotion generation mechanisms (e.g., [5], [20]). As soon as such IVAs start to communicate with each other, it will be useful for them to have insight in each other's emotions, and to make predictions about them. It may be expected that the generic setup of the model presented here allows it to be equally well applicable to software agents as to humans. Therefore, it may eventually be applied in larger systems where a number of real humans and virtual humans have to cooperate.

References

1. Aarts, E., Collier, R., van Loenen, E., de Ruyter, B.: EUSAI 2003. LNCS, vol. 2875, p. 432. Springer, Heidelberg (2003)
2. Aarts, E., Harwig, R., Schuurmans, M.: Ambient Intelligence. In: Denning, P. (ed.) The Invisible Future, pp. 235–250. McGraw-Hill, New York (2001)

3. Ball, G., Breese, J.: Modelling the emotional state of computer users. In: Proceedings of the Workshop on Personality and Emotion in User Modelling (1999)
4. Baron-Cohen, S.: Mindblindness. MIT Press, Cambridge (1995)
5. Bates, J.: The role of emotion in believable agents. Communications of the ACM 37(7), 122–125 (1994)
6. Bosse, T., Jonker, C.M., van der Meij, L., Treur, J.: A Language and Environment for Analysis of Dynamics by Simulation. International Journal of Artificial Intelligence Tools 16(3), 435–464 (2007)
7. Bosse, T., Jonker, C.M., Treur, J.: Formalisation of Damasio's Theory of Emotion, Feeling and Core Consciousness. Consciousness and Cognition Journal (in press, 2008); Fum, D., Del Missier, F., Stocco, A. (eds.), Proc. of the 7th International Conference on Cognitive Modelling, ICCM 2006, pp. 68–73 (2006)
8. Bosse, T., van Maanen, P.P., Treur, J.: A Cognitive Model for Visual Attention and its Application. In: Nishida, T., Klusch, M., Sycara, K., Yokoo, M., Liu, J., Wah, B., Cheung, W., Cheung, Y.-M. (eds.) Proceedings of the Sixth International Conference on Intelligent Agent Technology, IAT 2006, pp. 255–262. IEEE Computer Society Press, Los Alamitos (2006)
9. Bosse, T., Memon, Z.A., Treur, J.: A Two-Level BDI-Agent Model for Theory of Mind and its Use in Social Manipulation. In: Proceedings of the AISB 2007 Workshop on Mindful Environments, pp. 335–342 (2007)
10. Bosse, T., Pontier, M., Treur, J.: A Dynamical System Modelling Approach to Gross' Model of Emotion Regulation. In: Lewis, R.L., Polk, T.A., Laird, J.E. (eds.) Proceedings of the Eighth International Conference on Cognitive Modeling, ICCM 2007, pp. 187–192. Taylor and Francis, Abington (2007)
11. Busso, C., Deng, Z., Yildirim, S., Bulut, M., Lee, C.M., Kazemzadeh, A., Lee, S., Neumann, U., Narayanan, S.: Analysis of emotion recognition using facial expressions, speech and multimodal information. In: Proceedings of the ACM Sixth International Conference on Multimodal Interfaces, ICMI 2004, State College, PA (2004)
12. Cohen, I., Garg, A., Huang, T.S.: Emotion recognition using multilevel HMM. In: Proceedings of the NIPS Workshop on Affective Computing, Colorado (2000)
13. Damasio, A.: The Feeling of What Happens: Body, Emotion and the Making of Consciousness. Harcourt Brace (1999)
14. Frijda, N.H., Manstead, A.S.R., Bem, S. (eds.): Emotions and Beliefs: How Feelings Influence Thoughts. Cambridge Univ. Press, NY (2000)
15. Gärdenfors, P.: Slicing the Theory of Mind. In: Danish yearbook for philosophy, vol. 36, pp. 7–34. Museum Tusculanum Press (2001)
16. Goldman, A.I., Sripada, C.S.: Simulationist models of face-based emotion recognition. Cognition 94, 193–213 (2005)
17. Gross, J.J.: The Emerging Field of Emotion Regulation: An Integrative Review. Review of General Psychology 2(3), 271–299 (1998)
18. Ioannou, S.V., Raouzaiou, A.T., Tzouvaras, V.A., Mailis, T.P., Karpouzis, K.C., Kollias, S.D.: Emotion Recognition Through Facial Expression Analysis Based on a Neurofuzzy Network. Neural Networks 18, 423–435 (2005)
19. Kaber, D.B., Endsley, M.R.: The effects of level of automation and adaptive automation on human performance, situation awareness and workload in a dynamic control task. Theoretical Issues in Ergonomics Science 5(2), 113–153 (2004)
20. Marsella, S., Gratch, J.: Modeling coping behavior in virtual humans: Don't worry, be happy. In: Proceedings of Second International Joint Conference on Autonomous Agents and Multiagent Systems, AAMAS 2003, pp. 313–320. ACM Press, New York (2003)

21. Marsella, S.C., Pynadath, D.V., Read, S.J.: PsychSim: Agent-based modeling of social interaction and influence. In: Lovett, M., et al. (eds.) Proceedings of ICCM 2004, Pittsburg, Pensylvania, USA, pp. 243–248 (2004)
22. Pantic, M., Rothkrantz, L.J.M.: Automatic Recognition of Facial Expressions and Human Emotions. In: Proceedings of ASCI 1997 conference, ASCI, Delft, pp. 196–202 (1997)
23. Pelachaud, C., Martin, J.C., Andre, E., Chollet, G., Karpouzis, K., Pele, D.: IVA 2007. LNCS (LNAI), vol. 4722. Springer, Heidelberg (2007)
24. Vogt, T., André, E.: Comparing Feature Sets for Acted and Spontaneous Speech in View of Automatic Emotion Recognition. In: Proceedings of the IEEE International Conference on Multimedia & Expo, ICME 2005, Amsterdam, the Netherlands (2005)

End-User Software Engineering of Smart Retail Environments: The Intelligent Shop Window

Mark van Doorn[1], Arjen de Vries[2], and Emile Aarts[1]

[1] Philips Research,
High Tech Campus 34,
5656 AE Eindhoven, The Netherlands
{first name.last name}@philips.com
[2] Centre for Mathematics and Computer Science,
Kruislaan 413,
1098 SJ Amsterdam, The Netherlands
arjen.de.vries@cwi.nl

Abstract. This paper presents the concept of ambient narratives to represent dynamic open ambient intelligence environments and an end-user software engineering approach that supports retail designers to create, simulate, deploy and maintain interactive immersive retail spaces in this model. We present the user-centered design approach that led to this implementation and the user evaluation of the end-user authoring environment for an intelligent shop window installation with a group of retail designers, consultants and retailers.

1 Introduction

With the growing popularity of wireless home networking, mobile devices and other information appliances in our homes, the home forms a natural application domain for research on ambient intelligence and ubiquitous computing. Over the past decade, many Ambient Intelligence systems have been developed in a user-centered way to support specific types of tasks like programming the washing machine, checking goods in the fridge, listening to music, watching a movie and other activities inside and outside our homes e.g. [10,1,6,22]. In a typical Ambient Intelligence environment, multiple users at different locations are involved in several activities at a time and use a variety of networked computing devices and other tangible objects to support them in these tasks. This provides a major challenge for the design of such environments. Existing technology (e.g. context sensing, artificial intelligence and distributed computing infrastructure) is not mature enough. In addition, this approach raises questions about privacy and control. Rather than deciding for the end-users, much recent focus has gone into systems and applications that allow end-users to create and configure the way the environment responds and interacts with them [2,9,24].

In this paper we investigate how we can support end-users in the retail domain. There are a number of reasons for looking at this domain: First, shopping has become a major leisure time activity. People not just go to stores to buy things,

E. Aarts et al. (Eds.): AmI 2008, LNCS 5355, pp. 157–174, 2008.

they also go to stores and shopping malls to see and discover new things. Second, stores need to differentiate themselves from the competition in order to stay competitive. Each store has a unique brand identity it tries to convey through its products and the physical layout and architecture of the store. Third, retailers need to change the appearance of their store frequently for seasonal changes, new fashion trends, large events taking place and so on.

Electronic environments that are sensitive and responsive to the presence of shoppers have also been proposed for the retail domain. For example, the SMMART system [11] is a ubiquitous system for mobile interactive marketing that facilitates shoppers in finding correct matches between their buying preferences and the products on sale in a store. Smith describes Object AURAs [20], a mobile retail and product annotation system that associates a URL to products and objects on display in a store that can be read by a mobile device. In [23] the authors describe a set of display cubes that responds to the presence of people. Commercial solutions to track people and objects and log their actions also exist. VideoMining [28] offers a system based on computer vision that can track people in a store. WiseTrack [29] is an asset tracking and management system for objects tagged with RFID chips or bar codes. In contrast with the home domain, less work has been published on end-user customization and programming for retail environments.

This paper seeks to design a system that supports retail stakeholders (store owners, consultants and designers) in creating and customizing immersive, interactive retail environments that enhance the shopping experience. We focus particularly on the entire lifecycle of creating, simulating, deploying and maintaining such interactive retail experiences. Although end-user programming paradigms and strategies that have been validated for the home domain could also be suitable in a professional context like retail, many differences exist between these application domains in terms of users and their needs and goals. Therefore we conduct a number of interviews and workshops with retail designers to come up with user requirements placed on the design.

This paper is organized as follows. Section 2 presents the *ambient narrative concept* as a conceptual model to represent open, complex, dynamic Ambient Intelligence environments that should be authored by end-users. Section 3 discusses the results of a series of workshops and interviews conducted with this target user group to verifiy whether end-users can understand this concept and to collect feedback on four different end-user programming paradigms for writing such ambient narratives. Section 4 shows how these findings are translated into a system that enables end-users to create, simulate, deploy and share intelligent shop window environments as a subclass of smart retail environments. Section 5 presents the results of the user evaluation study, we conclude this paper in Section 6.

2   Authoring Ambient Narratives

The goal of Ambient Intelligence is to help people in performing their daily activities better, by making these activities more convenient and enjoyable using

ambient narrative

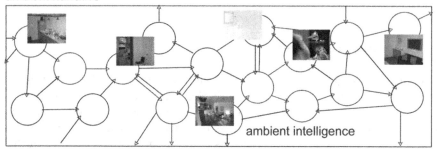

Fig. 1. Ambient narratives and ambient intelligence

technology. Performances are not just seen in the theatre, music, dance and performance arts in general but also in our everyday lives: We perform the role of a father or son in our private lives but maybe also that of a doctor, judge or police agent, for example in our professions. Goffman [7] already recognized in the 1950s that people follow culturally specified social scripts that influence each other. Viewing life as social theatre is interesting because if people behave according to social scripts, we may try to detect these scripts and connect actions to these events. The presence of social scripts is also recognized by service marketing and brand management professionals for commercial and public spaces. Fisk and Grove [8] describe a theatre framework for service marketing, in which services are seen as performances, front-end service personnel as actors, the service setting as the stage on which the service is performed, products used in the services as props and the business process of the service as the script. Just as lighting and sound effects add to the overall drama of a theatre play, Ambient Intelligence may thus be applied to enhance the performance described by these social scripts.

If we break down an Ambient Intelligence environment into these small, interrelated media-enhanced performances, the resulting structure can be seen as an ambient narrative, see Figure 1. With 'ambient narrative' we refer to the script of a story told in mixed reality. Or, to be more precise, as the exact story is not predefined but evolves in response to people's behaviour, it is really an *interactive narrative situated in mixed reality*. Ambient Intelligence and ambient narratives are related in the following way: By performing in the environment, i.e. by doing things, the reader of the ambient narrative implicitly sequences predefined ambient media presentations into a coherent personal story (depicted in blue in Figure 1) that is being perceived as ambient intelligence by the reader, provided the ambient narrative is designed well by its author. At the same time, multiple people can be active in the environment so multiple storylines can be active at any time. For more details we refer to [25].

Because social scripts differ from time to time and place to place, ambient narratives are also very much location and time dependent. Rather than designing for the end-user, we propose to place end-users in control and give them the tools and infrastructure they need to create, run and share their own ambient narratives in an easy way.

3   Learning from Users

This paper investigates the question whether retailers can understand this ambient narrative concept, and which authoring strategy they would prefer? To answer these questions we conducted a series of interviews and workshops with retailers, retail consultants and designers to generate user insights. The goal of the interviews was twofold. One goal was to get a better understanding of their current way of working with respect to designing, configuring and programming (interactive) lighting, media, ambient effects for as far as applicable and the different parties involved in this process. The other goal was to elicit feedback on four different end-user programming approaches. The purpose of the subsequent workshops was to find out if people could understand the ambient narrative concept and apply it to their own practice. In total we interviewed 17 participants in 13 sessions and organized 13 workshops (with the same people). Of this group 8 people were retailers running their own store or managing a chain of stores. 5 participants were professional consultants with a background in implementing retail, hospitality and general experience strategies and concepts. 4 people were lighting or interior designers with an interest in retail.

3.1   Ambient Intelligence in Retail

The design and implementation of new retail concepts and strategies can involve many different parties. This depends on the size of the store. If a large store or chain of stores is looking for a new store concept, they often hire a consultancy bureau. These consultants analyse the current business, identify business goals and translate these goals into a store concept and layout. The store layout and retail concepts are further worked out by interior and lighting designers. Once the design is completed and agreed upon by the retailer, a team of building constructors and installers will build up the new store or remodel the existing store and install and configure the immersive, interactive technology. This technology is supplied by component suppliers (lighting, LED panels, LCD display) and system integrators. For small stores, the retailer takes on one or more of these roles. Figure 2 shows these different parties involved in store concept design and implementation.

In terms of designing, configuring or programming interactive ambient effects, people commented that they had little or no experience except for setting the

Fig. 2. Parties involved in store concept design and implementation

lighting levels or basic climate control in their store. Although people report a clear wish to change the appearance of their stores at least four times a year, they wish they could do this faster because it is currently too cumbersome to change the environment. Lack of standard technology and high costs of developing tailor-made solutions are also seen as bottlenecks. An exception form the so-called flagship stores of companies like Apple, Nike and Nokia. In addition to selling products, these stores situated in strategic locations around the world are designed as places where people can see, hear and feel the story (brand) the company has tell. The interactive, immersive environments of these flagship stores are tailor-made and custom-built.

Workshop participants viewed ambient effects, interactive media and other software applications as an important part of the overall retail concept, and these should therefore be taken up from the concept phase. During the different stages in the design of a new store concept, there is a continuous dialogue between retailers, designers and consultants, on site or in the office. Designers use story and mood boards, drawings, lighting plans, and 3D visualizations to communicate their ideas to retailers. The designer checks with the installer if his light plan is implemented correctly. Another function of a system for designing and configuring interactive, immersive retail experiences is supporting communication between its different users.

3.2   Deriving Ambient Narratives Examples

The abstract notion of ambient narratives as multi-user, cross-modal, interactive narratives tightly integrated in a mixed reality environment is difficult to explain to non-technical people. Instead of trying to explain this concept directly, we took a more indifferent approach in the workshops we organized. First, we asked people to imagine their own store or a store concept and draw the layout of this store (concept) on a large piece of paper. Next, they had to write down a number of use-case scenarios from the shopper's point of view. From the interviews we knew that many designers and consultants already work with experience maps and story boards. Not all participants were equally good at coming up with user scenarios in the limited time we had. If people had difficulty in imagining scenarios, we helped them by asking them what would happen if somebody would walk by the store, stood still in front of the shop window display, entered inside, browsed through the store, stand still in front of a product etc. After this step we presented them with the theatre service marketing framework (see section 2) and asked them what they thought of this framework. Most of the participants liked this model and one of the consultants reported they used this idea of retail scripting already in their practice. Because an ambient narrative contains different intertwined storylines, we then asked them to decompose the user scenarios into theatrical scenes, each having an action and situation description, and write these scene descriptions on a post-it, which they had to position on the story layout. Although we structured the process to get results out, we gave the participants freedom to fill in the different tasks because we wanted to see how they would approach these tasks and how they would for example write down these

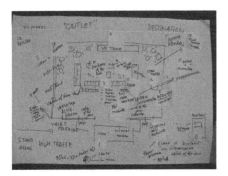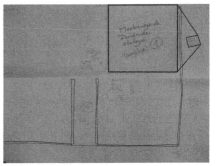

Fig. 3. Two example ambient narratives

scene descriptions. In total this approach resulted in 13 ambient narratives, each designed for a particular store. Figure 3 shows two examples we collected, one for a fish outlet store (left), the other for a furniture store concept (right).

Case 1. The idea behind the 'fish outlet store' ambient narrative was to transform an ordinary store where you can buy fish and other seafood into an experience store where people are educated about our relationship with the sea and fishing, learn how to prepare fish and other seafood, and, of course, buy sea products. Rather than replacing the real thing with 3D simulations or videos, the idea is to use immersive, interactive technology to emphasize the authenticity of the products on sale. In the center of the store, an aquarium with living fish and sea creatures gives shoppers the feeling that the products sold here will be fresh. In the top-left corner, there is a restaurant area where people can taste fish. In the top-right area there is a kitchen workshop where people can learn how to prepare seafood. This example shows that experience design takes a holistic approach that integrates product, interior and graphic design and ambient technologies. Many of the post-its in this example do not even require ambient technologies (e.g. fish tanks, in-store restaurant, kitchen workshop). This example also makes explicit how stores convey a message to bind people to them, by telling a story that resonates with shoppers. Clearly, the physical environment can play an important role here!

Case 2. The 'furniture store' example on the right is much more concrete. The first post-it for example (scene 1) (*meebewegende duidende etalage (langslopen)*) describes that if people walk past the store, moving images and sound in the shop window will try to attract attention. Scene 3 is a tunnel with projections on both sides where people walk through and learn what the store has inside. By interacting with the projections they indicate their preferences. In Scene 5 a shop employee gives shoppers a portable device that shows a personalized route through the store based on their preferences, very much like a guided audio-tour familiar from many museums. Scene 7 describes active zones that react with light, sound or tactile feedback if a person picks up a product from the table.

Discussion. The workshops resulted in dozens of use-case scenarios and over a hundred post-its with scene descriptions. We therefore have reason to believe that people can get used to the idea of writing ambient narratives to describe the how a store will react to the presence and activity of users.

The store layouts on paper, the text on the post-its and their positioning on the store layout reveal information for further analysis and research. We already mentioned that some examples were more on an abstract conceptual level whereas others were more concrete. We found that designers work top-down, they like to start from abstract vague descriptions and only worry about the details later. The place of the post-its in the shop layout is an indication for whether people think in terms of controlling devices or creating effects. As computer scientists we like to view devices and systems as state machines that can be set to different values, designers like to create a particular effect somewhere.

In the next section we will look deeper into the design of an ambient narrative system, but first we still need to find out how people would want to write such ambient narratives.

3.3   Feedback on End-User Programming Scenarios

As part of the retail interviews we proposed four different programming strategies to author ambient narratives to our group of users and asked them what they thought about these individual strategies. Three of these four end-user programming strategies came from the domestic domain so this was also a test to find out whether these approaches were also applicable to this domain. To make sure everybody understood it was not about the scenario but about the way the scenario was programmed, we choose the same scene to start from in each of the four cases and explicitly mentioned this. The scene we picked is one in which a transparent display on a shop window shows an interactive shop catalogue if a person is standing close in front of it.

Programming in a 3D Simulation. Figure 4 shows a scenario where the retailer or designer sits in front of his PC and looks at a 3D simulation of his store (left). The corresponding programming strategy is based on the idea of using a 3D simulation for rapid prototyping of context-aware system as put forward by e.g. Shirehjini and Klar [19]. The user sees the 3D environment and walks with his virtual character to the shop window and sees that nothing happens. The user switches to his programming environment and gets an overview of the location of people, devices and objects in his store and which scenes are

Fig. 4. Programming the shop window scene in a 3D simulation environment

Fig. 5. Programming the shop window scene in-situ on a portable device

currently active (middle). The user presses a button to create a new scene for the shop window. First he draws the stage in front of the shop window, then he associates a customer actor and shop window device prop to this stage. He then sets the shop window to 'interaction' and saves the newly created scene. The user switches back to the 3D simulation and sees a picture of the interactive shop catalogue on the virtual shop window (right).

Like many other examples of end-user programming systems, see e.g. [9,16, 21,24], scenario 1 involves using a graphical user interface for helping users comprehend the program structure through visualization. We follow however the performance metaphor discussed in Section 2, instead of modelling applications as jigsaw puzzles that can be connected as in [9], visual rule-based languages as in [21,17] or fridge door magnets [24]. The idea of a theater metaphor has been applied by Finzer and Gould [4] to help nonprogrammers create educational software. In their programming model, the components of the interface are performers who interact with one another on a stage by sending and responding to cues. Laurel [13] also uses a theater metaphor to describe human-computer interaction for graphical user interfaces. In our approach for ambient intelligence, we allow end-users to define context-aware rules by specifying the situation in terms of restrictions in terms of stage, performance, actor, prop and script and associate device actions to this situation description.

In-situ Authoring Using Portable Device. Instead of designing the interactive shop window scene behind a PC, Figure 5 presents a scenario where the retailer or designer is physically walking through the store and experiences the environment. The user is detected by the first shop window, but nothing happens (left). The user picks up a portable device and is presented with a real-time overview of the situation in the store and which scenes are currently active (middle). Like in the previous scenario, the user sets the context situation and device actions using the graphical user interface and saves the newly created scene. The user then walks up to the first shop window and sees that the transparent display in the shop window switches to the interactive shop window catalogue (right). The user interface for specifying the context-aware scenes is identical to scenario above but the programming takes place on location using a portable device. Examples of in-situ authoring environments have been described in [12,14] for mobile context-aware devices and showed good results in evaluations with users.

Tangible Programming. Figure 6 illustrates a scenario the retailer or designer is using a tangible programming language to specify the interactive shop

Fig. 6. Programming the shop window scene using tangible objects

window scene. The retailer or designer is physically walking through the store and experiences the environment as in the previous scenario (left). Instead of taking a portable device, the user walks up to a tabletop interface and sees an overview of the location of people, devices and objects in the store and which scenes are currently active. To create a new scene, the user demonstrates the desired context situation to the system by physically placing tagged objects that represent actors, props and stage corners (middle). When the user is done, he can save the scene and remove the tagged objects. The user walks up to the first shop window and sees that the transparent display in the shop window switches to the interactive shop window catalogue (right). The AutoHAN [2] system is one example in the domestic domain that employs tangible programming. Their Media Cubes language allows the user to associate behavior directly with a concrete representation. If e.g. an association has been made between a Media Cube and a CD player's play/pause function, pressing the button on the Media Cube will play/pause the music. The StoryRoom [15] and Pogo [5] systems are examples of tangible programming languages where children can create physical interactive environments that enhance storytelling.

Programming in Augmented Reality. The final scenario we presented to our target group is visualized in Figure 7. Sandor et al. [18] describe a demo where end-users can configure the setup of a distributed user interface based on a shared augmented reality. This scenario extends this idea further. The user puts on an augmented reality interface and sees through these glasses which scenes are currently active and deactive and real-time information about people, devices and objects (middle). To create a new scene, the user uses gestures to draw a zone in front of the first shop window and selects from a menu actors and props to associates to the newly defined stage. The user then takes off the augmented reality interface and walks up to the shop window to see that it presents the interactive shop window catalogue (right).

Fig. 7. Programming the shop window scene in augmented reality

Discussion. The participants prefered the 3D simulation and portable device scenarios. Designers had a slight preference for the 3D simulation programming strategy because they could do the design at home, retailers liked the portable device scenario more because it allowed them to see the effects in the real world. Light designers commented that realistic light rendering in 3D simulation was not nearly accurate enough to replace light setting customization in a real world environment. The augmented reality scenario was seen by most participants as too futuristic. The tangible programming strategy was considered to be time consuming and therefore not adding value to their way of working. This feedback confirmed our hypothesis that tangible programming would be more suitable for domestic environments and children than for professional environments where efficiency is important.

Both designers and retailers commented that they would also like to use the 3D simulation and portable device strategies in combination. They would use the 3D environment for creating and testing the desired interactivity of the retail environment and the in-situ authoring tool for finetuning later. This supports recent work in end-user software engineering where the idea is to be make end-user programming software more reliable using concepts from software engineering [3]. This is not done by transforming these end-users into software engineers, but by supporting these end-users with systems to create software in a software development paradigm that combines different stages in the software lifecycle (such as planning, specification, design, implementation, testing, deployment, maintenance) into an integrated environment. Another reason we believe end-user software engineering makes sense for retail environments in particular and business to business in general is total cost of ownership. If a system is easy to program but costly in terms of installation and maintenance, the overall costs may not lead to a positive return on investment in the end for the retailer. In the next section we will therefore look at how we can support the workflow and communication between retailers, consultants and designers using an end-user software engineering approach for retail ambient narratives that combines the 3D simulation and portable device scenarios.

4   Intelligent Shop Window System

To avoid spending a large amount of work implementing sensors and actuators we decided to limit ourselves to a subset of retail ambient narratives situated around an intelligent shop window application described in [27]. When nobody is close, the entire shop window front projects images that express the type and style of the shop (signage mode) on the transparent shop window displays, as shown in Figure 8. If a person stands still in front of one the windows, the shop window can be used to get additional information about the products in the store (interaction mode). Simply by looking at the products in the shop window or touching the screen, users can bring up extra product information. This intelligent shop window ambient narrative set-up in ShopLab, the feasibility

Fig. 8. Intelligent shop window set-up in ShopLab

and usability center for retail on the High Tech Campus in Eindhoven, received a lot of positive feedback of both retailers and users that were invited.

4.1   User Workflow

Figure 9 shows how the workflow and communication between different actors in the design process of smart retail environments is supported by the prototype system we implemented. Behind a dekstop PC, users can create and modify ambient narrative fragments that they can simulate in a 3D simulation of ShopLab (simulation phase). Once they are done testing, they can download the ambient narrative from the simulation environment and save it to a shared drive or web directory. The same tool (connected to the live system) can be used to upload an ambient narrative from this directory into the live system (deployment phase). Users can then experience the intelligent shop window ambient narrative as they programmed it in the simulation environment (operation phase). If the user wants to modify existing scenes or create new scenes, he can use the same authoring tool but now on the portable device to program the desired effects on location as well.

4.2   User Interface

The user interface of the authoring tool has two main functions. First, it gives a real-time overview of what is happening in the environment in order for users to be able to understand what the system is thinking that is going on. The user can see the location and identity (if available) of people, objects and devices on the shop layout. Furthermore, the user sees which ambient narrative fragments (scenes) are currently active and deactive.

Second, the tool allows users to manage the ambient narrative. Users can create new scenes, edit existing ones or delete scenes. If a scene is modified or created, a scene overview screen appears that enables the user to see in more detail what the scene is about. Each scene consists of a description, action timeline and context part. The description part gives users the possibility to change

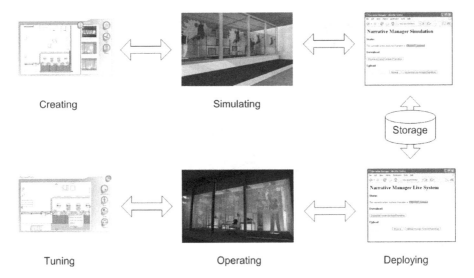

Creating   Simulating   Storage

Tuning   Operating   Deploying

Fig. 9. End-user software engineering support

the name of the fragment or take a visual snapshot. The action timeline part presents a timed list of device actions, similar to a time-based hypermedia presentations in a multimedia authoring tool. The context part enables the user to set the preconditions for scene activation and associate device actions. We let users articulate these context restrictions in a natural familiar way by presenting them with an interface where they can set the stage (location), performance (activity), actors (users), props (devices and objects) and script values (scenes dependencies). It is also possible to test on the non-existence of an actor or prop to write scenes that trigger when a user or device is no longer within a particular area in the store.

4.3   System Architecture

The system architecture is illustrated in Figure 10. The central component is the ambient narrative component, an interactive storytelling engine that determines given the available context information, session state and available plot material which scenes should become active and inactive. Each scene is stored in an XML document and can also be accessed through a web server. The rendering engine controls timing and synchronization of media, ambient effects and applications over the rendering devices based upon action fragments it receives from the narrative engine. The rendering devices and applications control how the commands from the rendering platform are executed. In total 24 rendering devices are used: Four shop window applications written in Java with a Flash UI running on four different PCs connected to a transparant holographic foil, four DMX LED wallwashers, ten DMX LED tiles, four directional audio devices and two spot lights. The context server collects, filters and aggregates sensor

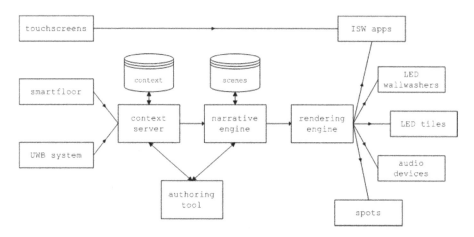

Fig. 10. System architecture

data for the ambient narrative engine. A pressure sensitive floor mat (Tekscan) and a tag-based UWB location system (Ubisense) provide sensor input (position and identification of people, objects) to the context server. The authoring tool updates its real-time overview of the people and objects in the environment using sensor data received from the context server. When a scene becomes active or inactive, the ambient narrative engine forwards this information to the authoring tool so that it can update its view (by parsing the document URL in the message). When a user adds a new scene or modifies an existing scene, the authoring tool updates the existing scene document or creates a new one and sends this to the ambient narrative. The ambient narrative engine recalculates which scenes should become active (or inactive). The same holds true when a user deletes a scene using the authoring tool.

For more information about the language model and ambient narrative engine we refer to [26].

5 Evaluation

To further validate the ability of our system to support people in creating and modifying scenes for the intelligent shop window environment, we conducted a user study with 18 participants. Again the participants were not computer scientists but retailers, designers or consultants, many of them had also participated in the workshops. We spent about 10 minutes with each individual user to explain the intelligent shop window environment and introduce them to the authoring environment. We gave each user the same four tasks: Modify an existing scene in the simulation, create a new scene in the 3D simulation, modify an existing scene in the live system using the portable device and creating a new scene in the live system using the portable device. The tasks differed slightly in terms of device settings for the 3D simulation and live system. In the 3D

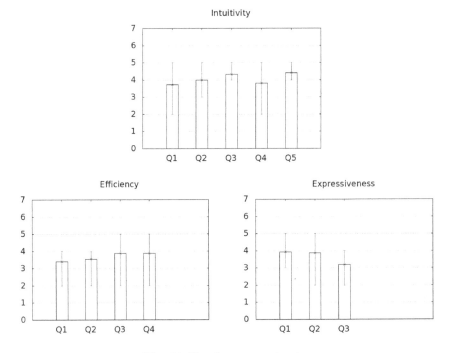

Fig. 11. Results user evaluation

simulation modification task we aksed them for example to set the light tiles behind the products to red while in the live system case they should set them to a blue color.

After they had conducted these four tasks we asked them to fill in a questionnaire with 12 questions about the intuitivity, efficiency and expressiveness of the authoring environment. Each question had to be given a score on a 5 point scale. The questions and results are stated below.

The questions in the intuitiveness category were: How clear did you find it to get an overview of the scenes present (Q1)? (Mean:3.73,St.Dev.:0.88). How easy did you find it to modify existing scenes (Q2)? (Mean:4.00,St.Dev.:0.53) How easy did you find it to create new scenes (Q3)? (Mean:4.33,St.Dev.0.49) How simple did you find it to set context restrictions for scenes (stage, actor, prop preconditions) (Q4)? (Mean:3.8,St.Dev.:0.94) How simple did you find it to set actions for scenes (Q5)? (Mean:4.4,St.Dev.:0.51)

For the efficiency category we asked the following questions: What did you think of the number of steps to modify existing scenes in the simulation (Q1)? (Mean:3.40,St.Dev.:0.82) What did you think of the number of steps to create new scenes in the simulation (Q2)? (Mean:3.53,St.Dev.:0.83) What did you think of the number of steps to modify existing scenes in the live system (Q3)? (Mean:3.87,St.Dev.:0.64) What did you think of the number of steps to create new scenes in the live system (Q4)? (Mean:3.87,St.Dev.:0.64)

The questions in the expressiveness category were: Does the system give you enough freedom to set scene preconditions (stage, actor, prop restrictions) (Q1)? (Mean:3.93,St.Dev.:0.46) Does the system give you enough freedom to set scene actions (Q2)? (Mean:3.87,St.Dev.:0.83) Does the system give you enough freedom to set the content of actions (Q3)? (Mean:3.2,St.Dev.:0.94)

In general participants appreciated both the 3D simulation and portable device authoring strategy in terms of ease of use, efficiency and possibilities. Although they had many remarks for improvement, they did not question the concepts and learned to use the system quickly. In terms of ease of use, people had some difficulty with setting the preconditions of a scene in terms of stage, actor and prop restrictions. Our user interface would allow people to add actors and props even if there was no stage defined. Our program however did not support this. Some people also said the overview screen could have been better if it would read from left to right and was larger. With respect to efficiency the scores were a little bit lower. To select the context situation screen from the scene overview screen we placed an icon in the top of the scene overview screen, people wanted to click directly on the context area in the scene overview screen to select this context situation screen. To set device actions for multiple devices, people had to redo the same actions. This also slows down the process. In terms of the expressive power, which is hard to evaluate because people can only tell what they see and not what the system could also do, participants were generally quite happy with the possibilities we showed them in terms of setting stage, actor and prop constraints and setting scene actions. The only aspect that was rated considerably less was the possibility to set the content of actions. We had no built-in editor or import function to change the content on the shop window display, people could only choose between presets.

6   Conclusions

In this paper we presented the concept of ambient narratives as a conceptual model to represent open dynamic Ambient Intelligent environments based on social theory. Because the social scripts ambient narratives augment with digital ambient media are highly situated and culturally dependent, it is difficult for the designer or producer of an intelligent environment to design ambient narrative in advance. To understand whether end-users could understand the ambient narrative concept and come up with examples, we conducted a series of workshops with retailers, retail designers and consultants which resulted in a dozen user-generated ambient narratives that we analyzed to come up with a hypertext model to represent ambient narratives. What we found was that many end-users found it useful to view their store as (improvisation) theatre and could therefore find themselves in the ideas of writing theatrical scenes.

One of the scenarios in the generated set was an intelligent shop window that would react to the presence of people and their activity. We decided to implement this intelligent shop window scenario in the ambient narrative system architecture and asked our target group which of four end-user programming strategies they would prefer. Designers had a preference for a 3D visualization scenario where they could write and simulate ambient narratives in advance while retailers liked an in-situ authoring tool that would help them to correct errors and finetune the interactive ambient experience on location. Based on these results we decided to implement both end-user programming strategies and connect the two to cover the entire lifecycle (create, run, share) of interactive scene-based immersive retail environments and support an end-user software engineering approach.

In a user satisfaction evaluation we tested both end-user programming environments by letting the participants perform four simple tasks and found that people were able to successfully accomplish these tasks in most cases. Although they had many remarks for improvements they did not question the concept and found the system intuitive to use. In terms of efficiency the two authoring environments scored slightly less, mainly due to some button choices and placement in the user interface. Our aim is to further lower the barrier for retail designers to create, simulate, run and adapt interactive immersive retail environments to improve the shopping experience.

Acknowledgements

The authors would like to thank Evert van Loenen, Vic Teeven, Frank van Tuijl for their help and Lars Kaijser, Rick van Haasen, Henk Sandkuyl, Tom Geelen, Roxana Frunza for their software support and all the retailers, designers and consultants that participated in the workshops and user evaluations.

References

1. Aarts, E., Marzano, S.(eds.): The New Everyday: Views on Ambient Intelligence. 010 Publishers (2003)
2. Blackwell, A., Hague, R.: AutoHAN: An Architecture for Programming the Home. In: Proceedings of the IEEE 2001 Symposia on Human Centric Computing Languages and Environments (HCC 2001), pp. 150–157 (2001)
3. Burnett, M., Engels, G., Myers, B., Rothermel, G. (eds.): End-User Software Engineering, 18.02. - 23.02.2007, volume 07081 of Dagstuhl Seminar Proceedings. Internationales Begegnungs- und Forschungszentrum für Informatik (IBFI), Schloss Dagstuhl, Germany (2007)
4. Cypher, A.: Watch What I Do: Programming by Demonstration. MIT Press, Cambridge (1993)
5. Decortis, F., Rizzo, A.: New active tools for supporting narrative structures. Personal Ubiquitous Computing 6(5-6), 416–429 (2002)
6. Gárate, A., Herrasti, N., López, A.: Genio: an ambient intelligence application in home automation and entertainment environment. In: Proceedings of the 2005 joint conference on Smart objects and ambient intelligence, pp. 241–245. ACM Press, New York (2005)
7. Goffman, E.: The Presentation of Self in Everyday Life. Garden City, Doubleday (1959)

8. Grove, S., Fisk, R.: The Dramaturgy of Services Exchange: An Analytical Framework for Services Marketing. In: Emerging Perspectives on Services Marketing, pp. 45–49. American Marketing Association (1983)

9. Humble, J., Crabtree, A., Hemmings, T.: "Playing with the Bits" User-Configuration of Ubiquitous Domestic Environments. In: Proceedings of the 5th International Conference on Ubiquitous Computing, pp. 256–263 (2003)

10. Kindberg, T., Barton, J., Morgan, J., Becker, G., Caswell, D., Debaty, P., Gopal, G., Frid, M., Krishnan, V., Morris, H., Schettino, J., Serra, B., Spasojevic, M.: People, places, things: Web presence for the real world. In: Proceedings of the Third IEEE Workshop on Mobile Computing Systems and Applications (WMCSA 2000), Washington, DC, USA, p. 19. IEEE Computer Society, Los Alamitos (2000)

11. Kurkovsky, S., Harihar, K.: Using ubiquitous computing in interactive mobile marketing. Personal Ubiquitous Computing 10(4), 227–240 (2006)

12. Lane, G.: Urban tapestries: Wireless networking, public authoring and social knowledge. Personal Ubiquitous Computing 7(3-4), 169–175 (2003)

13. Laurel, B.: Toward the Design of a Computer-Based Interactive Fantasy System. PhD thesis, Ohio State University (1986)

14. Li, Y., Hong, J., Landay, J.: Topiary: a tool for prototyping location-enhanced applications. In: Proceedings of the 17th annual ACM symposium on User interface software and technology, pp. 217–226. ACM, New York (2004)

15. Montemayor, J., Druin, A., Chipman, G.: Tools for children to create physical interactive storyrooms. Computers in Entertainment 2(1), 12–12 (2004)

16. Newman, M., Sedivy, J., Neuwirth, C., Edwards, W., Hong, J., Izadi, S., Marcelo, K., Smith, T.: Designing for serendipity: supporting end-user configuration of ubiquitous computing environments. In: Proceedings of the 4th conference on Designing interactive systems, pp. 147–156. ACM, New York (2002)

17. Repenning, A., Ioannidou, A.: Agent-based end-user development. Communications of the ACM 47(9), 43–46 (2004)

18. Sandor, C., Bell, B., Olwal, A.: Visual end user configuration of hybrid user interfaces. In: Proceedings of the 2004 ACM SIGMM workshop on Effective telepresence, pp. 67–68. ACM, New York (2004)

19. Shirehjini, A., Klar, F.: 3DSim: Rapid Prototyping Ambient Intelligence. In: Proceedings of the 2005 Joint Conference on Smart Objects and Ambient Intelligence, pp. 303–307. ACM, New York (2005)

20. Smith, M., Davenport, D., Hwa, H., Combs-Turner, T.: Object Auras: A Mobile Retail and Product Annotation System. In: Proceedings of the Fifth ACM Conference on Electronic Commerce, May 17-20, pp. 240–241 (2004)

21. Sohn, T., Dey, A.: icap: an informal tool for interactive prototyping of context-aware applications. In: CHI 2003 extended abstracts on Human factors in computing systems, pp. 974–975. ACM, New York (2003)

22. Streitz, N., Rocker, C., Prante, T., van Alphen, D., Stenzel, R., Magerkurth, C.: Designing smart artifacts for smart environments. IEEE Computer 38(3), 41–49 (2005)

23. Sukaviriya, N., Podlaseck, M., et al.: Augmenting a retail environment using steerable interactive displays. In: CHI 2003 extended abstracts on Human factors in computing systems, pp. 978–979. ACM, New York (2003)

24. Truong, K., Huang, E., Abowd, G.: CAMP: A Magnetic Poetry Interface for End-User Programming of Capture Applications for the Home. In: Proceedings of the 6th International Conference on Ubiquitous Computing, pp. 143–160 (2004)

25. van Doorn, M., van Loenen, E., de Vries, A.: Performing in Ambient Narratives: Supporting Everyday Life Performances with Technology. The Drama Review 51(4), 68–79 (2007)
26. van Doorn, M., van Loenen, E., de Vries, A.: Deconstructing ambient intelligence into ambient narratives: the intelligent shop window. In: Proceedings of the 1st international conference on Ambient media and systems, ICST, Brussels, Belgium, pp. 1–8 (2008) (Institute for Computer Sciences, Social-Informatics and Telecommunications Engineering)
27. van Loenen, E., Lashina, T., van Doorn, M.: Interactive Shop Windows. In: Ambient Lifestyle: From Concept to Experience. Bis Publishers, Amsterdam (2006)
28. VideoMining. Video Mining website (2008), http://www.videomining.com
29. WiseTrack. WiseTrack website (2008), http://www.wisetrack.com/

Collect&Drop: A Technique for Multi-Tag Interaction with Real World Objects and Information

Gregor Broll[1], Markus Haarländer[1], Massimo Paolucci[2], Matthias Wagner[2], Enrico Rukzio[3], and Albrecht Schmidt[4]

[1] Media Informatics Group, Ludwig-Maximilians-Universität München (LMU), Germany
gregor.broll@ifi.lmu.de
[2] DOCOMO Euro-Labs, Germany
{paolucci,wagner}@docomolab-euro.com
[3] Computing Department, Lancaster University, UK
rukzio@comp.lancs.ac.uk
[4] Pervasive Computing Group, University of Duisburg-Essen, Germany
albrecht.schmidt@acm.org

Abstract. The advancement of Ubicomp technologies leverages mobile interaction with physical objects and facilitates ubiquitous access to information and services. This provides new opportunities for mobile interaction with the real world, but also creates new challenges regarding the complexity of mobile applications, their interaction design and usability. In order to take advantage of this potential beyond simple interaction with single objects and tags, this paper investigates mobile interaction with multiple objects, tags and associated information. It introduces Collect&Drop as a generic technique for Multi-Tag Interaction that supports the collection, storage and management of information from the real world as well as its usage with different services. This paper describes the concept, architecture and interaction design of Collect&Drop and presents a user study that evaluates its features.

1 Introduction

Ever since 26th June 1974, when a pack of chewing gum was the first commercial product labeled with a barcode [1], everyday objects have been tagged for automated identification and access to associated information. Since then, the advancement of Ubicomp [2] technologies has increased the possibilities for mobile interaction with objects, information and services from the real world. NFC, RFID, visual markers or GPS make it possible to tag *"people, places and things"* [3], make them machine-recognizable and associate them with additional information. That way, physical objects can act as bridges into the digital domain, as they advertise ubiquitous information and services, facilitate their discovery and support the interaction with them. Complementary, mobile devices provide increasing technical capabilities for discovering, capturing and using information and services from the real world.

Physical Mobile Interaction (PMI) [4] takes advantage of these developments and uses mobile devices for physical interaction with tagged objects in order to facilitate

E. Aarts et al. (Eds.): AmI 2008, LNCS 5355, pp. 175–191, 2008.

the interaction with associated information and services. Due to its increased directness and simplicity, physical interaction can make mobile interaction more intuitive and convenient. Real world objects can serve as physical interfaces that complement mobile interfaces and adopt some of their features. Mobile applications are less confined to the constrained input/output facilities of mobile devices. Instead, users can interact with information and services by touching or pointing at physical objects, respectively by touching NFC-tags or by taking pictures of visual markers with their mobile devices.

Mobile interaction with physical objects is adopted by a growing number of applications for service discovery and invocation, ticketing, mobile payment, advertisement, information services or games: Visual markers are used as two-dimensional barcodes to identify consumer products or to tag objects with encoded URLs (e.g. Semapedia [5]). Mobile interaction with places is the foundation for location based applications and games like geo-tagging [6] or geo-caching [7]. NFC and RFID [8] are rapidly establishing as technologies for mobile ticketing (e.g. Octopus card [9]) or payment (e.g. iMode Felica [10]) as they reduce them to simply swiping a smart card or a mobile phone over a reader.

The further advancement of systems enabling or using PMI provides new opportunities for mobile interaction with a growing number of tagged physical objects and an increasing amount of information that is available from them. The impact of this development has been antedated by Mark Weiser: *"When almost every object either contains a computer or can have a tab [inch-scale machines that approximate active Post-It notes] attached to it, obtaining information will be trivial."* [2].

However, most *Physical Mobile Applications (PMA)* – mobile applications using PMI - make only little use of this growing potential. They are often restricted to the interaction with single tags to facilitate the first step in an interaction workflow which is then continued on the mobile device, suffering from its usability constraints. Further interaction with physical objects is usually neglected. In most cases, the information from a tag is coupled with a specific service and cannot be combined with other information or reused with different applications. Similarly, mobile services are often confined to specific tasks, are not interoperable and don't exchange information.

In order to take better advantage of the increasing opportunities for mobile interaction with objects and information from the real world beyond *Single-Tag Interaction (STI)*, Physical Mobile Applications have to be able to interact with multiple objects and tags, combine their information and (re)use it with different applications and services. This paper investigates *Multi-Tag Interaction (MTI)* - PMI with multiple tags that are targeted at the same interaction process. It presents Collect&Drop as a generic technique for MTI that facilitates the collection, management and usage of information and services acquired from the real world in order to improve their combination, reuse and interoperability.

The next section provides an overview of related work about enabling technologies and interaction techniques for mobile interaction with physical objects as well as different applications using Multi-Tag Interaction. Section 3 presents the concept and interaction design of Collect&Drop as a technique for MTI in more detail. Section 4 describes the design and features of its mobile and physical interfaces while section 5 explains the architecture of Collect&Drop. Section 6 presents an evaluation of Collect&Drop, its interaction design and its features. Section 7 concludes the paper.

2 Related Work

Physical Mobile Interaction relies on various enabling technologies to implement the tagging of objects with information as well as its acquisition with mobile devices: In 1999, Want et al. [11] presented one of the first systems for tagging objects like books, documents or business cards with RFID-tags. By touching an object with an RFID-reader, users could open a corresponding virtual representation, e.g. a website, with further information on an attached tablet-PC.

Cooltown [3] augments people, places and things with infrared beacons to transmit URLs that point to the web presence of an object. Mobile devices can use these URLs to get more information about objects from a web page or send them to web-enabled appliances for further usage.

The recognition of two-dimensional visual markers with mobile phone cameras has become one of the most established technologies for PMI: Rohs and Gfeller developed the Visual Codes system [12] that implements a lightweight visual code recognition algorithm that is adapted to the technical constraints of mobile phones (e.g. low resolution and image quality, limited processing power).

Another visual marker system is CyberCode [13] that has been used for direct-manipulation techniques in physical environments. One example is InfoStick [14] that implements a physical drag-and-drop operation. It uses CyberCodes to identify objects and pick up digital information from them with a wand-like camera device. That way, digital information can be moved between different physical objects and devices (e.g. monitors, printers, projectors) that are also identified by CyberCodes.

Välkkynen and Tuomisto [15] use a laser pointer attached to a PDA to implement the *PointMe* interaction technique which has light sensors in the physical object react to the laser beam. An advantage of using a laser pointer for interaction is the observable feedback that users get when pointing into the direction of an object.

Different techniques have been built on top of these and other technologies in order to make the interaction with them more familiar and intuitive: In [16] Rukzio et al. compare the interaction techniques *Touching* (using NFC) *Pointing* (using a laser-pointer) and *Scanning* (using Bluetooth) that are used for the selection and usage of smart-home appliances in different contexts of location and activity (e.g. sitting, lying or standing). The choice for an interaction technique was dependent on the location of the user, his motivation and his activity.

Several applications already show how to use the interaction with multiple objects and tags as input for mobile applications: Pac-Lan [17] implements an outdoor version of Pac-Man where RFID-tags in the real world replace the pills in the game. Players have to touch them in order to update their position. Players are also tagged with RFID-tags in order to identify them.

The mobile interaction technique Point&Shoot [18] relies on a coordinate system implemented with a grid of visual codes in order to determine the absolute position of objects on a large display.

The SmartTouch [19] project developed a multi-tag application that lets elderly people choose from alternative meals for home-delivery by touching different NFC-tags on a menu-card. In addition, the delivery personnel mark their delivery route by touching NFC-tags at different locations.

In [20], Reilly et al. present a prototype that allows the selection of different regions on a map by touching attached RFID-tags. The prototype also supports different techniques for the selection of tags including path-select, multi-select or lasso-select.

3   Introducing the Concept of Collect&Drop

Collect&Drop is a generic technique for Multi-Tag Interaction (MTI) - Physical Mobile Interaction with multiple tags that are targeted at the same interaction process. Multi-Tag Interaction increases the scope of mobile interaction with the real world: While Single-Tag Interaction is by definition confined to the interaction with single tags on single objects, Multi-Tag Interaction implies the interaction with multiple tags on the same or on different objects for a collective purpose. In this context, Collect&Drop tries to take advantage of the diversity of real world information that is provided by the interaction with multiple objects and tags. For that purpose, it implements a generic mechanism for the collection, management and usage of information and services from the real world in order to improve their interoperability and to enable their (re)use and combination across different objects and applications.

3.1   A Use Case Scenario for Multi-Tag Interaction

In order to illustrate the concept of Collect&Drop, this section gives a short overview of a use case scenario that was chosen for its implementation with a mobile client prototype. This scenario demonstrates mobile interaction with three augmented posters for mobile ticketing and sightseeing. Each poster is associated with a specific Web Service and comprises multiple tags that provide parameters for its invocation. Users can interact with these tags and use their mobile devices to collect information about services and parameters (see Fig. 1). Collect&Drop supports the management of this information as well as its usage for the invocation of the Web Services.

The movie ticket-poster (Fig. 2a) allows the interaction with a Web Service for ordering movie tickets and provides four groups of parameters (movie, cinema, time, number of persons) for invoking it. These groups are arranged in a numbered order to guide users through the interaction workflow.

Fig. 1. Collect&Drop enables mobile interaction with multiple objects and tags

Similarly, the public transportation-poster (Fig. 2b) offers the possibility to buy tickets for a public transportation system and is associated with a corresponding Web Service. The poster comprises numbered groups of parameters to select a departure zone, a destination zone, the validity of the ticket and the number of passengers.

Finally, the city guide-poster (Fig. 2c) presents 10 popular sights in Munich, Germany. Users can select the sights they are interested in and send them to a Web Service to receive additional information about each object. The design of the poster highlights the beginning and the end of the interaction workflow, but does not number the different sights or suggest any order in which users should interact with them.

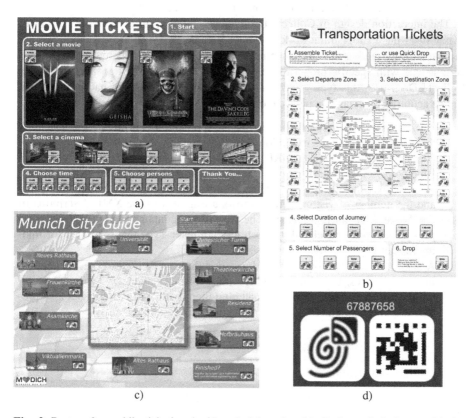

Fig. 2. Posters for mobile ticketing (a, b) and sightseeing (c). Each tag includes graphical symbols (d) to indicate and support the physical interaction with it by touching its NFC-tag, taking a picture of its visual marker or typing its numeric identifier into a form.

Each poster comprises multiple tags that contain or reference XML-encoded information that can be used to invoke the Web Service that is associated with the poster. Each tag is augmented with an NFC-tag, a visual marker and a numeric identifier which are indicated by different graphical symbols (see Fig. 2d). Users can interact with these tags and acquire their information by touching them with their NFC-enabled mobile device, taking a picture of the visual marker or typing the numeric identifier into a form.

3.2   Information Typing for Flexible Interaction

In order to allocate services, tags and parameters from the use case posters correctly and to enable their combination and usage across different objects, Collect&Drop builds upon the PERCI-framework [21] for PMI with Semantic Web Services and uses some of its technologies. The use case scenario for Collect&Drop reuses Web Services from the framework in order to guarantee the compatibility with these technologies. Opposite to the first mobile client for the PERCI-framework which implemented MTI in a rigid way (see [21]), Collect&Drop supports a much more flexible interaction with tags and information from physical objects.

The interaction design of Collect&Drop adopts the concept of *Abstract Parameter Types* from the PERCI-framework. Abstract Parameter Types are a generic typing-mechanism that adds semantic meaning to information from tags and marks it as a certain type with specific properties, e.g. as a cinema, movie or transportation zone. Collect&Drop uses this typing-mechanism with two kinds of information items that can be acquired from tags on physical objects:

- An *Action Item* describes a service or an application and provides information that is necessary for its execution. This information specifies a reference to the application/service (e.g. a URL), the interaction protocol (e.g. Web Service, Bluetooth ...) and the types of parameters that are necessary for its invocation. For example, the cinema service needs information about a movie, cinema, time and the number of visitors. Fig. 3 shows a fragment of the XML-description of the Action Item for this service. The *params*-tag contains each of the necessary parameters with a label and its Abstract Parameter Type that is needed for finding matching parameters.
- A *Data Item* contains parameter information that can be used to execute applications or services. Data Items use the same Abstract Parameter Types to specify the type of their information for matching them with Action Items but also provide a specific parameter-value, e.g. the title of a certain movie.

```
<actionItem protocol = "PERCIWebserviceAction">
  <label>Get movie ticket (Webservice)</label>
  <desc>This action invokes the Movie Ticketing Web Service with
      your data.</desc>
  <url>http://perci.medien.ifi.lmu.de:8080/axis/serviceDescription/
      extendedCinema/</url>
  <params>
    <param>
      <label>Movie Title</label>
      <abstype>http://perci.medien.ifi.lmu.de:8080/axis/domain/
          cinema/cinema.owl#MovieTitle</abstype>
    </param>

    ...

  </params>
</actionItem>
```

Fig. 3. XML-description of an Action Item including the parameters for its execution

Using the same typing-scheme for both Action and Data Items makes it possible to map applications/services and parameters to one another correctly. Information items can be independent from each other which again supports their combination and reuse - as long as their parameter types match. For example, a service from an Action Item can be invoked with any Data Item from any tag on any object, as long as their Abstract Parameter Types match. In the same way, Data Items that have been collected from one object can be reused with different Action Items to execute their services or applications. That way, Collect&Drop realizes mobile interaction with tags and information across different objects and improves the interoperability between information and services. Separating actions and parameters on the level of information items also makes it possible to combine Action Items and Data Items on the same tag (*Hybrid Tags*) and to map several of them to the same tag.

3.3 Basic Interaction Design of Collect&Drop

Fig. 4 shows the interaction workflow of Collect&Drop which is divided into two phases: During the Collect-phase, mobile devices interact with tags (indicated by a black frame) on physical objects in arbitrary order to acquire their Data Items and/or Action Items (blue and red squares). Each tag can contain or reference one or more Action Items and/or Data Items, respectively service-URIs and parameters. The current Collect&Drop client supports the interaction techniques Touching (using NFC), Pointing (using the recognition of Visual Code markers) and Direct Input (typing of numeric identifiers) for mobile interaction with tags on physical objects, respectively the use case posters.

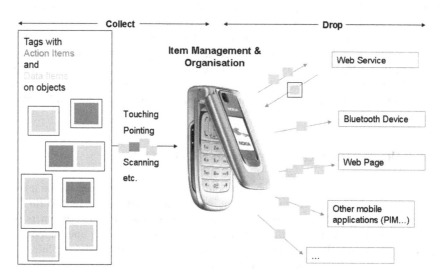

Fig. 4. The interaction workflow of Collect&Drop: collection, management and usage of information items

Collect&Drop stores and manages acquired Data Items and Action Items in *Collections* on the mobile device. Collections are data containers that facilitate the organization of information items and support the execution of applications and services specified by Action Items. Collect&Drop creates a new Collection for each Action Item that is acquired from a tag and adds Data Items according to their Abstract Parameter Types. This mechanism implements the matching between Action Items that require parameters of a certain type for their execution and available Data Items that provide these parameters. That way, an application that needs a certain type of information (e.g. a location) for its invocation, can use any Data Item as long as it matches the requested type. Whenever a new Data Item is collected, Collect&Drop automatically checks whether its Abstract Parameter Type matches the Abstract Parameter Type of all parameters that are required by any Action Item and adds matching Data Items to its collection. The system informs the user as soon as sufficient Data Items for the invocation of an action are available. Collections store information items beyond their immediate usage which provides the foundation for their combination and (re)use with different applications or services.

During the Drop-phase, Collect&Drop again relies on different technologies to execute applications or services from Action Items, respectively to "drop" Data Items from a collection to its Action Item. The name "Collect&Drop" tries to imply a certain mental model that when interacting with tags on a physical object, users can collect Data Items from different tags and then drop them to a tag with an Action Item in order to invoke its application/service. Technically, Collect&Drop does not really drop Data Items to a tag but rather picks up its Action Item to initiate the invocation of its application or service with collected Data Items. That way, a Web Service can be invoked via GPRS or UMTS, Data Items can be transferred to other devices via Bluetooth or NFC, a web page can be opened or information can be written to PIM-applications on the mobile device.

Applications and services can return a Data Item as the result of their invocation (see the return arrow from the Web Service action in Fig. 4). This item is again collected and stored by Collect&Drop and can be used with other applications. For example, the movie ticketing service returns a movie ticket-Data Item which can be used to order a transportation ticket to the cinema, using the location information from the ticket-Data Item.

4   Mobile and Physical Interfaces for Collect&Drop

The interface of Collect&Drop comprises both the Collection-interface on the mobile device as well as the physical interface that users interact with in the real world (e.g. the use case posters). The last section introduced Collections as data containers that manage information items acquired from tags on physical objects and support the execution of Action Items. For that purpose, the interface of the mobile Collect&Drop-client comprises four main elements:

- **Collection List:** The Collection List presents the different Collections to the user. Fig. 5a shows an example with three Collections for different services. When the user starts the application for the first time, an empty Collection List is displayed that briefly explains how to use the different interaction techniques.

As users interact with physical objects and their tags, different Collections for acquired information items are automatically added to the list to facilitate the interaction with them. Whenever information has been collected from a tag, Collect&Drop provides feedback through vibration and a visual pop-up.

- **Item List:** This interface shows all information items in a Collection when it is opened from the Collection List. All information items in a Collection are separated into Action and Data Items. As Fig. 5b shows, there is only one Action Item in a Collection which lists all parameters, respectively Data Items that are available or missing for its execution. A traffic light visualization informs users about the individual states of all information items. Data Items are always yellow. Action Items are marked as red as long as there are parameters missing for their execution. As soon as suitable Data Items have been collected, they are added to the Collection. When enough Data Items - either stored or collected - are available for executing the action, it is marked as green (see Fig. 5c). The purpose of this visualization is to provide a better overview of collected information items and the status of actions that can be executed with them.

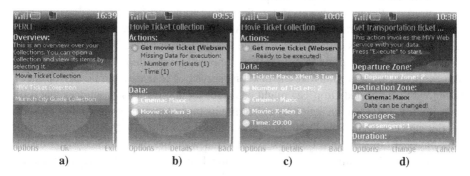

Fig. 5. Screenshots of a Collection List (a), two Item Lists (b, c) and an Action Execution Screen (d)

- **Action Execution Screen:** This interface asks users to confirm the execution of an action and presents an overview of the Data Items that have been selected for that purpose (see Fig. 5d). In case there are multiple Data Items with the same Abstract Parameter Type that can be used for the execution of the action, the item is highlighted with a yellow traffic light and the user can select from the alternatives.

- **Action Specific Screens:** After pressing the "Execute" command on the Action Execution Screen, the user interface control is handed over to the respective action component. Thus, it can present individual screens and control commands to the user, e.g. to indicate the transmission of data via GPRS or Bluetooth, to ask users to touch another NFC-device for data exchange or to execute additional steps in the interaction with a Web Service.

In order to fully realize MTI, the mobile Collect&Drop-client is complemented with physical interfaces that provide the input for the interaction with services and application. The separation of Data Items and Action Items, their association through the

Abstract Parameter Types as well as the concept of Collections to manage information items on the mobile device persistently makes the interaction design of Collect&Drop very flexible. The design of the use case posters relies on this flexibility to implement different features for the interaction with multiple tags and physical objects.

The movie ticket-poster uses Hybrid Tags that combine Action Items and Data Items on the same physical tag. Apart from its specific parameter-information, each tag on this poster contains the same Action Item that provides information for invoking the movie ticketing service. This Data Item is implicitly collected whenever the user interacts with any tag on the poster. The idea behind Hybrid Tags is to make the interaction process less complex for the users as they don't have to collect a separate tag that is dedicated to the Action Item for the service. Since all tags are the same, the users can interact with them in arbitrary order. In addition, the Data Items of the cinema tags on this poster also provide location information. The Web Service that is associated with the public transportation-poster can use these Data Items as input to provide tickets for getting to the cinema.

Contrary to the movie ticket-poster, the public transportation-poster does not use Hybrid Tags but separates Data Items and Action Items by putting them onto different tags. A tag that is thus dedicated to a single Action Item is called *Drop Tag*. Opposite to Hybrid Tags which provide Action Items implicitly, users have to collect the Drop Tag explicitly in order to invoke the ticketing service. The added complexity of interacting with a dedicated Drop Tag might be useful for applications or services that rely on explicitly triggering an action by collecting its tag, providing some kind of closure for this process. Dedicated Drop Tags also make it easier to use the same Data Item on a physical object with different services. That way, the movie ticket-poster could easily be extended with Drop Tags for additional services to get further information about its movies or to buy merchandising for them.

In addition to the dedicated Drop Tag, the public transportation-poster also features a so called *Quick Drop*-tag that includes all Action Items and Data Items for requesting a standard ticket (1 person, 1 day, start zone defined by poster location), except the Data Item that specifies the destination of the journey. This tag implements a shortcut that only requires its users to drop a single Data Item from the poster or other objects to complete the request to the Web Service. The missing Data Item can be taken from Collections on the mobile device. That way, a user who has interacted with the movie ticket-poster and has collected a Data Item for a movie or a ticket, can use the location information from this Data Item with the Quick Drop-tag to easily get a transportation ticket to the location of the cinema for which he bought a ticket.

The city guide-poster also features a dedicated Drop Tag in order to provide some kind of closure with which users can finish their interaction with the poster. All other tags provide Data Items about sights and Data Items about their location that can be used with the Public Transportation Poster.

The three use case posters offer a wide range of different features for MTI: The movie ticket-poster features implicit interaction with Hybrid Tags while the public transportation-poster and the city guide-poster implement explicit interaction with dedicated Drop Tags. Data Items from the movie ticket-poster and the city guide-poster can be reused with the Drop Tag and the Quick Drop-tag from the public transportation-poster thus realizing cross-object interaction.

5 Collect&Drop Architecture

The concept of Collect&Drop brings out three main requirements for its system architecture regarding the interaction with physical objects, data management as well as the execution of different actions (see Fig. 4). Collect&Drop is a client-side mechanism that was implemented as a J2ME-midlet on the Nokia 6131 NFC mobile phone. It handles the interaction with physical objects and uses their information to invoke associated Web Services that are part of the PERCI framework (see [21] for details). The architecture of the mobile Collect&Drop application (see Fig. 6) comprises the following components:

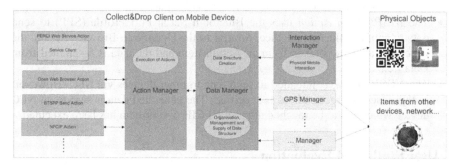

Fig. 6. The architecture of Collect&Drop including its components for PMI, data storage, management and the execution of actions

The *Interaction Manager* supports different PMI technologies and techniques through specialized sub-components and is responsible for receiving information through interaction with physical objects or other devices. The current implementation of the mobile Collect&Drop-client supports interaction through reading NFC-tags, taking pictures of visual markers and decoding them as well as the input of numeric identifiers. The Interaction Manager forwards information from tags to the *Data Manager* for further processing. When tags - especially visual markers - do not have enough capacity to store one or several information items directly, they only provide an identifier or a reference to this information, e.g. a URL. In that case, the Interaction Manager has to resolve this reference and download information items from a server.

The Data Manager provides different functionalities to parse and check information items, create new Collections and integrate new data with existing ones. The Data Manager must provide interfaces for other components to request or to delete data. It informs other components about the arrival of new data and the change or deletion of items and Collections. Other components can request data e.g. in order to present items and Collections to the user, to check whether new Data Items are available for an action or to use new items for action specific functionalities.

The *Action Manager* is responsible for mapping suitable Data Items to Action Items, checking whether Action Items are executable and finally organizing their final execution. This component has to manage the different Data and Action Items (which can be requested from the Data Manager) and check whether there are enough suitable Data Items for the execution of an Action Item. Actions can be executed automatically or manually from the user interface.

For every type of action there is an *Action Component* that describes the logic for executing a specific action. The Collect&Drop prototype currently supports the following actions, but can easily be extended with new ones:

- The *PERCI Web Service Action* component connects the Collect&Drop-client with Web Services from the PERCI-framework and handles their invocation.
- The *Open Web Browser Action* component uses the mobile device's standard web browser to open a website. The request is generated from an Action Item, providing the URL, and several Data Items, providing the request parameters. The resulting HTTP-GET request is processed by the server which generates and returns a web page according to the provided parameters.
- The *BTSPP Send Action* uses the Bluetooth Serial Port Profile (SPP) to send data to another Bluetooth device. Similar to the Open Web Browser Action, the Bluetooth address is taken from an Action Item and the data is assembled from Data Items.
- The *NFCIP action* is intended to send data to other devices via NFC. However, in this case no target address is specified. The generated data is sent to an NFC device which has to be touched after an NFCIP Action Item has been executed.

6 User Study and Evaluation

In order to evaluate Collect&Drop and its approach to Multi-Tag Interaction, a user study was designed and conducted with a working prototype and the use case posters. This section summarizes the design, setup and results of this study.

6.1 Scenario Design

For the evaluation of Collect&Drop, the subjects of the study had to carry out five different tasks for which they had to use the mobile Collect&Drop-client in order to interact with the use case posters.

- The first two tasks asked the subjects to interact with the movie and transportation posters separately. Apart from the overall interaction design and usability, these tasks tested whether the layout of the posters or the numbering of their options influenced the order in which the subjects collected them. In addition, the tasks tested whether users preferred interacting with dedicated Drop Tags (on the transportation poster) or with Hybrid Tags (on the movie poster).
- The third task evaluated cross-poster interaction as the subjects had to drop the movie ticket-Data Item they had received from the movie ticketing service to the Quick Drop-tag of the transportation poster.

- For the fourth scenario, the subjects had to drop the same movie ticket-Data Item to an NFC-tag that simulated a tag-reader at the entrance of a cinema. This task tested whether the subjects understood how to use a Data Item which they had received from a Web Service with other objects and applications.
- For the last task, the subjects had to collect tags for different sights from the sightseeing poster. Upon executing the action associated with the poster, Collect&Drop opened the web browser of the mobile phone and presented a web page with descriptions of these sights that was returned from a server. This task tested whether subjects got along with a different kind of action and a poster that allows the selection of an arbitrary amount of items.

6.2 Setup and Demography of the User Study

At the beginning of the study, each subject was shortly introduced to the Collect&Drop concept and the 5 tasks. The study was conducted with a panel of 15 subjects. Five of them were female, ten were male. The average age of the subjects was 25.5 years. 13 subjects were students: Nine of them had a background in computer sciences; four were studying other subjects like economics, geography, physics or statistics. The remaining two subjects worked as research associates that were not involved with the PERCI-project. All of the subjects owned a mobile phone and have done so for an average of about 6 years. The average skills with mobile phones were rated with 3.9 on a scale from 1 (not experienced at all) to 5 (very experienced). General technical skills were rated with an average of 4.1.

6.3 Results and Discussion

This section summarizes the results of the user study and the evaluation of Collect&Drop. Average values were calculated from Likert-scale ratings ranging from 1 ("do not agree at all") to 5 ("fully agree").

6.3.1 Collect&Drop Concept

The concept of Collect&Drop was accepted by the subjects, as 13 of 15 would use it if it was available. The subjects considered it to be very practical, easy, quick and time-saving. The comprehension of the Collect&Drop concept was rated with an average of 4.7. Several users stated that the whole application and the concept become clearer after the first usage. They said that it was a bit confusing at first and that they felt unconfident with the handling of the interaction and the application. But after they had seen how it worked, it became easier, clearer and more intuitive.

The design and the navigation of the Collection List and the Individual Item List were rated with an average of 4.1. Most subjects did not spend much time on the Individual Item Lists. During the interaction, the posters got more attention than the application. However, after every interaction with a tag, most of the subjects had a brief look at the list to check whether the collected Items had been added. The traffic light visualization did not get much attention and was not commented. The idea of managing information items in Collections was rated with an average of 4.5.

6.3.2 Comparison of Invisible Drop and Explicit Drop

A narrow majority of eight subjects was aware of the difference between posters with Hybrid Tags (movie poster) and a dedicated Drop Tag (transportation poster). A comparison between the two approaches shows that Hybrid Tags consistently got better results regarding simplicity, speed, intuitiveness and comprehensibility. Fig. 7 summarizes the results (rating from 1=worst to 5=best):

- **Simplicity:** Both systems are rated as easy to use, with Hybrid Tags scoring an average rating of 4.7 compared to 4.2 for the explicit Drop Tag.
- **Speed:** As expected, the results regarding the speed of both approaches show the biggest difference between them. The interaction experience without a dedicated Drop Tag is rated with 4.9, the one with a Drop Tag only with 3.4. This can be referred to the time that is needed to interact with the additional Drop Tag on the transportation poster.
- **Intuitiveness:** The explicit Drop Tag got an average rating of 3.7 and the Hybrid Tag 4.5 regarding intuitiveness of use. The results confirm that a Drop Tag does not make the system more intuitive, as assumed in the first place
- **Comprehensibility:** In terms of comprehensibility, the Drop Tag achieved a 4.1, the Hybrid Tags a 4.7. As Hybrid Tags always contain Action Items, their Collections always show information about their actions and missing parameters. One user stated that it was a very good idea to give such kind of feedback.

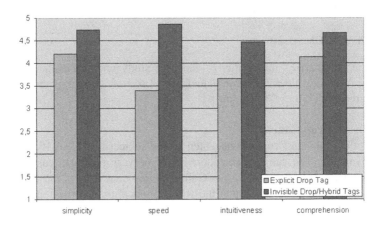

Fig. 7. Comparing Drop Tag and Hybrid Tags regarding simplicity, speed, intuitiveness and comprehension

When a Hybrid Tag has been collected, the usual pop-up showed the reception of two or more new information items. At the beginning, this information confused some users, as a single interaction resulted in the collection of two or more information items. However, after showing the Individual Item List, the concept became clearer or did not bother anymore.

6.3.3 Cross-Object Interaction and Quick Drop

Similar to the comparison of Hybrid Tags and Drop Tags, the subjects were asked to evaluate the concepts of Cross-Object Interaction between the posters and Quick Drop regarding speed, simplicity, intuitiveness and comprehension, again on a scale from 1 (worst) to 5 (best).

Cross-Object Interaction was rated as very quick with an average of 4.8, which can be explained with the fact that Data Items are already available on the phone and did not have to be collected again. The simplicity of Cross-Object Interaction was rated with an average of 4.2. Several users noted that it might get confusing if too many Data Items with suitable parameters were already on the phone. The average ratings for comprehension (3.9) and intuitiveness (3.3) were a bit lower. The posters were regarded as independent use cases and are more related to their individual services. Interoperability between posters seemed to be quite strange and unnatural at first. However, many subjects stated that the concept of Cross-Object Interaction became much clearer, more comprehensible and even quicker after the first try.

The results from the evaluation of Cross-Object-Interaction were similar to the results of the Quick Drop evaluation. This is not a surprise, since Quick Drop incorporates the idea of Cross-Poster-Interaction. The usefulness of Quick Drop was rated with 4.2. Problems appeared at the beginning of the Quick Drop scenario. Several subjects did not know how to start and asked if they were supposed to touch the Quick Drop tag first or do anything else. Another problem was that it was not clear to the subjects what would happen if more suitable Data Items were on the phone. If there are too many suitable Data Items for an Action Item to choose from, the users fear confusion and the loss of overview. Quick Drop still got a good rating for its simplicity (4.6). It might be an unnatural and unfamiliar process at first, but if somebody knows how to use it, it will be quite easy and practical. This was confirmed by many subjects, who said that after one try the functionality becomes much clearer and easier. The last category, speed, does not reveal any surprising results. As expected, the Quick Drop scored a high rating of 4.7 regarding the speed of interaction.

6.3.4 Poster Numbering

Four of the 15 subjects did not follow the numbering provided by the posters. In all cases, this phenomenon happened with the transportation poster during the first scenario. When asked about their preferences, all subjects advocated posters with numbering and a given order of interaction. They considered these as much easier and more intuitive as they are led through the process and no option can be forgotten. The provided orientation also prevents mistakes and is particularly helpful for beginners. Some subjects also stated explicitly that it was indeed a useful idea to provide a numbering, but it was also very practical that the order could be burst and an individual order of interaction could be applied.

6.3.5 Data Items as Output and Input

Receiving a ticket as the result of invoking a service and validating the movie ticket at the simulated tag reader caused no problems and was well understood (average 4.6). Subjects noted that it was a very good idea to have an electronic ticket on the phone as it avoids queuing at the cinema and is thus considered to be time-saving, very easy and intuitive.

7 Conclusion

This paper investigated the opportunities and challenges for mobile interaction with multiple physical objects, tags and information as it presented and explored the concept of Collect&Drop as a generic technique for Multi-Tag Interaction.

The evaluation of Collect&Drop provided interesting results about its own interaction design as well as MTI in general: One the one hand, the study showed that users basically understood and accepted the concept of Collect&Drop as well as its different features which confirms its approach to MTI. Users intuitively understood the rather abstract collection of information items on and between different objects and quickly learned how to use features that were unfamiliar to them at first. On the other hand there is still room for improving the interaction design and usability of Collect&Drop as some users still did not know how to start the interaction with the poster or had problems with the interaction workflow.

Probably the most interesting result of the study is that users quickly learn to use Multi-Tag Interaction, despite its increased complexity compared to Single-Tag Interaction. At different occasions during the study it could be observed that users did not understand the concept of MTI or the features of Collect&Drop at once. Nevertheless, users quickly learned how to use them and then even embraced them. In this context, the comparison between interaction with Hybrid Tags and a dedicated Drop Tag showed that MTI has to retain the simplicity of PMI, despite its added complexity.

Acknowledgement

The work presented in this paper was done within PERCI (PERvasive ServiCe Interaction) [22], a bilateral project between Ludwig-Maximilians-Universität München (LMU) and DOCOMO Euro-Labs which was funded by the latter.

References

1. Moeeni, F.: From Light Frequency Identification (LFID) to Radio Frequency Identification (RFID) in the Supply Chain. Decision Line, 8–13 (2006)
2. Weiser, M.: The Computer for the 21st Century. Scientific American, 94–104 (1991)
3. Kindberg, T., Barton, J.J., Morgan, J., Becker, G., Caswell, D., Debaty, P., Gopal, G., Frid, M., Krishnan, V., Morris, H., Schettino, J., Serra, B., Spasojevic, M.: People, Places, Things: Web Presence for the Real World. MONET 7(5) (2002)
4. Rukzio, E., Broll, G., Leichtenstern, K., Schmidt, A.: Mobile Interaction with the Real World: An Evaluation and Comparison of Physical Mobile Interaction Techniques. In: Schiele, B., Dey, A.K., Gellersen, H., de Ruyter, B., Tscheligi, M., Wichert, R., Aarts, E., Buchmann, A. (eds.) AmI 2007. LNCS, vol. 4794, pp. 1–18. Springer, Heidelberg (2007)
5. Semapedia, http://www.semapedia.org
6. Persson, P., Espinoza, F., Fagerberg, P., Sandin, A., Cöster, R.: GeoNotes: A Location-based Information System for Public Spaces. In: Höök, K., Benyon, D., Munro, A. (eds.) Readings in Social Navigation of Information Space. Springer, Heidelberg (2002)
7. Webb, R.M.: Recreational Geocaching: The Southeast Queensland Experience. In: Proceedings 2001 - A Spatial Odyssey- Australian Surveying Congress - Brisbane, Brisbane Convention Centre (September 2001)

8. Want, R.: An Introduction to RFID Technology. IEEE Pervasive Computing 5, 25–33 (2006)
9. Octopus website, http://www.octopuscards.com/enindex.jsp
10. NTT DoCoMo, iMode Felica,
    http://www.nttdocomo.com/corebiz/icw/index.html
11. Want, R., Fishkin, K.P., Gujar, A., Harrison, B.L.: Bridging physical and virtual worlds with electronic tags. In: CHI, pp. 370–377 (1999)
12. Rohs, M., Gfeller, B.: Using Camera-Equipped Mobile Phones for Interacting with Real-World Objects. In: Advances in Pervasive Computing, Austrian Computer Society (OCG), Vienna, Austria, pp. 265–271 (2004)
13. Rekimoto, J., Ayatsuka, Y.: CyberCode: Designing Augmented Reality Environments with Visual Tags. Designing Augmented Reality Environments 2000, 1–10 (2000)
14. Kohtake, N., Rekimoto, J., Anzai, Y.: InfoStick: An Interaction Device for Inter-Appliance Computing. In: Gellersen, H.-W. (ed.) HUC 1999. LNCS, vol. 1707, pp. 246–258. Springer, Heidelberg (1999)
15. Välkkynen, P., Tuomisto, T.: Physical browsing research. In: PERMID, pp. 35–38 (2005)
16. Rukzio, E., Leichtenstern, K., Callaghan, V., Schmidt, A., Holleis, P., Chin, J.: An Experimental Comparison of Physical Mobile Interaction Techniques: Touching, Pointing and Scanning. In: Dourish, P., Friday, A. (eds.) UbiComp 2006. LNCS, vol. 4206, pp. 87–104. Springer, Heidelberg (2006)
17. Rashid, O., Bamford, W., Coulton, P., Edwards, R., Scheible, J.: PAC-LAN: Mixed-Reality Gaming with RFID-enabled Mobile Phones. Computers in Entertainment 4(4) (2006)
18. Ballagas, R., Rohs, M., Sheridan, J., Borchers, J.: Sweep and Point & Shoot: Phonecam-Based Interactions for Large Public Displays. In: CHI 2005 Extended Abstracts, New York, NY, USA, pp. 1200–1203 (2005)
19. Häikiö, J., Isomursu, M., Matinmikko, T., Wallin, A., Ailisto, H., Huomo, T.: Touch-based User Interface for Elderly Users. In: Proceedings of MobileHCI, Singapore, September 9-12 (2007)
20. Reilly, D.F., Welsman-Dinelle, M., Bate, C., Inkpen, K.: Just Point and Click? Using Handhelds to Interact with Paper Maps. In: Mobile HCI 2005, pp. 239–242 (2005)
21. Broll, G., Siorpaes, S., Rukzio, E., Paolucci, M., Hamard, J., Wagner, M., Schmidt, A.: Supporting Mobile Service Usage through Physical Mobile Interaction. In: 5th Annual IEEE International Conference on Pervasive Computing and Communications, White Plains, NY, USA, March 19 - 23 (2007)
22. Perci (PERvasive ServiCe Interaction),
    http://www.hcilab.org/projects/perci

Tracking Outdoor Sports – User Experience Perspective

Aino Ahtinen[1], Minna Isomursu[2], Ykä Huhtala[1], Jussi Kaasinen[1],
Jukka Salminen[1], and Jonna Häkkilä[1]

[1] Nokia Research Center, Itämerenkatu 11-13, 00180 Helsinki, Finland
{aino.ahtinen,yka.huhtala,jussi.kaasinen,jukka.h.salminen,
jonna.hakkila}@nokia.com
[2] VTT, Kaitoväylä 1, 90571 Oulu, Finland
minna.isomursu@vtt.fi

Abstract. In this paper, the potential role of a sport tracking application is examined in the context of supporting tracking outdoor sporting activities. A user study with 28 participants was conducted to study the usage habits and user experiences evoked. The application consists of a mobile tracking tool and a related web service. It collects and stores workout data such as the route, speed and time, and compiles a training diary that can be viewed in many ways during the exercise and afterwards. Data can be uploaded into a web service for further analysis or for sharing it with others. The results show high interest in tracking outdoor sports with a mobile phone application – the participants used the application during almost all exercise sessions and stated that they would continue using the application after the study. Sharing data was not perceived as valuable, although some usage scenarios for social sharing arose.

Keywords: Sports, tracking, GPS, user experience, mobile application, web service.

1 Introduction

Use of computing devices for supporting everyday tasks has become common with mobile and personal computing devices. Digital tools help people by storing, distributing and processing information that is useful in managing the complexity of everyday life (even though sometimes themselves contributing to the complexity of everyday life). During recent years, mobile devices and applications that aim at supporting people doing sports and other physical activities have emerged – heart rate monitors and pedometers to name the most common ones. Being physically active is one of the most important factors in maintaining a good state of wellbeing. Digital tools can help, for example, in providing means for social support, visualizing the perceived benefits of being active, giving feedback about the workout and in setting appropriate goals. All these have been shown to contribute towards more satisfaction in sport activities [2, 21, 22, 23, 25, 38, 48]. In addition, tracking, saving and storing data of physical exercises motivates people to increase their level of physical activity and keep their current motivational level high [41, 43].

E. Aarts et al. (Eds.): AmI 2008, LNCS 5355, pp. 192–209, 2008.
© Springer-Verlag Berlin Heidelberg 2008

During the last decade, mobile phones have become an integrated part of everyday life. The high adoption rate of mobile phones means that they provide a computing platform that accompanies people in all their everyday activities, including sports. Mobile phones offer a suitable platform for applications supporting physical workout tracking, analysis and storing. Mobile phones typically fit comfortably into a pocket, and people have developed the habit of taking them along while on the move [18]. This eliminates the need to carry separate devices around while doing sports.

This paper examines the user experience evoked by the sports tracking application integrated in a mobile phone and the related web service. The research questions are:

- How can a mobile application and web service for sports tracking support the users in their outdoor activities – both in personal and social use?
- What are the design issues to be taken into account in the further design of similar systems?

In the following sections we describe the current state-of-the-art in the field of mobile sport applications, introduce the Sports Tracker mobile application and the web service, and present the results of a user study with 28 participants that was arranged to evaluate the application and service concept.

2 Related Work

During last decade, both commercial and research contributions on applications that can be used to support sport activities have emerged. Presented here are a summary of related work and a categorization of application features.

2.1 Current Practices and Beyond

Today, heart rate monitors have become common assistive technology for people during sport and fitness activities. They are used to increase awareness of the healthy training level, user's physical condition as well as calorie consumption and changes in these over time. In addition to information about the user's physical condition, location has become a key input for sport applications. GPS technology enables recording attributes of the route, speed and altitude. GPS and other positioning technologies have been used for location-aware mobile applications for several years now. These are generally used for navigation and route-planning, e.g., Navicore [31] and Route 66 [40]. Nowadays, there are also special services and devices for outdoor sports tracking. Several wrist computers can be used together with GPS receivers to track different aspects about the route. Garmin Forerunner 305 [15], for example, is a device with wrist-watch design meant for tracking speed, distance, heart rate etc. It works with a web portal where the workouts can be downloaded and viewed with various charts, pictures and maps. In addition, the workouts can be shared with other persons on the web portal. Other corresponding wrist computer models for outdoor sports are available, e.g., from Suunto [47] and Polar [39]. More advanced wearable sport products have also been introduced, by e.g., FRWD [14]. Also, applications that utilize the mobile phone as a location-aware platform have emerged, for example

SportsDo [44] that provides both mobile application for tracking and a web service to share the data with a community, and Bones In Motion [6].

In addition to the use of gadgets designed for collecting information of the physical activity, keeping a diary about personal performance is a common practice for many people devoted to their sports training. Typically, personal training logs containing a variety of information of the workout, e.g., date, duration, activity type and some additional notes exist both in paper and electronic format, such as Excel sheets. While the technology offers possibilities to track physical exercises automatically and in detail, several web services offer different kinds of training diaries [24, 30, 39]. There are various different ways to view and analyze the data, e.g., graphs and charts. The portals also support long-term data collection and observing the progress over time.

In addition to commercial products, the research community has introduced novel mobile concepts, e.g., for specific outdoor sports. In [16], Hachet et al. present a 3D mobile navigation assistant at a conceptual level. It is a location-based service meant for hikers, which offers a rendered panorama scene that fits with the real surroundings, and information nodes, e.g., names of mountains. Schöning et al. [42] present conceptual work with location-based services for climbers, which concentrates on navigation, communication, weather forecasts and the climbing community. Counts & Smith [12] have presented a prototype of sport tracking tools very similar with the application used in the study presented here. Consolvo et al. have studied motivational factors towards physical activity in different contexts with mobile phone applications called Houston [9] and UbiFit [11]. The former utilizes step counter information which is used in exercise goal setting and sharing the progress with other users and the latter presents a new visualization for the physical activity, i.e., the flower garden. Similar solution and study as Houston is presented also in [49]. Anderson et al. [1], on the other hand, present an application for tracking physical activity based on the GSM cell signal strengths.

2.2 Categorizing the Current Applications to Support Physical Activity

The features of current applications and solutions that are designed to support physical activity can be roughly categorized to four categories:

- Logger
- Virtual personal trainer
- Gaming and entertainment
- Community and social sharing

Logger is a simple approach for supporting physical exercise. They are able to measure one or several parameters related to the exercise, and store measurement information into logs. Pedometers offer easy to use and inexpensive tools for assessing physical activity. The basic models of the heart rate monitors also act as loggers, as they save the data about the pulse, but do not offer any tools for the analysis or interpretation, or do not give any guidance.

Virtual personal trainer-approach usually includes a logger feature and in addition, analysis functionality. Also, they can provide feedback on the performance. In [7], Buttussi et al. focus on the ability of GPS-enabled mobile devices to offer location-aware feedback. Their solution employs GPS for location information, and PDA is used for viewing maps and the animated, human-figured 3D fitness trainer. The trainer offers real-time feedback about how the user is proceeding during the exercise in graphical and audio format, and gives directions for the navigation and assistance of performing fitness tasks. Another example is presented by Asselin et al [3]. They developed a wearable Personal Wellness Coach to support a variety of activities such as health data collection, interpretation, feedback and self-monitoring. Mobile Coach [28] is a mobile application that assists users by giving training programs based on their current fitness and activity level. It analyzes how effective the workouts are and tunes the training program for the user when his/her schedules change.

Physical gaming and entertainment approach is utilized in many concepts related to physical activity. Mokka et al. [29] present the Virtual Fitness Center, which is a combination of an exercise bicycle, a computer and a large screen. The idea is that the user exercises while exploring new surroundings or playing fitness games in the environment seen on the screen. Physiological inputs have been used in [32] where real-time heart rate information controls an interactive biathlon computer game and in Shadow Boxer [17], a game that is controlled by body movements detected by a web camera. Commercial products that utilize physical gaming are, for instance, the Dance Dance Revolution and the Wii Fit [34]. Music can be used to help exercisers move in the correct way and reach their goals. Oliver & Flores-Mangas [37] present a mobile application that uses music in enabling users to reach their exercise goals more easily by fitting the tempo of the music with the heart rate of the user. A commercial example of combining music player and training is Nike+ IPod Sport Kit [33].

Social sharing of the exercise-related data is an important motivator to do more sports [48]. Encouraging results have been gained with a mobile phone prototype application sharing step count with a community consisting of friends [9, 49] and presenting auditory cues of a friend "jogging over distance" in another geographical location [35]. Bickmore et al. [5] report that even sharing information of physical activity with a PC-based animated conversational agent that acts as an exercise advisor increases the motivation to exercise more.

3   User Study

The goal of the user study was to collect and analyze user experiences evoked by the mobile sports tracking application, and related web service that can be used for sharing the workout data with other people. The focus was on subjective experiences that are dynamic [13] and highly context dependent [4]. The user experience findings can be used for deriving guidelines or design implications that can be used in designing applications that aim supporting sport activities. This chapter explains the technology and applications used in the study, how the participants were selected, and what research methods were used to collect user experience data.

3.1   Background

The mobile application that was used in this study is called Sports Tracker. At the time of the user study, the Sports Tracker mobile application had already been launched one year ago, and quite a few people were using it. The application features were updated in a regular basis during the first year after the launch. The participants for the user study were recruited based on how long they had been users of Sports Tracker, as we wanted to study user perceptions in the different phases of the usage lifecycle. The web service, on the other hand, had been launched only one month prior to the study, so at the time of the user study it was quite a new service for all participants.

3.2 Description of the Sports Tracker Application

Sports Tracker is a mobile application that runs on the Nokia S60 platform phones. The expected benefits of integrating the sports support application with a mobile phone were the following:s

o The platform offers an ultimately accessible way, enabled by the high penetration rate of mobile phones – close to 100% in many industrialized countries [50].
o The use of mobile phones offers a familiar user experience – people are already used to the input and output characteristics of mobile phones and have made it a habit to carry them along [18].
o Mobile phones have inbuilt communication features, i.e., data can be transferred between devices and shared with other people.
o Mobile phones offer additional, device-integrated applications which are sometimes considered useful when doing physical exercises or outdoors sports, e.g., a music player and a camera.

The main features of the application are the following:

o The application corresponds to people's *need for recording* personal exercise data.
o The application *provides feedback* to the users to support them in monitoring progress [7].
o The application provides an *engaging user experience* to motivate people to continue using the application. This can be created by offering gaming type features, e.g., beating your own records.
o The application *supports in sharing* personal exercise related data with others.

Technology. Sports Tracker is a GPS based activity tracking application which runs on Nokia S60 3.x mobile phones. Data measured by the application includes location, horizontal speed over ground as well as course over ground, altitude and exact time.

The application can broadcast live measurement data over a 2G or 3G data connection to the back-end server using ordinary IP traffic. Real time connection to a web server enables features like real time location sharing with other users by showing the user's positions on a dedicated web page. In several tests, it has been found that the latency is in the order of one second when live tracking is in use and location data is transferred from the measuring terminal to viewers via the web server. The live connection to network can also be used the other way around – the application can be updated over the air, for example, to provide new features.

User interface and features. The mobile application can be used for tracking, browsing, viewing, storing and comparing user's personal exercises in outdoor sports. It collects information such as the route, speed, pace, distance, time and altitude. The information is saved in a training diary and can be viewed in a variety of ways during the exercise and afterwards. The Sports Tracker application is available for downloading at [45].

Tracking is started by selecting 'New workout' on the main view. Users can then select the type of the exercise and make other settings, such as activate 'Auto lap-feature' or a previously saved route for comparison. After activation, the application informs about the GPS state. As the user starts tracking, the default view of the application shows the pace, distance and time of the ongoing workout (see Figure 1). The default view also shows a small map. User can scroll between different views both during and after the workout, for example between a full screen map, several graphical views (Figure 1) and views showing numerical data about the workout.

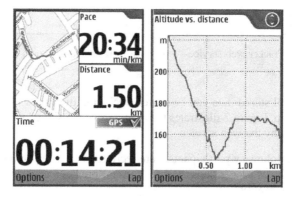

Fig. 1. Two examples of views during the workout: 1) a map and numeric information of the current workout and 2) a graph of the change of altitude vs. distance

The workouts are saved in a training diary, which can be opened on the main view of the application. The training diary offers a standard calendar monthly view where the workouts are indicated with colored squares. The different workouts of the same day appear in different colors. After selecting a workout, the user sees the workout summary as a default view and he/she is able to switch between similar screens as during the workout. Users can also view different kinds of workout summaries, i.e., per week, month, year and in total. In addition, users can to save workout routes, rename them and use them later for comparison while doing same exercises if they want to see their progress over time.

Configuration possibilities include, e.g., adding new sports types, switching between miles and metric system, selection of the map material source (no map, phone's default maps, maps downloaded from network), selection between street and satellite maps, and enabling a possibly built-in accelerometer for the step counting.

In the web portal [46], users can monitor and share their personal workout data with others after joining and logging in to the service. Uploading the data from the phone to the web can be done either in real time with 'live sharing' functionality or after the exercise with 'upload to service' feature. The user can define information to be publicly visible for all registered users, own pre-defined community or visible only

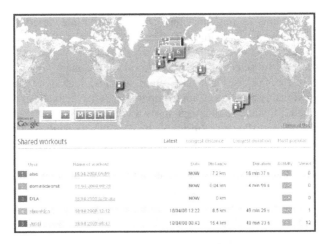

Fig. 2. The Sports Tracker web service - a page showing shared workouts of different persons on the map and list

for him/herself. All stored data can be shared, including the user's location and exercise route on a map. Figure 2 illustrates the overview of the shared workouts on a map interface provided by the web service.

Participants. 28 voluntary participants were recruited to participate in the study. We focused on 3 different user groups, based on users' previous experience in using the Sports Tracker application:

- Group 1: nine participants had used the application for less than one month. We call them *'Novice users'*. Their user experiences reflect the initial use of the application.
- Group 2: eight participants had used the application for between 1-6 months. They are called *'Experienced users'*. Their user experiences reflect relatively short-term use of the application.
- Group 3: 11 participants had used the application for more than six months. We call them *'Veteran users'*. Their user experiences reflect long-term use of the application.

The participants used the Sports Tracker application in the mobile phone they used daily, so it was easily available for them. All participants had daily access to internet as well. All participants were already Sports Tracker users, i.e., they had made the decision to start using the application independently from the study.

The participants were experienced mobile phone users. The age distribution of the participants was as follows: 21-30 years 30%; 31-40 years 50%; 41-50 years 20%. Participants were from all over the world, i.e., Scandinavia (43%), rest of the Europe (40%), North America (7%) and Asia (10%). 15% of them were females. Most of the participants had a technical background. All participants reported doing sports activities in their leisure time. Their average frequency of doing physical workouts was 4 times per week. 68% of them used heart rate monitors and 75% had previous experience in GPS devices.

Method. The study was arranged in field settings, where 28 participants used the Sports Tracker mobile application and the related web service. The goal was to disturb the usage patterns as little as possible, because altering the usage situation has effects on the user experience. Of course, this is impossible to achieve perfectly as there is strong evidence that mere knowledge of being studied affects user behavior and related user experience [26].

The participants were already users of the application, so they used the application with their own mobile phone, and they could continue using the application also after the study period. The hypothesis was that as the application is highly context dependent and is used as a tool that is highly intertwined and integrated into the everyday life of its user, collecting information from field settings can reveal experiences that cannot be explored in controlled or laboratory settings [10].

The data collection methods aimed at collecting user experience data about recent experiences [19] during the experiment to avoid recall problems. User experience data was collected by utilizing two methods: semi-structured interviews and text-message (SMS) questions. The data collection methods did not require the users to carry additional data collection instruments with them, and were designed to not to disturb the actual use.

Here, we explored only the subjective user experience expressed by the participants, i.e., we analyzed how the application was perceived by the participants directly. Application or server logs were not available at the time of the study.

Semi-structured interviews were conducted by phone, as the participants attending the study were located all over the world. The interviews focused on the following issues, including the mobile application and the service:

- In which sports activities is the application used and how well does it fit for them?
- The estimated frequency of use.
- What things on the Sports Tracker are liked most? Which features are used most actively? Why?
- What things on the Sports Tracker are disliked? Why?
- Motivational issues for the use of the Sports Tracker.
- Feedback for the future development.

Text-message based questionnaire inspired by Experience sampling method (ESM) [20] was used to collect user experience data over a period of two weeks. The questions were sent to the participants as text messages (SMS). The number of SMS questions sent was 8-10 depending on what participants replied to two questions; i.e., in certain cases they received an additional question. Following are some examples of the issues that the SMS questions focused on:

- Considered order of importance of the features.
- Usage of 'live sharing' feature.
- Usage of 'upload to service' feature.
- Most actively used features.
- Frequency of use for both the mobile application and the web service.
- Ideas for additional features.

Two questions were qualitative, and free text responses were expected. Others had 3 to 6 predefined choices, and the user only had to select one to answer. The response rate for the qualitative SMS-questions was 73%. For the multi-choice or quantitative questions it was even higher (89%).

The collected data was analyzed by the research group using content analysis methods.

4   Results

The findings related to usage habits and analysis of usage for personal versus social purposes is discussed here. To conclude, feedback for the future development of similar systems is given. All findings are based on the evaluation of the subjective user experience, e.g., application logs or other direct measurements of use were not used in this analysis.

4.1   General Usage Habits and Motivation

In order to understand the common use cases of the application and web service, data about typical use situations, their frequency and the most used features was gathered. Being designed for outdoor activities, the results reflect the common exercise forms there. The mobile application was clearly most used with biking by 80% of the participants. The second and third most popular sport activities were running (60%) and walking (40%), followed by hiking and skiing (both 15 %).

The SMS question *"During the last 7 days, how many times did you use the Sports Tracker A) mobile application and B) the web service* revealed that during that week (beginning of August 2007) the average weekly frequency for the mobile application was 3.3 times (Novices 2.9, Experienced 3.6, Veterans 3.3.), which is quite close to the initial estimation of the users about their average weekly exercise frequency, i.e., four times per week. For the web service the usage frequency was 1.5 times during that week (Novices 1.9, Experienced 1.9, Veterans 0.7). This indicates that they used the mobile application almost every time they were exercising but the web portal less frequently.

Half of the participants stated that they used the mobile application as a data logger during the exercise and viewed the results only after the workout. The most valued parameters of the exercise were the route, distance, speed, duration and altitude. 40% of the participants used the application both during and after the workout and 10% used it mostly during the exercise to check different aspects about the workout, especially the distance covered so far, speed, duration, altitude, lap time and location on map. The ability to get additional data to complement the information provided by the conventional equipment was valued:

"The altitude is quite interesting because it's not so easy to get the same information from map. On the map you can see where you are but not how high the place is."
(Male, 41-50, Japan)

There were basically three different positions where the participants kept the mobile phone during the workout: pocket, hand or backpack. Some of them had also built holders so that they could attach the phone to the bike. Some participants commented that Nokia N95, which at the time of the study was one of the rare models with integrated GPS, was too big and heavy to be carried along while running, because of the small pockets sizes of running pants. On the other hand, those participants who used a relatively small S60 mobile phone, e.g., Nokia 5500, commented that it was convenient to keep it along during the workout - it fit in the pockets of running pants and could even be kept in hand.

Participants seemed to be motivated to use the mobile application. In the interview, the participants were asked about their current perceived degree of motivation to use the application in a scale 0-10, where 0 referred to 'no motivation' and 10 'very high motivation'. The average degree of motivation for all participants was 8.3 and it was quite consistent between the groups - Novices 8.1; Experienced 8.3; and Veterans 8.6. The same parameters for the web service were 6.6 (whole sample) - 6.6. (Novices), 6.3 (Experienced) and 6.8 (Veterans). This indicates a higher perceived usage motivation for the mobile application than for the web service. All users stated that they would continue the usage of the Sports Tracker after the user study.

4.2 Personal vs. Social Use

This section presents the findings related to how the participants perceived the two different modes of use 1) using the application solely for *personal purposes*, e.g., tracking and viewing own exercises, and on the other hand 2) using the features supporting *social aspects*, e.g., sharing data with other users. The results indicate that, in general, for this sample of participants, the personal use seemed to be prevailing and more valuable.

Table 1 presents the three most common combinations of answers to the SMS question: *"What is the order of importance of the following features in Sports Tracker to you?"* (Options: A: Follow up on your own workouts, B: Share your workouts, C: View other users' workouts). The most important aspect of the system for the participants clearly was following up on their own workouts (option A). This is well illustrated by the fact that all three most common combinations start with option A, and the third most common combination was to select *only* option A. In fact, only two users rated some other feature more important over option A. For most Novices, viewing others' workouts was the second most important and sharing their own workouts was the least important aspect. For the Experienced and Veteran users, sharing their own workouts was the second most important and viewing others' was the least important.

Table 1. The distribution of answers to the question: " What is the order of importance of the following features in Sports Tracker to you?", n=25

	ABC (follow up own, share own, view others')	ACB (follow up own, view others, share own)	A only (follow up own)
Novices	1	5	1
Experienced	5	1	1
Veterans	5	3	3

Personal use. The automatic tracking and logging of own exercises seemed to be, simply enough, the main motive to use the application. Some of the participants commented that they would keep track of their exercises anyway, so the application on the mobile phone just offered an effortless way to do it. For some participants the mobile application replaced their former tracking techniques, such as noting down on paper, in Excel spreadsheets or bike speedometer. It was emphasized by the participants that the mobile phone was a natural device for workout tracking because in most cases the phone was carried along anyway when doing outdoor sports - for example for emergency purposes - so it did not cause an extra burden to have the device along. The participants also emphasized the benefit that only little action was required from the user while using the application. The application was considered quite easy to use. However, the Novices reported more usability problems than the other groups, for example related to the start-up of GPS and the terminology.

The training diary feature was valued highly by the participants. They considered it very important to get the exercises saved in the diary. The diary was used to check later what exercises they had done and where they had done them. Also, a possibility for creating mementos with the application was mentioned. Doing sports played an important role in the lives of the users, and many users sought unique experiences by exercising. For example, when taking part in an once-in-a-lifetime hiking trip, the trip could be saved to be recalled later on: *"Tracking hiking trips is like photos and videos – a way to remember an experience." (Male, 31-40 years, Singapore)*

The possibility to compare (own) previous and current workouts was considered an important aspect. Participants liked to challenge themselves with their previous workouts on the same route and see if they were faster or slower, and break their own records. The Veteran users seemed to value more than the other user groups the possibility to do trend analysis by comparing their own data with the personal history data. Also, they used the personal history data for setting goals for personal development: *"I can challenge myself with my previous workouts, to see if I'm faster or slower." (Male, 41-50 years, Denmark)*

Social use. With an SMS question the participants were asked about *the use of 'Live sharing' function*, i.e., the possibility to share the exercise-related data in real time (options and the counts among all participants: A: never tried – seven users, B: tried once or twice but not using actively – six users, C: using occasionally – 10 users, D: using frequently – two users, E: do not know what it does – no-one). A relatively high number of users had not tried this function at all. Most of them had tried it but were not using it frequently. The interviews revealed that quite a few participants had a negative attitude towards 'Live sharing'. They were suspicious why anyone would be interested in following their workout, because they could not imagine who would like to see, for example, where they are running at the moment. And if there was no one to view this information, they saw no value using the feature. On the other hand, a couple of users saw possible value in 'Live sharing' in emergency situations: *"If I got lost in the forest and was sharing the route with a trusted person, he could save me." (Female, 21-30 years, Finland)*

The participants were also asked about *the use of 'Upload to service' function*, i.e., the possibility of transferring the exercise data to the web service (Options and the counts among all participants: A: never tried – three users, B: tried once or twice but

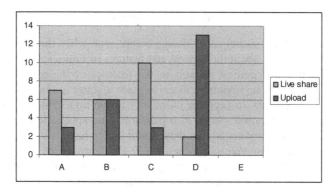

Fig. 3. The distribution of answers to the questions: "Your use of 'Live sharing' function in Sports Tracker" (n=25) and "Your use of 'Upload to service' function in Sports Tracker" (n=25). The options: A) never tried, B) tried once or twice but not using actively, C) using occasionally, D) using frequently, E) do not know what it does.

not using actively – six users, C: using occasionally – three users, D: using frequently – 13 users, E: do not know what it does – no-one). Half of participants stated that they frequently uploaded their data to the web service. They commented that it was nice to be able to look at their routes and maps on the bigger screen and also share the routes with other persons. Figure 3 presents the distribution of answers to the questions about the use of 'Live sharing' and 'Upload to service'. The 'Upload to service' seems to be more popular among the participants than 'Live sharing' feature.

The participants seem to be divided into two groups based on their opinions about the social use: 1) *those that do not see any value in sharing their exercises* and 2) *those who consider the social aspect as a motivating factor.* The first group of users seemed to feel that the exercise related data is private, and did not see value in sharing it. These participants did not obviously use the sharing functionalities of the application. Some participants also considered sharing as a security risk. On the other hand, those who considered the social aspect as a motivating and interesting issue, stated several reasons for sharing their workouts. First, sharing own data with familiar persons and viewing their data can be seen to be an additional new way for keeping in touch with friends and other people the users already knew and maintaining social networks. Also, competing against others was mentioned several times. Second, some users found it interesting to see if anyone had been exercising in the same area or even taken the same routes. Third, the users mentioned situations when they had travelled to an unfamiliar place and in those cases it was useful to be able to look at where people have been exercising there, and plan their own routes accordingly (supporting findings in [12]).

An important aspect of the social use was that a *large enough community of familiar persons* was needed before that could act as a motivating factor. Most users found it interesting to follow the exercises of other people only if they already knew the persons they were following. The participants were not, in general, interested in viewing workout data of strangers. However, many users found it interesting to see routes of other people (including strangers) in the areas they were doing sport themselves, or in new areas they were planning to visit.

4.3 Participant Feedback for Future Development

The interview included a participatory design component, when the participants were asked to brainstorm ideas about the aspects and features of future sports applications.

The participants liked getting updates to the features of the mobile application. They stated that it would be important to *get regular updates to the content*, i.e., new features and improvements, to keep the usage motivation high. This is possible when taking into account the mobile phone as a platform - the application can be updated over the air. They also commented that they would like to have *better possibilities for personalizing the sports application to better suit their own sports activities*. Not all of the currently available data was necessary in all sports activities, and on the other hand, in some sports activities even more information would be beneficial. For example, using the application for tracking regular running activities differs a lot from tracking a hiking trip - different features and views are needed in these activities.

Automatic acquiring of data from different sensors, e.g., heart rate monitors and biking meters was requested by several participants. That would allow all the data related to the exercise to end up being analyzed and stored in one application. During the development of the Sports Tracker, the usage of the sensors was demonstrated. These sensors included heart rate to give additional useful information during sports exercises.

Users who did *indoor sports* in addition to outdoor exercise wished that they could also track these with the same application and device.

5 Discussion

The user experiences revealed several factors that indicate that combining the sport tracking application with a mobile phone has its benefits. Especially, the following issues were mentioned by several participants:

- Mobile phone is carried along anyway when doing sports. Combining sports tracking application with a mobile phone removed stress as users did not need to remember to take extra equipment with them when doing sports, provided an easy-to-access storage space for the exercise related data, and lessened difficulties in finding suitable places to store multiple devices while doing sports.
- In-built communication features make uploading data and updating the features of the application easy and transparent. Several participants stated that new features raised motivation to do exercise for a short period of time. Therefore, the possibility to update the product features was valued.

Only the largish size of certain phone models was seen as a barrier for tracking sports with a mobile phone.

Users valued the data that was stored about the workout, e.g., route, distance and length. Many of them had recorded similar information manually and had used other technical solutions prior the use of the application. The application saved their time and effort in automating tasks related to storing exercise related data, and provided better means for analyzing and visualizing the information. In addition, amount of details and the quality of the saved information were considered better than manual recording, and the phone was considered an easy-to-access integrated storage space for exercise related data.

Using the Sports Tracker for personal use, i.e., tracking and logging own exercises to be viewed during and after the workout, and comparing with their own previous workouts was the primary use case and clearly the most valued feature of the application. The following benefits were observed:

- The application created new opportunities by providing detailed, concrete data, that was used to support the users to make new kinds of concrete goals (such as real time comparison of lap times) that help them attain more abstract goals related to doing sports, and raise motivation by introducing new ways for monitoring exercised and progress (e.g., monitoring data about altitude).
- Reliable and relevant data about exercise can help the users to make performance corrections in time, or it can provide the user the feeling of being in control. Both increase the feeling of satisfaction during and towards exercise. More reliable and detailed cues on the progress can increase the possibilities of success in pursuing goals, as in goal-oriented actions, humans automatically monitor, appraise and evaluate goal-relevant external and internal cues for evaluating progress [27] and correct performance to meet their goals [8].

The users were clearly divided into two groups according to their attitudes towards the social features of the application – the first group of users thought that they only exercise for themselves and would not like to anyone else to see the exercise related data. Their attitude towards the social features was rather indifferent; they saw no value in sharing exercise data with anyone. However, the other group considered the social use, i.e., sharing and viewing other users' exercises valuable, and thought that social sharing could motivate them in exercising. The most valued social features (by the latter group) were: 1) sharing data with familiar persons, 2) viewing if anyone has been exercising nearby and what kinds of routes he/she has taken, 3) viewing what kinds of routes people have taken in unfamiliar areas and planning own routes based on this information. For the first case, a large enough community consisting of familiar persons was needed. This finding is in line with other studies, such as [9] and [49] who studied the motivating aspects of the friend groups attending physical activity.

Generalizations about the findings related to the perceived value of social features of the sports tracking solution should be made cautiously. At the time of the study, the web service for social sharing had been launched only one month ago, while the mobile application had been available for a year. Being more accustomed to using the mobile application for personal purposes, rather than the social features, might have affected the user perceptions of personal vs. social aspects. However, the perceived value of the web service did not differ significantly between the novice and more experienced users, even though for novice users the service had been available from the beginning of their Sports Tracker usage time. More research is needed to study the personal and social aspects with different user groups, e.g., those who are not active in doing sports, as they might seek for group support in pursuing their goals for being more active.

Our results have raised design considerations that can be exploited by designers and researchers who are exploring the design space of mobile applications that support people in doing sports. To summarize, our findings indicate that the most valuable features and support functionalities that should be addressed by a sports tracking application are the following: 1) supporting personal use, e.g., by offering a comprehensive training diary feature and possibilities to compare the ongoing exercise with the previously recorded ones, 2) supporting the social use by enabling community building especially with familiar persons, 3) offering content and feature updates for the software to keep the usage motivation high and 4) supporting proper customization possibilities for the application, as different sport activities require different data sets and views.

6 Summary and Future Work

This paper presents findings on the use of mobile application integrated with a web service that can be used to support exercising outdoors. The application can be used as a personal tool, or it can be additionally used for sharing exercise related data with others. The findings indicate that a mobile application can both replace and enhance existing practices related to exercising (such as keeping an exercise diary) and provide new features that can support and provide sources of motivation for the end user (such as planning tracks).

As a future work, the authors are planning to conduct more research on the domain of sports applications. A more controlled setup will be arranged with a more versatile user group to study the aspects related to personal and social use of sport applications. Ongoing and future work will include, for example, exploring the use of sport applications in different cultures, and exploring the features that can contribute towards motivating users for being more active in sports.

Acknowledgments

The authors would like to thank the developers of the Sports Tracker application, who provided us with information and details about technical implementation issues, and all anonymous Sports Tracker users who invested their valuable time and effort as they shared their experiences and insights related to the application with us.

References

1. Anderson, I., Maitland, J., Sherwood, S., Barkhuus, L., Chalmers, M., Hall, M., Brown, B., Muller, H.: Shakra: Tracking and Sharing Daily Activity Levels with Unaugmented Mobile Phones. Mobile Netw. Appl. 12, 185–199 (2007)
2. Annesi, J.J.: Effects of Computer Feedback on Adherence to Exercise. Perceptual and Motor Skills 87(2), 723–730 (1998)
3. Asselin, R., Ortiz, G., Pui, J., Smailagic, A., Kissling, C.: Implementation and Evaluation of the Personal Wellness Coach. In: Proceedings of the 25th IEEE International Conference on Distributed Computing Systems Workshops, pp. 529–535 (2005)
4. Battarbee, K.: Co-experience. Understanding user experiences in interaction. PhD Thesis. University of Art and Design Helsinki (2004)
5. Bickmore, T.W., Caruso, L., Clough-Gorr, K.: Acceptance and Usability of a Relational Agent Interface by Urban older Adults. In: Extended abstracts of the Conference on Human Factors in Computing Systems, pp. 1212–1215 (2005)

6. Bones In Motion, http://bonesinmotion.com
7. Buttussi, F., Chittaro, L., Nadalutti, D.: Bringing Mobile Guides and Fitness Activities Together: A Solution based on an embodied virtual trainer. In: Proceedings of the 8th conference on Human-computer interaction with mobile devices and services, pp. 29–36 (2006)
8. Carver, C., Scheier, M.: Feedback Processes in the Simultaneous Regulation of Action and Affect. In: Handbook of Motivation Science, pp. 308–324. The Guilford Press, New York (2008)
9. Consolvo, S., Everitt, K., Smith, I., Landay, J.A.: Design Requirements for Technologies that Encourage Physical Activity. In: Proceedings of the Conference on Human Factors in Computing Systems, pp. 457–466 (2006)
10. Consolvo, S., Harrison, B., Smith, I., Chen, M., Everitt, K., Froehlich, J., Landay, J.: Conducting In Situ Evaluations for and With Ubiquitous Computing Technologies. International Journal of Human-Computer Interaction 22(1&2), 103–118 (2007)
11. Consolvo, S., McDonald, D.W., Toscos, T., Chen, M.Y., Froehlich, J., Harrison, B., Klasnja, P., LaMarca, A., LeGrand, L., Libby, R., Smith, I., Landay, J.A.: Activity Sensing in the Wild: A Field Trial of UbiFit Garden. In: Proceedings of the Conference on Human Factors in Computing Systems, pp. 1797–1806 (2008)
12. Counts, S., Smith, M.: Where Were We: Communities For Sharing Space-Time Trails. In: Proceedings of the 15th annual ACM international symposium on Advances in Geographic Information Systems (2007)
13. Forlizzi, J., Ford, S.: The building blocks of experience: an early framework for interaction designers. In: Proceedings of the 3rd conference on Designing interactive systems: processes, practises, methods, and techniques, pp. 419–423 (2000)
14. Frwd, http://www.frwd.fi
15. Garmin, http://www.garmin.com
16. Hachet, M., Pouderoux, J., Knödel, S., Guitton, P.: 3D Panorama Service on Mobile Device for Hiking. In: Extended abstracts of the Conference on Human Factors in Computing System (2007)
17. Höysniemi, J., Aula, A., Auvinen, P., Hännikäinen, J., Hämäläinen, P.: Shadow Boxer – A Physically Interactive Fitness Game. In: Proceedings of NordiCHI 2004, pp. 389–392 (2004)
18. Ichikawa, F., Chipchase, J., Grignani, R.: Where's the phone? A study of Mobile Phone Location in Public Spaces. In: Proceedings of The International Conferences on Mobile Technology, Applications and Systems (2005)
19. Kahneman, D., Krueger, A., Schkade, D., Schwarz, N., Stone, A.: A Survey Method for Characterizing Daily Life Experience: The Day Reconstruction Method. Science 306(5702), 1776–1780 (2004)
20. Larson, R., Csikszentmihalyi, M.: The experience sampling method. New Directions for Methodology of Social and Behavioral Science 15, 41–56 (1983)
21. Laverie, D.A.: Motivations for Ongoing participation in Fitness Activity. Leisure Sciences 20, 277–302 (1998)
22. Leslie, E., Owen, N., Salmon, J., Bauman, A., Sallis, J., Lo, S.K.: Insufficiently Active Australian College Students: Perceived Personal, Social, and Environmental influences. Preventive Medicine 28, 20–27 (1999)
23. Locke, E.A., Latham, G.P.: The Application of Goal Setting to Sports. Journal of Sport & Exercise Psychology 7(3), 205–222 (1985)
24. Map My Run, http://www.mapmyrun.com/

25. Martin, J.E., Dubbert, P.M., Katell, A.D., Thompson, J.K., Raczynski, J.R., Lake, M., Smith, P.O., Webster, J.S., Sikora, T., Cohen, R.E.: Behavioral Control of Exercise in Sedentary Adults: Studies 1 Through 6. Journal of Consulting and Clinical Psychology 52(5), 795–811 (1984)
26. Morwitz, V., Johnson, E., Schmittlein, D.: Does measuring intent change behavior. Journal of consumer research 20(1), 453–469 (1993)
27. Mikulincer, M., Shaver, P.: Contributions of Attachment Theory and Research to Motivation Science. In: Handbook of Motivation Science, pp. 201–216. The Guilford Press, New York (2008)
28. Mobile Coach, http://www.firstbeattechnologies.com
29. Mokka, S., Väätänen, A., Heinilä, J., Välkkynen, P.: Fitness Computer Game with a Bodily User Interface. In: Proceedings of the second international conference on Entertainment computing (2003)
30. Motion Based, http://www.motionbased.com/
31. Navicore, http://www.navicoretech.com
32. Nenonen, V., Lindblad, A., Häkkinen, V., Laitinen, T., Jouhtio, M., Hämäläinen, P.: Using Heart Rate to Control an Interactive Game. In: Proceedings of the Conference on Human Factors in Computing Systems, pp. 853–856 (2007)
33. Nike, http://www.nike.com
34. Nintendo, http://www.nintendo.com
35. O´Brien, S., Mueller, F.: Jogging the Distance. In: Proceedings of the Conference on Human Factors in Computing Systems, pp. 523–526 (2007)
36. Ojala, K.: Validity of Two Electronic Pedometers for Assessment of Number of Steps and Distance. Publications of UKK Institute, Finland (2004)
37. Oliver, N., Flores-Mangas, F.: MPTrain: A Mobile, Music and Physiology-Based Personal Trainer. In: Proceedings of the 8th conference on Human-computer interaction with mobile devices and services, pp. 21–28 (2006)
38. Paschali, A.A., Goodrick, G.K., Anastasia, K., Papadatou, D.: Accelerometer Feedback to Promote Physical Activity in Adults with Type 2 Diabetes: A Pilot Study. Perceptual and Motor Skills 100, 61–68 (2005)
39. Polar electro, http://www.polar.fi
40. Route 66, http://www.66.com/route66/
41. Schlenk, E.A., Dunbar-Jacob, J., Sereika, S., Starz, T., Okifuji, A., Turk, D.: Comparability of daily diaries and accelerometers in exercise adherence in fibromyalgia syndrome. Measurement in Physical Education & Exercise Science 4(2), 133–134 (2000)
42. Schöning, J., Panov, I., Kessler, C.: No vertical limit – Conceptual LBS design for climbers. In: Extended abstracts of the Conference on Human Factors in Computing Systems (2007)
43. Speck, B.J., Looney, S.W.: Effects of a Minimal Intervention to Increase Physical Activity in women: Daily Activity Records. Nursing Research 50(6), 374–378 (2001)
44. SportsDo, http://www.sportsdo.net
45. Sports Tracker,
46. http://research.nokia.com/research/projects/SportsTracker
47. Sports Tracker beta web service,
    http://sportstracker.nokia.com/nts/main/index.do
48. Suunto, http://www.suunto.com

49. Ståhl, T., Rütten, A., Nutbeam, D., Bauman, A., Kannas, L., Abel, T., Lüschen, G., Rodriquez, D., Vinck, J., van der Zee, J.: The importance of the social environment for physically active lifestyle – results from an international study. Social Science and Medicine 52, 1–10 (2001)

50. Toscos, T., Faber, A., Connelly, K., Upoma, A.M.: Encouraging Physical Activity in Teens – Can technology help reduce barriers to physical activity in adolescent girls? In: Proceedings of the 3rd International Conference on Pervasive Computing Technologies for Healthcare (2008)

51. Wikipedia, http://en.wikipedia.org/wiki/Mobile_phone

Rich Tactile Output on Mobile Devices

Alireza Sahami[1], Paul Holleis[1], Albrecht Schmidt[1], and Jonna Häkkilä[2]

[1] Pervasive Computing Group, University of Duisburg Essen,
Schuetzenbahn 70, 45117, Essen, Germany
[2] Nokia Research Center, Yrttipellontie 1, 90230, Oulu, Finland
{Alireza.Sahami,Paul.Holleis,Albrecht.Schmidt}@uni-due.de,
Jonna.Hakkila@nokia.com

Abstract. In this paper we assess the potential of rich tactile notifications on mobile phones. Many mobile phone users use vibration output for various types of notification on their phone. Currently, tactile output in phones is limited to one single actuator that can potentially present patterns based on different vibration intensity over time. To explore the possible design space, we conducted experiments with up to 6 actuators included in a phone prototype to find out about the user experience that can be created with multi-vibration output in a handheld device. The dimensions of the resulting design space are comprised of the location of the active actuators, the intensity of the vibration, and the variation of these parameters over time. Based on several user studies and interviews, we suggest design guidelines for rich tactile output facilitated by several distinct actuators. We show where vibration motors should optimally be placed and that different information can be reliably communicated by producing different patterns of vibration output using a small number of actuators.

1 Introduction

For mobile phones, notification is of great interest as many functionalities of a phone are triggered externally and require the attention of the user. Audio notification is the most commonly-used form of notification; however it is not suitable in many contexts as it may disturb others or may be inaudible due to environmental noise.

As audio engineering on mobile phones has become more and more sophisticated, using ringtones have become a popular way to personalize one's cell phone and therefore became a standard feature offered by cell phone providers. According to M:Metric[1], who measures the consumption of mobile content and applications, the number of users who say they made their own ringtone grew from 11.3 percent in May to 12.3 in November 2006 in Germany, from 10.2 to 12.6 percent in France, from 17.1 percent to 19.1 percent in the UK, and from 5.1 percent in to 6.6 percent in the U.S. Another standard feature of recent mobile phones is the option to configure different ringtones as event notification (e.g. incoming call, SMS, and alarm). With

---

[1] http://www.mmetrics.com/press/PressRelease.aspx?article=20070110-ringbacks (accessed July 2008)

E. Aarts et al. (Eds.): AmI 2008, LNCS 5355, pp. 210–221, 2008.

incoming calls, ringtones can even reveal a caller's ID by using different ringtones for individuals or contact groups.

In contrast, the means of personalization with tactile output is still very limited and not commonly used. Tactile output is used as a means of discreet notification and offers an alternative to audio output. Tactile or cutaneous sense is defined as a combination of various sensations evoked by stimulating the skin [14]. In combination with kinesthesia, tactile feedback is often referred to as haptic [19] and is crucial for us to interact with our physical environment. The vibration stimulus is an unobtrusive way to find out about incoming calls, messages, or reminders without disturbing others. Vibration pulses are a widely-used output mechanism in current phones and a common part of the phone interface.

Haptic interaction offers many potential benefits for the users of mobile devices, as these devices are designed to be carried or worn by users wherever they go. This may include noisy and busy environments where users have to multiplex their visual, auditory, and cognitive attention between the environment and the information device [1]. In such cases, haptic interaction offers another channel. Due to nature of tactile reception, it is a private medium that provides for unobtrusive modality for interaction. So by redirecting some of the information processing from the visual channel to touch, we can take advantage of this ability to reduce the cognitive load and make it easier to operate mobile devices. Skin is the largest human sensory organ ($\sim 1.8 m^2$) and with the exception of water and heat regulation, most of it is unused [14]. Since touch receptors can be found all over the body, it is usually possible to find a suitable location to provide a haptic stimulus without environmental interference [2].

2   Design Space for Multitactile Output

Skin sensation is essential for many manipulation and exploration tasks. To handle flexible materials like fabric and paper, we sense the pressure variation across the fingertip. In precision manipulation, perception of skin indentation reveals the relationship between the hand and the grasped tool. We perceive surface texture through the vibrations generated by stroking a finger over the surface.

Geldard et al. [15] in 1956 developed a vibrotactile language called *Vibratese* to transmit single letters and digits as well as the most common English words and demonstrated that trained subjects were able to receive a complex message up to 38 words per minute. This showed that with proper encoding, messages could be transmitted through the skin. We can take advantage of this while designing mobile interfaces. The message, however, does not necessarily need to be symbolic: touch has a strong emotional impact. Running a finger into a splinter, touching a cat's fur, or immersing into some unknown sticky substance all bring intense, though very different, emotional responses. Hence, touch is a very strong "break-in" sense: cutaneous sensations are highly attention demanding especially if they are used in unusual patterns [16]. Tactile feedback provides superior temporary discrimination, e.g. when rapidly successive data needs to be resolved, the feel of touch is about five times faster than vision [17]. Hence, it allows for precise and fast motor control: When we roll a pencil in our fingers, we can quickly and precisely readjust the 3D positions and grasping forces of our fingers by relying entirely on touch [18].

Particularly, mobile phones typically are still not aware of the contexts in which they are being used. Many cell phones support profiles that allow the user to manually set an appropriate response for different context, however the user should remember to set the correct profile. So providing vibration (silent) feedback and output is needed in mobile phones. There are many possibilities for tactile feedback in mobile interfaces. Here, we are particularly interested in a small subset of this design space: using touch as the ambient, background channel of output and feedback. In a mobile setting the user's attention is not fixed on the device, but on real-world tasks.

To understand the current use of audio and vibration feedback with mobile phones, we surveyed 30 people about their personal use of each type of notification. Our surveys consisted of 13 females, 17 males, 21 to 42 years in age with an average age of 26. We found that 80% use vibration as a form of notification for incoming call (as silent mode). However, a great majority of the users used the preset vibration output. Furthermore, 70% of the participants were not aware that their own phone model supported the use of different vibration alerts for different events such as incoming calls, receiving SMS or MMS, and low battery.

Vibration alerts found in mobile phones are generated based on a vibration actuator made of a small motor with an eccentric weight on its shaft. The rotation of the motor then generates the vibration stimuli. The control signal can switch the motor on and off; and in some cases; it is possible to control the intensity of the vibration by controlling the speed of the motor (typically using pulse-width modulation). Thus, using different pulse intensities and timings with a single motor, as present in many current phone models, seems to either leave little impression on users or is processed subconsciously.

The idea in this research was to integrate more than a single vibration motor in a mobile phone and to find out if multi-tactile output/feedback is achievable and can be used to enhance the interaction between users and the device. As previous research showed that providing tactile feedback and output increased the performance of interaction (see the next section), our hypothesis is that multi-tactile feedback in different locations on a mobile phone is feasible for users. Having more than a single motor for generating the vibration alert helps us to have stimulus all over the surface on the phone (of course it depends on how the motors are integrated in the mobile phone), and provide multi-tactile output and feedback as well as different vibration patterns. Based on how many motors are used, different patterns can be defined and each one can be associated to a special feedback, output, or event.

Looking conceptually at tactile output we can discriminate 3 distinct dimensions that describe the basic design space:

- Temporal change in the vibro-tactile output signals
- Spatial arrangement of vibro-tactile output elements
- Qualitative sensation created by an output element

To create rich tactile output, those dimensions are combined. In Fig. 1 this is explained for temporal and spatial aspects.

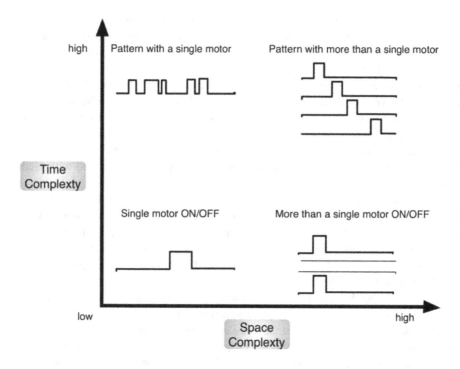

Fig. 1. Time-Space complexity to generate vibration stimuli. By increasing the number of the motors, the space complexity is increased too. Also providing vibration patterns has a higher time complexity than simple vibration output.

With a larger number of motors it is obvious that the space complexity is increased. However the overall number of motors is limited by the physical properties of the device and the ability of the user to discriminate different vibrating locations. On the other hand, the time complexity of a single motor setup is limited by the switching frequency that is feasible (with regard to the device capabilities and the user's ability to recognize it). Having a larger number of motors and generating a distributed vibration pattern has the highest complexity in terms of time and space (Fig. 1).

To explore the design options in detail, a series of experiments were conducted. We created a prototype with multiple vibration actuators in the form factor of a current mobile phone matching dimensions as well as weight and report on two studies. In our work, we investigate ways to increase the options for tactile output to provide a richer and more personalized user experience.

3 Related Work

If we look at previous research, it is widely recognized that haptic interaction offers another channel to provide output to users as they may be in a context where they have to multiplex their cognitive attention between the device and context, and that performance can be improved in interactions with mobile phones and handhelds.

Brewster *et al.* [4] investigated the use of vibrotactile feedback for touch screen keyboards on PDAs to simulate the physical button presses. They found out that with tactile feedback users made fewer errors, and corrected more of the errors they made. They also designed a tactile progress bar indicating the progress of a download and found out that users performed better with tactile progress bars than standard visual ones [4]. Brown and Kaaresoja developed a set of distinguishable vibrotactile messages by using Tactons (tactile icons) to customize alerts for incoming calls, SMS, and MMS [5]. Poupyrev *et al.* [7] embedded a TouchEngine – a thin miniature low-power tactile actuator – in a PDA and conducted user studies that demonstrated 22% faster task completion when the handheld's tilting interface is enhanced with tactile feedback.

One example that uses different sequences in buzzing is the VibeTonz[2] technology developed by Immersion for enhancing ringtones and games in mobile phones. Other examples integrate vibration with sound, such as with Motorola's Audio-Haptic approach, which enhances ringtones with haptic effects using a multifunction transducer [13]. Williamson *et al.* [11] designed a system for mobile phones called *Shoogle*, which implements different real-world metaphors that reveal information about the state of the phone. For example, using *Shoogle*, users can determine the content of their SMS inboxes by shaking their phones, which activates vibration feedback.

All these approaches show that there are clear opportunities and advantages for using tactile output. The aforementioned projects focus on a single vibration actuator and look at the design space that is given by changing the intensity of the vibration. A more complex example is described by Chang *et al.* [6] who designed a tactile communication device called *ComTouch*. The device is designed to augment remote voice communication with touch, to enrich interpersonal communication by enriching voice with a tactile channel. In this case, tactile patterns and timings are immediately taken from the user and do not need to be generated. In [12], a tangible communication system using connected roles is described. The author demonstrates that having such a channel could improve the user experience in remote collaboration setting.

Haptic output has already been successfully applied in other areas. Tan *et al.* [8] combined the input from pressure sensors mounted on the seat of an office chair with tactile actuators embedded in the back of the seat to create an input device with haptic feedback. They also integrated the system into a driving simulator to determine when the driver intended to change lanes and alerted the driver with vibrotactile pulses about danger based on observed traffic patterns. This is an example of how haptic feedback can communicate information with low cognitive overhead, and this motivated us to further investigate the design space of mobile devices. In the domain of wearable computing, there have been projects, such as [9] and [10] that suggest using vibrotactile output for communicating information discreetly without disturbing others. Similar to our approach, multiple actuators were used. However, the authors required the actuators to be at a specific position on the body (e.g. around the waist or in the hands).

---

[2] Immersion ViboTonz system, http://www.immersion.com/mobility/

Our motivation to further investigate multi-tactile output for mobile devices is based on the results of existing systems using single or multiple actuators mounted to specific places on the body. For our investigation we designed and implemented a prototype mobile phone with actuators as descried in the next section.

4 Prototype for Rich Tactile Output

We decided to develop a prototype that allowed us to create rich, tactile output in a device equivalent in size and shape to a typical mobile phone. As current mobile phones are highly integrated and tightly packed, we chose to use a dummy phone and concentrate on the vibration output functionality, see Fig. 2. A dummy phone is a plastic mobile phone with the same dimensions as a real one without any functionality and electronic boards inside. With this prototype, we set out to explore the impact of multi-tactile output on the user experience.

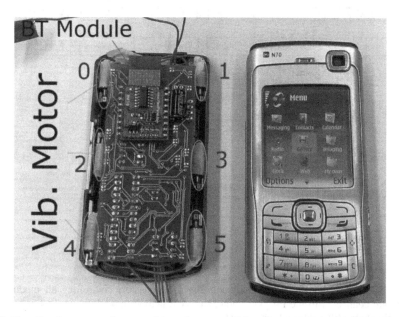

Fig. 2. Six vibration motors integrated in a dummy mobile phone, placed to maximize the distance between them. The motors can be controlled using a Bluetooth connection.

For the prototype, we designed a printed circuit board with one microcontroller (MCU), six controllable vibration motors and one Bluetooth module. The Bluetooth module was chosen so that the microcontroller, and hence the vibration motors, could be remotely controlled over a Bluetooth connection using another phone or a PC. We took a Nokia N-70 dummy phone, removed all its internal parts and integrated our multi-vibration system. Therefore, the resulting prototype looks and feels just like a real Nokia N70 mobile phone without any phone functionality. The N-70 Nokia mobile phone's physical specifications are:

- Volume: 95.9 cm³
- Weight: 126 g
- Length: 108.8 mm
- Width (max): 53 mm
- Thickness (max): 24 mm

The actuators are standard vibration motors that are used in mobile phones to generate vibration alert. Four motors are located at the four corners of the phone, and two more in the center of the phone (see Fig. 2). Within the device, the actuators are located close to the back cover. The location of the actuators was chosen to maximize the distance between them. Using the prototype, we can therefore generate vibration pulses on the body of the mobile phone in six different areas and with varying intensity. During our experiments, we used a Bluetooth connection to control the vibration sequences of the motors.

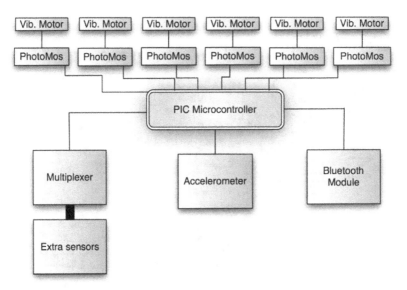

Fig. 3. PCB Architecture: a PIC microcontroller is responsible controlling all modules. Six motors are connected to the PIC via PhotoMos. A Bluetooth module is used to establish the connection to the PIC and send/receive data.

The microcontroller unit (a PIC18F2550) runs at 20MHz, and each motor is controlled using a PhotoMOS switch connected to the microcontroller. After a Bluetooth connection is established, the vibration intensity of all six motors can be controlled independently with no perceivable delay. The intensity is controlled using pulse-width modulation (30%-100%). The software running on the microcontroller receives commands that specify which motors should be switched on with what intensity over the Bluetooth connection. A Java-based application was implemented to run on another mobile phone and generate these commands. Using the prototype, we can generate vibration pulses on the body of the mobile phone in six different areas and can control duration and intensity. The architecture of the board is shown in Fig. 3.

5 Experiments

To explore the design space in detail, we conducted two studies using the prototype. In the first study, we investigated how easy it is for users to identify individual actuators. The second study looked at the user experience provided by different vibration patterns and how easy it is to distinguish between them. In both cases we asked users to hold the device in their prefer hand. We also considered having a condition where users have the phone in a pocket; however, the variation in how people prefer to carry their phone would seemingly require a very large sample to make useful conclusions. If the phone is carried in a pocket or bag, the initial vibration is felt there. Then the users can seize the phone but do not necessarily have to take it out or even look at it as it was argued in [11]. Hence testing in the hand appears reasonable.

Study 1: Locating a specific actuator
In the first study, we asked the participants to tell the position of the vibration stimuli. This three-part study was conducted with 15 persons (5 females and 10 males), aged 21 to 30 with an average of 26 years.

In the first part, the users were asked if the vibration pulse was on the right or left side of the phone. In the second part, users were asked if the stimulus was on the top, middle or bottom of the mobile phone. Finally, in the last part, users were asked the position of the pulse in two dimensions: top/middle/bottom (on the y-axis) and right/left (on the x-axis). In this part the stimulus was generated just with a single motor. For example the pulse could be addressed like top-right (if motor 1 was on) or middle-left (if motor 2 was on). The motors' configuration is shown in Fig. 2. Turning motors 1, 3, and 5 on, simultaneously generated the stimulus on the right side and motors 0, 2, and 4 generated the stimulus on the left side. The stimulus on top was generated by turning motors 0 and 1 on, in the middle by turning motors 2 and 3 on, and on the bottom by turning motors 4 and 5 on at the same time. The experiment was repeated 10 times (5 times each for the right and left sides) in the first part, 15 times (5 times each for the top, centre, and bottom) in the second part, and 30 times (5 times for each motor) in the last part. All the vibrations were triggered randomly and remotely. The duration of each stimulus was chosen to be 300ms.

The experiment showed that users could discriminate between left and right, as well as top and bottom, with a recognition rate of 75% on average. Participants showed a similar detection rate for actuators in the four corners (with an average rate of 73%). However, recognition for the actuators in the middle of the device (as a group or individually) was significantly lower. One reason could be the lack of enough space between the motors in the middle and motors in top and bottom of the phone although in our design the motors were located with maximum distance from each other.

Therefore, the overall recognition rate of locating the vibration of a single actuator was only 36%. In Fig. 4, an overview of the results is given. The results indicate that it is preferable to place actuators for vibration in the corners of the device. One point

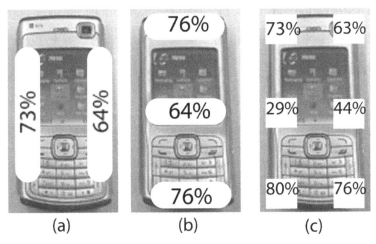

Fig. 4. The results show that users could better locate the active actuators in the corners than in the middle of the device

that was not taken into account here in processing the result and drawing conclusions were potential differences between holding the phone in the right and left hand (in our survey, 80% of the participants were right-handed and held it in their preferred hand). As shown in Fig. 4, recognition rates between actuators on the right and left side are close. On the other hand, the results also depend on the motors' configuration which we will consider and test in future work.

Study 2: Discriminating between vibration patterns
In the second study, three vibration patterns were defined and the focus was on how well the participants can distinguish between these patterns. The main difference between the patterns is the number of motors that are switched on in a particular point in time. The first pattern called *"Circular"* meant that in each moment one motor was on, the second one was *"Top-Down"* with two motors on, and the last pattern was *"Right-Left"* with three motors on at the same time. To generate the patterns, each set of motors (1, 2, or 3 motors, depending on the pattern) was switched on for 300ms and then followed by the next set.

This study was conducted with 7 users from the previous study and 6 new users (in total 4 female, age range 20-42, average age 27 years). At the beginning of the experiment, all patterns were played to the users and they asked to memorize them. Additionally we include random patterns to see whether the user could locate the predefined patterns. First we tested the recognition of each pattern separately against random patterns. During this phase in the experiment, users indicated if the played pattern was the pattern shown at the beginning or not. Each experiment was repeated 10 times (i.e. 5 times the predefined pattern and 5 times a random pattern, in random order). Overall users correctly identified the specified patterns and the random patterns with 80% accuracy for all three patterns.

In the next phase, we compared the detection of the patterns using all patterns in the experiment. Users had to indicate if the vibration stimuli constituted one of the predefined patterns or random vibration and potentially identify the pattern. In this part, each pattern appeared 5 times at random places in the sequence. Based on the results, the accuracy rate for the first pattern *"Circular"* was 82%, the second pattern

"Top-Down" 51% and the last one *"Right-Left"* 68%. The results show that the recognition is independent of the number of active vibration actuators in one particular moment. This showed that different patterns could be defined as default in mobile phones and could be used as feedback or any other usage in mobile devices as users could understand and discriminate different patterns. For instance, most mobile phones have a feature that let users assign a specific ring-tone to a number or group of numbers in the contact list. Instead of that, they can use patterns and assign different patterns to different contact items.

Limitations
During the user studies, we could not explore the interaction with real mobile phones as these devices are tightly integrated and is hardly possible to integrate extra actuators without altering the form factor. Once integrated within a functional phone, we expect that there are interesting aspects with regard to multimodality (e.g. visual navigation relating to tactile output).

Although the user studies were conducted with a limited set of users, we see a clear trend that shows the potential of rich tactile output. In our experiment, we focused on situations where users have the device in their hand and the results only apply to these use cases. As we are aware that people often have their phones in pockets or bags, we are currently looking into experiments to assess how feasible rich tactile output is for such scenarios.

The generated sensations and the quality of the tactile output are strongly dependent on the actuators used. In our prototype, we used common actuators present in typical mobile phones to show that rich tactile output can be achieved with these components. Nevertheless, we expect that specifically designed output elements may even improve the user experience. Hence our results can be seen as a bottom-line from which to improve. Such improvements could be achieved on all dimensions introduced earlier.

The vibration stimuli created in a device are not exactly limited to the spot where they are created. These signals also pass through the shell of the phone depending on the material. Hence, stimuli from different motors may influence each other. Again, a more targeted design of the device covers may help to reduce ambiguities and create a better user experience.

6   Conclusion and Future Work

One of the main issues in user interface engineering is presenting clear and understandable feedback and output during the interaction with a system. Advances in technology made mobile devices ubiquitous and enabled users to employ them in many contexts. However, they often employ naive alerting policies that can transform them into nuisances as users of mobile devices are bombarded with alerts and notifications.

Rich tactile output creates new options for providing information to the user. Currently, this modality is used only in its very basic form. Analogous to the developments in ringtones, there is a potential for personalization in tactile notification. Using a customized prototype with multiple, independently-controllable vibrating actuators, we explored the effectiveness of multiple haptic output in a suite of experiments.

From our experiments we conclude that multiple actuators can be used to create a richer user experience and users are able to feel and recognize different forms of tactile output in a single handheld device. Users were able to understand stimuli generated with motors in different locations in a mobile phone while holding it in their hands. In particular, based on the motor's configuration, our research findings indicate that the corners of the handheld device provide the most effective places for mounting vibration actuators.

While testing dynamic actuation patterns with different durations, we found out that discriminating between vibration patterns is feasible for users. We consider this a new potential mechanism for providing tactile output and personalizing the mobile phone in parallel with audio ring-tones and offer a new dimension for a richer user experience.

The results of our study and the interviews carried out indicate that having several vibration elements in a handheld device is feasible and understandable and can be suggested to be used as an effective way to provide richer tactile feedback and output, improve the user interface, and offer a new dimension for a richer user experience. In our future work, we are investigating the use of multiple vibration output elements as a feedback mechanism also during visual interaction on mobile devices. In addition to the tests we have conducted, we look at the recognition rate of multi-tactile output on a mobile phone when it is in a pocket or bag attached to the body.

So far this research shows the potential tactile output for mobile devices. To explore it further, we suggest testing other configurations with different numbers of motors.

Acknowledgement

This work was performed in the context of the DFG (Deutsche Forschungsgemeinschaft) funded research group 'Embedded Interaction'.

References

1. Oulasvirta, A., Tamminen, S., Roto, V., Kuorelahti, J.: Interaction in 4-second Bursts: The Fragmented Nature of Attentional Resources in Mobile HCI. In: Proc. CHI 2005, pp. 919–928 (2005)
2. Luk, J., Pasquero, J., Little, S., MacLean, K., Levesque, V., Hayward, V.: A Role for Haptics in Mobile Interaction: Initial Design Using a Handheld Tactile Display Prototype. In: Proc. CHI 2006, pp. 171–180 (2006)
3. Brewster, S., Chohan, F., Brown, L.: Tactile Feedback for Mobile Interactions. In: Proc. CHI 2007, pp. 159–162 (2007)
4. Brewster, S.A., King, A.J.: An Investigation into the Use of Tactons to Present Progress Information. In: Costabile, M.F., Paternó, F. (eds.) INTERACT 2005. LNCS, vol. 3585, pp. 6–17. Springer, Heidelberg (2005)

5. Brown, M.L., Kaaresoja, T.: Feel Who's Talking: Using Tactons for Mobile Phone Alerts. In: Proc. CHI 2006, pp. 604–609 (2006)
6. Chang, A., O'Modhrain, S., Jacob, R., Gunther, E., Ishii, H.: ComTouch: Design of a Vibrotactile Communication Device. In: Proc. DIS 2002, pp. 312–320 (2002)
7. Poupyrev, I., Maryuyama, S., Rekimoto, J.: Ambient Touch: Designing Tactile Interfaces for Handheld Devices. In: Proc. UIST 2002, pp. 51–60 (2002)
8. Tan, H., Lu, I., Portland, A.: The Chair as a Novel Haptic User Interface. In: Proc. Workshop on Perceptual User Interface, pp. 56–57 (1997)
9. Tsukada, K., Yasumura, M.: ActiveBelt: Belt-Type Wearable Tactile Display for Directional Navigation. In: Davies, N., Mynatt, E.D., Siio, I. (eds.) UbiComp 2004. LNCS, vol. 3205, pp. 384–399. Springer, Heidelberg (2004)
10. Bosman, S., Groenendaal, B., Findlater, J.W., Visser, T., de Graaf, M.: Panos Markopoulos: GentleGuide: An Exploration of Haptic Output for Indoors Pedestrian Guidance. In: Proc. Mobile HCI 2003, pp. 358–362 (2003)
11. Williamson, J., Murray-Smith, R., Hughes, S.: Shoogle: Excitatory Multimodal Interaction on Mobile Devices. In: Proc. CHI 2007, pp. 121–124 (2007)
12. Brave, S., Ishii, H., Dahley, A.: Tangible Interfaces for Remote Collaboration and Communication. In: Proc. CSCW 1998, pp. 169–178 (1998)
13. Chang, A., O' Sullivan, C.: Audio-Haptic Feedback in Mobile Phones. In: Proc. HCI 2005, pp. 1264–1267 (2005)
14. Cholewiak, R.W., Collins, A.A.: Sensory and physiological bases of touch. The Psychology of Touch, pp. 23–60 (1996)
15. Geldard, F.A.: Adventure in Tactile Literacy (1956)
16. Gault, R.H.: Progress in Experiments on Tactual Interpretation of Oral Speech. Journal of Abnormal Psychology (1965)
17. Geldard, F.A.: Some Neglected Possibilities of Communication. Science 131(3413), 1583–1588 (1960)
18. Annaswamy, A.M., Srinivasan, M.A.: The Role of Compliant Finger pads in Grasping and Manipulation and Control 5. Essays on Mathematical Robotics (1998)
19. Appelle, S.: Haptic perception of form: Activity and stimulus attributes. The psychology of touch, pp. 169–187 (1991)

An Ambient Agent Model Exploiting
Workflow-Based Reasoning to Recognize Task Progress

Fiemke Both, Mark Hoogendoorn, and Jan Treur

Vrije Universiteit Amsterdam, Department of Artificial Intelligence
De Boelelaan 1081, 1081 HV Amsterdam, The Netherlands
{fboth,mhoogen,treur}@cs.vu.nl

Abstract. For an ambient intelligent agent to support a human in demanding tasks it is important to be aware of the progress made in a given workflow. It would be possible to interact with the human about this, but this may disturb task performance. In this paper an ambient agent model is presented that is able to obtain such an awareness of the human's progress in a workflow by performing model-based analysis using available workflow models and available observation information. Simulation experiments for the presented the ambient agent model for a case study are discussed, and evaluated by automated formal verification.

Keywords: Ambient agent, workflow model, task progress, awareness, model-based reasoning.

1 Introduction

Ambient agent systems may provide means to support a human in demanding tasks (e.g. [3; 2; 13]). To realise these potentials it is useful if such an agent system has some awareness of how the human task is progressing. This awareness enables dedicated support by the ambient agent system. For example, the ambient agent system can provide dedicated support for the task being performed, and while performing a very intensive task the human is not disturbed. Not always a registration system is available where it is documented on the fly at which points in time a certain (sub)task is started and at which time it is finished. Direct communication about this with the human often would disturb the human's process. One of the challenges for ambient intelligent agents is to obtain such information about a human's progress by an analysis based on observation information and a workflow model. In some other approaches the use of objects in activities is exploited; detecting an object reveals information about the activity of the human; see, e.g., [12], [16]. In contrast, the approach put forward in the current paper does not assume any use of objects, but exploits available workflow models.

Often workflow models are nondeterministic, and the human's choice for a certain branch may depend on circumstances and on his or her preferences, which may be unknown. Therefore it may not be clear at forehand which of the branches of such a workflow model are actually followed, and at least some observation information is

E. Aarts et al. (Eds.): AmI 2008, LNCS 5355, pp. 222–239, 2008.
© Springer-Verlag Berlin Heidelberg 2008

needed. In this paper an ambient agent model is presented that is able to perform model-based analysis using available workflow models and available observation information, to obtain more detailed information on the human's progress in task execution. The (possibly partial) observation information may come from sensors detecting location, posture, movements of the user, or when a computer system is used.

The model has been designed as a specialisation of the generic agent model for human-like ambience presented in [5], and incorporates formally specified model-based reasoning methods as presented in [4]. As part of these reasoning methods, a focussing approach was applied to control the reasoning. This allows the ambient agent to limit the amount of processing and information within itself. An important aspect of the approach developed is that model-based reasoning methods, as known within Artificial Intelligence and usually applied to causal models, are now applied to workflow models. To this end a representation format for workflow models was chosen that unifies with usual formats for model-based reasoning.

This paper is organized as follows. In Section 2 the case study is introduced. Thereafter, Section 3 introduces the formal modelling language that has been used, whereas Section 4 uses this language to express the reasoning method used. Section 5 addresses how to use focusing mechanisms, and in Section 6 a simulation model is presented. Simulation results are shown in Section 7, and verified in Section 8. Finally, Section 9 is a discussion.

2   The Case Study Addressed

In order to get a better understanding of the idea, the case study is introduced first. It concerns two mechanics on board of a naval vessel, namely Michael and Pete. The ambient agent of Michael has knowledge of the workflow Michael is currently in, as shown in Figure 1. Hereby, the nodes indicate states whereas the arrows represent possible transitions. Furthermore, the specific control mechanism Michael uses to go through the workflow is represented by the box in the figure, connected to the workflow via dashed arrows. It is assumed that this control mechanism is a black box, i.e. it is not known by the ambient agent. The mechanic Michael is currently trying to solve an alarm about a critical system when Pete wants to call him to ask for advice about his own task. That triggers Michael's ambient agent to start reasoning (using the workflow) about what Michael is doing at the moment in order to determine whether to disturb him with the call or not. The current time is 10:04; the last time the ambient agent received input on what Michael was doing 9 minutes ago at 09:55, when Michael accepted the alarm and started working on it (subtask B1 in the figure below). The average time in minutes it takes Michael to perform the different processes are shown in Figure 1. Note that these times can be determined depending on the specific situation (e.g. subtasks performed before, the particular human's state, etc.). Given the scenario sketched, the example leaves two possible positions in the workflow: O5 (path 1: B1, O1, B3, O3, B5, O5) and B6 (path 2: B1, O1, B2, O2, B4, O4, B6). Furthermore, the ambient agent knows that Michael cannot be disturbed during tasks B2, B3, B4 and O5 (shown in figure 1 by the grey nodes).

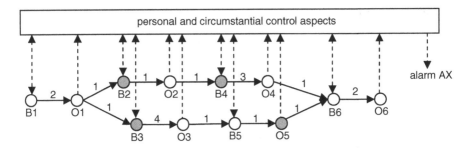

Fig. 1. Representation of a workflow. The numbers above the arrows indicate the average time it takes to complete one task and start the next. The grey nodes represent subtasks during which the operator cannot be disturbed.

The next sections describe a formal approach how the ambient agent can reason to derive what Michael has been doing.

3   Formal Languages Used

In order to execute and verify human-like ambience models, the expressive language TTL is used [7]. This predicate logical language supports formal specification and analysis of dynamic properties, covering both qualitative and quantitative aspects. TTL is built on atoms referring to states, time points and traces. A *state* of a process for (state) ontology Ont is an assignment of truth values to the set of ground atoms in the ontology. The set of all possible states for ontology Ont is denoted by STATES(Ont). To describe sequences of states, a fixed *time frame* T is assumed which is linearly ordered. A *trace* γ over state ontology Ont and time frame T is a mapping $\gamma : T \to$ STATES(Ont), i.e., a sequence of states γ_t ($t \in T$) in STATES(Ont). The set of *dynamic properties* DYNPROP(Ont) is the set of temporal statements that can be formulated with respect to traces based on the state ontology Ont in the following manner. Given a trace γ over state ontology Ont, the state in γ at time point t is denoted by state(γ, t). These states can be related to state properties via the formally defined satisfaction relation $\models$, comparable to the Holds-predicate in the Situation Calculus: state(γ, t) $\models$ p denotes that state property p holds in trace γ at time t. Based on these statements, dynamic properties can be formulated in a sorted first-order predicate logic, using quantifiers over time and traces and the usual first-order logical connectives such as $\neg, \wedge, \vee, \Rightarrow, \forall, \exists$. A special software environment has been developed for TTL, featuring both a Property Editor for building and editing TTL properties and a Checking Tool that enables formal verification of such properties against a set of (simulated or empirical) traces. Especially the possibility to use variables and quantifiers, also over numbers, makes TTL more useful in practical applications, compared to, for example, propositional and modal temporal languages.

Executable Format. To specify simulation models and to execute these models, the language LEADSTO [8], an executable sublanguage of TTL, is used. The basic building blocks of this language are causal relations of the format $\alpha \twoheadrightarrow_{e, f, g, h} \beta$, which means:

if state property α holds for a certain time interval with duration g, then after some delay (between e and f) state property β will hold for a certain time interval of length h.

where α and β are state properties of the form 'conjunction of literals' (where a literal is an atom or the negation of an atom), and e, f, g, h non-negative real numbers. Also for the language LEADSTO, the possibility to use variables, (e.g., over numbers), makes it more useful for practical application, compared to, for example, propositional or qualitative causal modelling languages.

4   Reasoning Methods Enabling Workflow-Based Analysis

A first step in deriving what task an agent is currently doing is by specifying the workflow of the agent. The workflow is represented in the ambient agent as a collection of rules that state which node follows which node. The set of rules are of the form

belief(leads_to_after(node1, node2, duration)).

When the ambient agent believes that the human has performed a specific subtask at some time point, it has a belief of the form belief(at(node, time)). A set of generic reasoning methods has been developed to derive more beliefs based on the leads_to_after rules and one or more beliefs about active nodes; cf. [4]. Below is a summary of these methods.

4.1   Forward Reasoning Methods

Reasoning methods that reason forward in time are often used to make predictions on future states, or on making an estimation of the current state based on information acquired in the past. The first reasoning method is one that occurs in the literature in many variants in different contexts and under different names. This varies from, for example, computational (numerical) simulation based on difference or differential equations, qualitative simulation, causal reasoning, execution of executable temporal logic formulae, and forward chaining in rule-based reasoning, to generation of traces by transition systems and finite automata. The basic specification of this reasoning method can be expressed as follows (note that for the sake of clarity the subscript below the LEADSTO arrow has been omitted since the same values for e,f,g, and h are used namely 0,0,1,1).

Belief Generation based on Positive Forward Simulation
If it is believed that I holds at T and that I leads to J after duration D, then it is believed that J holds after D.

$\forall$I,J:INFO_EL $\forall$D:REAL $\forall$T:TIME
belief(at(I, T)) $\land$ belief(leads_to_after(I, J, D)) $\twoheadrightarrow$ belief(at(J, T+D))

If it is believed that I1 holds at T and that I2 holds at T, then it is believed that I1 and I2 holds at T.

belief(at(I1,T)) ∧ belief(at(I2, T)) → belief(at(and(I1, I2), T))

Note that, if the initial beliefs are assumed correct, belief correctness holds for leads to beliefs, and positive forward correctness of leads to relationships holds, then all beliefs generated in this way are correct. A second way of belief generation by forward simulation addresses the propagation of negations. This is expressed as follows.

Belief Generation based on Single Source Negative Forward Simulation

If it is believed that I does not hold at T and that I leads to J after duration D, then it is believed that J does not hold after D.

∀I,J:INFO_EL ∀D:REAL ∀T:TIME
belief(at(not(I), T)) ∧ belief(leads_to_after(I, J, D)) → belief(at(not(J), T+D)))

If it is believed that I1 (resp. I2) does not hold at T, then it is believed that I1 and I2 does not hold at T.

belief((at(not(I1),T))) → belief(at(not(and(I1, I2)), T))
belief(at(not(I2),T)) → belief(at(not(and(I1, I2)), T))

Note that this only provides correct beliefs when the initial beliefs are assumed correct, belief correctness holds for leads to beliefs, and single source negative forward correctness holds for the leads to relationships.

Belief Generation based on Multiple Source Negative Forward Simulation

If for any J and time T, for every I that is believed to lead to J after some duration D, it is believed that I does not hold before duration D, then it is believed that J does not hold.

∀I,J:INFO_EL ∀D:REAL ∀T:TIME
∀I, D [belief(leads_to_after(I, J, D)) → belief(at(not(I), t-D))] → belief(at(not(J), T))

If it is believed that I1 (resp. I2) does not hold at T, then it is believed that I1 and I2 does not hold at T.

belief(at(not(I1),T)) → belief(at(not(and(I1, I2)), T))
belief(at(not(I2),T)) → belief(at(not(and(I1, I2)), T))

This provides correct beliefs when the initial beliefs are assumed correct, belief correctness holds for leads to beliefs, and multiple source negative forward correctness holds for the leads to relationships.

4.2 Backward Reasoning Methods

The basic specification of a backward reasoning method is specified as follows.

Belief Generation based on Modus Tollens Inverse Simulation

If it is believed that J does not hold at T and that I leads to J after duration D, then it is believed that I does not hold before duration D.

∀I,J:INFO_EL ∀D:REAL ∀T:TIME
belief(at(not(J), T)) ∧ belief(leads_to_after(I, J, D)) → belief(at(not(I), T-D))

If it is believed that not I1 and I2 holds at T and that I2 (resp. I1) holds at T, then it is
believed that I1 (resp. I2) does not hold at T.

belief(at(not(and(I1, I2), T)) ∧ belief(at(I2, T)) → belief(at(not(I1), T))
belief(at(not(and(I1, I2), T)) ∧ belief(at(I1, T)) → belief(at(not(I2), T))

Belief Generation based on Simple Abduction

If it is believed that J holds at T and that I leads to J after duration D, then it is
believed that I holds before duration D.

∀I,J:INFO_EL ∀D:REAL ∀T:TIME
belief(at(J, T)) ∧ belief(leads_to_after(I, J, D)) → belief(at(I, T-D))

If it is believed that I1 and I2 holds at T, then it is believed that I1 holds at T and that
I2 holds at T.

belief(at(and(I1, I2), T)) → belief(at(I1,T)) ∧ belief(at(I2, T))

As another option, an abductive causal reasoning method can be internally
represented in a simplified form as follows.

Belief Generation based on Multiple Effect Abduction

If for any I and time T, for every J for which it is believed that I leads to J after some
duration D, it is believed that J holds after duration D, then it is believed that I holds at T.

∀I:INFO_EL ∀T:TIME
∀J [belief(leads_to_after(I, J, D)) → belief(at(J, T+D))] → belief(at(I, T))

If it is believed that I1 and I2 holds at T, then it is believed that I1 holds at T and that
I2 holds at T.

belief(at(and(I1, I2), T)) → belief(at(I1,T)) ∧ belief(at(I2, T))

Belief Generation based on Context-Supported Abduction

If it is believed that J holds at T and that I2 holds at T and that I1 and I2 leads to J
after duration D, then it is believed that I1 holds before duration D.

∀I,J:INFO_EL ∀D:REAL ∀T:TIME
belief(at(J, T)) ∧ belief(at(I2, T-D)) ∧ belief(leads_to_after(and(I1, I2), J, D))
    → belief(at(I1, T-D))

If it is believed that I1 and I2 holds at T, then it is believed that I1 holds at T and that
I2 holds at T.

belief(at(and(I1, I2), T)) → belief(at(I1,T)) ∧ belief(at(I2, T))

5   Focussing the Reasoning

When the ambient agent uses these methods to derive more beliefs, the number of beliefs can quickly get out of control. For example, in the scenario above the ambient agent could derive beliefs about all nodes in the workflow that follow the first node, because there is no reason to select one path and not the other. Therefore, this section introduces a selection mechanism that can control which beliefs are derived and which beliefs are not. For the belief generation reasoning methods this means that an antecedent is added stating which selection criteria must be met. This idea is shown for the reasoning method *positive forward simulation*.

If the belief that I holds at T was selected and it is believed that I leads to J after duration D, and selection criterion s1 holds, then the belief that J holds after D is selected.

∀I,J:INFO_EL ∀D:REAL ∀T:TIME
selected_belief(at(I, T)) ∧ belief(leads_to_after(I, J, D)) ∧ s1 → selected_belief(at(J, T+D))

Selection criteria needed for controlled belief generation can be specified in different manners. A simple manner is by assuming that the ambient agent has knowledge about which beliefs are relevant, expressed by a predicate in_focus. If this assumption is made, then the selection criterion s1 in the example above can be expressed as in_focus(I), where I is the property for which a belief is considered. The general idea is that if a belief can be generated, it is selected (only) when it is in focus. This section explains how foci can be generated dynamically within an ambient agent.

Focussing the reasoning is useful when, for example, the ambient agent has a belief about one node being true at some time point and it only needs to know what has happened after that time point and not before that time point. Another example is when two nodes are believed to have been true. Reasoning about one of the nodes may lead to two different possible paths, while reasoning about the other node within a specific path may lead to only one possibility. In principle the ambient agent only needs to derive the beliefs necessary for fulfilling its desire (e.g. interrupting the human as in the case study described in Section 2, or giving advice).

Many types of information provide possible selection criteria. The ambient agent can use these to determine the focus. As an example, using *competences* of the human is one type of information that can be used (and has actually been used in the case study). It can be used to focus the reasoning on a path that fits most to the competence profile of the human. It can also be used to decide if and when the human may need additional information about the problem he/she is solving. A human might, for instance, be competent to use a certain set of tools, but be incompetent to use other tools. Of course, other criteria can be used as well, depending on the particular context the ambient agent is designed to operate in.

Given that the ambient agent wants to know what the human (i.e., the mechanic) is doing now and that it knows some state in the past, there are several possible reasoning strategies to find out where the human is at the moment. The first strategy is focusing on the existing belief about the past and reasoning forward towards the current time. For this method, for example, the selection criterion competence can be used to choose between different paths. Since the starting point is a belief about a specific node and a specific time, the competences possible for this node can be taken as an indication. All nodes with the same competences can be in focus.

A second reasoning strategy is starting from the current time point and reasoning backwards until the ambient agent arrives at the belief about the past. Assumptions must be made about the possible states that the human is in now, therefore this method is useful when the number of possibilities is limited.

Beliefs about the competences of the human and about the allowed competences for the tasks are required, for example:

```
belief(competence_level_operator(0.8));
belief(allowed_competence(B4,0.8));
belief(allowed_competence(B5,0.4)).
```

The value for competence represents the ability of the human to perform the action without help. Using these beliefs as selection criteria for focus generation:

```
if      belief(allowed_competence(I, X)) & belief(competence_level_operator(X)
then    in_focus(I, HIGH)

if      selected_focus_level(Y) & in_focus(I, Y)
then    in_selected_focus(I)
```

Again, any reasoning method can be used to actually derive a belief about the node in selected focus. In case the competence level focus selection does not lead to a single path to be explored, the reasoning will be done on the set of paths with the closest competence level. Another option may be to involve another criterion in the selection mechanism such that after using this additional criterion again a single path results.

6 Overview of the Ambient Agent Model

To assess the human's task execution state, the ambient agent performs model-based reasoning of the type discussed in Section 4. However, it does so in a focused manner, where foci are determined using criteria of the type discussed in Section 5. This means that the overall reasoning pattern is an alternation of generation of a focus, and generation of beliefs within a given focus. As the criteria for focus generation have a heuristic character, it is not guaranteed that deriving beliefs within a focus will lead to a successful outcome. Therefore sometimes an earlier generated focus set has to be abandoned and a new focus set has to be generated. This is modelled by distinguishing different levels of foci. First the highest level is chosen, but if after model-based reasoning to generate beliefs this does not lead to an appropriate outcome, the highest level is disqualified and the one but highest level is chosen, and so on. More specifically, the following process is followed to model the overall reasoning process.

1   set highest focus level

2   while there are no selected foci
3   generate focus levels for all nodes
4   while there is no selected focus level

```
5        if the highest focus level is disqualified
6                selected focus level = next focus level
7        else
8                selected focus level = highest focus level
9        end if
10       end while
11       select foci for selected focus level
12   end while

13   derive beliefs based on selected foci and the model

14   if there is an observed belief inconsistent with the current foci
15       disqualify selected focus level and start focus generation
16   end if
```

The first line of the reasoning process description is applied only once at the start of the simulation. The second part, lines 2 to 12, describes the process of generating foci, selecting the highest not disqualified focus level, and selecting the foci corresponding to the selected focus level. The third part of the process, line 13, covers all generic belief generation methods described in Section 4. The last part, lines 14 to 16, continuously checks for (new) observed beliefs that are inconsistent with the current selected focus set. If there is such a belief, the current focus level is disqualified. Since selected foci are only generated when there is a selected focus level, all selected foci do not hold any longer and the reasoning process continues with line 2.

This process has been formally modelled in the directly executable LEADSTO format. Examples of formalisations for some of the lines above are:

Focus Generation based on Competence Level (line 3)

If it is believed that I needs competence level X and that the focus level for competence level X is Y and that the current phase is focus generation, then I is in focus with focus level Y.

$\forall$I:INFO_EL $\forall$X:COMPETENCE_LEVEL $\forall$Y:FOCUS_LEVEL
belief(competence_for(I,X)) $\wedge$ competence_focus_level(X,Y) $\wedge$ focus_generation
$\quad \rightarrow$ in_focus(I,Y)

Selected Focus Generation based on Selected Focus Level (line 11)

If it is believed that I needs competence level X and that the focus level for competence level X is Y and that the current phase is focus generation, then I is in focus with focus level Y.

$\forall$I:INFO_EL $\forall$X: FOCUS_LEVEL
in_focus(I,X) $\wedge$ selected_focus_level(X) $\wedge$ focus_generation $\rightarrow$ in_selected_focus(I)

Focus Level Disqualification upon Inconsistent Belief (lines 14-16)

If it is believed that I holds at T and that I is in focus at level X and that the selected focus level is Y and that X is not equal to Y and that I is not in focus at level Y, then X is disqualified and focus generation is true.

∀I:INFO_EL ∀X,Y:FOCUS_LEVEL ∀D:REAL ∀T:TIME
observed_belief(at(I, T)) ∧ in_focus(I, X) ∧ selected_focus_level(Y) ∧ X≠Y ∧ not(in_focus(I, Y)
→ disqualified(X) ∧ focus_generation

7 Simulation Results

A number of scenarios have been simulated based on the case study described in Section 2. In the first scenario, the ambient agent of Michael receives a communication request from the ambient agent of Pete at time point 6. The agent has one belief about a subtask of the human at time point 1. Using this belief and the competence levels of the two possible paths, the agent first derives the bottom path: it believes the current task is B3. Since B3 is a task that cannot be interrupted, the ambient agent takes no action. After the reasoning process, the beliefs of the ambient agent are confirmed by an observation about task B3.

In scenario 2, the ambient agent receives the communication request at time point 10 and has a belief about subtask B1 at time point 1. The ambient agent focuses on the path with the highest competence level and derives beliefs about the bottom path. The conclusion is that Michael's current task is O5. Because O5 is not an interruptible task, the ambient agent does not forward the call. At some later time point, a new observation is made involving subtask O4. The agent revises its beliefs and foci, and derives the top path: it believes the current task is B6. Since B6 is a task that can be interrupted, the ambient agent transfers a new attempt by Peter to call Michael.

In scenario 3, Pete tries to contact Michael at a later time point. Therefore, the ambient agent starts reasoning at time point 12, at which the belief about subtask O4 already exists. In this scenario, the agent soon disqualifies the highest focus level, because the belief about O4 is inconsistent with the bottom path. The ambient agent derives the top path first and concludes that the human is currently performing O6. The call is transferred by the agent, because Michael can be disturbed during execution of task O6.

The traces resulting from applying the presented reasoning method on the three scenarios are shown in Figures 2, 3 and 4. In the Figures, the left side indicates the atoms that occur over time, whereas the right side of the figures indicate a timeline where a dark box indicates that the atom is true, and a grey box indicates false. Note that the time on the x-axis is the simulation time which is not related to the time points in the atoms.

The current time in the first scenario depicted in Figure 2 is 6 (current_time(6)), which is an atom that is known during the entire simulation (simulation time 0 to 14). The agent starts with an observation about subtask B1 at time 1 (observed_belief(at(B1, 1))). The agent thereafter starts with the focus generation phase. In this case study, two paths exist in the workflow. Using the set of beliefs about the allowed competence levels of the two paths and a belief about the competence level of the mechanic, the ambient agent derives two sets of foci (in_focus(O1, high) and in_focus(O1, low)) for the two focus levels: high and low. Since the level 'high' is the highest and not disqualified, it is selected (selected_focus_level(high)). At the same time, the observed belief about task B1 becomes a selected belief. Now that a focus level is selected, the foci can be used to derive selected foci matching the selected focus level: all nodes in the bottom path (in_selected_focus(B1), etc.). The belief generation methods described in Section 4 are

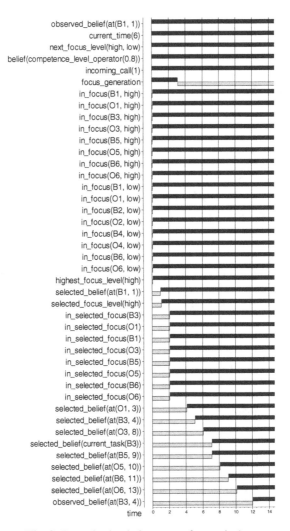

Fig. 2. Example simulation trace of scenario 1

used to derive selected beliefs. When the time points of selected beliefs match the current time, the ambient agent derives that B3 is the current task of the human (selected_belief(current_task(B3))). After this derivation, the ambient agent observes that the mechanic was indeed working on subtask B3 (observed_belief(at(B3, 4))). Since B3 is a task during which Michael cannot be disturbed, the call of Pete is not forwarded to Michael.

In Figure 3, the trace of the second scenario is shown. The current time is 9 minutes after the time of the first belief (current_time(10) and observed_belief(at(B1, 1))). The first half of this trace is the same as trace 1, except for the current time and current task: because the current time is 10, the ambient agent believes that the current task is the interruptible task O5. The two sets of foci the agent derives are not shown in this figure. The ambient agent does not forward the call from Pete to Michael at time 10.

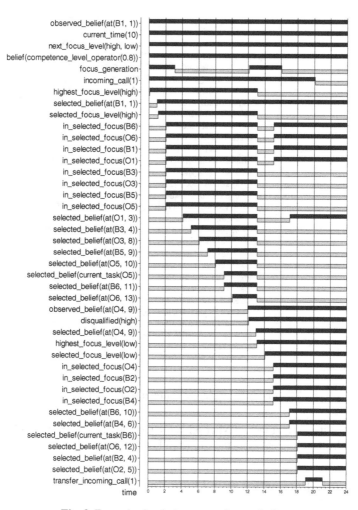

Fig. 3. Example simulation trace of scenario 2

At simulation time 12, a new observation is made by the agent that subtask O4 was executed at time 9 (observed_belief(at(O4, 9))). This belief is inconsistent with the selected focus level, because the competence level for O4 is low. Therefore, the focus level 'high' is disqualified and all beliefs and foci based on this level do not hold any longer. The focus generation phase starts again, the other focus level is selected, new selected foci are derived and the agent reasons about the top path. The ambient agent now derives that the current task of the human is B6. Michael can be interrupted during execution of B6, therefore the agent transfers the call from Pete.

The trace of the third scenario is shown in Figure 4. The current time in this scenario is 12 and the ambient agent already believes that task O4 has been executed at time point 9. Since O4 is inconsistent with the path that matches Michael's competences, the agent disqualifies the highest focus level (with the best matching competence level) and continues focussing on and reasoning about the path containing task O4. The agent

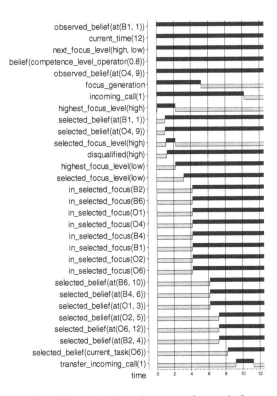

Fig. 4. Example simulation trace of scenario 3

believes that the current task of Michael is O6 (selected_belief(current_task(O6))), which is interruptible, therefore transfers the call from Pete.

8 Dynamic Properties and Their Verification

For the model a number of overall properties have been identified, formally specified and automatically verified against the simulation traces of the three scenarios:

P1: Observed facts will become selected beliefs
If at time point t a new observed belief exists, and the current set of derived beliefs does not comply to this observed belief, then eventually the set of derived beliefs will change such that it complies to the observed beliefs.

∀γ:TRACE, t:TIME, l:INFO_EL, T:TIME
[[state(γ, t) |= observed_belief(at(l, T)) &
   ¬state(γ, t-1) |= observed_belief(at(l, T)) &
   ¬state(γ, t) |= selected_belief(at(l, T))]
       ⇒   ∃t2:TIME ≥ t state(γ, t2) |= selected_belief(at(l, T))]

This property is satisfied for all three traces considered.

P2: Derived beliefs are within one path in the workflow model

When a set of beliefs is derived, then this set contains at most one execution path of the workflow.

∀γ:TRACE, t:TIME, I1, I2:INFO_EL, T1, T2:TIME
[state(γ, t) |= selected_belief(at(I1, T1)) &
  state(γ, t) |= selected_belief(at(I2, T2)) &
  I1 ≠ I2 & T2 > T1]
    ⇒ path_between(γ, I1, I2)

Hereby (with te the last time point of the trace),

path_between(γ, I1, I2) ≡ state(γ,te) |= path_between(I1, I2)

Here state properties path_between(I1, I2) can be generated in the trace as additional information (i.e., a form of trace enrichment):

belief(leads_to_after(I1, I2, D)) → path_between(I1, I2)
belief(leads_to_after(I1, I2, D)) ∧ path_between(I2, I3) → path_between(I1, I3)

This information is easily derived during or after the simulation using the predicates already present in the trace.

This property distinguishes traces without revision from traces with revision. Property 2 is satisfied for trace 1 and 3, but not for all time points in trace 2. Due to the occurrence of a new observation result, temporary a node in another path is selected as a belief, resulting in the property not being satisfied. At the last time point however, the property is satisfied, since then the inconsistencies are no longer present.

P3: Most plausible beliefs are generated first

If one path is more likely to be followed than another path according to the background information, and there are no observed beliefs that distinguish either path, then this path will be explored first by deriving beliefs along that path.

∀γ:TRACE, t:TIME, I, J:INFO_EL, T:TIME, D:DURATION, V:VALUE
[state(γ, t) |= selected_belief(at(I, T)) &
  state(γ, t) |= belief(leads_to_after(I, J, D)) &
  state(γ, t) |= belief(competence_for(J, V)) &
  consistent_with_observations(γ, t, J, T+D) &
  ¬∃J2:INFO_EL, D2:DURATION, V2:VALUE
  [state(γ, t) |= belief(leads_to_after(I, J2, D2)) &
  state(γ, t) |= belief(competence_for(J2, V2) & V2 > V &
  consistent_with_observations(γ, t, J2, T+D2)]
      ⇒ ∃t2:TIME state(γ, t2) |= selected_belief(at(J2, T+D))]

Here:
consistent_with_observations(γ:TRACE, t:TIME, I:INFO_EL, T:TIME) ≡
[∀I2:INFO_EL, T2:TIME state(γ, t) |= observed_belief(at(I2, T2))
    ⇒ [[I = I2 & T = T2] OR path_between(γ, I2, I) OR path_between(γ, I, I2)]

This property is satisfied for all traces.

P4: Only beliefs consistent with observations are derived
If beliefs are derived, then these beliefs need to be consistent with the observations.

∀γ:TRACE, t:TIME, l:INFO_EL, T:TIME
state(γ, t) |= selected_belief(at(l, T)) ⇒ consistent_with_observation(γ, t, l, T)

Also this property distinguishes traces without revision from traces with revision. This property is satisfied for trace 1 and 3, but not for all time points in trace 2, due to the updating process of beliefs as mentioned for property P2. Before the observation is received, and after the reasoning has been conducted, the property is satisfied.

P5: Immediate correct derivation
If a set of beliefs is derived at time t, then there does not exist a time t' > t where the derived belief is not consistent with the observations.

∀γ:TRACE, t:TIME, l:INFO_EL, T:TIME
[state(γ, t) |= selected_belief(at(l, T)) ⇒ ∀t2:TIME > t consistent_with_observation(γ, t2, l, T)]

Again, this property distinguishes traces without revision from traces with revision. It is satisfied for traces 1 and 3, but not for trace 2 since in that case a conflicting belief comes in that requires revision.

9 Discussion

This paper addressed one of the challenges for ambient intelligent agents (e.g., [3; 2; 13]), to support a human in demanding tasks, namely to be aware of which (sub)tasks the human is doing, and how much progress is made, without direct communication about this. Some other work on subjects related to this theme can be found in, for example, [11], [12], [15], [16].

A formally specified executable ambient agent model was introduced that is able to perform model-based analysis using available workflow models and available observation information. Thus it obtains awareness of the human's progress in task execution. Hereby, a focused reasoning method has been used whereby the most likely path is evaluated first, avoiding having to pass all possible paths, hence, improving the scalability. In addition, the scalability of the approach can be improved by choosing an appropriate abstraction level for the workflow. Some simulation experiments for a case study concerning the question what the human is doing at the current time point have been discussed and evaluated. This information has been used by the ambient agent to decide whether the human can be disturbed at this time point or not. In case it was derived that the human was working on a task during which it could not be disturbed, calls were not forwarded whereas in the other cases the calls were forwarded. Since the approach presented in this paper is a heuristic approach, a safer option might be to choose a less intrusive manner of forwarding the call (e.g. a message on the screen) instead of not forwarding it.

Another question that the ambient agent can ask itself in the context of the case study is: what has the human been doing until now? The ambient agent might want to find out which path the human has taken to reach his/her goal in order to store this information as experience, for example, or to store this as information for future reference (when the same workflow needs to be executed advice can be given about the previous solution). Yet another question that can be addressed is: what should the human be doing in the future? If the ambient agent needs to determine the shortest path between two states, it can use a breadth-first search mechanism. The ambient agent determines the next location that can be reached in all paths after a fixed amount of time (1 minute for example). The path that reaches the last node first is the shortest one.

In the case study of Section 2, the action the ambient agent can take as a result of the reasoning process is to disturb the operator with a phone call. Other possible actions are to support the operator in performing the task by providing documentation or by removing tasks from the task list. Interaction between the ambient agent and the operator can take place for example, via a visual or auditory interface, or with a virtual character (see e.g. [14]).

The model was designed as a specialisation of the generic agent model for human-like ambience presented in [5], which also was taken as a point of departure for an ambient agent model for assessment of driving behaviour; cf. [6]. Furthermore, it includes formally specified model-based reasoning methods adopted from [4]. In the current approach it is assumed that the observations are deterministic. Another option would be to obtain observations with a certain probability. The approach presented in this paper can handle such probabilistic observations by simply assuming the one with the highest probability. More advanced methods are future work.

The approach followed incorporated not only simulation but also analysis, formal specification and automated verification of requirements for the overall process. In Section 8 a number of such (required) formally specified dynamic properties of the overall process and their verification were discussed. For specification of these properties the expressive predicate logic temporal language TTL was used [7]. As this language allows the use of variables (also over numbers) and quantifiers, for practical applications it is more useful than, for example, propositional and modal temporal languages.

Specification of the workflow of a human can be done using a variety of methods, e.g. [9] and [10]. For a comparison of these methods, see [1]. The advantage of the representation used throughout the current paper is that it is a rich specification format, enabling the usage of the generic model-based reasoning methods as specified in this paper.

In other work such as [11] and [15] also temporal relationships between activities are exploited to recognize plan execution states, based on relational Markov networks and causal networks, respectively. These papers address the theme from a probabilistic angle, whereas the current paper addresses it from a logical reasoning perspective. For future work it will be interesting to explore how such probabilistic approaches can be integrated within a logical reasoning approach. Other approaches exploit the use of objects in activities; e.g., [12], [16]. In contrast, the approach put forward in the current paper does not assume any use of objects, but exploits available work flow models. However, when additional information is available via the use of objects, it can be integrated within the reasoning approach as observations.

In further future work, extensions will be made on the model and the application of it. For example, different focus generation methods will be explored. Moreover, within focus generation different domain aspects will be incorporated, such as statistical information about how often in the past a certain path was chosen. For example, if one path was followed in 90% of the cases, the ambient agent can use that information to focus on that path first. A challenge here is the ambient learning part: for the ambient agent to learn which path is often taken, without disturbing the human with questions.

References

[1] van der Aalst, W.M.P., ter Hofstede, A.H.M., Kiepuszewski, B., Barros, A.P.: Workflow Patterns. QUT Technical report FIT-TR-2002-02, Queensland University of Technology, Brisbane (2002)

[2] Aarts, E., Collier, R., van Loenen, E., Ruyter, B. (eds.): Ambient Intelligence. Proc. of the First European Symposium, EUSAI 2003. LNCS, vol. 2875, p. 432. Springer, Heidelberg (2003)

[3] Aarts, E., Harwig, R., Schuurmans, M.: Ambient Intelligence. In: Denning, P. (ed.) The Invisible Future, pp. 235–250. McGraw Hill, New York (2001)

[4] Bosse, T., Both, F., Gerritsen, C., Hoogendoorn, M., Treur, J.: Model-Based Reasoning Methods within an Ambient Intelligent Agent Model. In: Mühlhäuser, M., Ferscha, A., Aitenbichler, E. (eds.) Proceedings of the First International Workshop on Human Aspects in Ambient Intelligence. Constructing Ambient Intelligence: AmI 2007 Workshops Proceedings. Communications in Computer and Information Science (CCIS), vol. 11, pp. 352–370. Springer, Heidelberg (2008)

[5] Bosse, T., Hoogendoorn, M., Klein, M., Treur, J.: An Agent-Based Generic Model for Human-Like Ambience. In: Mühlhäuser, M., Ferscha, A., Aitenbichler, E. (eds.) Proceedings of the First International Workshop on Model Driven Software Engineering for Ambient Intelligence Applications. Constructing Ambient Intelligence: AmI 2007 Workshops Proceedings. Communications in Computer and Information Science (CCIS), vol. 11, pp. 93–103. Springer, Heidelberg (2008)

[6] Bosse, T., Hoogendoorn, M., Klein, M., Treur, J.: A Component-Based Ambient Agent Model for Assessment of Driving Behaviour. In: Sandnes, F.E., Zhang, Y., Rong, C., Yang, L.T., Ma, J. (eds.) UIC 2008. LNCS, vol. 5061, pp. 229–243. Springer, Heidelberg (2008)

[7] Bosse, T., Jonker, C.M., van der Meij, L., Sharpanskykh, A., Treur, J.: Specification and Verification of Dynamics in Cognitive Agent Models. In: Nishida, T., et al. (eds.) Proc. of the Sixth International Conference on Intelligent Agent Technology, IAT 2006, pp. 247–254. IEEE Computer Society Press, Los Alamitos (2006); Extended version to appear. Int. Journal of Cooperative Information Systems

[8] Bosse, T., Jonker, C.M., van der Meij, L., Treur, J.: A Language and Environment for Analysis of Dynamics by Simulation. International Journal of Artificial Intelligence Tools 16, 435–464 (2007)

[9] Ellis, C.A., Nutt, G.J.: Modelling and Enactment of Workflow Systems. In: Ajmone Marsan, M. (ed.) ICATPN 1993. LNCS, vol. 691, pp. 1–16. Springer, Heidelberg (1993)

[10] Georgakopoulos, D., Hornick, M., Sheth, A.: An Overview of Workow Management: From Process Modeling to Workow Automation Infrastructure. Distributed and Parallel Databases 3, 119–153 (1995)

[11] Liao, L., Fox, D., Kautz, H.: Location-Based Activity Recognition using Relational Markov Networks. In: Proceedings of the Nineteenth International Conference on Artificial Intelligence, IJCAI 2005 (2005)

[12] Patterson, D., Fox, D., Kautz, H., Philipose, M.: Fine-Grained Activity Recognition by Aggregating Abstract Object Usage. In: Noma, H., Kogure, K., Nakajima, Y., Shimonomura, H., Ohsuga, M. (eds.) ISWC 2005, pp. 44–51. IEEE Computer Society Press, Los Alamitos (2005)

[13] Riva, G., Vatalaro, F., Davide, F., Alcañiz, M. (eds.): Ambient Intelligence. IOS Press, Amsterdam (2005)

[14] Thalmann, D.: The Role of Virtual Humans in Virtual Environment Technology and Interfaces. In: Earnshaw, R., Guejd, R., van Dam, A., Vince, J. (eds.) Frontiers of Human-Centred Computing, Online Communities and Virtual Environments, pp. 27–38. Springer, London (2001)

[15] Qin, X., Lee, W.: Attack Plan Recognition and Prediction Using Causal Networks. In: Proc. of the 20th Annual Conference on Computer Security Applications, pp. 370–379 (2004)

[16] Wu, J., Osuntogun, A., Choudhury, T., Philipose, M., Rehg, J.M.: A Scalable Approach to Activity Recognition based on Object Use. In: Proc. of the 11th Int. IEEE Conference on Computer Vision, ICCV 2007, pp. 1–8 (2007)

An Architecture to Automate Ambient Business System Development*

Pau Giner and Vicente Pelechano

Centro de Investigación en Métodos de Producción de Software
Universidad Politécnica de Valencia
Camino de Vera s/n, 46022 Valencia, Spain
{pginer,pele}@pros.upv.es

Abstract. Business Processes in organizations usually involve real-world objects. A tight integration of these elements from the physical world into business process can improve process automation. This paper introduces a software architecture that allows this integration. The presented architecture is defined following an architectural process that decouples architectural concepts from technological solutions and stresses the relevance of automating the development process. Several case studies have been developped using the introduced architecture to experiment their benefits. In addition, modelling techniques have been used to automate the development of this kind of systems.

1 Introduction

Business processes in organizations usually deal with physical objects such as products in a supermarket or baggage pieces in an airport. This supposes a gap between the physical world and the Information System. When physical objects participate actively in business processes, this gap between physical and virtual worlds is reduced [1]. Thanks to Ambient Intelligence (AmI [2]) technologies, the linkage between physical elements and their digital counterparts can be automated, and people can focus on their real world activities, while the system is hidden in the background, controlling the process in an unobtrusive way.

Automatic Identification (Auto-ID) technologies enable real-world objects to be taken automatically in consideration by a software system, thus objects become "smart" as they are not human-dependent anymore [3]. People, places and things can be identified in a myriad of different ways. Radio Frequency Identifications (RFID), Smartcards, barcodes and magnetic strips to name a few, are some Auto-ID enabler technologies with a different degree of automation.

From the Business Process Management (BPM) area several initiatives have emerged to automate business processes. Modeling notations to specify processes, and execution engines that keep track of the state of long-running business processes, are some examples. However, these initiatives are almost exclusively

* This work has been developed with the support of MEC under the project SESAMO TIN2007-62894 and cofinanced by FEDER.

E. Aarts et al. (Eds.): AmI 2008, LNCS 5355, pp. 240–257, 2008.

focused in activities that occur in the digital space –i.e., systems exchanging information–, while physical elements have received few attention –with the exception of human participants and printed documents–.

The term Ambient Business [4], defines the application of AmI technologies to business process to take advantage of the information gathered ubiquitously from various sources including physical objects. To obtain the benefits of bridging real and virtual worlds, there is a need for software infrastructure that allow an easy integration between business process support systems and Auto-ID mechanisms.

This work defines a software architecture to support business processes that integrate physical elements. The architecture has been defined following an architectural process introduced in [5]. This process is designed to obtain software architectures that are minimally affected by technological cycles, permit an easy evolution of requirements and promotes automation in the software development.

By following this architectural process, the contribution of this work is twofold. On the one hand, the present work is offering a technological solution that allows the integration of real-world objects in business process. So software systems that fit this application domain can be built with less effort. On the other hand, a more general contribution is offered to the community since architectural concepts have been also defined in a technology-independent fashion. This encourages communication with stakeholders and permits the realization of these architectural concepts in many different technological solutions.

The remainder of the paper is structured as follows. In Section 2 the architectural process followed is described. In Section 3 the defined architecture for the integration of physical elements in business processes is introduced. Section 4 provides some results from the application of the architecture to two case studies. Section 5 gives some insights about the automation of the development process for systems based on the defined architecture. Related work is presented in Section 6. Finally, Section 7 presents conclusions and further work.

2   The Architectural Process

The present work deals with Information Systems that integrate real-world elements to support business processes in an organization. This definition is quite broad but we are focused on applications where this linkage is highly exploited and identification –specially Auto-ID– is relevant. These systems contain several elements suitable to be identified by means of potentially different technologies.

An example of such a systems could be a library in which clients can borrow books just by picking them. If a non-member –or a member with an expired card– takes some book, the member first, and then, the security personnel are warned. By using Auto-ID technologies, there is no need for librarians to transfer the data about book loans to the Information System. So, the process becomes more efficient.

The present work defines an architecture to integrate Auto-ID mechanisms in business processes. In order to offer support to business processes that involve real-world elements, many technological aspects should be considered related to both, business process management and Auto-ID. Some examples include Business process execution engines –based on different specifications like WS-BPEL or XPDL–, interoperability solutions –such as Web Services or CORBA– to integrate different systems, and middleware to integrate Auto-ID devices – such as RFID antennas, barcode readers and the like–. The involved technologies are many in both fields, and new ones are expected to appear.

Since we do not want our architecture to be affected by the high technology diversity in service orchestration and Auto-ID solutions, we propose to abstract from technological details. Based on the foundations of Model Driven Engineering (MDE [6]) we propose the use of models –abstract technology-independent description of systems– to face the automatic construction of this kind of systems. In order to define an architecture that supports this automatic development paradigm, we followed the architectural process introduced by Völter in [5]. Völter proposes an architectural process composed of the following steps:

1. First, the **elaboration** phase of the architecture defines the architecture by decoupling the technology independent concepts form the actual technological solutions.
2. The iteration phase serves to **consolidate the architecture** receiving feedback from its use.
3. Finally, the use of the architecture can be improved by avoiding repetitive programming tasks with **automation**. In this way, software development for the architecture becomes more effective.

3   Elaboration of the Architecture

According to the architectural process followed, the elaboration of the architecture defines the architecture first at a conceptual level. This constitutes a **technology-independent architecture**. Then, usage guidelines for the defined concepts are established in a **programming model**. The **technology mapping** defines how artifacts from the programming model are mapped to a particular technology. A **mock platform** facilitates testing tasks to developers. Finally, the development of a **vertical prototype** helps to evaluate the architecture and provide feedback about non-functional requirements.

3.1   Technology-Independent Architecture

In this section we present a technology-independent description of the architecture introduced in this paper. By using a description based on technology-neutral concepts we obtain **a sustainable software architecture**. This is, an architecture that is not affected by technological hypes and can evolve in time along several technological cycles.

For the definition of the architecture we rely on the *component* concept. Components become the basic software pieces that will conform the system. Component functionality is described by means of *interfaces*. Components are connected

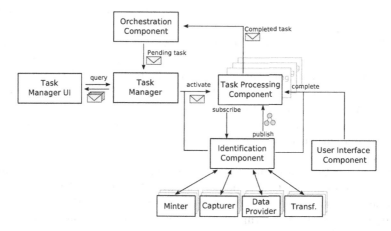

Fig. 1. Architecture component overview

by *wires*, and they offer asynchronous communication. We have opted for asynchronous communication since business processes considered are usually long-running and tend to involve human participation. In addition, a subscription mechanism following the Observer Pattern [7] is used to deal with identification events for Auto-ID related components.

It is worth noting that several instances of a process are usually running at the same time, so correlation mechanisms are needed. For example, in a library requesting new books and receiving them happens asynchronously. When new books arrive, it is important to determine to which of the many active requests they correspond to.

Since we are considering the integration of Auto-ID mechanisms in business processes, the presented architecture has to balance the message-based approach usually associated with business processes with the event-based approach of Auto-ID mechanisms. The presented architecture considers events as low-level messages that are processed –e.g., filtered, aggregated, etc.– to generate business-level messages. Fig. 1 illustrates the components involved in this process. More detail about these components is given below.

Orchestration Component: This component is in charge of managing the state of the long-running business process. It interchanges messages with different systems in order to orchestrate the process. It is in charge of creating new process instances, keep track of the different process instances and perform message correlation –i.e., find the process instance related with the received message–.

Task Manager: This component gives support to the asynchronous communication of systems that participate in the business process. It receives messages from the *Orchestration Component* and waits for components to process them. The *Task Manager* can be queried to obtain the pending tasks that conform certain criteria –e.g., targeted to a certain user–. Pending tasks can be added and cancelled by the *Orchestration Component* and completed by a *Task Processing Component*.

Task Processing Component: This component receives a message corresponding to a pending task when it is *activated*. Then it retrieves information and composes a response message. When the task is *completed*, the response message is send to the *Orchestration Component*. To complete the response, the required information can be provided by the user or by some *Identification Component*. The Task Processing Component has to subscribe to the different Identification Components –subscription is active until the task is completed–.

Identification Component: This component provides the mechanisms to bridge physical and digital spaces. Physical elements are detected and their associated information can be used to (1) trigger the activation or (2) provide complementary information of a *Task Processing Component*. In addition, new identifiers can be generated and transferred to the physical space using this component.

This component relies in a set of components identified in a previous work [8]. These are *Capturers*, *Minters*, *Transformations* and *Data Providers*. Capturers –such as a barcode reader– can acquire identifiers from the Physical Space to the Digital Space. Minters are in charge of generating physical representations of an identifier –such as a printing device that produces a barcode label–. Transformations define conversion operations between different codifications. Data Providers provide the functionality required to obtain the information associated to an identifier, modify this information and create new instances –e.g., obtain the book details from its ISBN number–.

These components can have a *User Interface Component* associated to them to permit user participation or just display some helpful information. Although process automation is one of the main goals of this kind of systems, sometimes it is not possible to obtain a complete automation using sensors and user interfaces are required.

3.2   Programming Model

Once defined a technology-independent architecture, we define how this architecture is used from the developer perspective. More detail about the definition of the basic components that conform the architecture is given below. In addition some insights on aspects such as task life-cycle and error management are given.

Create the Building Blocks. First, the business process that the system is going to support should be defined. The *Orchestration Component* should be provided a description of the process. This description represents the composition of the functionality of different systems. When the system that provides the desired functionality does not exist, this system should be built. The presented architecture gives support for the development of these systems when real-world objects are involved.

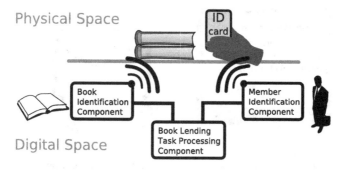

Fig. 2. Two task processing components

A *Task Processing Component* should be defined for each task that is supported by the process and there is no existing system handling it automatically. Given an input message for a pending task, the logic that determines how the resulting response message is constructed should be defined.

When defining the Task Processing Component, information dependencies are detected, this determines the required *Identification Components*. For example, in a library, the "lend book" task can require the identification of the client and all the books the client is borrowing. So two Identification Components –implementing the *Identification Component interface*– are required, one for detecting *clients* and another for *books* as illustrated in Fig. 2.

Identification Components are developed by choosing the adequate Capturers, Minters, Data Providers and Transformations. All these elements implement different interfaces, and normally wrap the functionality offered by the specific technological solution.

Once the required elements are defined, they are connected together. In addition, a specific *User Interface Component* offering a customized view of the Task Manager for each particular task can be defined to provide specific information required for a certain task in order to improve user experience.

Defining Task Life-Cycle. When defining *Task Processing Components* the origin of task life-cycle events –initiation and termination of the tasks– should be identified.

For example, in a library when a package of books arrive –see Fig. 3–, the completion of the reception task can be notified explicitly by the user –using a User Interface Component– or implicitly using Auto-ID mechanism–by means of an Identification Component–. When Auto-ID events guide task life-cycle, the process becomes more fluent since the system is notified as the task is performed.

Error Management. Since Information Systems have not full control of the physical world, there is a need to define error conditions when the detected elements are not the ones expected. Error management is essential when implementing the access to data providers. We have detected the following error

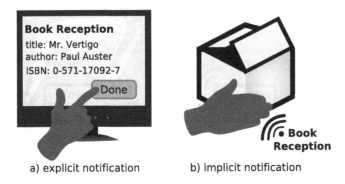

Fig. 3. Explicit and implicit task life-cycle

patterns, depending on the chosen pattern error management should be implemented in a different way for each Identification Component. The detected error patterns are described below.

Error when not found: In the normal case is considered an error that an element lacks associated information. The physical identifier can be read by the system but the system has no information about this element. This error is probably caused by skipping some process step where information about the element is created.

Error when found: This approach expects that elements are not associated with any information when they are identified in order to create this information. In this case an error is considered when information is found. The detection of an element triggers the creation of a new piece of information attached to this element.

Avoid errors: A combination of both behaviors is also possible. If a piece of information is found for an element, this information is selected. In case it is not found, a new piece of information is created.

3.3   Technology Mapping

Once defined the technology-independent concepts that conform the architecture and the programming model that defines how to use this architecture, we elaborate the technology mapping. The technology mapping defines how artifacts from the programming model are mapped to a particular technology. More detail about the **target technology selected** and how **architectural concepts can be mapped to the technological solution**.

Target Technology. We have chosen Service Component Architecture (SCA) as the target technology. SCA is a vendor, technology and language neutral model for implementing Service Oriented Architectures (SOAs). We have adopted this technology for the following reasons:

Component model: the SCA component model fits with our technology-independent architecture concepts. SCA components declare explicitly their references in terms of required interfaces and are resolved following the Dependency Injection pattern. Components are injected by a container to solve these dependencies according to a configuration file.

Support for asynchronous communication: asynchronous communication is supported by SCA by means of the bidirectional interface concept. A bidirectional interface is composed by a pair of interfaces, the provided and the callback interface. A component implementing the bidirectional interface should implement the methods defined in the provided interface, while clients of this component should implement the callback interface.

Data abstraction: For data handling, SCA can use Service Data Objects (SDO). SDO makes it possible to hide the back-end data source, as it offers homogeneous access for XML, relational or file based data sources among others. In addition, SDO permits disconnected data access patterns with an optimistic concurrency control model. These properties are also adequate for the considered application domain. Since data portions from many sources are combined and updated.

Support for distribution: the systems this work is dealing with usually expand across organizations and they involve diverse computing resources. Labels are commonly produced by one system and read by many different systems with the potential need to share information among them. SCA components can be distributed easily in different computing nodes, from different threads in the same machine to different computers. This flexibility is desirable for our application domain.

Technological integration: SCA allows the use of different technologies for the implementation of components and their communication. This favours the integration of different systems. For the purpose of this work we are specially interested in the possibilities of integrating Business Process Execution engines and Auto-ID middleware solutions.

From the different available implementations of SCA and SDO specifications[1] we have chosen Apache Tuscany[2] since it is an open source solution in a mature state.

Mapping to a Technological Solution. Once SCA has been chosen as the target technology, we define how the technology-independent concepts described in Section 3.1 are mapped to implementation assets.

Orchestration Component: Since Business Process Management community is familiar with the WS-BPEL standard, we considered the implementation of the *Orchestration Component* in WS-BPEL. A WS-BPEL definition of the business process activities and its interface –by means of a WSDL

---

[1] http://www.osoa.org/display/Main/Implementation+Examples+and+Tools
[2] http://tuscany.apache.org/

definition– are required. Apache Tuscany supports the implementation of components using WS-BPEL by means of Apache ODE Orchestration Engine. However, since the *Task Manager Component* is exposed as a Web Service, other process execution engines and Web Service-based software – such as Enterprise Service Buses or Messaging Middleware– can be used to drive the business process execution.

Task Manager: This component is implemented in Java. It is a repository for pending tasks. Query capabilities are provided thanks to the XPath support that SDO offers. Pending tasks are formed by a header that includes some metadata –reception date, user group in charge of completing the task, ect.– and the payload – domain-specific data that the *Task Processing Component* will handle–. When designing data structures, meta-information included in tasks should be defined. The more meta-data considered, the more fine-grained queries could be. On the other hand, including great amounts of metadata supposes to move complexity to the *Orchestration Component* since this is the component in charge of providing this information.

Task Processing Component: Components of this kind define a set of references according to the information elements they require –or they need to generate– to complete a specific task. SDO API is used to compose the resulting message that is returned to the Orchestration Engine. In the component specification, wires are defined to determine which *Identification Components* are providing the defined references.

Identification Component: This component provides a bidirectional interface to allow for subscriptions. Task Processing components that are subscribed to a particular *Identification Component* should implement the corresponding callback interface. Identification Components can be connected to the *Task Manager* to trigger the activation of certain tasks. They can be also connected to Task Processing Components to trigger their completion.

For the definition of Capturers, Minters, Data Providers and Transformations an implementation of the corresponding interfaces should be provided. These components can be implemented with several technologies. In addition to Java, for our implementations OSGi is considered to obtain some dynamic capabilities that are quite interesting for Minters and Capturers.

User Interface Components: Apache Tuscany allows the implementation of components using HTML and Javascript. We have used these components offering with a json-rpc[3] based communication.

3.4 Mock Platform

Once the technology for the architecture has been decided, it is important to define a mock platform for developers. With a mock platform, developers can run tests locally as early as possible. The choice of SCA and SDO as target technologies offers good properties to be used as a mock platform.

SCA is based on the Dependency Injection Pattern. Components declare their dependencies and the application wiring is defined in an external asset. Thus,

---

[3] http://json-rpc.org/

components are easily interchangeable as far as the replacing component provides the same interface than the replaced one. This allows for an easy definition of mock components for test purposes.

At the data level, SDO makes it possible to hide the back-end data source, as it offers homogeneous access for XML, relational or file based data sources among others. This allows a seamlessly migration from a mock platform –e.g., based on static XML files– for testing to a production environment –e.g, based on Web Services–.

3.5   Vertical Prototype

In order to validate the defined architecture we have implemented an application based on the Smart Toolbox [9] case study, a representative application in this domain. This case study consists in monitoring the tools used for aircraft maintenance tasks. During aircraft reparations, the system should prevent tools from being lost and causing potential damage. In order to do so, the content, the location and the carrier of the toolbox is sensed automatically in real-time. This application improves the aircraft Maintenance, Repair, and Overhaul (MRO) process in an unobtrusive manner, so it fits perfectly in the application domain targeted in this work.

In this stage of the architecture development we are interested in testing the non-functional requirements, so only a small subset of the functional requirements were considered for the development. Only two tasks of the process –namely *planning* and *repairing task*– are supported. First, in the *planning task*, mechanics are assigned a plane to repair and a set of tools. Then, they proceed with the *repairing task*. During reparation, the toolbox content is monitored. When the reparation is completed, the system checks that the toolbox contains all the previously assigned tools –avoiding tools to be accidentally forgotten and causing any damage–. Repairing task completion is automatically informed by a location change. When the toolbox detects that the mechanic is leaving a certain location, the task is automatically considered as completed.

Fig. 4 shows an screenshot of the developed prototype. This prototype integrates different identification technologies. Mechanics and locations are

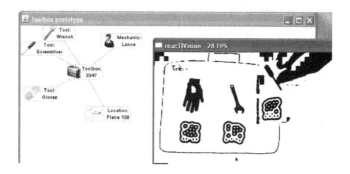

Fig. 4. Smart Toolbox prototype

identified by textual labels while tools contained in the toolbox are identified by fiducials [10] –two-dimensional barcodes specially designed for real-time video camera recognition–.

Printed labels are transferred to the system using a web interface. The *Fiducial Capturer Component* wraps the reacTIVision framework [4]. A wide-angle lens webcam was used as a capturing device. For the minting of text labels and fiducials a common printer was used.

Since the support for WS-BPEL in Tuscany is quite recent, we encountered some problems with the Orchestration Component, so we opted for the use of an external Process Execution Engine –Intalio BPMS[5] was used–, using the Web Service based communication with the Task Manager.

This solution increased the reliability of the system but performance was sacrificed by the use of Web Services. Since the architecture is intended to support long-running processes, this performance reduction was not considered meaningful.

4   Consolidation of the Architecture

In order to stabilize the architecture concepts, define better the programming model and adjust the technology mapping; we have applied the architecture to two existing case studies. These case studies came from both, Business Process Management area –not dealing with real-world elements– and the AmI area –not considering business process aspects–.

Introducing the defined architecture for the development of these case studies offers two complementary visions of the benefits this architecture provides. On the one hand, BPMs can be extended to consider real-world elements. On the other hand, AmI systems can be process-aware; adapting to the user specific needs for each task. The comparison with the original systems was useful as feedback to improve the architecture. More detail about both case studies is given below.

4.1   Incidence Management Process

This case study –introduced in [11]– defines a business process that describes the protocol followed by a company in order to manage the infrastructure incidences reported by company members.

It defines the set of activities that need to be performed and how these are organized among the different participant roles –see Fig. 5–. In this case, the involved roles are members, the infrastructure manager and the technicians. We have modified the case study to consider that (1) department members are identified by an identity card and (2) material requests are labeled by the provider.

For example, when something is broken, it is reported by a company member. Then, the infrastructure manager contacts with the provider to get the required

---

[4] http://reactable.iua.upf.edu/?software
[5] http://bpms.intalio.com/

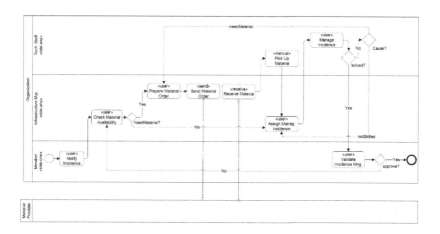

Fig. 5. BPMN diagram of the Incidence management business process

materials to fix the incidence. Finally, members of the technical staff are in charge of the reparation.

Considering this, Auto-ID mechanisms are used for the tasks where requested materials and members participate. The *Pick up material* task for example can be completely automated since the detection of a requested material by means of Auto-ID mechanisms can trigger task completion making the process more fluent.

As a result, the introduction of the developed platform increased the automation level of the process avoiding human intervention for some tasks that were previously manual. There were no noticeable performance lost by the introduction of the new architecture components for the tasks that did not involve real-world elements. So the integration of real-world objects in the process did not suppose any significant drawback.

4.2   Pervasive Meeting Room

This case study was introduced in [12] as an example of AmI system. This case study defines pervasive services provided in a meeting room –see Fig. 6–. The meeting room provides two kind of lighting services: the main lighting service, which covers all the room, and a specific service for lighting a projector screen. Users must be able to switch these lighting services manually using some kind of device. When anybody is near the screen, the intensity of the specific lighting must be decreased in order to provide a better visibility. Moreover, a security system must record what happens in the room if anybody is there when the security is activated.

The detection of people in the original case study was done by a presence sensor, for the purpose of this work we replaced it with an Auto-ID system. This allows to retrieve the user preferences and customize the offered services. We

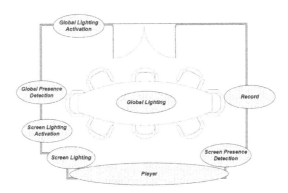

Fig. 6. Diagram of the services involved in the Meeting room case study

have defined a business process in order to adjust the environment conditions for the activities performed during a talk. When the speaker arrives at the meeting room, light flashes to indicate the beginning of the talk, then, light is adjusted and the recording system is activated according to the speaker preferences. When slides arrive at the end, the talk is considered finished and illumination is changed again.

In this case study new value is created by the coordination of available services to cover specific user needs with an adaptive service.

5   Automating the Development

One of the main reasons of following the current architectural process is that it is focused on automation. Business process requirements change quite often, and systems need to evolve accordingly. By automating the development process, the system can adapt to requirement changes without losing quality. Thus, changes in requirements can be mapped automatically to the particular technology the system relies on, facilitating its evolution.

In order to automate the development process, system descriptions should be machine-processable. To allow the description of a system based on the architecture concepts introduced in this work, these concepts must be precisely defined. How the architectural concepts have been formalized in the **architecture metamodel** to obtain machine-processable models, and which steps compose an **automated development process** is detailed below.

5.1   Architecture Metamodel

MDE proposes the use of metamodels to formalize concepts and their relationships. A metamodel defines the constructs that can be used to describe systems. Using a metamodel, system descriptions become unambiguous at least at syntactic level. This makes the descriptions machine-processable.

We have defined an **architecture metamodel** as the first step towards the automation of the development process. This metamodel captures the concepts defined in Section 3.1 such as the *Identification Component* or the *Task Processing Component*, and the constraints for their composition.

By using the constructs defined in the metamodel, different systems can be modeled. This enables the resulting models to be processed automatically by different MDE tools. So, models can be used in the development process as it will be illustrated in next section.

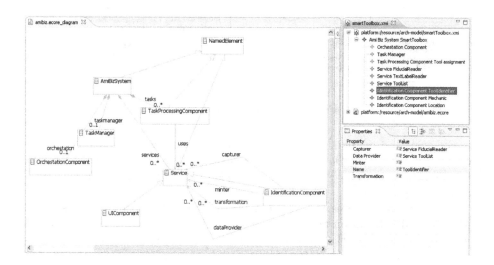

Fig. 7. Architecture metamodel

For the definition of the architecture metamodel, concepts have been formalized using Ecore. Ecore, part of the Eclipse Modeling Framework[6] (EMF), is a language targeted at the definition of metamodels with precise semantics. EMF provides tool support for the definition of metamodels and the edition of models.

Fig. 7 shows the defined metamodel using the Eclipse based tool set. At the right hand side of the figure, a model defined for the Smart Toolbox case study is shown using the default tree-based editor EMF generates.

5.2   Defining a Model-Driven Development Process

The definition of a precise architecture metamodel and a clear technology mapping for Ambient Business systems makes development process suitable for automation. A model-based development process is proposed –see Fig. 8– to achieve this automation. Models are the main assets in the process and different kind of model transformation techniques are used to move from high level system specifications to particular technology solutions.

---

[6] http://www.eclipse.org/modeling/emf/

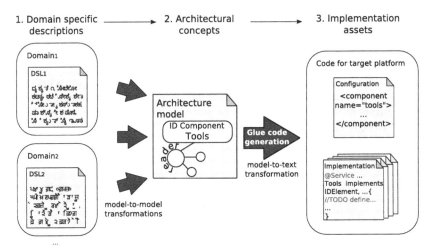

Fig. 8. MDE development process

Following the method, systems are specified using familiar notations for the domain experts using Domain Specific Languages (DSLs [13]), the system can be validated prior to its construction and code for specific platforms is generated automatically.

The method proposes three stages: DSL-based specification of the system, Model-based verification and glue code generation. The definition of DSLs and validators falls out of the scope of the present work since they depend on particular domain needs. Thus, further research is required to capture the specific requirements for a given domain. However, glue code generation support was faced in the present work since it provides an automation of the technology mapping which is valid for any domain.

DSL-based specification: Requirements can be expressed in a brief and concise manner by means of a DSL. In order to facilitate the specification of systems in different domains, a DSL can be defined for each domain of interest. DSLs are specifically suited to domain needs, and based on concepts familiar to the domain experts.

In order to enable a DSL-based specification for different domains, DSL concepts should be captured in a metamodel and a mapping should be established between the DSL metamodel and the architecture metamodel. This mapping can be defined by a model-to-model transformation.

Model-based verification: One of the most important use of models is to reason about the system they describe. Model-based verification can ensure that the system is valid prior to its construction. Model-to-model transformations can be used to check models [14] for their compliance with some properties. For example, from a model conformant to our architecture it is interesting to validate that objects are tagged before they are read and technologies used for identification are compatibles –reading technologies used for an object should be compatible with the technologies used for labeling it–.

Glue Code Generation: The technology mapping generally involves several repetitive tasks. For our target technology, the definition of each Identification Component involves actions like the definition of a Java class that extends the IDComponent interface, the use of SCA annotation to indicate the SCA container that an identification service is provided and the definition of the component in the XML configuration file. This boilerplate code can be automatically generated by the information captured in system models. In this way, developers can focus on implementing only relevant business-logic. From the description of a system following our defined metamodel, source code can be generated with model-to-text transformations.

Glue code generation have been implemented using Xpand templates from openArchitectureWare[7]. The application of templates to models is similar to the way templates are used to generate dynamic web pages in the web application development area. Model elements can be iterated and pieces of code can be produced instantiating them with values obtained from the model.

The current implementation generates the SCA configuration file for the system, and the Java classes that are required for the implementation of the different components. SCA annotations and method declaration is also generated. Although full code generation is not provided for component implementation, the provided code skeletons let developers focus on the implementation of the business-logic behavior, avoiding to deal with particular details of the target technology.

6 Related Work

Object tagging applications have been studied for a long time [15]. Tagged products bring benefits in different business areas [3] such as source verification, counterfeit protection, one-to-one marketing, maintenance and repair, theft and shrinkage, recall actions, safety and liability, disposal and recycling as well as mass customizing.

The need for defining architectures that support Auto-ID has lead to the development of frameworks and middleware to abstract from the filtering and aggregation tasks needed when tags are processed. Some middleware is specific to RFID such as Accada [16] or SAP's Auto-ID infrastructure [17]. However, one of our main goals is to support the heterogeneity in identification technologies.

Support for Auto-ID in a technology independent fashion has been also developed [18,19,20] in order to reduce the technological heterogeneity of identification technologies. All these proposals have a shared goal with the present work. However, these approaches do not consider the integration with business-process support systems, which is a key point of our work. In addition, these approaches are particular technological solutions while, thanks to the architectural process followed in the development of our architecture, we have also considered the architecture definition at conceptual level.

---

[7] http://www.eclipse.org/gmt/oaw/

Spieß in [21] proposes an architecture similar in scope. Spieß proposes a five layer architecture to filter aggregate and notify identification events. This architecture is based on rule processing for routing events, while our approach defines customized Task Processing elements that can elaborate richer messages of business level and control task life-cycle. In addition, the most characteristic point of our architecture design is that it has been defined to enable automatic development.

7   Conclusions and Further Work

The present work introduces an architecture for the support of business processes where real-world elements are involved. The architectural process followed decouples the architectural concepts from the particular technological choices, improving the evolution capabilities of the resulting systems. The architecture has been used in several case studies and has been proven suitable for the automation of the development.

The presented development method raises the abstraction level for the development of this kind of systems. In order to facilitate system specification, DSLs can be defined for particular domains, avoiding architectural concepts. Further research is required to capture specific domain needs in order to define DSLs and validators. However, since the defined architecture metamodel is based on open metamodelling technologies, an opportunity is offered to the MDE community for the development of DSLs and validators suited to specific domains.

Obtaining tool support for the automatic generation of these kind of systems guiding the whole development process becomes the final goal of this research.

References

1. Strassner, M., Schoch, T.: Today's impact of ubiquitous computing on business processes. In: Mattern, F., Naghshineh, M. (eds.) Short Paper Proc. International Conference on Pervasive Computing, Pervasive 2002, pp. 62–74 (April 2002)
2. Aarts, E., Harwig, R., Schuurmans, M.: Ambient intelligence. The invisible future: the seamless integration of technology into everyday life, pp. 235–250 (2002)
3. Römer, K., Schoch, T., Mattern, F., Dübendorfer, T.: Smart identification frameworks for ubiquitous computing applications. Wirel. Netw. 10(6), 689–700 (2004)
4. Schmitt, C., Fischbach, K., Schoder, D.: Towards ambient business: Value-added services through an open object information infrastructure. In: Proceedings of the CollECTeR Europe, pp. 141–148 (2006)
5. Völter, M.: Software architecture patterns – a pattern language for building sustainable software architectures (March 2005)
6. Schmidt, D.C.: Guest editor's introduction: Model-driven engineering. Computer 39(2), 25–31 (2006)
7. Gamma, E., Helm, R., Johnson, R., Vlissides, J.: Design Patterns. Addison-Wesley Professional, Reading (January 1995)
8. Giner, P., Albert, M., Pelechano, V.: Physical-virtual connection in ubiquitous business processes. In: Proceedings of the 10th International Conference on Enterprise Information Systems, Barcelona, Spain, vol. 2, pp. 266–271 (June 2008)

9. Lampe, M., Strassner, M., Fleisch, E.: A ubiquitous computing environment for aircraft maintenance. In: SAC 2004: Proceedings of the 2004 ACM symposium on Applied computing, pp. 1586–1592. ACM, New York (2004)

10. Bencina, R., Kaltenbrunner, M.: The design and evolution of fiducials for the reactivision system. In: Proceedings of the 3rd International Conference on Generative Systems in the Electronic Arts (3rd Iteration 2005), Melbourne, Australia (2005)

11. Torres, V., Giner, P., Pelechano, V.: Modeling ubiquitous business process driven applications. In: Eder, J., Tomassen, S.L., Opdahl, A.L., Sindre, G. (eds.) CAiSE Forum (2007) ISSN: 1503-416X

12. Muñoz, J., Pelechano, V., Cetina, C.: Implementing a pervasive meeting room: A model driven approach. In: IWUC, pp. 13–20 (2006)

13. van Deursen, A., Klint, P., Visser, J.: Domain-specific languages: an annotated bibliography. SIGPLAN Not. 35(6), 26–36 (2000)

14. Bézivin, J., Jouault, F.: Using atl for checking models. In: Int. Workshop on Graph and Model Transformation (GraMoT) (2005)

15. Want, R., Fishkin, K.P., Gujar, A., Harrison, B.L.: Bridging physical and virtual worlds with electronic tags. In: CHI 1999: Proceedings of the SIGCHI conference on Human factors in computing systems, pp. 370–377. ACM Press, New York (1999)

16. Floerkemeier, C., Roduner, C., Lampe, M.: Rfid application development with the accada middleware platform. IEEE Systems Journal, Special Issue on RFID Technology (December 2007)

17. Bornhövd, C., Lin, T., Haller, S., Schaper, J.: Integrating automatic data acquisition with business processes experiences with sap's auto-id infrastructure. In: vldb 2004: Proceedings of the Thirtieth international conference on Very large data bases, VLDB Endowment, pp. 1182–1188 (2004)

18. Aberer, K., Hauswirth, M., Salehi, A.: Middleware support for the "internet of things". In: 5th GI/ITG KuVS Fachgespräch, Stuttgart, Germany (2006)

19. Langheinrich, M., Mattern, F.: First steps towards an event-based infrastructure for smart things. In: Ubiquitous Computing Workshop, PACT 2000, Philadelphia (October 2000)

20. Vermeulen, J., Thys, R., Luyten, K., Coninx, K.: Making bits and atoms talk today: A practical architecture for smart object interaction. In: First international workshop on Design and Integration Principles for Smart Objects (DIPSO 2007), Innsbruck, Austria (September 2007)

21. Spieß, P., Bornhövd, C., Lin, T., Haller, S., Schaper, J.: Going beyond auto-id: a service-oriented smart items infrastructure. Journal of Enterprise Information Management 20(3), 356–370 (2007)

C-NGINE:
A Contextual Navigation Guide for Indoor Environments

Manolis Kritsotakis, Maria Michou, Emmanouil Nikoloudakis, Antonis Bikakis,
Theodore Patkos, Grigoris Antoniou, and Dimitris Plexousakis

Abstract. Location-based services have evolved significantly during the last few years and are reaching a maturity phase, relying primarily on the experience gained and the utilization of recent technologies. Taking advantage of these opportunities, this paper presents a context-aware navigation guide, strongly connected to the semantics behind user profile. Our approach, which focuses on indoor environments, uses OWL ontologies to capture and formally model profile and context information, and reasons on the ontology data using rules in order to support personalized context-aware navigation services. To test and demonstrate the approach, a prototype has been developed that documents the flexibility of the design.

Keywords: context modeling, user profiles, user modeling, spatial representation, path-finding, user tracking, path deviation.

1 Introduction

Technological advances in mobile devices and applications during the last few years have caused a boost in the emergence of location-based and mobile ubiquitous services. This new emerging Ambient Intelligence paradigm commands the interaction of user in a new personalized, context-aware and content-adaptive environment. Mobile guides and navigation systems have come a long way since their first release, but certain challenges have yet to be addressed, while new requirements are continuously becoming apparent. Location based services are typically encountered in outdoor environments and rely on Geographical Information Systems (GIS) in order to correlate a wealth of data to the present location of a mobile terminal. Comparing the information needs of car drivers and pedestrians Rehrl & Leitinger [1] conclude that the main differences are in the degrees of freedom in movement, the velocity of movement and thus the opportunity for perceiving the environment and the resolution of space is larger. Little focus has been given to indoors navigation, and even less to semantically enriched navigation. Most existing approaches are based exclusively on geometric information and neglect important aspects like semantics bound to building areas and user profiles. Hence, the derived applications do not reach the intelligence level anticipated by modern users. Thereby, new methodologies and advanced technologies are being developed that focus on providing flexible and extensible design models, proposing efficient solutions for dynamic environments, structuring solid context-aware infrastructures, as well as promoting openness and interoperability in response to the current highly heterogeneous reality.

E. Aarts et al. (Eds.): AmI 2008, LNCS 5355, pp. 258–275, 2008.

Considering recent trends, the present paper proposes a framework for structuring advanced location-based and context-aware services that integrates up-to-date technologies and develops novel mechanisms and interactive interfaces by applying techniques and formalisms from the Semantic Web and Ambient Intelligence domains. The objective is to explore the intelligent pedestrian navigation by implementing a contextual guide for users in indoor environments. Contextual Navigation Guide for INdoor Environments (C-NGINE) focuses on modeling and representing context using Semantic Web technologies for efficient processing and dissemination of context-based knowledge in order to develop services for mobile users. Integrating web ontology languages, such as OWL, with context-aware applications has manifold benefits. These languages offer enough representational capabilities to develop a formal context model that can be shared, reused, extended for the needs of specific domains, but also combined with data originating from other sources, such as the Web or other applications. Moreover, the development of the logic layer of the Semantic Web is resulting in rule languages that enable reasoning about the user's needs and preferences and exploiting the available ontology knowledge.

C-NGINE enriches indoor navigation with many capabilities which realize the Ambient Intelligence paradigm. The adaptation of the spatial domain to dynamic changes (e.g. obstacles, operational malfunctions etc.) is one of them. Moreover the proposed platform has the ability to track user's movement on the suggested path, ensuring he/she follows it and providing information about user location and motion state. In case of user deviation, the system highlights a new optimal path from the location of the deviation to the same desired destination by activating a dynamic re-planning of the proposed route.The generation of dynamic tours, which take into account personal user interests and preferences, relative contextual information and available time, is another one in the list of features. However, the major contribution is the flexibility of the design of the proposed framework. C-NGINE easily adapts to a wide range of applications, without the need of structural or architectural modifications, based on ontology modeling and rule-based proactive and reactive reasoning. General contextual navigation requirements for a system such as the one presented in this paper, are met in hospitals, conference centers, museums, campus premises etc. As a use-case we have developed a prototype for dynamic user navigation on the premises of our institute research facilities.

Related Work

This subsection is an effort to describe some of the major navigation systems which have already been integrated, to highlight their weaknesses and to uncover the innovative chances that led to the development of C-NGINE.

A navigation solution which takes into consideration the human factor and contains human-centric criteria is Navio system [2]. Navio, stands for Pedestrian Navigation Systems in Combined Indoor/Outdoor Environments. Using an ontology-based model, it provides guiding information to the users describing the criteria, the actions and the reference objects that pedestrians use during their routing. The project mainly focuses on the information aspect of location-based services, especially on the user's tasks and the support of the user's decisions by provided information.

Ontonav is an integrated navigation system for indoor environments which uses a hybrid space model, both geometric and symbolic [3]. OntoNav is purely user-centric in the sense that both the navigation paths and the guidelines that describe them are provided to the users depending on their physical and perceptual capabilities as well as their particular routing preferences. The proposed navigation scheme is largely based on semantic descriptions of the constituent elements of navigation paths, which, in turn, enable reasoning with the available space information.

myCampus [4] is a Semantic Web environment for context-aware mobile services aimed at enhancing everyday campus life. The environment revolves around a growing collection of task-specific agents capable of automatically accessing a variety of contextual information about their users. A central element of the myCampus architecture is the Semantic eWallets that support automated discovery and access of contextual resources subject to privacy constraints specified by their users.

In an effort to highlight the major differences between our system and those mentioned above, we can state the following.

• Systems designed according to the semantic location model (e.g. Navio) and targeted to the optimal user interface creation, have weakened the geometric enrichment of the path finding part.
• Systems which introduce the hybrid location model (e.g. OntoNav) are mostly dedicated on the user-centric navigation services and don't fully exploit the semantics potential, such as the relation representation between users and space elements.
• Systems which aim in context-aware modelling (e.g. myCampus), don't include user characteristics that are subject to navigation dimensions such as possible user impairments and means of guidance. As a result, myCampus doesn't emphasize on the proper design of navigation techniques.
• Independently of the location model, almost all the systems fairly neglected the user tracking part during navigation, the deviation detection and dynamic path replanning procedure.

The rest of the paper is structured as follows: Section 2 presents a detailed scenario which uncovers the major part of C-NGINE functionality, whereas section 3 describes the basic skeleton of the system's architecture. Sections 4, 5 and 6 describe in detail the three main components of the system; User Modeling, Contextual Path-Finding and User Tracking. Section 7 overviews the implementation tools used for the development of the application prototype. Finally, section 8 contains the concluding ideas and briefly summarizes some future goals.

2 Scenario

Below, we present a typical scenario, which takes place in the premises of a research institute, and takes advantage of the capabilities of C-NGINE. Professor Smith has arrived in town for a business meeting. After the meeting he realizes that he has a little time to spare and decides to visit the nearby research center, where he has many professional connections. Upon entering the main gate of the building he is provided with a PDA through which he can have access to C-NGINE. After logging in, Prof. Smith fills in a form that describes his profile. He chooses one of the default profiles, and in particular one describing him as a male visitor, and then fills in some more specific details. Being motor impaired, he defines himself as impaired user assisted by wheelchair. He selects from a list "machine learning" and "computer vision" as his scientific fields of interest and goes on to using the navigation system.

The first screen Prof. Smith views provides him with a description of the events taking place during that day, along with the time and maybe a list of people participating in. He notices that there is a series of lectures on machine learning algorithms all day long, and considers paying a visit if he has time later on. But before proceeding, he decides that he would better go to the restroom, to freshen up. He asks for a path to the closest restroom. The navigation system highlights a path on the navigation map, from his current location to the closest restroom for men, along with a simple textual description of the path he must follow. While moving towards the desired destination, the system visualizes his current location and the motion direction using both textual description (e.g. located in Corridor X, moving northeast) and landmark highlighting (e.g. showing an arrow depicting direction on the spatial element he is currently located). While moving towards the restroom, he realizes that the suggested path is blocked, as a crew of electricians performs maintenance operations and has blocked the whole corridor. Prof. Smith uses the navigation map, to denote that this particular corridor is blocked, and moves out of the suggested path. The system senses that the user has deviated from the selected path and tries to figure out another way to the restroom. However, the path leading to the same restroom and avoiding that corridor is now too long; therefore, the system suggests a new restroom and Prof. Smith finally reaches his destination.

Prof. Smith feels tired of wandering around and decides he should catch up with some of his friends in the institute. Since he has not visited the Institute for a long time, he is not sure where the office of his friend Dr Anderson is. So, he asks the system for a list of people who have a public profile. Dr Anderson is indeed, in the list, but through his public calendar, Prof. Smith realizes that his friend must be in a meeting and probably will not be able to meet him at that particular time. But one of the options in the list of public profiles is Prof. Heinz, who is also a friend and seems to be in his office. So, Prof. Smith asks for directions to his office, which is located on the second floor. The system, being aware that Prof. Smith cannot make use of stairways, suggests a path that leads him to the second floor, through an elevator that fulfils the specifications for carrying wheelchairs. Prof. Smith follows the path and meets with his friend.

After catching up with Prof. Heinz, Prof. Smith realizes that time has passed and he really should go. He makes a phone call, and the taxi agency informs him that the taxi in closest proximity will be there in at least 30 minutes, so Prof. Smith finds the perfect chance to wander around the research center. He denotes to the system that he has 30 minutes to spend and asks for a route that starts from the building entrance, where he is currently located, and returns him back there in time. The system, using information about Prof. Smith's interests, suggests a route that walks through a corridor with posters showing the latest achievements of the computer vision laboratory. Another point of interest is also the conference room where the talking session on machine learning algorithms is now taking place. Prof. Smith follows the suggested route, and after about 30 minutes is located in the main entrance, where the taxi waits for him.

3 Overall System Architecture

C-NGINE is an integrated contextual navigation system for indoor environments. C-NGINE consists of five fundamental components; a *User Interface*, a *Knowledge Base (KB)*, a *Services Layer*, a *Reasoner* and a *Rule Engine*. These components form our system's architecture as depicted in Fig. 1.

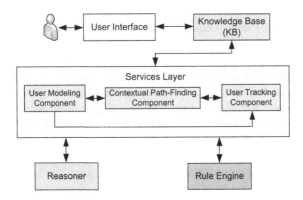

Fig. 1. C-NGINE Architecture

- *User Interface:* Each user interacts with a User Interface; the system takes feed-back from the user and displays essential data. The user inserts data in order to create a unique user profile and edit his/her privacy preferences. Additionally, the user is enabled to customize various parameters for path-finding and deviation purposes. For example, a user may instruct the system to interrupt him/her if he/she deviates from the proposed path. Through the same interface, the system also provides responses to user queries, such as: "Which is the quickest way to the restaurant?" or "Where is my colleague John?"
- *KB:* All information is stored in KB, in the form of semantic web rules and on-tologies, which contains the schema and instances of our modeled classes and properties. For usability and clarification purposes, we split KB into three on-tologies; the User Profile Ontology (UPO), the Spatial Ontology for Path-Finding (SOP) and the User Tracking Ontology (UTO), which are further analyzed in the corresponding sections.
- *Services Layer:* C-NGINE's main functionality is represented by the *Services Layer*, which is decomposed into three mutually dependant components; the User Modeling Component, the Contextual Path-Finding Component, and the User Tracking Component.
- *Reasoner:* Reasoner is a mechanism for inferencing logical consequences from a set of asserted facts and axioms. The main services of a Reasoner are consistency checking, taxonomy classification and computation of inferred types.
- *Rule Engine:* Rule Engine is an environment which enables reasoning on the available context using knowledge supplied in the form of rules.

We also use an application programming interface (API) as middleware between *KB, Reasoner* and *Rule Engine*. API provides *KB* as input to both the *Reasoner* and the *Rule Engine*. Respectively, derived results from the *Reasoner* and the *Rule Engine* are stored to *KB* through the API.

Below, we analyze the information flow between the three components in *Services Layer*. The first important task that the system confronts, during execution, is the creation of an appropriate user profile. During this procedure, User Modeling component receives information from SOP ontology in order to associate users with space elements (e.g. associating a user with his/her office). Respectively, Contextual Path-Finding component communicates with User Modeling in order to provide the optimal navigation path and the guideline information according to user's profile and preferences. The User Tracking component when triggers dynamic re-planning process, calls Contextual Path-Finding to calculate a new optimal path from user's current position to the same desired destination.

4   User Modeling Component

The User Modeling component includes the user model, which describes the user's profile and context information, and the classification of users into various user groups. User Modeling uses two autonomous processing segments; the Reasoner, which classifies the user into various user groups, and the Rule Engine which executes user classification (static) rules and user defined (dynamic) rules. Each of these segments requires input from users (through a user interface) and a Knowledge Base which stores the users' profiles. For the User Modeling component, we will refer to Knowledge Base as the User Profile Ontology (UPO).

4.1   User Profile Ontology (UPO)

User modeling techniques used in prior works include various modeling approaches, such as key-value models, markup scheme models, graphical models, object oriented models, logic based models and ontology based models [5]. In our case, we concluded that the most promising assets for context modeling for ubiquitous computing environments can be found in the ontology based models, because semantics-based technology is widely considered the most enabling research direction.

The aim of User Modeling is to capture all user-related information. As a result, we model not only the users' profiles, but also their context. UPO is developed as an extension of OntoNav's ([6] [7]) User Navigation Ontology (UNO) to give emphasis on context-awareness and modeling of users' dimensions. Such characteristics are essential for the development of group-oriented services, such as semantic notes, semantic alerts, and single-user/group calendars.

The schema of UPO includes classes that describe different types of user, and other information which is required for classifying users under specific user groups. The taxonomy of main classes and their corresponding subclasses is depicted in Fig. 2.

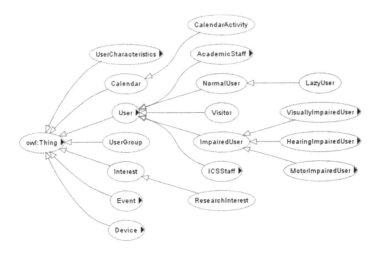

Fig. 2. Main classes of User Profile Ontology (UPO)

- *User*: this superclass includes the user groups a user may belong to according to parameters such as gender (*MaleUser/FemaleUser*), occupation (*AcademicStaff* or *ICSStaff* and *Visitor*) and impairments (*NormalUser*, *HearingImpairedUser*, *MotorImpairedUser* or *VisualImpairedUser*). *NormalUser* class is further analyzed into *LazyUser*; users in this user group do not have any disability but have expressed specific routing preferences such as elevator and escalator.
- *UserGroup*: this class contains user groups that are dynamically created from users' instances that have common interests, work projects, etc.
- *UserCharacteristics*: this class describes the information that is required to classify the users into dynamic user groups, such as gender (male of female), interests (research or general interests), means of guidance (audio, text, and graphical) and routing preferences (elevator, escalator, stairs and ramp).
- *Device*: in addition to main user groups and the user's characteristics, we model the devices the user interacts with. For device modeling, we use the CC/PP [8] vocabulary in UPO. Based on the Semantic Web and RDF technologies, CC/PP allows the creation of extensible, non-centralized vocabularies, enhancing the management of device capability and user preference profiles. For our purposes, CC/PP is only used for device modeling.
- *Event*: this class describes all activities carried out in the premises of a building.
- *Calendar*: each user owns one personal calendar. Each calendar contains at least one task, in the form of activities. Calendar activities have the same characteristics as event activities. Additionally, a user owns user group calendars, which are dynamically generated when an event is created. A user can have as many user group calendars as the dynamic user groups he/she belongs to (according to the projects he/she may be involved in, the events that might be interested in, etc). The user group calendars combine the characteristics of the groups' participants (if allowed by their privacy preferences), and enable the creation of a common electronic board of alerts about new events or projects, group meetings, etc. The publication of alerts is always conformed to the users' privacy preferences.

4.2 Classification of Instances into Classes

A key feature of the OWL language is the *Open World Assumption*, i.e. if there is a statement that we don't have the knowledge for, we cannot infer that is true or false. As a consequence, the Reasoner classifies instances into classes that have a strict definition, named *defined* or *complete* classes, as opposed to *primitive* or *partial* classes. A defined class in UPO is *MaleUser*. An instance of this class would be read as: "if a user instance belongs to *MaleUser* class then he is also a member of *User* class and his gender is male" and vice versa: "if a user belongs to *User* class and his gender is male, then he is also a member of *MaleUser* class". On the other hand, a primitive class in UPO is *ImpairedUser*. An instance of this class would be read as: "if a user belongs to *ImpairedUser* class, then he/she must have a disability". The opposite doesn't necessarily apply i.e. "If a user has a disability then he/she belongs to *ImpairedUser* class". In our case, some of our classes are defined and some are not. As we already stated, the Reasoner undertakes classification into defined classes only. For the classification into primitive classes, we have to define specific classification rules, which are executed by the Rule Engine immediately after the Reasoner has completed its tasks. Some representative examples of such rules, which we call *static rules* are given below:

- *VisuallyImpairedUser(?x) → hasMeansOfGuidance(?x, profiles:AudioGuidance)*
  Description: A visually impaired user is guided with audio assistance.
- *NormalUser(?x) ∧ hasRoutingPreferences(?x,Elevator) → LazyUser(?x)*
  Description: If a user doesn't have any impairment and his/her routing preferences include elevator, then he/she is a member of *LazyUser* class.

4.3 Privacy Preferences

Our system enables users to express their privacy preferences in terms of rules. Specifically, users can edit predefined rules to determine what segment of their profile is visible and to whom. Initially, the users select if they want their profile to be visible. If this is the case, they can choose which parameters will be visible and to which user groups or individuals. We also have to note that they cannot use arbitrary groups, but exclusively those they belong to. For example, a user may want his/her personal data to be visible to all users, while his/her calendar to be visible only to his/her colleagues. Another category of rules is about notifications depending on a users' status. For example, if a user is busy, then he/she may wish to be notified only via email. Below, we further explain some user-defined (*dynamic*) rules:

- *User(jdoe) ∧ hasStatusAction(jdoe, ?s) ∧ hasStatus(?s,away) → hasAction(?s,sms)*
  Description: When user's 'jdoe' status is away, he/she wants to be notified via sms.
- *User(jdoe) ∧ hasStatusVisibility(jdoe, ?v) ∧ hasStatus(?v,online) ∧ User(?b) ∧ hasBuddies(jdoe,?b) → isVisibleTo(?v,?b)*
  Description: Only jdoe's buddies see him/her online.

- *User(jdoe) ∧ hasStatusVisibility(jdoe, ?v) ∧ hasStatus(?v,busy) ∧ User(?u) →*
  isVisibleTo(?v,?u)

  Description: All users see jdoe's status as busy.

Notice that the second and the third rule are conflicting, because jdoe's buddies are also members of the User class. To resolve this type of conflicts, we define priorities depending on a user's status. For example, we define that the 'online' status makes the rule stronger than 'busy' status. If the weaker rule fires before the stronger rule do, i.e. the third rule fires before the second does, then we have no conflicts. Using the priority definition, the interpretation of rules becomes: "All users except jdoe's buddies see jdoe busy, while only jdoe's buddies see him/her online".

5   Contextual Path-Finding component

This component is responsible for providing the "best traversable" path, according to the parameters analyzed in the previous section. Moreover one of the tasks accomplished by this component is the population of SOP, and the creation of a spatial graph by using floor maps and a series of steps whose analysis is out of the scope of this paper. The user options concerning path-finding are:

- Typical path-finding: We become aware of the desired user destination in one of the following ways:
    o   The user clicks on the desired destination directly on the map
    o   The user chooses to go to a spatial element that is closest to him/her from a selection list (e.g. printer, bathroom)
- Time-based tour: The user denotes that he/she has a particular amount of time available and requests the system to provide him/her with a tour. This tour must include elements that may be of interest to him/her. Also the destination point is considered to be the same as the starting one and the requirement is that the user is back there in time provided as input. The time needed to traverse the requested route, is actually affected by the user's profile and in particular by his physical capabilities/ impairments. (e.g. an impaired user with a wheelchair is considered to move with lower speed when compared to a user with no impairments).

5.1   Spatial Ontology for Path-Finding (SOP)

The navigation ontology that we use is largely based on the Indoor Navigation Ontology (INO) [6]. INO relies, to a large extent, on the semantic description of paths and their structural elements. This description, in conjunction with the semantic/ symbolic space description, facilitates the reasoning and the enforcement of restrictions during user navigation. Following these guidelines, SOP supports both path search and the presentation tasks of a navigation system. A core part of our ontology is depicted in Fig. 3.

The main spatial concepts behind semantic path-finding are *path elements*, which are classified to *passages* and *path points*. A *passage* is any spatial element that is part of a *path* and has specific accessibility properties. We can classify passages to *horizontal* (connecting corridors in the same floor), *vertical* (connecting corridors in different floors) and *motor passages* (a passage that operates with motor power). The

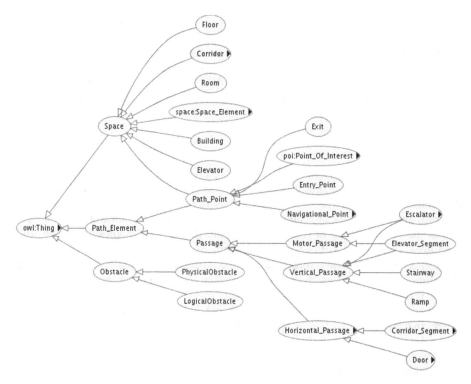

Fig. 3. The Spatial Ontology for Path-finding (SOP)

main types of vertical passages are *elevator segments*, *stairways* and *escalators*. The main types of horizontal passages are *ramps*, *doors*, and *corridors* (actually parts of corridors). A passage always connects exactly two path points.

Path points can either be *exits*, *entry points*, *navigational points* or *points of inter- est*. An *exit* is a point which signifies the transition from the interior to the exterior (and vice versa) of a spatial element such as a *building*, a *floor* or a *room*. An *entry point* is actually used, only when we want to navigate to the interior of a room. This point defines the start of a *virtual corridor*, namely a corridor of non-physical exis- tence, a conceptual construct used to navigate to points of interests inside a room. As a *point of interest*, we define any object of virtual or physical existence on a path, which may be of importance to a user (e.g. an entrance to a room, a printer). Also a user may define any spatial element as an *obstacle*, namely anything that may block his/her way. Based on this definition, an obstacle may be of physical or logical nature. A *physical* obstacle may be an object whose dimensions block a passage or a corridor or any object with certain properties that denote that access is prohibited or not possi- ble (closed door, non operating elevator). Logical objects on the other hand enable the definition of *dynamic* and *non-physical* obstacles. The latter imply either some-non permanent conditions (e.g. security policies that prevent access to some particular space) or some user-specific preferences (a user may desire not to pass from a particu- lar passage).

The aforementioned set of concepts cannot provide all the desired model expressiveness by itself. For that purpose we have to import elements of other spatial ontologies which define spatial concepts and topological relations between them (e.g., we need the concepts of *room, floor* and *building*). The same principle applies for the Points of Interest which partly depend on the application scenario. Apart from the virtual points of interest, that a particular user may define, we may need to define the concepts of *printer, scanner, poster* etc.

5.2 Path-Finding

There are several research works focusing on path-finding algorithms. A representative example oriented on pedestrian navigation is [9] where an algorithm calculating the "simplest" path between two points, is described. The main concept here is that the form and complexity of route instructions may be as important to human navigators as the overall length of route. So the author defines as "simplest" the path with the lowest complexity with respect to the complexity of the instructions. Another interesting approach is also presented in [10]. The paths composed by the routing algorithm are presented as "less risk paths". The most important feature of this approach is the lowest probability of getting lost.

The main element of our navigation scheme is also the path-finding algorithm, which, in conjunction with a set of production rules, is responsible for the calculation of the *best* navigation path between two locations. Our algorithm is applied on a topological graph, which is created based on the instances of the navigation ontology. The vertices of the graph are instances of *Path_Point*, while the edges are instances of *Passage*. The weight marked on edges can either be the *total length* of the passage or the *average time* needed to traverse the passage. These two are actually both attributes of *Passage*, while *time* is also an attribute of *Path_Point*. The notion of *length* is quite intuitive and does not depend on user's profile. On the contrary the *time* needed to traverse a passage is different in special cases of impaired users (e.g. an impaired user with a wheel chair is considered to move in lower speed than a user with no disabilities and thus needs more time). When *time* refers to an instance of *Path_Point,* we consider it to model *observation time* (e.g. average time needed to study a poster mounted on a wall).

The geometric model (*graph*) of our system represents the paths that are accessible by any user. The length (or the time needed to traverse accordingly) of a path is a parameter that we consider being of concern to any type of user and this attribute is used for the initial calculation of the possible paths. Namely, any mathematical path-finding algorithm applied on this graph returns a set of paths that are traversable by any user. The only ranking parameter is the sum of weights of the edges the route comprises of. In our implementation, we use a k-shortest path algorithm based on an implementation of J.Y Yen [11]. This step provides us with a super-set of all the traversable paths, with their end-to-end weight.

5.3 Semantic-Driven Navigation

The semantic-driven selection of the *Best Traversable Path* is achieved through rule-based reasoning. The rules combine the semantics of the spatial elements of the navigation ontology with that of UPO. To support the desired functionality, we define three different and disjoint classes of attributes.

- The class of *physical capabilities* (i.e., attributes related to user's physical capabilities). The rules based on this class define which path elements are accessible by physically handicapped users. The system applies these rules to all path elements, so that inaccessible ones are excluded.
- The class of *perceptual capabilities* (i.e., attributes related to user's understanding of navigation guidelines). The rules based on this class are responsible for the selection of elements of the finally selected path, which may be used for the navigation guidelines.
- The class of *routing preferences* (i.e., attributes related to various user preferences regarding the path selection process). A user may for example prefer paths that do not contain stairways. Also we must also reward path elements that seem to be of interest to the user.

The rules applied on the last two types of attributes are used to reward or penalize path elements, rather than exclude them. For instance, some rules of this type are presented below:

- *Physical rule*
  $MotorImpairedUser(?u) \land Escalator(?s) \rightarrow isExcludedFor(?s, ?u)$
  Description: If a user is disabled and makes use of a motor powered vehicle, exclude all escalators
- *Perceptual rule (penalization)*
  $HearingImpairedUser(?u) \land hasDescription(?pass, ?descr)$
  $\land Audio\_Description(?descr) \rightarrow hasPerceptualPenaltyFor(?pass, ?u)$
  Description: If a user is hearing impaired then penalize all path elements that have audio description
- *Routing preference rule (reward)*
  $LazyUser(?u) \land Motor\_Passage(?p) \rightarrow hasPreferentialBonusFor(?p, ?u)$
  Description: If a user has been classified as lazy, then reward any passages powered by motor.
- *Routing preference rule (reward)*
  $Room(?room) \land hasPoint(?room, ?exit) \land hasInterest(?room, ?interest) \land User(?user) \land hasInterest(?user, ?interest) \rightarrow hasPreferentialBonusFor(?user, ?exit))$
  Description: If a user has defined his/her field of interest and a room matches some of these interests, then reward path points that belong to this room.

The classification of rules into different classes demands a conflict resolution method, so that it is clear which one is applied first. The main features of our method are the following:

- The physical rules are mandatory and should always supersede other types. They are always applied before searching for possible paths, namely they are applied on the whole navigation space and not on specific path elements. They are the only type of rules applied for exclusion.

- For the calculation of the best traversable paths we use the above sum formula:

$$total\ path\ weight = a * total\ path\ length +$$
$$b * total\ perceptual\ reward +$$
$$c * total\ preference\ reward$$

The values of *a*, *b*, *c* determine the level at which the navigation is semantic-driven, and can be modeled in the user's profile as a custom percentage. In case of time-driven navigation the total path length is replaced by total path time.

6 User Tracking Component

This specific system component is responsible for tracking user's movement on the suggested path and providing with useful information about user location and motion state. For example, when a user enters an elevator in order to move from the ground floor to the first floor of a building, the information provided by the system will be: "User is inside elevator and moves upwards". Furthermore, the component is responsible for checking whether a user is following the proposed path and for detecting any deviations. In case of a path deviation, the User Tracking component dynamically re-plans the user's suggested path from his/her current position. Another case, in which the tracking mechanism executes the dynamic re-planning process, is upon receiving user feedback. For example, in case a user finds an obstacle blocking the way, he/she sends feedback to the application about the collision point and the system proposes a new, collision-free, path to user's desired destination.

6.1 User Tracking Ontology (UTO)

In Fig. 4 below, the diagrammatic representation of ontology's classes is depicted, expressing the hierarchy and inheritance that exist between general classes and their subclasses.

- *LocationDescription*: expresses the type of relation between users and path elements or POIs.
    - o *DynamicDescription*: contains all the dynamic types of relations, such as *towards, away from* etc.
    - o *StaticDescription*: contains all the static types of relations, such as *at, inside* etc.
- *Motion*: models user's movement.
    - o *Direction*: models user's movement orientation which can be distinguished in *ClockDirection* (movement according to the rotation of clock hands), *CompassDirection* (movement according to a magnetic compass), *RelativeXYDirection* (movement according to the X and Y axis), *RealtiveZDirection* (movement according to the Z axis) and *Relative0Direction* (immobility).
    - o *MotionState*: describes user's movement state, which can be either *Standing* or *Walking*.

- *NavigationalPreferences*: models user's navigation preferences, which can be either *AutonomousNavigation* or *AssistedNavigation*.
- *NaviCharacteristics*: models user's navigation characteristics and information.
  - o *DeviationState*: models user's state according to the number of times he/she has deviated from the proposed path, which can be *RareDeviate* (0 to 5 deviations), *OftenDeviate* (6 to 10 deviations) and *TooOftenDeviate* (11 and above deviations).
  - o *NavigationalState*: models user's state according to his/her navigation behavior, which can be either *FollowingPath* or *DeviatingFromPath*.

Fig. 4. Diagram of User Tracking & Location Modeling Ontology

User Location Modeling and Dynamic Feedback

The original intention for user's location modeling is to create a relation of the following type: "*John is inside roomA*". This expression implies the existence of a 3-ary relation, which will connect user class (*John*) with the static descriptions class (*inside*)

and with the space element class (*roomA*). In similar way, we create dynamic and static relations with users and space elements.

The system handles user feedback about factors which block his/her navigation route using the three following ontology properties: *reportsLock*, *reportsMalfunction* and *reportsObstacle*. For example, *reportsLock* property connects the user with the specific door which is reported as locked.

6.2 Proactive and Reactive Rules for User Tracking and Dynamic Re-planning

Reactive rules have the structure "ON Event IF Condition DO Action" and specify to execute the Action automatically when the Event happens, provided the Condition holds. Proactive (production) rules are of the form WHEN Condition DO Action and specify to execute the Action if an update to the local data base makes the Condition true. This shows that the similarities in the structure of these two kinds of rules come with similarities, but also some differences, in the semantics of the two rule paradigms.

The most important proactive rules designed for the user tracking component control are listed below. These rules are referred to the user motion modeling, the user relative location modeling and the classification of user according to the number of deviations.

- *User(?x) ∧ hasXTimesDeviated(?x,?y) ∧ lessThanOrEqual(?y, 5) ∧ RareDeviate(?z) → hasDeviationState(?x, ?z)*
  Description: If user has deviated y times and y is up to 5, then user x has deviation state z where z is *RareDeviate*. In similar way, the rules for *OftenDeviate* and *TooOftenDeviate* classes are designed.
- *User(?x) ∧ CompassDirection (?y) ∧ Walking(?z) ∧ hasDirection(?x, ?y) → hasMotionState(?x, ?z)*
  Description: If user has moving direction y and y is the state of motion according to a magnetic compass, then user has motion state z, where z is *Walking*. In similar way, the rules for *CompassDirection*, *RelativeXYDirection* and *RelativeZDirection* classes are designed.

Apart from the proactive rules developed in all three system components, the user tracking procedure requires the existence of reactive rules which are dynamically triggered only in special occasions (i.e. deviation, path obstacle). These rules are designed based on JESS definition rules architecture and target to cover two main theme categories, user feedback and user deviation. The main characteristic of the JESS rules is the operation of JavaBeans in rule's body. Two basic reactive rules are described below:

- *(defrule lockRule (User { reportsLock == TRUE } (specificUser ?usr))*
  => (printout ?usr "reported lock")(calling DynamicReplanning ?usr))
  Description: From the entity User, if the boolean field 'reportsLock' (JavaBean property) becomes true, then print out which user (stored in variable usr) reported the locked door and call DynamicReplanning process, with argument the specific user (i.e. the variable usr). In similar way, the rules for path obstacle and malfunctioning motor passage are designed.

- *(defrule deviationRule (User { deviates == TRUE }(specificUser ?usr)) => (print-out "Deviation Detected for "?usr)(calling DynamicReplanning ?usr))*
  Description: From the entity *User*, if the boolean field *'deviates'* becomes *'true'*, then print out which user deviates and call DynamicReplanning process, with argument the specific user.

6.3 Dynamic Re-planning Process

Dynamic re-planning procedure is strongly connected with the Contextual Path-Finding component and the incorporated algorithm. The specific algorithm takes as arguments path points (e.g. junctions, exits); therefore the most important issue that re-plan process handles is the correct calculation of these arguments. The arguments refer to the start and destination points of user's route. Of course, the calculation of the destination point is trivial, because it is the same destination as before dynamic re-plan triggering.

However, the specification of the starting point is a little more complicated. The general confrontation of the issue is to retract the path element that the user has static relation with, before the triggering of dynamic re-planning. For this purpose the system takes this information from the *hasRelativeLocation* property of the ontology model.

There are two different occasions in which the system triggers dynamic re-plan; the first is user deviation. When system receives coordinates that correspond to a path element that does not belong to the proposed path or that has already been overlapped by the user, it suggests that user has deviated from the proposed path. The second occasion is the user feedback; when user finds an obstacle blocking his/her navigation, reports it to the tracking system. The obstacle could be a locked door, a malfunctioning motor passage or a blocked path element. In both occasions, tracking system proposes a new optimal route.

7 Implementation Characteristics

In the second section, the presented scenario uncovers the major part of our system functionality. Specifically, the implemented prototype of our navigation guide is referred to the premises of a research institute. In the following paragraphs, the main implementation tools used to develop this particular prototype are described.

For the ontology modeling we use Protégé-OWL [13], an open-source ontology editor. Protégé, besides the editor, provides a suite of tools that support the creation, visualization, and manipulation of ontologies in various representation formats. In order to establish communication between the designed ontology and the application's API, we use the Protégé-OWL API, an open-source Java library for OWL and RDF(S). The API provides classes and methods to load and save OWL files, to query and manipulate OWL data models, and to perform reasoning based on Description Logic engines.

The OWL [14] sublanguage that we chose is OWL-DL, which supports complicated context and also defines rules in owl format, without referring to another language. It is expressive enough to cover our needs (i.e. it doesn't have cardinality constraints), without increasing the complexity of reasoning as in OWL-Full. One of the major advantages using an ontology described in OWL-DL is that it can be processed by a Description Logic Reasoner. For our purpose we use Pellet [15] Reasoner, an open source OWL DL Reasoner in Java which communicates with Protégé through the DIG [16] interface.

Protégé integrates the SWRLTab plug-in in Protégé-OWL that supports the execution of SWRL [17] proactive rules using the Jess rule engine [18]. SWRL rules are of the form: "if antecedents then consequent". Jess is a rule engine and scripting environment written in Java that has the ability to "reason" using knowledge supplied in the form of rules. A category of reactive rules is the Jess definition rules which are used to apply reactivity to our system. Jess rules are of the type: "on event, if condition is satisfied, then action is triggered" and are executed whenever their conditional parts are satisfied.

The map graphics and the spatial representation are implemented with the aid of SVG files. SVG is a language for describing two-dimensional graphics and graphical applications in XML which allows designers to create dynamically generated, high-quality graphics from real-time data with precise structural and visual control.

Finally, the system receives user coordinates through a positioning mechanism that locates user in the environment. This particular mechanism is the Collaborative Location Sensing system [12] that exploits the IEEE802.11 wireless network infrastructure for positioning.

8 Conclusion

Our Contextual Guide aims at providing a navigation tool for indoor environments, which directly depends on human profiles, exploiting information about user's physical and mental status and preferences. Using such kind of data, the guide adapts the path-finding algorithm, through the aid of predefined rules, in order to provide the "best traversable" and not necessarily the quickest route. Moreover, the guiding system is responsible to track user's movement, ensuring he/she follows the suggested path and providing useful information about user location and motion state.

A task of crucial importance for our guide is the imminent evaluation testing of the application. The testing results would be very helpful in order to succeed the optimal interaction for the user without inconveniencies from latency factors. In addition, the modeling of a generic way to provide the guideline instructions and user location and motion information is one of our future priorities.

Due to the fact that C-NGINE is a semantics-enriched system, we will be able to develop more group-oriented services that user groups will exploit, not necessarily belonging to the scientific field, e.g. user groups concerning sports activities. Also, user model is subject to more context enhancement by increasing the user's dimensions without affecting its flexibility. The enrichment of the user model could lead us to conceive various context-aware scenarios. However, the more semantics we add in user model, the more control we wish to have in privacy and security issues. As a result, as expressiveness of knowledge representation increases, we have to enhance privacy and security customizations.

References

[1] Rehrl, K., Leitinger, S.: The SemWay Project – Towards Semantic Navigation Systems. In: Proceedings of the 4th International Symposium on LBS & TeleCartography, Hong Kong (2007)

[2] Gartner, G., Frank, A., Retscher, G.: Pedestrian Navigation System in Mixed Indoor/Outdoor Environment- The NAVIO Project, CORP 2004 and Geomultimedia 2004, Vienna, Austria (2004)

[3] Anagnostopoulos, C., Tsetsos, V., Kikiras, P., Hadjiefthymiades, S.: OntoNav: A Semantic Indoor Navigation System. In: Proceedings of the 1st Workshop on Semantics in Mobile Environments (SME), MDM 2005, Cyprus (2005)

[4] Gandon, F., Sadeh, N.: Semantic web technologies to reconcile privacy and context awareness. J. Web Sem. 1(3), 241–260 (2004)

[5] Strang, T., Linnhoff-Popien, C.: A context modeling survey. In: First International Workshop on Advanced Context Modelling, Reasoning And Management (2004)

[6] Kikiras, P., Tsetsos, V., Hadjiefthymiades, S.: Ontology-based User Modeling for Pedestrian Navigation Systems. In: ECAI 2006 Workshop on Ubiquitous User Modeling (UbiqUM), Riva del Garda, Italy (2006)

[7] Tsetsos, V., Anagnostopoulos, C., Kikiras, P., Hadjiefthymiades, S.: Semantically enriched navigation for indoor environments. Int. J. Web and Grid Services 2(4), 453–478 (2006)

[8] Composite Capability/Preference Profiles (CC/PP): Structure and Vocabularies 1.0. W3C Recommendation (January 15, 2004), http://www.w3.org/TR/2004/REC-CCPP-struct-vocab-20040115/

[9] Duckham, M., Kulik, L.: "Simplest" Paths: Automated Route Selection for Navigation, COSIT (2003)

[10] Grum, E.: Danger of getting lost: Optimize a path to minimize risk. In: 10th International Conference onUrban Planning & Regional Development in the Information Society (CORP 2005), Vienna, Austria (2005)

[11] Yen, J.Y.: Finding the k shortest loopless paths in a network. Management Science 17, 712–716 (1971)

[12] Fretzagias, C., Papadopouli, M.: Cooperative location-sensing for wireless networks. In: Second IEEE International conference on Pervasive Computing and Communications 2004, Orlando, Florida (2004)

[13] The Protege Ontology Editor and Knowledge Acquisition System. Stanford Center for Biomedical Informatics Research, http://protege.stanford.edu/

[14] OWL Web Ontology Language Reference. W3C Recommendation (February 10, 2004), http://www.w3.org/TR/owl-ref/

[15] LLC, Clark & Parsia. Pellet: The Open Source OWL DL Reasoner, http://pellet.owldl.com/

[16] (DIG), DL Implementation Group. DL Implementation Group (DIG), http://dl.kr.org/dig/index.html

[17] SWRL: A Semantic Web Rule Language Combining OWL and RuleML. W3C Member Submission (May 21, 2004), http://www.w3.org/Submission/SWRL/

[18] Friedman-Hill, Ernest. Jess, the Rule Engine for the Java Platform. Sandia National Laboratories, http://herzberg.ca.sandia.gov/

Creating Design Guidelines for a Navigational Aid for Mild Demented Pedestrians

F.N. Hagethorn[1], B.J.A. Kröse[1], P. de Greef[2], and M.E. Helmer[2]

[1] University of Amsterdam, Kruislaan 403, 1098 SJ Amsterdam, The Netherlands
[2] Eindhoven University of Technology, P.O. Box 513, 5600MB, Eindhoven,
The Netherlands

Abstract. In this paper we describe our project in which we study design options for a GPS-based navigation aid for elderly with beginning dementia. In a user centered approach we first studied problems of the target group. Results were used in the design of a WoZ prototype. The method proved to work very well in designing a prototype that is tuned to the needs of the user. This prototype was used in experiments in which we studied the performance of landmark vs. left right instructions in navigation. We found that landmark based instructions resulted in less errors and less hesitation with the users.

1 Introduction

Nowadays, finding the right way to a destination is getting easier because of the broad range of navigation systems on the market. The user can enter his desired destination and the system will point the user in the right direction. At every decision point, like a junction, the system uses verbal instructions and/or visual support on a screen, like directions on a map. Such systems are available for most people who take part in traffic, like motorists, cyclists and pedestrians. Currently research is focusing more and more on specific target groups. Studies have been done in order to explore the most effective form of auditive aid for the blind and the visually challenged [8,15,5,9]. Another category that may benefit from such systems is the elderly pedestrian, especially the elderly pedestrian with mild dementia. Alarm systems exist that let the elderly get in touch with a caregiver when they are lost, for example the alarm medallion that with a press on a button can warn the caregiver who then will accompany the person to his or her desired destination. Prototype systems have been tested only for indoor navigation [11]. Andersen et al.[2] found that good support for pedestrians with mild dementia can lead to a better quality of life, especially in terms of independence and freedom to move around outdoors. The physical and mental fitness of a patient can also improve and the deterioration of the dementia process can be postponed [12]. With this extended independence and freedom the patient can continue to live at home for an endured period of time and medical expenses can be reduced as well as the work pressure of the caregiver.

We study the design considerations for a navigation system for the target group. We took a user centered approach because we feel that nobody better

E. Aarts et al. (Eds.): AmI 2008, LNCS 5355, pp. 276–289, 2008.

than the dementia patients themselves can indicate the problems they encounter while taking an independent walk outdoors. Next to the findings in literature it is essential to learn about the experiences in the field and needs the patients and their caregivers have in relation to wayfinding. For this we contacted several care centers in the Netherlands and undertook outdoor walks with patients who suffer from mild dementia. We had group discussions and interviews with patients and caregivers about their experiences with wayfinding and about the possible functionality of the aid. We also took several walks with a test system which we designed to find out what the patients thought about it and to see if walking with our system is helping them to find their way.

The goal of our study is to gain insight into 1) frequently made mistakes that people with mild dementia make in wayfinding, while taking an independent walk. 2) which functionalities a navigational aid for this target group should have or should not have 3) how the target group feels about such a navigational aid 4) test the difference between landmark based and left/right based instructions for navigation.

2   Dementia and Wayfinding

The term dementia represents a number of illnesses which increasingly weakens the patient's memory functions and cognitive skills. This can lead to problems in wayfinding [4]. Dementia can affect the area of language (aphasia or the disability to use language correctly), the motor area (apraxia or the disability to execute targeted operations or movements correctly), the perception area (agnosia or the disability to recognize impressions of the senses) and/or the area for executing functionalities (planning, organizing and consecutive acting). The symptoms significantly contribute to impairments in social and professional handling and show a clear decrease in former cognitive level.

Wayfinding is the process that involves making decisions about which direction to choose while taking a walk [1]. It is heavily based on the memory and perception functions of a person. As discussed in the previous paragraph, these functionalities are the ones which deteriorate when the dementia progresses. A logical result is that patients with dementia perform worse at wayfinding and learning new routes [4,1,18]. They also more frequently fail to execute a planned wayfinding task than people who do not suffer from dementia. Patients also seem to get confused more easily by conventional navigation aids, like street nameplates [11], not so much because they do not know how to use these but because of problems with understanding language or sight. It was reported often that patients who suffer to dementia make use of salient objects in the surroundings, or 'landmarks', while taking a walk outdoors [1,18]. Passini et. al [14] studied design criteria for indoor environments to let patients with Alzheimer's disease find their way better. Their study shows that performance of reaching a predefined destination depends on the structure of the building and the number of reference points. Examples of these reference points are spaces with a certain function, like the lobby, the living room or medical staffroom but also smaller objects like a clock. Deviations in form, function or meaning of an object in contrast to other objects in its surrounding form the characteristics of a reference point.

It seems that 'landmark objects', or 'reference points' play an important role in the spatial cognition of dementia patients. In the following we will focus on our design procedure for our landmark-based navigation device for elderly with beginning dementia.

3   Design of a Simple Navigational Aid

With the target group in mind, the interaction between the aid and the patient must be as simple as possible. This way the patient can more easily learn to handle the aid and is distracted by it as little as possible. We base the design on existing navigational aids that are used in cars, like TomTom, since we do not have urgent reasons not to do so, at this point in the study. To design such an aid using a user centered approach, we need to view the design in a few levels. The first level is that of the experienced problems and hindrance we try to aid with the system. The second level consists of the functionalities of the system. The third level consists of the dialog between the aid and the user and the fourth level consists of the physical form of the system itself.

Level 1: problems in wayfinding. To address the first level of the design, which covers the retrieval of information about what problems or hindrance the system may aid, we contacted different care centers in The Netherlands and spoke with mild demented patients and caregivers about their experiences with wayfinding. To gain more insight we also took several outdoor walks (as of now: "Introduction walks") with patients. The main goal of these walks was to gain insight into the reoccurring mistakes which people with mild dementia make while finding their way when taking an independent walk outdoors. We've paid close attention to the ability of the patient to find the correct way to a predefined destination and to problems that occur in relation to their independence. We also paid attention to the correct use of the rules in traffic by the patient. During the walks we recorded frequently made mistakes and hindrance the patients experience, by using observation and making conversation with every participant after the walk. While taking the introductions walks, no use was made of electronics to navigate. The routes we walked were not predefined. The patient chose the destination, for example the market place and the way that he or she thought was the correct one. Table 1 shows the demographic characteristics of the participants and the locations where the walks took place.

During the introduction walks we found that the most frequently made mistakes were: choosing the wrong direction at a decision point, not recognizing the destination, incorrect use of the rules in traffic and portraying dangerous behavior by, for example, not taking the rest of traffic into account while crossing the street. The hindrance pointed out most by the participants was the feeling of uncertainty or agitation while choosing a direction to go into. Also the sudden

Table 1. Demographic characteristics of the participants and the locations the walks took place. Par.= Participant, M= Male, F= Female, Diagn.= Diagnose, AD = Alzheimer's disease, VD = Vascular Dementia.

Par.	Sex	Diagn	Remark	Location
1	F	AD	-	Amsterdam
2	F	VD	Has difficulties with walking	Hilversum
3	M	AD	Has difficulties with walking	Hilversum
4	F	VD	Has difficulties with visual perception	Hilversum
5	M	AD	Young demented	Utrecht
6	M	AD	Young demented	Leusden
7	M	AD	Young demented	Leusden

loss of memory or understanding of their whereabouts is pointed out as being problematic. It must be said that the wayfinding performance during the walks greatly differ from patient to patient while for the most part the diagnosed disease was the same. In this part of our research we concentrate on the first stated problem; the decision making process involving the directions about the way in which to proceed a walk. If some kind of guidance is given, the user could feel less uncertain or agitated while choosing a direction.

Level 2: functionalities of the aid. In any case, the system is meant to aid the user in navigating to a predefined destination. However at this point, it is still undecided if the future system will use geographical maps to navigate with, just like navigational aids for cars do, or that the routes are specifically programmed for a certain user. In this particular part of our research, we've used predefined routes with a destination where the patient is navigated to. From the user's point of view, we can say that there are decision points along the way, like crossings, where the user has to decide in what direction he or she should proceed. A simple navigational aid will assist the user by giving instructions to go left or right when arriving at decision points. If the user doesn't follow up the instruction and makes a mistake, he or she will get the instruction to turn around, so the user will get back on the predefined route. If the user has reached the destination, he or she will be informed about that by the system.

Level 3: dialog with the user. Instructions could appear on a display, like text or a map, but the display for information about a route can also be in the form of auditive instructions. We choose to use the latter because it requires the least attention and offers the least distraction [7]. In this part of our research we have used the same syntax as used in car navigation. For example, the TomTom navigational aids have a speech display. Approximately 50 meters prior to a decision point an instruction is giving like: "In 50 meters turn [left/right]." It also has an instruction to turn around when going in the wrong direction and the arrival at the destination will also be announced. We did not use distance information, and in experiments reported later in this paper we compare left/right instructions to landmark based instructions.

Level 4: physical aspects of the aid. The navigational aid will be built in a small box that can be carried around easily. The auditive display will be realized with an earphone, a speaker system would be less discrete. We used a male voice for the spoken instructions. Our decision about the voice was based on a study by Lines and Hone (2006) [10]. They found that a male voice was preferred for spoken instructions.

4   Evaluating the Design

To determine the effect of a simple electronic navigational aid, we need a working system that we can use to let participants perform tasks. At the time of this writing we do not have such a system. In user-centered design such a dilemma is dealt with using the Wizard of Oz approach.

4.1   Wizard of Oz Approach

In a Wizard of Oz (WoZ) approach, a simulation of the future system is constructed. The system is not fully autonomous but some parts, often the reasoning part or the perception part, are carried out by a human behind the screen (the 'Wizard'). The WoZ system is evaluated by users as if it were a real working implementation of the system. In other projects on technology acceptance by elders we had a positive experience with WoZ approaches [6]. Figure 1 shows the Wizard of Oz approach we took to simulate a simple navigational aid. To perform the Wizard role accurately is a demanding job and requires prior training to get acceptable and consistent behavior [16]. Preparations for our Wizard of Oz walks consist of defining a route near the care centre of the participant, defining decision points within the route, defining the points in the route were the spoken instruction is given, recording the spoken instructions and practicing with the WoZ setup on site without participants because we didn't want to stress the patients while practicing.

Fig. 1. Wizard of Oz method for the walks with a simple navigational test system

4.2   Apparatus

The test system consists of a ASUS A636N PDA with Windows Mobile 5. This PDA has Bluetooth version 2 software with Advanced Audio Distribution Profile (A2DP). The earphones, the Jabra BT320s, can be connected to the PDA with A2DP. We used the Windows Mobile 5 Windows Media Player to play the spoken instruction sound files. We configured the PDA control buttons so we can play the sound files by using the buttons instead of having to use the stylus while walking. Using the stylus while walking could result in accidentally tapping the wrong sound file. Also, we muted all the theme sounds in Windows Mobile 5.

4.3   Routes

Two routes were set out. One route went through the town of Leusden (from now on: Town-route) and the other went through a park in Leusden (from now on: Park-route). Both routes begin and end at the building of the care center for young demented patients. Both routes took approximately 50 minutes to walk, with an average speed of 3 kilometers an hour. The town-route holds 24 audio instructions and the park-route had 22 audio instructions.

4.4   WoZ Walks with the Participants

A total of four young demented patients took part in our WoZ-walks. Table 2 shows their demographic characteristics.

Table 2. Demographic characteristics of the patients who participated on the WoZ-Walks. P= Participant, S= Sex, M= Male, F= Female, D= Diagnose, AD = Alzheimer's disease, VD = Vascular Dementia, YD= Young demented.

P	S	D	Walk Type	Remark	Location
8	M	VD	WoZ (park)	YD	Leusden
9	F	VD	WoZ (town)	YD	Leusden
10	M	AD	WoZ (park)	YD	Leusden
11	M	AD	WoZ (town)	YD	Leusden

We chose a group of young demented patients because this group can put in more effort and often has better vision and hearing that an older group of patients with mild dementia, apart from exceptions that is. Also, fourteen participants, including the participants shown in table 1 and 2, have taken part in the group conversations about our Audioguide study.

4.5   Procedure WoZ-Walk

The Wizard of Oz enactment of the town-route and the park-route are equal to each other. The only difference is the route itself. The described procedure we describe in this paragraph thus applies to both types of WoZ-walks.

In consultation with the caregivers of the care center, two participants per WoZ-walk were asked to take part. The first participant gets a short briefing about what is going to happen, where emphasis is laid that the participant only has to follow up the instruction he or she hears, as best as he/she can. The earphone is placed in the participant's ear and we begin to walk. During the walk, the caregiver and the second participant walk behind the first participant at a short distance.

The researcher who controls the PDA, sending the audio instructions (the wizard) walks approximately two meters behind the participant who receives the instructions. This way the wizard can determine when to send the audio instruction and take action when the participant threatens get him or herself into a dangerous situation. When he participant gets confused while choosing a direction, the wizard can take action by asking the participant what the system told him of her over the earphone. The wizard will try to help by encouraging the participant to choose a direction which he or she thinks is the right one.

The observer also walks approximately two meters behind the participant who receives the audio instructions. This way he can hear remarks and see reactions better then walking further away. Halfway the first participant switches with the second participant who walked further behind with the caregiver. The short briefing is given to the second participant and the earphone is placed in his or her ear.

After the walks, both participants talk about their experience. One of the researchers summarizes what the participant told and asks the participants if he understood them correctly

4.6   Evaluation during and after the Walks

The most frequent made mistakes while taking an independent walk, the hindrance one experienced and the attitude patients and caregivers have toward the audioguide were taken in stock in three ways. By having group discussions prior to the introduction walks and WoZ-walks, by observing during the introduction walks and the WoZ-walks and by having a discussion about the experience after both types of walks.

Group discussions. We have had several group discussions to clarify our goal and learn about the mistakes patients make and hindrances they experience while taking on independent walk outdoors. During these group discussions, we asked no explicit questions. We encouraged the patients and caregivers to ask us anything about the project and share their walking and wayfinding experiences with us and the other patients.

Observation during the walks. We made observations during the walks to complement the information we gained from the group discussions, to learn which mistakes are made most frequently and which hindrances the patients experience while walking. We have looked at the behavior or impairment that has a negative effect on the patient's independence. We also observed if the patient acted out the rules in traffic for pedestrians correctly, mainly for the patient's own protection.

Discussion after the walks. To get an idea about what the participants think about the electronic navigational aid after they took part in the WoZ-walk, we had a short discussion with them. We asked them if they could tell us what they thought about the walk with the electronic navigational aid. Most of the participants started the conversation by themselves. When the participant was done sharing his or her story, one of the researchers would sum up the most important points according to the patient and asked if he had understood the patient correctly. In the end we always asked the patient to tell us if they have a positive or negative feeling about walking with an aid like this and if they are skeptical about such an aid.

5   Discussion

We have formulated three research questions prior to this study.

1. What are the frequently made mistakes and hindrances people with mild dementia experience while taking an independent walk?
2. Which functionalities and audio messages of the test system are and are not appreciated or missed by people with mild dementia and their caregivers?
3. How do people with mild dementia feel about the electronic navigational aid?

With the findings and information we described in the prior chapters we can answer these research questions.

5.1   Frequent Made Mistakes and Experienced Hindrance

As we expected based upon the discussed literature in the introduction and section 1, several patients were having trouble interpreting and using language. This showed during the walks when they tried to read or interpret street nameplates, house numbers and direction indicators. For the group of (mild) demented patients it is difficult to use conventional wayfinding aids to navigate from point A to point B. This combined with the feeling of anxiety to lose the way results in most of the patients always taking the same route when they decide to take a walk outside. Also, as can be found in literature, acts that are more frequently performed and are stored in the long term memory more easily performed then acts that are almost never performed [3]. These inabilities result in serious restrictions in the freedom of choice and independency of the patient. During our research we had a growing concern about the safety of the patients during the walks. A number of times we observed unsafe behavior, like crossing the street without paying attention to the traffic and pedestrian aids like traffic lights, level-crossings and sidewalks. A solution to this problem may be to equip the audioguide with safety warning instructions like "Pay attention to the traffic" or "Proceed using the sidewalks". During the group discussions several patients and the caregivers pointed out that this addition would be very preferable.

5.2 Functions and Audio Instructions for an Electronic Navigational Aid

We have asked the patients and caregivers which functions they think a future pedestrian navigational aid must have. With the development of an interface for this aid, the following matters should be kept in mind:

- The aid must have only a few buttons that can be used to control it. This because of the deteriorating perception of the patient.
- The buttons on the aid must be big. This because of the deteriorating motor skills of the patients.
- The aid must be easy to use. The patient should be able to select or program a route himself.
- It would be appreciated if the patient could make a "free" walk. By free walk we mean a walk where the patient can randomly choose a direction but will be directed back to his or her starting point if they ask for it, or get to far away from where they initially came from.
- The aid must have an alarm function so the patient can call for help when needed.
- The aid must have a tracking function for the caregivers to see where their patient is.

The patients pointed out that an aid without these functions would not be that interesting to have. In the matter of the audio instructions, patients and caregivers wanted additional information about landmarks in the instructions. They feel that this would give them extra confirmation in choosing the right direction at a decision point. Also, the timing in which the instructions are given must be correct. It would be confusing and cause agitation and disorientation for the patients, if the instructions follow each other in a fast pace.

5.3 Attitude towards an Electronic Navigational Aid

We have had very positive reactions from the patients and caregivers to the idea of an electronic navigational aid. They pointed out that it would increase their freedom and independence if they would have an aid like the intended Audioguide. We must point out that one must bear in mind the used sample of young demented patients. Although this group of young demented patients does not have many differences in comparison to an older group of demented patients, the young age of the group might have influenced the attitude towards an electronic navigational aid. None of the patients in the group were older than 65 years and might have gotten more used to using of technology in their daily life then an older group of demented patients. So it could very well be that these findings about attitude towards the aid cannot be generalized to the general group of demented patients in the Netherlands, but to the smaller group of young mild demented patients.

6   The Use of Visual Landmarks

Current pedestrian navigation systems predominantly use distance-to-turn information and directional information to enable a user to navigate. However, [4] showed that dementia patients performed better on recognition of landmarks compared with recognition and recall of spatial layout. Studies have been carried out on the quality of landmarks [13,17]. Here we focus on the performance of such a navigational system for elderly and defined the following research question:

Does the use of landmarks lead to better performance of using a navigation system and a better acceptance of the system by the elderly patient with beginning dementia?

We present an experiment which is carried out to compare landmark based navigational instructions with navigational instructions based only on left/right turn information.

6.1   Set-Up

Conditions and routes. We compare the following conditions:

- Navigation information is given as directional (left/right/straight) instructions on decision points
- Navigation information is given as directional instructions augmented with landmark information.

We have set out two routes in the vicinity of the day care centre, each approximately 750 meters long. Each route had 13 decision points at which navigational information had to be given. Both routes are as similar as possible with respect to difficulty and the number of instructions. Both contain a shopping area, residential area and a park-like area. In the first route we used only directional information. In the second route we used directional information augmented with landmark based instructions.

Fig. 2. Left: typical decision point. Right: participant with earphone.

Instructions. The instructions were as short as possible, and spoken by a male voice. The instructions are 'pre-recorded speech', and not computer generated. The use of a landmark is always an addition to the directional information, where the landmark was always used at the end of the sentence [4], e.g. 'Turn left at the IKEA'. Given the limited number of participants it was not possible to use elderly patients to find the best names for the landmarks, as was suggested by [3].

Participants and design. We used participants with beginning dementia from a day care centre, 4 males and 2 females. Each walked both routes in a random order.

Performance measure. We compared the two conditions on the navigation performance and on the attitude of the users. During the walk we registered at each decision point whether an error was made, and whether the participant was sure about its direction or hesitated. A navigation error is counted if the participant takes the wrong direction and has to be corrected by the wizard. He does this by giving an audio instruction 'Please try to turn around'. When the participant sees that he or she is going wrong before the correction instruction is given, this is not counted as error. We also measured the hesitation of the participant by observation (0 points for no hesitation, 1 for a little and 2 for much hesitation). At the end of each route we also measured the acceptance and the participant's attitude toward the navigational system. We used a small questionnaire with 10 questions with a 7-points Likert scale. The questionnaire was taken after the first part of the tour, and again after the second part.

6.2   Results

Table 3 summarizes the results for the conditions. The landmark condition resulted in a lower number of errors then the left/right condition. The amount of hesitation was lower for the landmark condition then for the left/right condition. The attitude of the participants toward the system was only slightly more positive for the landmark condition. Under both conditions an overall high positive evaluation of the system was given

Table 3. Results for the 6 participants

Participant	Errors		Hesitation		Attitude	
	Left/right	Landmark	Left/right	Landmark	Left/right	Landmark
P1	1	0	2	1	67	69
P2	2	1	7	0	48	58
P3	1	0	0	1	68	68
P4	1	1	0	1	67	67
P5	1	1	1	0	69	69
P6	2	1	1	3	65	62
Total	8	4	11	6	64	65.5

6.3   Discussion

A further analysis of the data learned that the 4 errors in the landmark condition were made at the same decision point, where the route instruction was not optimal. The instruction was to turn left at the landmark, while the landmark itself was placed after the decision point. For landmark based navigation, a careful formulation of the instructions is needed. In the final discussion with the participants the overall consensus was that the system is very helpful indeed. Even the use of earphones was not considered a problem.

7   Conclusion

After the findings of this study, we can conclude that an electronic navigational aid (our 'Audioguide'), can be a very valuable supplement in the lives of patients who suffer from mild dementia. The feeling of freedom and independence could be effected positively by offering the patient the possibility to go outside and take an independent walk with an aid like the intended Audioguide. The aid should prevent the patient from getting lost and it is maybe possible to let the patient live at home for a longer period of time before he or she gets transferred to a care center. Also, with this aid even the caregiver's job can be made a bit easier. The most important conclusion is that by involving the target group, in this case the young mild demented patients, in the preliminary research and evaluation of a new system, one can create an aid that is exactly tuned to fit the needs of the future user, which will be appreciated. On a small sample of participants we showed that landmark based navigation causes less errors and less hesitation then left/right navigation.

We are aware of the fact that the design of a future Audioguide will not eliminate all the problems and hindrance in a patients' life. We are also aware of the fact that not all of the patients in the target group with the same diagnose of dementia also experience the same problems. The main goal of this Audioguide project is to design a navigational aid that makes an independent walk for people with individual impairments possible. No matter if errors are made, the person should be able to reach his or her destination in a safe and reliable fashion. This means that the system should be designed in a way that the individual problems can be preempted as well as possible. Having a form of dementia brings a lot of stress, doubts and insecurities in the lives of the patients and if aids like the Audioguide can help to reduce these feelings while the patients is taking an independent walk, then our goal is for the better part fulfilled.

Performing a study with a sample of mild demented patients has not always been easy. Like we pointed out before, we had difficulties finding participants that were diagnosed with a form of dementia and which were physically fit enough and had well enough motor and perception skills. Because we had difficulty finding the right participants, we choose to look for young mild demented people, which is a smaller group of demented patients in the Netherlands. This group was also difficult to find because not all of the young mild demented patients have joined a care centre. Nevertheless, it seems wise to further study the design of a navigational aid for a bigger group of mild demented patients. The participants in this study were very enthusiastic about the test system they walked with. It gave them freedom, independence and it made the job of the caregiver a little less hard. They stated that an Audioguide like the intended test system, could be a good solution to the wayfinding issue.

In further studies one could concentrate on adding safety and warning instructions to the default left and right instructions of the current navigational aids for pedestrians. However, it should be taken into account that the length of an instruction cannot be too long, this could cause confusion.

It is also important to study the technical aspects of an Audioguide system. For example, more study is needed to find out what the user interface for the patient and caregiver should look like and how it should function in an user friendly fashion. Also, the Audioguide needs to have a robust GPS-signal in order to work with the precise location of the patients whereabouts. With this one should for example keep in mind that a GPS satellite fix is lost when one walks through a tunnel. The power supply is also very important. Studies should be done on how to manage the power of a Audioguide system. And last but not least, other studies can point out what exciting technology can added to the Audioguide system, like alarm and /or tracking functions.

References

1. Allen, G., Golledge, R., Hopkins, J.: Spatial Abilities, Cognitive Maps and Wayfinding - bases for individual differences in spatial cognition and behavior. In: Cognitive Mapping and Other Spatial Processes, pp. 46–80. JHU Press (1999)
2. Andersen, C., Wittrup-Jensen, K., Lolk, A., et al.: Ability to perform activities of daily living is the main factor affecting quality of life in patients with dementia. Health and Quality of Life Outcomes 2(1), 52 (2004)
3. American Psychiatric Association. DSM-IV-TR: Diagnostic and Statistical Manual of Mental Disorders. American Psychiatric Press Inc. (2000)
4. Cherrier, M., Mendez, M., Perryman, K.: Route learning performance in alzheimer disease patients. Neuropsychiatry, Neuropsychology, & Behavioral Neurology 14(3), 159–168 (2001)
5. Gaunet, F., Briffault, X.: Specifications of a localized wayfinding verbal aid for blind pedestrians: Simple and structured urban areas. Human-Computer Interaction 20, 267–314 (2005)
6. Heerink, M., Kröse, B.J.A., Wielinga, B.J., Evers, V.: The influence of a robot's social abilities on acceptance by elderly users. In: Proc. RO-MAN, Hertfordshire, pp. 521–526 (September 2006)
7. Holland, S., Morse, D.R., Gedenryd, H.: Audiogps: Spatial audio navigation with a minimal attention interface. Personal and Ubiquitous Computing 6(4), 253–259 (2002)
8. Hoyle, B.S., Fowler, J.M., Waters, D.A., Withington, D.J.: Development of the electronic guide cane for enhanced primary mobility for the vision impaired. In: Conference and Workshop on Assistive Technologies for Vision and Hearing Impairment (2004)
9. Ladetto, Q.: In step with ins: Navigation for the blind, tracking emergency crews. In: GPSWorld, pp. 30–38 (2002)

10. Lines, L., Hone, K.S.: Multiple voices, multiple choices: Older adults' evaluation of speech output to support independent living. Gerontechnology 5(2), 78–91 (2006)
11. Liu, A.L., Hile, H., Kautz, H., Borriello, G., Brown, P.A., Harniss, M., Johnson, K.: Indoor wayfinding: developing a functional interface for individuals with cognitive impairments. In: Proceedings of the 8th international ACM SIGACCESS Conference on Computers and Accessibility, pp. 95–102 (2006)
12. Loh, J., Schietecat, T., Kwok, T., et al.: Technology applied to address difficulties of alzheimer patients and their partners. In: Proceedings of the conference on Dutch directions in HCI, Amsterdam (2004)
13. May, A., Ross, T.: Presence and quality of navigational landmarks: effect on driver performance and implications for design. Human Factors 48(2), 346–361 (2005)
14. Passini, R., Pigot, H., Rainville, C., et al.: Wayfinding in a nursing home for advanced dementia of the alzheimer's type. Environment and Behavior 32(5), 684–710 (2000)
15. Ross, D.A., Blasch, B.B.: Wearable interfaces for orientation and wayfinding. In: Proceedings of the fourth international ACM conference on Assistive technologies (2000)
16. Salber, D., Coutaz, J.: A wizard of oz platform for the study of multimodal systems. In: Proceedings of INTERACT 1993 (1993)
17. Bechinie, M., Müller, R., Seibert-Giller, V., Messer, P., Sefelin, R., Tscheligi, M.: Landmarks: Yes; but which? five methods to select optimal landmarks for a landmark- and speech-based guiding system. In: ACM - Mobile HCI 2005, pp. 287–290 (2005)
18. Sheehan, B., Burton, E., Mitchell, L.: Outdoor wayfinding in dementia. Dementia 5(2), 271–281 (2006)

Context-Aware Indoor Navigation

Fernando Lyardet[1], Diego Wong Szeto[2], and Erwin Aitenbichler[2]

[1] SAP Research CEC Darmstadt, Darmstadt 64283, Germany
[2] Darmstadt University of Technology, Hochschultrasse 10, 64289 Darmstadt, Germany

Abstract. Over the past few years, several technological advances have been made to enable locating people in indoor settings, where way finding is something we do on a daily basis. In a similar way as it happened with GPS and today's popular outdoor navigation systems, indoor navigation is set to become one of the first, truly ubiquitous services that will make our living and working environments intelligent. Two critical characteristics of human way finding are destination choice and path selection. This work focuses on the latter, which traditionally has been assumed to be the result of minimizing procedures such as selecting the shortest path, the quickest or the least costly path. However, this path approximations are not necessarily the most natural paths. Taking advantage of context-aware information sources, this paper presents an easy to deploy context-aware indoor navigation system, together with an efficient spatial representation, and novel approach for path adaptation to help people find their destination according to their preferences and contextual information. We tested our system in one building with several users to estimate first an assessment of preference values, and later to compare how the paths suggested by our system correspond to those people would actually follow. The positive results of this evaluation confirm the suitability of our models and algorithms.

1 Introduction

Many people, especially business travelers, are often confronted with the situation that they are visiting new places and have to figure out how to navigate to the places where they want to go. Because path finding is a frequently occurring real-world problem, many studies and applications have been done on this subject over the last years. These studies provide several interesting insights, e.g., primary criteria for human path selection [1], or how people often prefer routes that are easier to describe and follow over routes that are optimal in a theoretical sense. An important indicator of perceived easier-to-follow routes are those with fewer instructions. In order to achieve this goal, different non-optimal algorithms that provide simpler paths were proposed, e.g., by Liu [2] and Richter [3]. However, these approaches were focused on street navigation, where the movement of people and vehicles follow the rules of street orientation.

We believe an aspect that is hardly covered by current research literature is the need of adapting to the current situation of the user, and to the condition of the environment in indoor navigation applications. The variation of conditions people may encounter in environments such as airports, museums, corporate campuses, shopping malls, factories, etc. is so diverse that they play a deciding role on the criteria to which path would be the one people would actually follow.

E. Aarts et al. (Eds.): AmI 2008, LNCS 5355, pp. 290–307, 2008.

For this reason, we have developed a user-centric approach for indoor navigation. In this paper, we first describe our hybrid indoor location model required to efficiently calculate possible paths between two given locations. Then we present a novel user model that includes information about physical capabilities, access rights, and a flexible modeling of user preferences based on Multiattribute Decision Theory (MAUT). We also describe in detail, how these preferences are analyzed and how context information is used to select the most appropriate path for the user.

Finally, we describe the architecture of the implemented CoINS system which can work with several different local positioning systems (LPS), such as WLAN, Ubisense, or Elpas. A particularly interesting deployment scenario is based on camera smart-phones and QR-Codes for locating users. This solution provides a low-entry technology threshold and allows to use CoINS on any recent smartphone without the need to deploy any proprietary software components on the phone.

1.1 CoINS Overview

The aim of the Context-aware Indoor Navigation System (CoINS) is to provide efficient user navigation in buildings with a strong emphasis on the "human factor". When considering the human as part of the system, the term *efficient* does not longer simply correspond to the shortest path calculated by some mathematical method. To efficiently navigate users to their destinations, it is also vital that they can quickly comprehend and execute the navigation instructions they receive from the navigation system. For example, a good route description would consist of a low number of turns, turns would be at "landmarks" the user can easily identify, and would always clearly indicate the directions in which the user is supposed to walk. The user model and the path selection algorithm presented in this paper allow to include such considerations into route planning.

An important subcomponent of CoINS is *path calculation*, which only considers the "geometric" aspects of route planning. In our earlier work [4] we only used models and algorithms based on quadtrees [5]. This limited the scalability of the system to larger buildings. The present CoINS system is able to efficiently find the geometrically shortest paths because of the following two extensions: First, the symbolic part of our hybrid location model is based on a hierarchical graph. Second, we improved the search path algorithm with an heuristic to further reduce the search space. These two factors allow to keep the single graphs small to reduce pathfinding complexity to $O(|L| - 1) + O(|V_i|)$ in the average case, and $O(|V_i|^2)$ in the worst scenario (see 2.1).

2 World Model

The CoINS world model is a hybrid model that combines symbolic graph-based models with geometric models. A symbolic model is required for indoor navigation, because *room numbers, corridor names, floor numbers*, etc. have an intuitive semantic to users. Using geometric coordinates for end-user interaction would not be suitable. The geometric model is needed for determining the shortest paths and to obtain orientation information for guiding users into the correct directions.

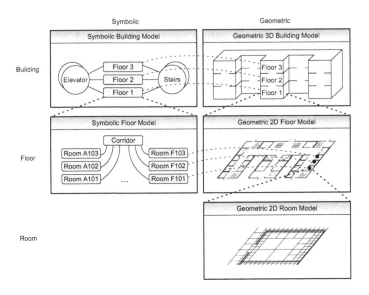

Fig. 1. Hybrid world model of CoINS

The world model serves two main purposes. First, it supports transformations between geometric coordinates and symbolic locations and vice versa. When a 3D tracking system is used that provides geometric coordinates to locate users, the model must be able to transform this coordinate into a symbolic location, such as a room number. The pathfinding algorithm of CoINS starts with the symbolic models to create a coarse plan of the route. After that, the geometric models are used for fine-planning. At the transition between using symbolic and geometric models, the world model must also support transforming symbolic into geometric coordinates.

Second, the model enables efficient pathfinding. The design of the CoINS world model has been refined over several iterations to ensure that the search sets are as small as possible and that the basic relations needed by the pathfinding algorithm can be checked efficiently. In most cases, users will mostly move in two dimensions. Movements in the height dimension usually only occur when changing floors, which is modeled by using separate maps for each floor.

The world model of CoINS is shown in Figure 1. According to modeling level and model type, the world model consists of five parts:

Geometric Building Model: This is a detailed geometric 3D model of the entire building. All other model parts are created at design time from this model. At run time, this model is not needed by the pathfinding algorithm of CoINS. However, if a 3D local positioning system is used in the building, the model is needed to transform metric coordinates to symbolic locations.

Geometric Floor Model: The floor model is a geometric 2D model of a single floor. Here, the term *floor* denotes some part of the building at the same level that is connected. It does not necessarily have to correspond to the whole story of a building. On the same floor, users will only be able to move in two dimensions. When guiding a user on a floor,

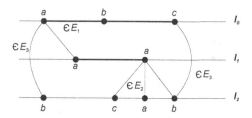

Fig. 2. A vertex-labeled universal hierarchical graph

a 2D representation is sufficient. The reduction to 2D space simplifies path calculation and increases performance significantly.

Geometric Room Model: The room model is a geometric 3D model of a room or a corridor. While it is not necessary to model rooms in detail, the geometry of corridors is important for finding shortest paths and to obtain direction information for navigation.

Symbolic Building Model: This is a symbolic graph-based model of the whole building. Its nodes are *floors* and *connecting structures*, such as elevators and stairs. Each floor node holds a reference to its symbolic floor model.

Symbolic Floor Model: This is a symbolic graph-based model of a floor. Its nodes are *rooms* and *corridors*, connected by entrances and exits.

2.1 Graph-Theoretical Model

This new model can be formalized using a recently specified graph class called universal hierarchical graphs [6]. In [6], undirected universal hierarchical graphs have been introduced to calculate the topological entropy of such graphs. After this, the graph class has been extended to the directed case [7]. Also, it was shown that these graphs can be efficiently classified by transforming them into certain property strings capturing important structural information.

In the following, we extend the definition given in [6] to vertex-labelled graphs and state a special edge type specification.

Definition 1. *Let*

$$V := \{v_{0,1}, v_{0,2}, \ldots, v_{0,|V_0|}, v_{1,1}, v_{1,2}, \ldots, v_{1,|V_1|},$$
$$v_{2,1}, v_{2,2}, \ldots, v_{2,|V_2|}, \ldots, v_{|L|-1,1}, v_{|L|-1,2}, \ldots, v_{|L|-1,|V_{|L|-1}|}\}, \quad (1)$$

be the vertex set, $|V| < \infty$ *and let*

$$A_V^U := \{l_1, l_2, \ldots, l_{|A_V^U|}\}, \quad (2)$$

be the unique vertex alphabet. $l_V : V \longrightarrow A_V^U$ *represent the corresponding vertex labeling function.* $L := \{l_0, l_1, \ldots, l_{|L|-1}\}$ *defines the level set.* $|L|$ *denotes its cardinality.* $\mathcal{L} : V \longrightarrow L$ *is a surjective mapping that is called a multi level function if it assigns to each vertex an element of the level set L. The graph* $U = (V, E)$ *is called a vertex-labelled universal hierarchical graph* $\Leftrightarrow$ *its edge set can be represented by the union* $E := E_1 \cup E_2 \cup E_3$. *We specify the sets* E_i *as follows:*

- E_1 denotes the set of horizontal Across-edges. A horizontal Across-edge does not change a level i.
- E_2 denotes the set of edges which change exactly one level. .
- E_3 denotes the set of edges which overjump at least one level.

The set of undirected labelled universal hierarchical graphs is denoted by $\mathcal{G}_{LUHG}$.

As an example, Figure (4) shows an undirected labelled universal hierarchical graph. Here, it holds $A_V^U := \{a, b, c\}$. For example, it is $l_V(v_{0,1}) = a$ and $l_V(v_{2,4}) = b$. We see that our objects we deal with can be described by graphs $U \in \mathcal{G}_{LUHG}$. The relationship to general graphs can be understood by recalling that an arbitrary graph is not necessarily hierarchical (the hierarchies must be induced). Generally, hierarchies can be induced by selecting a distinct root and applying algorithms based on shortest path, see, e.g., [8]. In our case, the hierarchy is given naturally because the building we want to model is hierarchical.

In the following, we consider a special class $\mathcal{G}_{LUHG}^\star$ of undirected labelled universal hierarchical graphs such that E_2 can be written as

$$E_2 = \{\{v_{0,i_0}, v_{1,i_1}\}, \{v_{1,i_1}, v_{2,i_2}\}, \dots, \{v_{|L|-2,i_{|L|-2}}, v_{|L|-1,i_{|L|-1}}\}\} \cup E_2^\star, \quad (3)$$

where $1 \leq i_0 \leq |V_0|, 1 \leq i_1 \leq |V_1|, \dots, 1 \leq i_{|L|-1} \leq |V_{|L|}| - 1$. Speaking informally, that means we assume that there always exists at least one directed path starting from at a vertex $v_{0,i_0} \in V$ and ending at $v_{|L|-1,i_{|L|-1}} \in V$ (e.g. as it is the case with stairs connecting floors). $E_2^\star$ is assumed to contain the remaining edges $e \in E_2$. By using this assumption, we easily derive the following assertion.

Theorem 1. *Let $U = (V, E) \in \mathcal{G}_{LUHG}^\star$. The time complexity for finding an arbitrary vertex $v \in V$ is $O(|L| - 1) + O(|V_i|)$.*

Proof: Let $U = (V, E) \in \mathcal{G}_{LUHG}^\star$ and arbitrary $v \in V$. Because there exists a path $P = (v_{0,i_0}, v_{1,i_1}, \dots, v_{|L|-1,i_{|L|-1}})$, the worst case time complexity to calculate the distance for vertices on this path is consequently $O(|L| - 1)$. The time complexity for finding a vertex on level i is $O(|V_i|)$.

Corollary 1. *Let $U = (V, E) \in \mathcal{G}_{LUHG}^\star$. In case there exists a vertex on each level i which connects all remaining vertices on this level, the time complexity for finding an arbitrary vertex $v \in V$ is $O(|L| - 1) + O(1)$.*

Theorem 2. *Let $U = (V, E) \in \mathcal{G}_{LUHG}^\star$. Without the assumptions we made in Theorem (1), the time complexity for finding an arbitrary vertex $v \in V$ (starting from another vertex) is $O(|V|^2)$.*

Proof: Let $U = (V, E) \in \mathcal{G}_{LUHG}^\star$. We always assume that our graphs we deal with are connected. To start from an arbitrary vertex and calculating the shortest distance to another vertex, any shortest path algorithm can be used, e.g., Dijkstra-algorithm [8]. For this, the complete adjacency matrix must be parsed. But this requires time complexity $O(|V|^2)$.

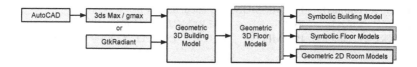

Fig. 3. Generation of the World Model

2.2   Generation of the World Model

Figure 3 shows the generation of the CoINS world model and its parts.

CoINS currently uses the Quake III map format [9] as input for the world descriptions, since it is widely known and open source tools are available to create world descriptions. To create models for CoINS we have used the GtkRadiant kit [10] and Autodesk Gmax [11] which allows us to import AutoCad drawings. A detailed discussion of describing the world using Quake maps, and the further processing required to map into 2D maps and identify rooms is presented in [4].

3   A Model for User Centric Adaptation

The user model we have developed and applied in our indoor navigation technology combines three key aspects besides user identification data: physical capabilities, user preferences, and location access rights.

3.1   Physical Capabilities

Physical capabilities are represented using the International Classification of Functioning, Disability and Health (ICF) of the World Health Organization (WHO) [12]. The ICF has been developed by the WHO as a framework for measuring health and disability, and proposes several types of qualifiers depending on the kind of impairment evaluation. For body functions, a qualifier shows the presence of an impairment which is measured on a five point scale: no impairment, mild, moderate, severe and complete. For the sake of simplicity, only voluntary leg movement-related functions involved in walking are considered, although this model can be extended with other body functions.

3.2   Location Access Rights

Location access rights control the entrance of users to certain locations or places. In CoINS, a user can enter a location, if her access rights are available. This is modeled according to the Role Based Access Control (RBAC) model [13]. A user profile is a set of roles. Each role has a set of permissions that grant or restrict access to locations. User profiles and roles are managed within a session, in which user, profiles, roles and the permissions are assigned. Concretely,

USER:	{users}	SESSION:	$\subseteq USER \times PROFILE \times 2^{ROLE}$
PROFILE:	{Profiles}	PERMISSION:	{ granted, denied }
ROLE:	{Roles}	ROLE:	$USER: \times PROFILE \mapsto 2^{ROLE}$
LOCATION:	{Locations}	PERMIT:	$ROLE \times LOCATION \mapsto PERMISSION$

3.3 Preferences

The user preferences influence the selection of paths. These preferences describe the desire or predisposition of a user in favor of something. In this case, the preferences take the attributes of paths into account. Some examples of such attributes are temperature, luminosity, distance and crowdedness (Table 1). Since such preferences can be arbitrary, we need to measured them with a numerical scale so that the preference is quantifiable [14]. The range of the preference scale varies from 0 to 100, where 0 is equivalent to least and 100 the most preferable. In Table 2, we show different user preferences in their natural scales together with their upper and lower bounds. The upper bound values of Path length and number of turns is different for every building, therefore an estimation was done by calculating the longest path possible in the building minimizing repetition of places. On the other hand, other maximum values such as path crowd density and variance are standards already documented elsewhere [15].

On certain occasions the construction of a natural scale is not possible. For instance, the beauty of a path is hard to measure with a scale, since it involves aspects such as color combination, layout, among others. For those scenarios, it is necessary to substitute the attribute with other(s) that are easier to quantify. For instance, beauty can be replaced with attributes like homogeneity of the locations layouts and the height of walls.

3.4 Modeling User Preferences with Multiattribute Utility Theory

This model presents a Multiattribute Utility Theory (MAUT)-based architecture that enables decision making according to user interests (Table 3). Each user has a different setting of preferences, and each with a different priority to the user. The strength of a preference is given by an assessment function f. Let's define F as the set of all assessment functions f. Nevertheless, every user has different preferences when faced

Table 1. User preference assessment for (a) distance, (b) turns, and (c) temperature variation

(a)		(b)		(c)		
Distance (m)	Assessment Value	Number of turns	Assessment Value	ADRT range	Category	Assessment Value
0	100	0	100	0°C - 10°C	Low	100
10	95	5	80	11°C - 20°C	Medium	40
30	85	10	40	20°C - higher	High	0
60	45	18	1			
125	20					
200	3					

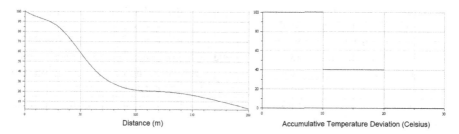

Fig. 4. The first curve shows an example of a polynomial approximation with distance values in meters. Preferences can also be categorized as "low", "medium" and "high", resulting in the step function on the right

Table 2. Natural scales of path preference attributes

Attribute	Lower bound	Upper bound
Path length (m)	0	3780
Number of turns	0	246
Number of visual aids	0	75
Acum. temperature deviation ($^{\circ}$C)	0	100
Path crowd density $(persons/m^2)$	0	6
Crowd density variance $(persons/m^2)^2$	0	0.2

in several different situations. As a result, an assessment function f holds if certain conditions apply. Let's define E as our set of possible events e. An event e represents a situation of the user like for instance, the user is carrying heavy luggage or the location is on fire.

Depending on the application domain, every assessment function f quantifies the preference strength of some criterion c. These criteria comprise several aspects concerning the application. In the domain of indoor navigation, criteria such as *path length, number of turns* or *crowdedness* are relevant.

Each of these criteria may also be subject to user specific trade-off behavior. One way to solve this is to assign priority weights to the assessment functions, which is conventionally done in standard Multiattribute Utility Theory (MAUT) techniques.

Even though preference strength is measured by assessment functions, the preference priority can change when events occur. Someone walking in an airport with empty

Table 3. Multiattribute Utility Theory definitions, and attribute examples

F	$= \{f \mid f$ is an assessment function$\}$	COND	$= \{$STATE, ACTIVITY,
E	$= \{e \mid e$ is an event$\}$		LOCATION, TIME$\}$
X	$= \{x \mid x$ can be assessed with some $f \in F\}$	STATE	$= \{$ happy, busy, available, $\dots\}$
		ACTIVITY	$= \{$ run, read, work, $\dots\}$
where	$f : \mathcal{P}(E) \times X \rightarrow \{0, \dots, 100\}$	LOCATION	$= \{$room a036, kitchen, $\dots\}$
And:			
E	$= $ (SUBJ, COND)	TIME	$= \{$starttime, endtime$\}$
SUBJ	$= \{$user 1, user 2, room a036, $\dots\}$		

hands could probably care less about the path length than after picking his luggage. In that situation, the importance weight of the path length criteria increases from not being empty handed and having luggage. Therefore, preference priority weights should be adjustable to different circumstances when events happen. An Event Listener notifies the client about an incoming event e_i (1). Upon receiving the event notification, the client updates the preference functions by forwarding the notification message to every criteria. As a result, every criteria knows what events affects them and by how much the preference priority is increased or decreased.

4   Path Calculation and Selection

To select the most suitable path for a specific user we use the Simple Multi-Attribute Rating Technique (SMART). Under this technique, every path can be described by individual preference attributes and through the value functions of each single attribute, the preference strength can be measured.

The process of decision making can be influenced by the user's consideration of what attributes are more important or relevant to him. For this reason, importance weights are given to attributes in order to model this kind of situation. The importance weight alters the output of an attribute's value function.

The measured preference strength of every single attribute of a path can be aggregated to return an overall path evaluation value. This resulting value will be later used to compare against other possible paths.

4.1   Assessment of Preferences with Simple Multiattribute Rating Technique (SMART)

Our optimal path selection problem using SMART is formalized as follows:

Let P be the set of all feasible paths, then $P = \{p|p$ is a path over the location model$\}$ and a_n all attributes with importance weights w_n and value functions v_n. Then, the optimal path $p \in P$ maximizes

$eval(p) = aggregate(w_i(v_i(a_i(p))))$ for i = 1,..., number of attributes

The following five steps describe how the path selection using the SMART method is conducted:

1. **Define the feasible paths and attributes for evaluation.** All feasible paths are generated. Given that locations are connected as a graph in the location model, all paths can be generated by traversing the graph using a depth first search, A^* or Dijkstra. User constraints (e.g. physical disabilities) can be used at this stage to avoid traversing unnecessary paths thus filtering them out from the selection process.

2. **Assign the importance weights to the attributes.** The importance of attributes to the user are established by assigning importance weights to attributes. These weights are normalized,which means in this case that the sum of all weights equals one. This weight assignation allows an ordering of attributes according to their relevance and therefore the preference strength of an attribute with a high importance

Table 4. Assessment of path attributes. Path 2 is the selected path

Attribute	Importance	Path 1	Path 2	Path 3
Path length	0.4	39.31 (65m)	51.67 (55m)	18.6 (138m)
Number of visual aids	0.2	99.29 (19)	96.52 (18)	3.09 (50)
ADRT	0.1	100 (4°C)	100 (6C)	0 (29°C)
Number of turns	0.1	94.03 (2)	94.03 (2)	80 (5)
Path Crowd Density	0.05	89.7 ($0.11p/m^2$)	91.66 ($0.09p/m^2$)	87.69 ($0.13p/m^2$)
Crowd Density Variance	0.15	99.22 ($0.012(p/m^2)^2$)	86.51 ($0.008(p/m^2)^2$)	98.86 ($0.017(p/m^2)^2$)
Evaluation value		74.35	**76.93**	35.27

weight will have a higher impact on the path evaluation than those with lower. Importance weights can be constants or functions. The latter is necessary when no constant ordering of path attributes can be modeled. For example, if the importance depends on the preference strength of some other path attributes.

3. **For every path, assess the path attributes separately.** At this step the iteration of value measurement over all attributes for every path generated in the first step is performed.
4. **Calculate evaluation value by aggregating all attribute assessments under consideration of importance weights.** In the fourth step, assessment values of paths attributes from step three are aggregated. Different aggregation models exist to approach this. For SMART, a very common model is the additive, which sums up all assessment values from attributes multiplied by its respective importance weight, i.e. $eval(p) = \sum_{i=1}^{n} w_i d(a_i(p))$.
5. **Select the path with the best evaluation value.** In the last step, path selection can be done by searching for the path with a target evaluation value. How the target evaluation value is defined can depend on how the value scales were created during path attribute assessment. For example, if the assessment functions map into numerical values between 0 and 100 where 0 means the least desirable and 100 the most, then path selection will concentrate on paths with highest evaluation values.

5   CoINS Architecture

Figure 5 shows the architecture of the CoINS system. The *Presentation* component of CoINS can be either accessed as web interface through a web server or from rich clients. The web-based solution has the advantage that no software deployment is necessary on clients, but location tracking is limited to QR codes or purely infrastructure-based solutions. In contrast, rich clients can provide more customized user interfaces and support additional local positioning systems.

The *Path Calculation* component determines all possible routes from a given source location to a given destination location. In addition, it provides the geometric length of each route. This component only considers the location model.

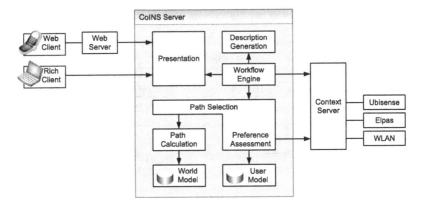

Fig. 5. CoINS System Architecture

The *Path Selection* component uses *Preference Assessment* to calculate all non-location related metrics for all candidate routes and then selects the best route. The candidate routes have been previously determined by Path Calculation. Preference Assessment uses the route, the user model, and the current context as inputs.

The whole process is controlled by a small *Workflow Engine*. Using a workflow allows us to decouple the guidance process from the CoINS core system. CoINS server, the Context Server, the location tracking systems, and rich clients are based on our communication middleware MundoCore. MundoCore and the Context Server are described in more detail in the following sections.

5.1 MundoCore Middleware and Software Architecture

MundoCore [16] is an open-source communication middleware specifically designed for AmI applications. It supports automatic discovery of peers in the network and provides a peer-to-peer publish/subscribe system. The middleware has mechanisms to handle network failures and handovers between different networks, allowing users to transparently continue accessing services in such conditions. In addition, MundoCore implements an Object Request Broker on top of publish/subscribe to achieve location and execution transparency.

Therefore, programmers of an application do not need to know about the address of its communication partners (a server, for instance). The distribution of client and server components can be determined at deployment time or even changed at runtime.

For the implementation of CoINS, we adopted a service-oriented architecture, because it allows deploying application components according to different scenarios and improve their reuse by other applications. For example, if a client only supports a web browser, all components of CoINS can run on a server in the Internet. A more powerful client such as an Ultra Mobile PC could already run the whole CoINS system locally.

5.2 The Mundo Context Server

The Mundo Context Server [17] is responsible for transforming raw sensor readings into information that is meaningful to applications. It is an application-independent and reusable component that aims to decouple applications from sensors such that sensors become interchangeable and that new sensors can be added without requiring to change applications. The context server provides the following functionality:

- Interpreting data received from sensors and transforming this data into a common representation.
- Maintaining a geometric world model of the environment and supporting geometric operations and queries.
- Inferring "higher-level" context from "lower-level" context.
- Notifying applications when certain context properties change.
- Storing histories of sensed and inferred context and supporting queries in those histories.

CoINS uses the Context Server to track the locations of users. Because the Context Server provides an abstraction layer above the physical sensors, CoINS can use standardized queries and does not have to be aware of the underlying sensor technology. The Context Server is based on the notion of widgets to process context information. A processing chain for a location sensor usually consist of the following steps:

1. **Sensor:** The first widget in the chain obtains the raw sensor data. In most cases, it is a MundoCore Subscriber that receives messages from a remote sensor in the network.
2. **Normalization:** Normalization transforms a system-specific message into a normalized, system-neutral message. The classes of normalized messages are composed by "multiple inheritance" and implement an ID part and a location part.
3. **Transformation:** This step handles entity/ID transformations, e.g. to translate from tags to users, or from base stations to rooms, or positions between coordinate systems.
4. **Inference:** This step infers relations from messages. A relation typically consists of two entities and describes a relationship between those two entities. Relations are expressed as RDF statements.
5. **Storage:** The relation store stores relations and is based on the Tuplespace concept.
6. **Query/Subscription:** Applications can query the relation store or subscribe to the store. A query operation returns all relations matching a specified pattern. When an application subscribes to the store, it will be notified each time a tuple matching the specified pattern is inserted into the space.

The current implementation of the CoINS system can work with the following tracking systems:

- **Ubisense:** Ubisense [18] is an UWB-based high-resolution 3D tracking system. For this system, the processing chain consists of a normalization to a common representation for 3D tracking systems, coordinate system transformation, tag-to-user ID mapping, transformation to symbolic coordinates using the *Geometric Building Model*.

- **Elpas:** Elpas [19] is a badge-based system that combines IR, LF, and RF. It can cover entire buildings and depending on the amount of infrastructure deployed, its accuracy varies between 25m and 2m. Elpas provides symbolic location in a system-specific format. The processing chain consists of a normalization to a common representation for badge-based systems, tag-to-user ID mapping, and sensor-to-room ID mapping.
- **WLAN:** WLAN-based tracking [20] can utilize WLAN infrastructures that often already exist. WLAN-based systems can reach an accuracy of about 2-3m, given that the necessary RSS fingerprint maps are accurate.
- **QR:** Quick Response (QR)-Codes are two-dimensional barcodes that were standardized by ISO in the year 2000 (ISO/IEC 18004). To date, QR reading software is available for almost any smartphone. QR codes can be used to create *physical world hyperlinks*: A user having a camera phone can scan the image of a QR Code causing the phone's browser to launch and redirect to the programmed URL. When using QR codes as a location source, the physical location of the QR code is encoded into the URL. The context server is then used to map location codes to symbolic locations.

The Context Server would support even more tracking systems. However, these systems either cover areas too small for indoor navigation applications (IRIS [21]) or they are not accurate enough (Cellphone tracking [22]).

6   User Guidance

6.1   Customizable Guidance Process

The CoINS system decouples the process of guiding a user by including a small, embeddable workflow engine called Micro workflow [23]. In this way, both the supporting services and the process of indoor user guidance can be further modified. Another advantage is that this approach also enforced further separations of responsibilities in order to allow a possible change of the workflow engine if required. Figure 6 shows the implementation of a guidance workflow.

6.2   Giving Directions to the User

Different techniques and requirements have been studied for guiding users indoors with mobile platforms [24,25]. Guiding techniques includes floor maps, schemas, and spatial landmarks [26] together with their spatial relationships to help build a "mental trip" on the guided user.

The user guidance in the current version of CoINS is realized through a visual modality, where instructions are displayed in the user's terminal. We have so far developed 2 different versions for the user terminal. The latest one is a "thin" client, in order to support the common situation where no software deployment can be done on the user terminal.

In a typical scenario, a user enters the building and points with the mobile's camera to any of the QR-Codes available in every door (Figure 7). A URL is encoded that

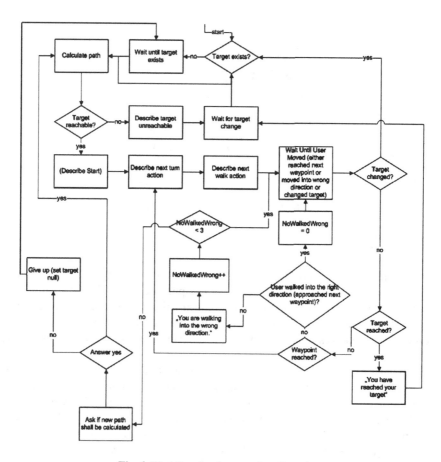

Fig. 6. Workflow Implementation Overview

takes the user to a welcome page where information of the current location (people to contact, office hours, contact information) is displayed, and the question is the user requires directions. When the user selects this option, she can either type the name of the person or room number, and the system starts the guiding process (current location is assumed to be where the QR-Code was read).

The user continues receiving instructions everytime she requires it. Along the way, the user may feel insecure about the current location and how to proceed. In such cases, just by scanning any QR-Code, CoINS resumes que navigation from the current possition to the originally specified.

Indoor location systems are seldom installed in large scale settings, and can be either very expensive or impractical following the building construction characteristics. Therefore, the choice of a standard such as QR-codes appears as a natural solution. Clearly, the limitations of the thin client and QR-Codes as a location systems makes it difficult for proactive guidance. However, we are currently experimenting with new approaches to overcome these restrictions.

Fig. 7. A user scanning a QR-Code

7   Evaluation

Two different experiments have been carried out to study the paths people follow to reach a given destination in indoor settings. The purpose of the first evaluation was to gather information to find a common profile for the experiment, that is, a set of assessment functions (three of them are shown in table 1(a),(b) and (c)) and a ranking of the different criteria to estimate their weight in the path selection assessment procedure (shown in table 4).

For the first experiment 8 subjects where scheduled, all of them familiar with the Piloty Building at the University of Darmstadt, a 4-story building, that offers in every floor five different stairs and 2 elevators to change floors (see figure 5). A set of pairs of origins and destinations were carefully selected, and the subjects were asked to carry out simple tasks that implied walking between the selected destinations(e.g. *"You need to pick up a form in office XXX"*, *"Take the form to Mr. YYY in office XYZ"*, *"Go to the library"*,*"Get a Coffee at the Bistro"*, etc.). To start the experiment, subjects were met at the origin for their assigned route and then were read the appropriate directions. Afterwards, the subjects began walking to the given destinations as a part of the assignments given. The routes every participant followed were recorded in separate maps of the area, and all possible paths were coded to record every time a particular path was followed. Subjects then completed a questionnaire on the criteria they used in selecting a path.

The second experiment involved 9 subjects (5 female, 4 male) that did not participate in the first experiment. We chose the same set of destinations as in the first experiment, and assigned the same tasks to the subjects, following the first experiment's procedure. We also used the data and user preference profile information gathered during the first experiment for the algorithm to calculate for every participant the suggested path, in order to take into account the contextual characteristics at the moment where the experiment would take place, and compare it to the one actually followed by the subject. The results of this first evaluation of the system are shown in table 6. These results suggests that the proposed paths by system matches those chosen by people at a particular contextual setting. In table 5 we show an schema of the building, with the proposed paths by the system and the alternatives performed by the users. Although encouraging,

Table 5. (a) Shows the structure of the Piloty building, and the paths proposed for evaluation. (b)Table shows for each participant and path, whether the path followed by the subject matches the path proposed by the system.

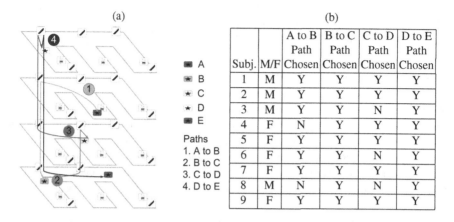

(a)

(b)

		A to B Path	B to C Path	C to D Path	D to E Path
Subj.	M/F	Chosen	Chosen	Chosen	Chosen
1	M	Y	Y	Y	Y
2	M	Y	Y	Y	Y
3	M	Y	Y	N	Y
4	F	N	Y	Y	Y
5	F	Y	Y	Y	Y
6	F	Y	Y	N	Y
7	F	Y	Y	Y	Y
8	M	N	Y	N	Y
9	F	Y	Y	Y	Y

A
B
C
D
E

Paths
1. A to B
2. B to C
3. C to D
4. D to E

Table 6. Generated paths and evaluation results

	Path 1	Path 2	Path 3	Path 4	Σ
♯ Dijkstra's generated Paths	24	9	24	57	
♯ CoINS heuristic's generated Paths	9	9	1	1	
Users that followed path as predicted	7	9	6	9	31
Users that followed a different path	2	0	3	0	5

this study must also be performed in our future work in large indoor scenarios such as airports, where users may have more options of movement according to the context.

In Table 6 we show the result of the reduced search space done by the heuristic implemented in CoINS allowed a reduction of potential paths to be analyzed of more than 82% (114 found by the general Dikjstra vs. 20 from CoINS spearch space reduction + Dijkstra). The results of the user behavior are encouraging: more that 86,1% of the users actually followed the paths suggested by the algorithm.

8 Related Work

Human way finding has been studied from many different perspectives. Understanding human way finding and navigation has been done in architecture and geography studies. How human convey information to guide and orient others with verbal instructions [27]. Different studies have shown the relative importance of path optimality: people would accept a less optimal (in terms of distance) path, in favor of routes that are potentially easier to describe or follow. Perhaps the closest related system is by Tsetsos et al. [28] presenting Ontonav , a system that introduces the use of ontologies in indoor navigation to describe and reason over the user preferences, and annotate the world model, in order to determine the path users must follow. Finally, Yao et al. [29] also proposes a navigation system using geo-coded QR-codes for individuals with cognitive impairments.

Other relevant systems are Drishti developed by Lisa Ran, Sumi Helal and Steve Moore in [30]. Drishti is an integrated indoor/outdoor navigation system for visually impaired people that uses commercial off the shelf soft- and hardware. And finally the Navio Project [31] from the Vienna University of Technology, a pedestrian navigation system in mixed indoor and outdoor environment. It addresses several important aspects like positioning, route planning, and communication of pedestrian navigation services.

9   Summary and Future Work

We have developed CoINS, a context-aware indoor navigation system with efficient route planning. A key element to the efficient calculation of routes between two given locations is the hybrid location model presented in this paper. We have also discussed the application of QR codes for easy to deploy indoor navigation, without having to deploy any specific software on the end-user terminal. Finally, the selection of the most suitable path is done through a process of assessing user preferences according to the context information.

As future work we plan to add automatic customization of the preferences to each user, as well as the set of preferences to be evaluated and the ranking among them. On the technology side, we will extend the current web-based user client to a rich application, and take advantage of compass-enabled smartphones.

References

1. Golledge, R.G.: Path selection and route preference in human navigation: A progress report. In: COSIT, pp. 207–222 (1995)
2. Liu, B.: Intelligent Route Finding: Combining Knowledge, Cases and an Efficient Search Algorithm. In: Proceedings of ECAI 1996, 12th European Conference on Artificial Intelligence, pp. 149–155. John Wiley & Sons, Chichester (1996)
3. Richter, K.F., Duckham, M.: Simplest Instructions: Finding Easy-to-Describe Routes for Navigation. In: Cova, T.J., Miller, H.J., Beard, K., Frank, A.U., Goodchild, M.F. (eds.) GI-Science 2008. LNCS, vol. 5266. Springer, Heidelberg (2008)
4. Lyardet, F., Grimmer, J., Mühlhäuser, M.: CoINS: Context sensitive Indoor Navigation System. In: Proceedings of IEEE International Symposium on Multimedia (ISM), pp. 30–37. IEEE Press, Los Alamitos (2006)
5. Samet, H.: The Quadtree and Related Hierarchical Structures. ACM Computing Surveys (CSUR) (June 1984)
6. Emmert-Streib, F., Dehmer, M.: Information theoretic measures of uhg graphs with low computational complexity. Applied Mathematics and Computation 9, 1783–1794 (2007)
7. Dehmer, M., Emmert-Streib, F.: Structural similarity of directed universal hierarchical graphs: A low computational complexity approach. Applied Mathematics and Computation 194, 7–20 (2007)
8. Dijkstra, E.W.: A note on two problems in connection with graphs. Numerische Mathematik (51), 161–166 (1950)
9. Proudfoot, K.: Unofficial Quake 3 Map Specs (March 2000),
   http://graphics.stanford.edu/~kekoa/q3/
10. Radiant, G.T.K. (March 2006) (last visited: July 03, 2008),
   http://www.qeradiant.com

11. Autodesk: Gmax (2008) (last visited: July 03, 2008),
    `http://www.autodesk.com/gmax`
12. World Health Organization: International Classification of Functioning, Disability and
    Health (last visited: July 03, 2008), `http://www.who.int/classifications/icf/en`
13. Ferraiolo, D., Kuhn, R.: Role-Based Access Control. In: Proceedings of the 15th National
    Computer Security Conference, pp. 554–563 (1992)
14. Edwards, W., von Winterfeldt, D.: Decision Analysis And Behavioral Research. Cambridge
    University Press, Cambridge (1986)
15. Neufert, E., Neufert, P.: Architect's Data. Blackwell Science, Malden (2000)
16. Aitenbichler, E., Kangasharju, J., Mühlhäuser, M.: MundoCore: A Light-weight Infrastruc-
    ture for Pervasive Computing. Pervasive and Mobile Computing 3(4), 332–361 (2007)
17. Aitenbichler, E., Lyardet, F., Mühlhäuser, M.: Designing and Implementing Smart Spaces.
    Cepis Upgrade VIII(4), 31–37 (2007)
18. Ubisense: Homepage. The Smart Space Company (2008) (last visited: July 03, 2008),
    `http://www.ubisense.net/`
19. Visonic Technologies: Elpas (2007) (last visited: July 03, 2008), `http://www.visonictech.com/elpas.html`
20. Song, Y.: In-House Location Tracking. Master's thesis, Darmstadt University of Technology
    (2002)
21. Aitenbichler, E., Mühlhäuser, M.: An IR Local Positioning System for Smart Items and De-
    vices. In: Proceedings of the 23rd IEEE International Conference on Distributed Computing
    Systems Workshops (IWSAWC 2003), pp. 334–339. IEEE Computer Society, Los Alamitos
    (2003)
22. Hartl, A.: A Provider-Independent, Proactive Service for Location Sensing in Cellular Net-
    works. In: GTGKVS Fachgespräch (Online Proceedings) (2005)
23. Manolescu, D.: Workflow Enactment with Continuation and Future Objects. In: OOPSLA
    2002. ACM, New York (2002)
24. Butz, A., Baus, J., Krüger, A., Lohse, M.: A Hybrid Indoor Navigation System. In: IUI 2001:
    International Conference on Intelligent User Interfaces, pp. 25–32. ACM Press, New York
    (2001)
25. Fraunhofer: Messe Navigator (accessed, April 2006), `http://www.iis.fraunhofer.de/ec/navigation/indoor/projekte/messe`
26. Sorrows, M., Hirtle, S.: The Nature of Landmarks for Real and Electronic Spaces. In: Freksa,
    C., Mark, D.M. (eds.) COSIT 1999. LNCS, vol. 1661, pp. 37–50. Springer, Heidelberg (1999)
27. Streeter, L.A., Vitello, D., Wonsiewicz, S.A.: How to Tell People Where to Go: Comparing
    Navigational Aids. International Journal of Man-Machine Studies 22(5), 549–562 (1985)
28. Tsetsos, V., Anagnostopoulos, C., Kikiras, P., Hasiotis, P., Hadjiefthymiades, S.: A Human-
    Centered Semantic Navigation System for Indoor Environments. In: Proceedings of Interna-
    tional Conference on Pervasive Services, ICPS 2005, pp. 146–155 (July 2005)
29. Chang, Y.J., Tsai, S.K., Chang, Y.S., Wang, T.Y.: A Novel Wayfinding System Based on Geo-
    Coded QR-Codes for Individuals With Cognitive Impairments. In: Assets 2007: Proceedings
    of the 9th international ACM SIGACCESS conference on Computers and accessibility, pp.
    231–232. ACM, New York (2007)
30. Ran, L., Helal, S., Moore, S.: Drishti: An integrated indoor/outdoor blind navigation system
    and service. In: PERCOM 2004: Proceedings of the Second IEEE International Conference
    on Pervasive Computing and Communications (PerCom 2004), Washington, DC, USA, p.
    23. IEEE Computer Society, Los Alamitos (2004)
31. Gartner, G., Frank, A., Retscher, G.: Pedestrian Navigation System in Mixed Indoor Outdoor
    Environment The NAVIO Project (2004)

Distributed Defeasible Contextual Reasoning in Ambient Computing

Antonis Bikakis and Grigoris Antoniou

Institute of Computer Science, FO.R.T.H., Heraklion, Greece
{bikakis,antoniou}@ics.forth.gr

Abstract. The study of ambient computing environments and pervasive computing systems has introduced new research challenges in the field of Distributed Artificial Intelligence. The imperfect nature of context, the different viewpoints from which the ambient agents face the available context, and their heterogeneity with respect to the language and inference system that they use cannot be efficiently handled by the classical centralized reasoning approaches followed by most of the systems presented so far. The current paper proposes a distributed reasoning approach from the field of Multi-Context Systems (MCS) that handles these requirements by modeling ambient agents as peers in a P2P system, local context knowledge as local rule theories, and mapping rules through which an ambient agent imports context knowledge from other ambient agents as defeasible rules. To resolve potential inconsistencies that may derive from the interaction of context theories through the mappings, it uses a preference relation, which may express the trust that an agent has in the knowledge imported by other ambient agents. The paper also describes a specific distributed algorithm for query evaluation in the proposed MCS framework, analyzes its formal properties, and demonstrates its use in three use case scenarios from the Ambient Intelligence domain.

1 Motivation

The study of ambient computing environments and pervasive computing systems has introduced new research challenges in the field of Distributed Artificial Intelligence. These are mainly caused by the imperfect nature of context information and the special characteristics of the agents that provide and process this knowledge. Henricksen and Indulska in [1] characterize four types of imperfect context information: *unknown*, *ambiguous*, *imprecise*, and *erroneous*. Sensor or connectivity failures (which are inevitable in wireless connections) result in situations, that not all context data is available at any time. When the data about a context property comes from multiple sources, the context information may become ambiguous. Imprecision is common in sensor-derived information, while erroneous context information arises as a result of human or hardware errors.

The agents that operate in an ambient environment are expected to have different goals, experiences and perceptive capabilities. They may use distinct vocabularies; they may even have different levels of sociality. Due to the highly

E. Aarts et al. (Eds.): AmI 2008, LNCS 5355, pp. 308–325, 2008.

dynamic and open nature of the environment (various entities join and leave the environment at random times), they are not able to know a priori all other entities that are present at a specific time instance nor can they communicate directly with all of them.

Considering these requirements, three main challenges of knowledge management in Ambient Intelligence are to enable:

1. Reasoning with the highly dynamic and ambiguous context data.
2. Managing the potentially huge piece of context data, in a real-time fashion, considering the restricted computational capabilities of some mobile devices.
3. Collective intelligence, by supporting information sharing, and distributed reasoning between the entities of the ambient environment.

So far, most ambient computing frameworks have followed fully centralized approaches (e.g. [2,3,4,5,6,7,8,9,10,11]), while others have used models based on the *blackboard* and *shared memory* paradigms (e.g. [12,13,14]). Collecting the reasoning tasks in a central entity certainly has many advantages. It achieves better control and better coordination between the participating entities. However, such solutions cannot meet the demanding requirements of ambient environments. The dynamics of the network and the unreliable and restricted (by the range of the transmitters) wireless communications inevitably lead to fully distributed solutions.

In the current study, we present a fully distributed approach for reasoning in ambient computing environments, which is based on the Multi-Context Systems paradigm. Our approach models ambient agents as autonomous logic-based peers in a P2P system and context knowledge possessed by an ambient agent as a system peer's local rule theory, while information exchange between agents is achieved through *mapping* rules that associate their local context knowledge. Even if it is assumed that each context theory is locally consistent, the same assumption will not necessarily hold for the global knowledge base. The unification of local theories may result in inconsistencies that are caused by the mappings. For example, a local theory A may import conflicting context information from two different agents, B and C, through two competing mapping rules. In this case, even if the three different theories are locally consistent, their unification through the mappings defined by A may contain inconsistencies. To deal with this type of inconsistencies (*global conflicts*), we model mappings as defeasible rules, and use context and preference information to resolve the conflicts.

With this model, we aim to capture the three fundamental dimensions of contextual reasoning, as these were formulated in [15]:

- *Partiality.* Each agent may not have immediate access to all available information, so a local theory can be thought as a partial representation of *the world*.
- *Approximation* Each local theory differs at the level of detail at which a portion of *the world* is represented.
- *Perspective* Each local theory encodes a different point of view on *the world*.

Furthermore, the P2P paradigm enables us to model: (a) Information flow between different ambient agents as message exchange between the system peers; (b) context changes using the dynamics of a P2P system; and (c) confidence in the knowledge of other agents as trust between the system peers.

The rest of the paper is structured as follows. The next section discusses prominent recent studies on reasoning in Multi-Context Systems and Peer Data Management Systems. Section 3 describes the proposed reasoning model. Section 4 presents *P2P_DR*, a specific reasoning algorithm for distributed query evaluation in Multi-Context Systems, and Section 5 analyzes its formal properties. Section 6 demonstrates the application of the algorithm in three use case scenarios from the Ambient Intelligence domain. The last section summarizes and presents the next steps of this work.

2   Background

A Multi-Context System consists of a set of *contexts* and a set of inference rules (known as *mapping* or *bridge* rules) that enable information flow between different contexts. A context can be thought of as a logical theory - a set of axioms and inference rules - that models local context knowledge. Different contexts are expected to use different languages and inference systems, and although each context may be locally consistent, global consistency cannot be required or guaranteed. Reasoning with multiple contexts requires performing two types of reasoning; (a) *local reasoning*, based on the individual context theories; and (b) *distributed reasoning*, which combines the consequences of local theories using the mappings. The most critical issues of contextual reasoning are the *heterogeneity* of local context theories, and the potential conflicts that may arise from the interaction of different contexts through the mappings.

The notions of *context* and *contextual reasoning* were first introduced in AI by McCarthy in [16], as an approach for the problem of *generality*. In the same paper, he argued that the combination of non-monotonic reasoning and contextual reasoning would constitute an adequate solution to this problem. Since then, two main formalizations have been proposed to formalize context: the propositional logic of context (*PLC*) ([17,18]), and the Multi-Context Systems introduced in [19], which later became associated with the Local Model Semantics proposed in [20]. The second formalism was the basis of two recent studies that were the first to deploy non-monotonic reasoning approaches in MCS: (a) the non-monotonic rule-based MCS framework [21], which supports default negation in the mapping rules allowing to reason based on the absence of context information; and (b) the multi-context variant of Default Logic [22]. The latter models the bridge relations between different contexts as *default rules*, and has the additional advantage that is closer to implementation due to the well-studied relation between Default Logic and Logic Programming. However, the authors do not provide specific reasoning algorithms (e.g. for query evaluation), and their model does include the notion of priority, which we use for conflict resolution.

A relevant problem researched by several recent studies is the semantic characterization of mappings in peer data management systems. Two prominent early approaches were the first-order logic interpretation, followed in [23,24], and the epistemic logic semantics proposed in [25]. The main problem of both approaches is that they do not handle inconsistency. Three recent studies that deal with inconsistencies are [26], [27], and [28]. The first one is based on autoepistemic semantics and handles only local inconsistency. The second is based on non-monotonic epistemic logic, and enables handling peers that may provide mutually inconsistent data. Finally, the propositional P2P inference system proposed in the third study deals with conflicts caused by mutually inconsistent information sources, by detecting them and reasoning without them. A common deficiency of the two latter studies is that the conflicts are not actually resolved using some external trust or priority information, but they are rather isolated.

3   Reasoning Model

Our approach models a Multi-Context System P as a collection of distributed local rule theories P_i in a P2P system:

$$P = \{P_i\}, i = 1, 2, ..., n$$

Each system peer (context) has a proper distinct vocabulary V_i and a unique identifier i. Each local theory is a set of rules that contain only local literals (literals from the local vocabulary). These are of the form:

$$r_i^l : a_i^1, a_i^2, ...a_i^{n-1} \rightarrow a_i^n$$

where i denotes the peer identifier. These rules express local knowledge and are interpreted in the classical sense: whenever the literals in the body of a local rule $(a_i^1, a_i^2, ...a_i^{n-1})$ are consequences of the local theory, then so is the conclusion of the rule (a_i^n). Local rules with empty body are used to express factual knowledge.

Each peer also defines mappings that associate literals from its own vocabulary (*local literals*) with literals from the vocabulary of other peers (*foreign literals*). The acquaintances of peer P_i, $ACQ(P_i)$ are the set of peers that at least one of P_i's mappings involves at least one of their local literals. The mappings are modeled as defeasible rules (rules that can be defeated in the existence of adequate contrary evidence) of the form:

$$r_i^m : a_i^1, a_j^2, ...a_k^{n-1} \Rightarrow a_i^n$$

The above mapping rule is defined by P_i, and associates some of its own local literals with some of the local literals of P_j, P_k and other system peers. a_i^n is a local literal of the theory that has defined r_i^m (P_i).

Finally, each peer P_i defines a trust level order T_i, which includes a subset of the system peers, and expresses the trust that P_i has in the other system peers. This is of the form:

$$T_i = [P_k, P_l, ..., P_n]$$

A peer P_k is considered more trusted by P_i than peer P_l if P_k precedes P_l in this list. The peers that are not included in T_i are less trusted by P_i than those that are part of the list.

4   The *P2P_DR* Algorithm

P2P_DR is a distributed algorithm for query evaluation in Multi-Context Systems following the model that we described in the previous section. The specific reasoning problem that it deals with is: *Given a MCS P, and a query about literal x_i issued to peer P_i, find the truth value of x_i considering P_i's local theory, its mappings and the context theories of the other system peers.* The algorithm parameters are:

x_i: the queried literal
P_0: the peer that issues the query
P_i: the local peer
SS_{x_i}: the Supportive Set of x_i (a set of literals that is initially empty)
CS_{x_i}: the Conflicting Set of x_i (a set of literals that is initially empty)
$Hist_{x_i}$: the list of pending queries ($[x_1, ..., x_i]$)
Ans_{x_i}: the answer returned for x_i (initially empty)

The algorithm proceeds in four main steps. In the first step, the algorithm determines if the queried literal, x_i, or its negation $\neg x_i$ are consequences of P_i's local rules. To do that it calls a local reasoning algorithm (*local_alg*, described later in this section), which returns a positive answer, in case x_i derives from the local rules, or a negative answer in any other case. Below, we denote as $R_s(x_i)$ the set of rules that support x_i (as their conclusion); and as $R_c(x_i)$, the set of rules that contradict x_i (those that support $\neg x_i$)

P2P_DR$(x_i, P_0, P_i, SS_{x_i}, CS_{x_i}, Hist_{x_i}, Ans_{x_i}, T_i)$
  if $\exists r_i^l \in R_s(x_i)$ **then**
    $localHist_{x_i} \leftarrow [x_i]$
    call $local\_alg(x_i, localHist_{x_i}, localAns_{x_i})$
    if $localAns_{x_i} = Yes$ **then**
      return $Ans_{x_i} = localAns_{x_i}$ and terminate
  if $\exists r_i^l \in R_c(x_i)$ **then**
    $localHist_{x_i} \leftarrow [x_i]$
    call $local\_alg(\neg x_i, localHist_{x_i}, localAns_{\neg x_i})$
    if $localAns_{\neg x_i} = Yes$ **then**
      return $Ans_{x_i} = \neg localAns_{\neg x_i}$ and terminate

If Step 1 fails, the algorithm collects, in the second step, the local and mapping rules that support x_i. To check which of these rules can be applied, it checks the truth value of the literals in their body by issuing similar queries (recursive calls of the algorithm) to P_i or to the appropriate neighboring peers $P_j \in ACQ_{P_i}$. A rule is considered applicable if all the literals in its body have positive truth values. To avoid cycles, before each new query, it checks if the same query has been issued before, during the same algorithm call (using $Hist$). For each applicable supportive rule r_i, the algorithm builds its supportive set SS_{r_i}; this derives from the unification of the set of the *foreign literals* (literals that are defined by peers that belong in $ACQ(P_i)$) that are contained in the body of r_i, with the Supportive Sets of the local literals that belong in the body of the same rule. In the end, in case there is no applicable supportive rule ($SR_{x_i} = \{\}$), where SR_{x_i} is the set of applicable rules that support x_i , the algorithm returns a negative answer for x_i and terminates. Otherwise, it computes the Supportive Set of x_i, SS_{x_i}, as the *strongest* of the Supportive Sets of the applicable rules that support x_i, and proceeds to the next step. The *strongest* Supportive Set is computed using the *Stronger* function (described later in this section), which applies the preference relation defined by P_i, T_i, on the given sets.

$SR_{x_i} \leftarrow \{\}$
for all $r_i^{lm} \in R_s(x_i)$ **do**
    $SS_{r_i} \leftarrow \{\}$
    for all $b_t \in body(r_i^{lm})$ **do**
        if $b_t \in Hist_{x_i}$ **then**
            stop and check the next rule
        else
            $Hist_{b_t} \leftarrow Hist_{x_i} \cup b_t$
            call $P2P\_DR(b_t, P_i, P_t, SS_{b_t}, CS_{b_t}, Hist_{b_t}, Ans_{b_t}, T_t)$
            if $Ans_{b_t} = No$ **then**
                stop and check the next rule
            else if $Ans_{b_t} = Yes$ and $b_t \notin V_i$ **then**
                $SS_{r_i} \leftarrow SS_{r_i} \cup b_t$
            else
                $SS_{r_i} \leftarrow SS_{r_i} \cup SS_{b_t}$
    if $SR_{x_i} = \{\}$ **or** $Stronger(SS_{r_i}, SS_{x_i}, T_i) = SS_{r_i}$ **then**
        $SS_{x_i} \leftarrow SS_{r_i}$
    $SR_{x_i} \leftarrow SR_{x_i} \cup r_i^{lm}$
if $SR_{x_i} = \{\}$ **then**
    return $Ans_{x_i} = No$ and terminate

In the third step, in the same way with the previous step, the algorithm collects the rules that contradict x_i and builds the conflicting set of x_i (CS_{x_i}). In case there is no applicable rule that contradicts x_i, the algorithm terminates by returning a positive answer for x_i. Otherwise, it proceeds with the last step. Below, we denote as CR_{x_i} the set of the applicable rules that contradict (support the negation of) x_i.

$CR_{x_i} \leftarrow \{\}$
for all $r_i^{lm} \in R_c(x_i)$ **do**
    $SS_{r_i} \leftarrow \{\}$
    for all $b_t \in body(r_i^{lm})$ **do**
        if $b_t \in Hist_{x_i}$ **then**
            stop and check the next rule
        else

$Hist_{b_t} \leftarrow Hist_{x_i} \cup b_t$
call $P2P\_DR(b_t, P_i, P_t, SS_{b_t}, CS_{b_t}, Hist_{b_t}, Ans_{b_t}, T_t)$
if $Ans_{b_t} = No$ then
    stop and check the next rule
else if $Ans_{b_t} = Yes$ and $b_t \notin V_i$ then
    $SS_{r_i} \leftarrow SS_{r_i} \cup b_t$
else
    $SS_{r_i} \leftarrow SS_{r_i} \cup SS_{b_t}$
if $CR_{x_i} = \{\}$ or $Stronger(SS_{r_i}, CS_{x_i}, T_i) = SS_{r_i}$ then
    $CS_{x_i} \leftarrow SS_{r_i}$
$CR_{x_i} \leftarrow CR_{x_i} \cup r_i^{lm}$
if $CR_{x_i} = \{\}$ then
    return $Ans_{x_i} = Yes$ and SS_{x_i} and terminate

In the last step, the algorithm compares SS_{x_i} and CS_{x_i} using again the *Stronger* function. If SS_{x_i} is *stronger*, the algorithm returns a positive answer for x_i. In any other case, it returns a negative answer.

if $Stronger(SS_{x_i}, CS_{x_i}, T_i) = SS_{x_i}$ then
    return $Ans_{x_i} = Yes$ and SS_{x_i}
else
    return $Ans_{x_i} = No$

The local reasoning algorithm *local_alg* is called by *P2P_DR* to determine whether a literal is a consequence of the local rules of the theory. The algorithm parameters are:

x_i: the queried literal
$localHist_{x_i}$: the list of pending queries in P_i
$localAns_{x_i}$: the local answer for x_i

local_alg$(x_i, localHist_{x_i}, localAns_{x_i})$
    for all $r_i^l \in R_s(x_i)$ do
        if $body(r_i^l) = \{\}$ then
            return $localAns_{x_i} = Yes$ and terminate
        else
            for all $b_i \in body(r_i^l)$ do
                if $b_i \in localHist_{x_i}$ then
                    stop and check the next rule
                else
                    $localHist_{b_i} \leftarrow localHist_{x_i} \cup b_i$
                    call $local\_alg(b_i, localHist_{b_i}, localAns_{b_i})$
            if for every b_i: $localAns_{b_i} = Yes$ then
                return $localAns_{x_i} = Yes$ and terminate
    return $localAns_{x_i} = No$

The *Stronger(S, C, T)* function is used by *P2P_DR* to check which of S and C sets is *stronger*, based on T (the preference relation defined by the peer that the algorithm is called by). According to T, a literal a_k is considered to be *stronger* than a_l if P_k precedes P_l in T. The strength of a set is determined by the weakest literal in this set.

Stronger(S, C, T)

$a^w \leftarrow a_k \in S$ s.t. *for all* $a_i \in S : P_k$ *does not precede* P_i *in* T
$b^w \leftarrow a_l \in C$ s.t. *for all* $b_j \in C : P_l$ *does not precede* P_j *in* T
if P_k precedes P_l in T **then**
   $Stronger = S$
else if P_l precedes P_k in T **then**
   $Stronger = C$
else
   $Stronger = None$

Below we demonstrate how the algorithm works through an example. In the system depicted in Figure 1, there are six peers, each one with its local context theory, and a query about x_1 is issued to P_1.

P_1
$r_{11}^l : a_1 \rightarrow x_1$
$r_{12}^m : a_2 \Rightarrow a_1$
$r_{13}^m : a_3, a_4 \Rightarrow \neg a_1$

P_2
$r_{21}^l : c_2 \rightarrow a_2$
$r_{22}^l : b_2 \rightarrow a_2$
$r_{23}^m : b_5 \Rightarrow b_2$
$r_{24}^m : b_6 \Rightarrow b_2$

P_3
$r_{31}^l :\rightarrow a_3$

P_4
$r_{41}^l :\rightarrow a_4$

P_5
$r_{51}^l :\rightarrow b_5$

P_6
$r_{61}^l :\rightarrow b_6$

Fig. 1. A MCS of Six Context Theories

Given the query about x_1, P_1 calls $P2P\_DR$, which proceeds as follows:

- In the first step, it fails to compute the truth value of x_1 based on P_1's local theory, so the algorithm proceeds to the second step.
- It successively calls rules r_{11}^l and r_{12}^m, and issues a query about a_2 to P_2.
- In P_2, a_2 does not derive from the local theory, and the algorithm successively calls the two rules that support a_2; r_{21}^l and r_{22}^l.
- c_2 is not supported by any rule, so r_{21}^l is not applicable.
- To check whether rule r_{22}^l can be applied, the algorithm computes the truth value of literal b_2. b_2 is supported by two mapping rules; r_{23}^m and r_{24}^m.
- To determine whether these rules can be applied, the algorithm queries P_5 about b_5, and P_6 about b_6.
- P_5 and P_6 return positive answers for b_5 and b_6 respectively, as these literals are consequences of their local theories.
- As there is no rule in P_2 that contradicts b_2 or a_2, the algorithm computes a positive answer for a_2, and constructs the Supportive Set of a_1, which contains literal a_2 ($SS_{a_1} = \{a_2\}$).
- The next step is to check the only rule that contradicts a_1, rule r_{13}^m. Using a similar process, the algorithm ends up with a conflicting set that contains literals a_3 and a_4 ($CS_{a_1} = \{a_3, a_4\}$).

– To compare SS_{a_1} and CS_{a_2}, the algorithm uses the trust level order defined
by P_1, T_1. Assuming that $T_1 = [P_4, P_2, P_3]$, a_2 and a_3 are respectively the
weakest elements of SS_{a_1} and CS_{a_1}, and a_3 is weaker than a_2. Consequently,
the algorithm computes a positive answer for a_1, and, as there is no rule that
contradicts x_1, it eventually returns a positive answer for x_1.

5   Properties of *P2P_DR*

In this section we describe some formal properties of *P2P_DR* with respect to its
termination (Proposition 1), complexity (Propositions 2-3), and the possibility
to create an equivalent unified defeasible theory from the distributed context
theories (Proposition 4). Proposition 1 holds as cycles are detected within the
algorithm.

Proposition 1. *The algorithm is guaranteed to terminate returning either a
positive or a negative answer for the queried literal.*

Proposition 2 is a consequence of two states that we retain for each peer, which
keep track of the incoming and outgoing queries of the peer.

Proposition 2. *The total number of messages that are exchanged between the
system peers for the computation of a single query is $O(n^2)$ (in the worst case
that all peers have defined mappings that contain literals from all system peers
and the evaluation of the query involves all mappings defined in the system),
where n stands for the total number of system peers.*

It is interesting to compare our approach with a centralized reasoning approach
with regard to the total number of messages exchanged between the system
peers for the evaluation of a single query. As Proposition 2 states, in the case of
P2P_DR, this number equals $O(n^2)$, but only in the worst case that all peers
have defined mappings that contain literals from all other system peers and
the evaluation of the query involves all mappings defined in the system. In a
centralized approach, where all peer theories should be collected in a central
entity before query evaluation, the required number of messages would be in
any case $O(\log n)$. The size of the messages would be however much bigger. In
the centralized approach, these messages should contain whole peer theories.
P2P_DR, on the other hand, requires the peers to exchange single boolean
values.

Proposition 3. *The computational complexity of the algorithm on a single peer
is in the worst case $O(n^2 \times n_l^2 \times n_r)$, where n stands for the total number of system
peers, n_l stands for the number of literals a peer may define, and n_r stands for
the total number of (local and mapping) rules that a peer theory may contain.*

Proposition 4. *Using a standard process, it is possible to unify the local context
theories into a global defeasible theory, which produces the same results with
P2P_DR. In this theory, local rules are modeled as strict rules, mapping rules
are modeled as defeasible rules, and trust information from the system peers is
used to derive priorities between conflicting rules.*

The latter property, which shows the equivalence with a defeasible theory, enables resorting to centralized reasoning by collecting the distributed context theories in a central entity and creating an equivalent defeasible theory. In addition, this result is typical of other works in the area of Peer-to-Peer reasoning, in which the distributed query evaluation algorithm is related to querying a single knowledge base that can be constructed (see, e.g. [29]). Via Proposition 4, $P2P\_DR$ has a precise semantic characterization. Defeasible Logic has a proof-theoretic [30], an argumentation-based [31] and a model-theoretic semantics [32]. The proof of Proposition 4 is particularly complex, as it has to take into account matters as how provability in the case of $P2P\_DR$ is interpreted in defeasible provability of Defeasible Logic, and how trust information from the distributed system peers is translated into the priority relation of Defeasible Logic. Details about Proposition 4, as well as the proofs for Propositions 1-4 will be presented elsewhere due to space limitations.

6   Three Use Case Scenarios from Ambient Intelligence

In this section, we illustrate how $P2P\_DR$ works in three use cases scenarios from the Ambient Intelligence domain, where the MCS model that we described in Section 3 is used to represent local knowledge of various ambient agents, and interaction between the agents is achieved through mapping rules that associate their local context knowledge.

6.1   Context-Aware Mobile Phone in an Ambient Classroom

The first scenario involves a context-aware mobile phone that has been configured by professor Dr. Amber to make decisions about whether it should ring or not (in case of incoming calls) based on Dr. Amber's preferences and context. Dr. Amber has the following preferences: His mobile phone should ring in case of an incoming call, unless it is in silent mode or Dr. Amber is busy with some important activity. One such important activity is a lecture for one of the courses he teaches at the university. These preferences are expressed in Dr. Amber's mobile phone as follows:

$r^l_{11} : incoming\_call, \neg silent\_mode, \neg important\_activity \Rightarrow ring$
$r^l_{12} : lecture \rightarrow important\_activity$

Consider the case that Dr. Amber is located in the 'RA201' classroom of the university reading his emails on his laptop. It is Tuesday, the time is 7.50 p.m. and he has just finished with a lecture for course CS566. The context-aware mobile phone receives an incoming call, but it is not in silent mode. The latter two facts are described by the following two strict local rules in Dr. Amber's mobile phone:

$r^l_{13} :\rightarrow incoming\_call$
$r^l_{14} :\rightarrow normal\_mode$

In this case, the mobile phone cannot decide whether it should ring or not based only on its local context knowledge, as it is not aware of other important context parameters (e.g. whether Dr. Amber is currently busy with an important activity). Therefore, it will attempt to use its mapping rules, through which it can import context information from other ambient agents, and use this information to infer further knowledge about Dr Amber's current context. The mobile phone connects through the wireless network of the university with Dr. Amber's laptop, the wireless network localization service, and the classroom manager (a stationary computer installed in the 'RA201' classroom). Dr Amber has predefined the following mapping rules:

- Rule r_{15}^m, which states that if there is a scheduled lecture for course CS566, and Dr. Amber (actually his mobile phone) is currently located in classroom 'RA201', then Dr. Amber is possibly giving a lecture. Information about scheduled events is imported from Dr. Amber's laptop (agent P_2), while information about his current location is imported from the wireless network localization service (agent P_3).

$$r_{15}^m : scheduled\_CS566_2, location\_RA201_3 \Rightarrow lecture$$

- Rule r_{16}^m, which states that if there is no class activity taking place in the classroom, Dr. Amber is rather not giving a lecture. Information about the state of the classroom is imported from the classroom manager (agent P_4).

$$r_{16}^m : \neg class\_activity_4 \Rightarrow \neg lecture$$

Dr. Amber's personal laptop contains knowledge about the current day and time, as well as, Dr. Amber's personal calendar. Specifically, using the following rules, it can infer that at the current time (Tuesday, 7.50 p.m.), there is a scheduled class event.

$$r_{21}^l :\rightarrow day(tuesday)$$
$$r_{22}^l :\rightarrow time(19.50)$$
$$r_{23}^l : day(tuesday), time(X), 19.00 \leq X \leq 20.00 \rightarrow scheduled\_CS566$$

The localization service context knowledge base contains one fact describing Dr. Amber's mobile phone current location.

$$r_{31}^l :\rightarrow location\_RA201$$

The classroom manager possesses context knowledge about the state of the classroom. Specifically, it uses a local strict rule with empty body to describe the state of the projector installed in the classroom, and a mapping rule which imports information from an external person detection service (agent P_5) about the presence of people in the classroom, to determine about whether there is a class activity in progress.

$$r_{41}^l :\rightarrow projector(off)$$
$$r_{42}^m : persons\_detected(X)_5, X < 2, projector(off) \Rightarrow \neg class\_activity$$

Finally, the person detection service describes its local context information regarding the number of persons detected in the classroom using one fact:

$r_{51}^l :\rightarrow persons\_detected(1)$

Assuming that the trust level order defined by Dr. Amber for his mobile phone is $T_1 = [P_3, P_4, P_2]$, where P_2 stands for Dr. Amber's laptop, P_3 stands for the classroom manager, and P_4 stands for the localization service, given the query about whether the mobile phone should ring or not, the $P2P\_DR$ algorithm called by the mobile phone will proceed as follows:

- Using the local context theory of the mobile phone, it cannot reach to a decision as it has no knowledge about Dr Amber's current activity. It can derive a positive value for *incoming_call* and a negative truth value for *silent_mode*, but it cannot determine about the applicability of rules r_{11}^l and r_{12}^l. To do that, it has to determine the truth value of *lecture*.
- For *lecture*, the mobile phone contains two conflicting mapping rules (r_{15}^m and r_{16}^m). Through r_{15}^m, the algorithm accesses the local knowledge of P_2 (the laptop) and P_3 (localization service), computes positive truth values for both *scheduled_CS566* and *location_RA201*, and determines that r_{15}^m is applicable.
- Through rule r_{16}^m, the algorithm accesses the local knowledge of P_4 (classroom manager) and through P_4's mapping rule r_{42}^m, it also uses the knowledge of P_5 (person detection service) to determine that ¬*class_activity* is true and r_{16}^m is applicable.
- The algorithm uses the trust level order of P_1 to determine which of the two conflicting mapping rules (r_{15}^m and r_{16}^m) is *stronger*. P_4 precedes P_2 in T_1, so the algorithm determines that r_{16}^m is stronger, and computes a negative truth value for *lecture* and consequently for *important_activity* as well.
- The algorithm determines that r_{11}^l is applicable and reaches to the *ring* decision.

6.2 Ambient Intelligence Home Care System

The second scenario takes place in an apartment hosting an old man, Mr. Jones. Mr. Jones, a 80 year old widower, is living alone in this apartment, while his son resides in close proximity. A nurse visits Mr. Jones 8 to 10 hours daily, while his son also visits him for some hours every couple of days. Mr Jones' apartment is equipped with an Ambient Intelligence Home Care System, which consists of:

- A position tracking system, which localizes Mr. Jones in the apartment.
- An activity tracking system, which monitors the activities carried out by Mr. Jones; activity can take values such as *sitting, walking, lying*, etc.
- A data monitoring system, in the form of a bracelet, which collects Mr. Jones' basic vital information, such as pulse, skin temperature and skin humidity.
- A person detection system, which is able to recognize Mr. Jones, his son and the nurse.
- An emergency monitoring system, identifying emergency situations. This system has a wired connection with the position tracking system, the activity tracking system, the person detection system and the emergency telephony system, and a wireless connection with the data monitoring bracelet.

- An emergency telephony system, which makes emergency calls to Mr. Jones' son in case of emergency.

Assume that neither the nurse nor Mr. Jones' son are located in the apartment, and Mr Jones is walking through a hall of the apartment to his bedroom. He suddenly stumbles, falls down and loses his consciousness, while the data monitoring bracelet that he wears in his wrist is damaged, transmitting wrong data to the emergency monitoring system.

The emergency telephony system agent (P_1) determines about whether it should make an emergency call to his son using the following rule:

$$r_{11}^m : emergency_2, \neg detected(nurse)_3, \neg detected(son)_3 \Rightarrow emergency\_call$$

Using this rule, the telephony agent imports information about emergency situations from the emergency monitoring agent (P_2), and information about the people that are present in the apartment from the person detection agent (P_3). P_3 preserves presence information in terms of local rules. In this case, it tracks only the presence of Mr. Jones and expresses this knowledge using the following rule:

$$r_{31}^l :\rightarrow detected(jones)$$

The emergency monitoring agent (P_2) includes the following rules for determining emergency situations: Rule r_{21}^l states that any abnormal situation is an emergency situation. Rule r_{22}^m imports data from the data monitoring agent (P_4), and states that if temperature, skin humidity and pulse have normal values then there is no case of emergency situation. Rule r_{23}^l imports Mr. Jones' activity information from the activity tracking agent (P_5) and position information from the position tracking agent (P_6) and states that in case Mr. Jones is lying in a place different than his bed, then this is an abnormal situation.

$$r_{21}^l : abnormal\_situation \rightarrow emergency$$
$$r_{22}^m : normal\_temperature_4, normal\_skin\_humidity_4, normal\_pulse_4 \Rightarrow \neg emergency$$
$$r_{23}^m : activity(lying)_5, \neg position(bed)_6, \Rightarrow abnormal\_situation$$

The data monitoring agent (P_4) reports the following wrong values about Mr. Jones' temperature, skin humidity and pulse:

$$r_{41}^l :\rightarrow normal\_temperature$$
$$r_{42}^l :\rightarrow normal\_skin\_humidity$$
$$r_{43}^l :\rightarrow normal\_pulse$$

Finally, the activity tracking and the position tracking agents use respectively the following two local rules to encode current Mr. Jones' activity and position:

$$r_{51}^l :\rightarrow activity(lying)$$
$$r_{61}^l :\rightarrow position(hall)$$

Assuming that the trust level order defined for the emergency tracking system is $T_2 = [P_6, P_5, P_4]$, given the query about whether the emergency telephony system (P_1) should make an emergency call, the $P2P\_DR$ algorithm called by P_1 will proceed as follows:

- Using the local context theory of P_1, it cannot reach to a decision as it has no knowledge about the people that are present in the apartment nor about the current situation.
- Through rule r_{11}^m, the algorithm imports information from P_3 about the presence of Mr. Jones in the apartment (and the absence of his son and the nurse).
- Through the same rule, the algorithm attempts to import information about Mr. Jones' situation from P_2.
- For *emergency*, P_2 contains two conflicting rules (r_{21}^l and r_{22}^m). Through rule r_{23}^m, the algorithm accesses the local knowledge of P_5 (activity tracking agent) and P_6 (position tracking agent), computes positive truth value for *activity(lying)* and negative truth value for *position(bed)*, and determines that r_{21}^l is applicable.
- Through rule r_{22}^m, the algorithm accesses the local knowledge of P_4 (data monitoring agent) and determines that r_{22}^m is also applicable.
- The algorithm uses the trust level order of P_2 to determine which of the two conflicting rules (r_{21}^l and r_{22}^m) is *stronger*. P_5 and P_6 both precede P_4 in T_2, so the algorithm determines that r_{21}^l is stronger than r_{22}^m, and computes a positive truth value for *emergency*.
- The algorithm determines that r_{11}^m is applicable and, as there is no conflicting rule, reaches to the *emergency_call* decision.

6.3   Mushroom Hunting in an Ambient Natural Park

The scenario takes place in an ambient environment of mushroom hunters, who collect mushrooms in a natural park in North America. The hunters carry mobile devices, which they use to communicate with each other through a wireless network, in order to share their knowledge on edible and non-edible mushrooms.

People interested on picking mushrooms typically do not know every specie and family of mushrooms in detail. They know that a deadly mushroom can be very similar to an edible one, e.g., the "amanita phalloides" (deadly) and the "amanita caesarea" (edible and one of the best mushrooms) that look very much alike. In general, a mushroom hunter has to respect certain rules imposed by the natural park legislation such as the limited quantity of mushrooms that can be picked. Since the limitation on the allowed quantity, there is the need of establishing the specie of an unknown mushroom during the picking itinerary instead of bringing the picked ones to an expert and discovering, after some days, that the picking has been useless due to the high number of non-edible picked mushrooms. Furthermore, the picking has not been simply useless but it has also vainly cheated the ecosystem of a part. Moreover, even in the case of an irrelevant quantity of non-edible picked mushrooms, it might happen that a small chunk of a deadly mushroom (e.g., "amanita phalloides" also known as *The Death Cap*) mixes with edible ones and accidentally eaten. By keeping in mind the above discussed motivations, let us consider the scenario in which a mushroom hunter finds an interesting mushroom but it is unclear if it is edible.

Suppose that the mushroom in question has the following characteristics: It has a stem base featuring a fairly prominent sack that encloses the bottom of the stem (*volva*) and a pale brownish cap with patches, while the margin of the cup is prominently lined, and the mushroom does not have a ring (*annulus*). The description of the mushroom is expressed in terms of facts as follows:

$\rightarrow amanita$
$\rightarrow volva$
$\rightarrow \neg ring$
$\rightarrow brownish\_cap$
$\rightarrow patches$
$\rightarrow lined\_margin$

The hunter has some knowledge on the description of specific species, such as the *Destroying Angel*, the *Death Cap* and the *Caesar's Mushroom* (rules r^l_{11}-r^l_{13}). He also knows which of them are poisonous, and which are not (rules r^l_{14}-r^l_{16}).

$r^l_{11} : volva, ring, white\_cap, \neg patches \rightarrow destroying\_angel$
$r^l_{12} : volva, ring, patches, greenish\_cap, \neg lined\_margin \rightarrow death\_cap$
$r^l_{13} : volva, ring, patches, orange\_cap, lined\_margin \rightarrow ceasars\_mushroom$
$r^l_{14} : destroying\_angel \rightarrow poisonous$
$r^l_{15} : death\_cap \rightarrow poisonous$
$r^l_{16} : ceasars\_mushroom \rightarrow \neg poisonous$

The description of the mushroom in question does not fit with any of these species, so the hunter uses the wireless network to contact other mushroom hunters that are located nearby. His wireless device establishes connection with the devices of three other hunters (P_2, P_3 and P_4). We assume that the first hunter has predefined the following mappings that associate his vocabulary with the vocabularies used by the three hunters: Non-edible mushrooms defined by P_2 imply poisonous mushrooms (rule r^m_{11}), non-toxic mushrooms defined by P_3 imply mushrooms that are not poisonous (rule r^m_{12}), while dangerous mushrooms defined by P_4 imply poisonous mushrooms (r^m_{13}).

$r^m_{11} : non\_edible_2 \Rightarrow poisonous$
$r^m_{12} : non\_toxic_3 \Rightarrow \neg poisonous$
$r^m_{13} : dangerous_4 \Rightarrow poisonous$

P_2 uses a generic rule, which states that mushrooms with a volva are non-edible (rule r^l_{21}). P_3 has knowledge of some specific species that are not toxic, including *springtime amanita* (rule r^l_{31}), but does not know how to describe them. P_4, on the other hand also uses a very generic rule, which states that amanitas are dangerous (rule r^l_{41}). Using the same wireless network, P_3 establishes a connection with P_5. P_3 has predefined a mapping rule that associates *springtime amanita* with *amanita velosa* defined by P_5 (rule r^m_{31}). The local knowledge base of P_5 contains a detailed description of this specific specie, which fits the description of the mushroom in question (rule r^l_{51}).

$r_{21}^l : volva \rightarrow non\_edible$

$r_{31}^l : springtime\_amanita \rightarrow non\_toxic$

$r_{31}^m : amanita\_velosa_5 \Rightarrow springtime\_amanita_3$

$r_{41}^l : amanita \rightarrow dangerous$

$r_{51}^l : volva, \neg ring, brownish\_cap, patches, lined\_margin \rightarrow amanita\_velosa$

Assuming that the description of the mushroom is shared between the involved hunters (e.g. through a picture taken by the first hunter), and that the trust level order of P_1 is $T_1 = [P_3, P_2, P_4]$, the algorithm proceeds as follows:

- Using the local context theory of P_1, it is not able to determine whether the mushroom is *poisonous* or not.
- For *poisonous*, P_1 has defined two mapping supportive rules: r_{11}^m and r_{13}^m. Through r_{11}^m, the algorithm accesses the local knowledge of P_2, computes positive truth value for *non_edible* and determines that r_{11}^m is applicable.
- Through r_{13}^m, the algorithm accesses the local knowledge of P_4, computes positive truth value for *dangerous* and determines that r_{13}^m is also applicable.
- P_1 has also defined a mapping rule that contradicts *poisonous*; rule r_{12}^m. Through this rule, the algorithm queries P_3 about *non_toxic*. The instance of *P2P_DR* called by P_3 uses its mapping rule r_{31}^m to import information about *amanita_velosa* from P_5. Successively, P_5 returns a positive value for *amanita_velosa*, P_3 returns a positive value for *non_toxic*, and the algorithm determines that r_{12}^m is also applicable.
- Using T_1, the algorithm computes $SS_{poisonous} = SS_{r_{11}^m} = \{non\_edible_2\}$ (P_2, which has defined *non_edible* is more trusted than P_4) and $CS_{poisonous} = SS_{r_{12}^m} = \{non\_toxic_3, \}$. It, then, compares $SS_{poisonous}$ with $CS_{poisonous}$ using T_1, and as P_3 is more trusted than P_2, the algorithm eventually returns a negative answer for *poisonous*.

7   Conclusion

In this study, we proposed a totally distributed approach for reasoning in Ambient Computing environments based on the Multi-Context Systems paradigm. To handle inconsistency in the distributed context knowledge, we added non-monotonic features in Multi-Context Systems. In the proposed model, local context knowledge is expressed using local rule theories, and a preference relation is used to resolve conflicts that derive from the interaction of the distributed context theories through the mappings. We also described a distributed query evaluation algorithm for MCS, and analyzed its formal properties with respect to termination, complexity and the possibility to create an equivalent global defeasible theory from the distributed contexts. Finally, we demonstrated the use of the algorithm in three use case scenarios from the Ambient Intelligence domain. Part of our ongoing or future work includes:

- Implementing the algorithm in Logic Programming, using the equivalence with Defeasible Logic, and the well-studied translation of defeasible knowledge into logic programs under Well-Founded Semantics [33].

- Implementing the described scenarios in a real ambient peer-to-peer environment with peers lying on a variety of stationary and mobile devices (such as PDAs or cell phones).
- Studying alternative methods for conflict resolution, which differ in the way that a peer evaluates the answers returned by its peers; e.g. we could associate the quality of an answer not only with the trust level of the queried peer, but also with the confidence of the queried peer on the answer it returns.
- Adding non-monotonic features in the local context theories to support uncertainty in the local context knowledge.
- Extending the algorithm to support overlapping vocabularies, which will enable different contexts to use elements of common vocabularies (e.g. URIs).
- Studying more applications in the Ambient Intelligence and Semantic Web domains, where the theories may represent ontological context knowledge, policies and regulations.

References

1. Henricksen, K., Indulska, J.: Modelling and Using Imperfect Context Information. In: Proceedings of PERCOMW 2004, Washington, DC, USA, pp. 33–37. IEEE Computer Society, Los Alamitos (2004)
2. Chen, H., Finin, T., Joshi, A.: Semantic Web in a Pervasive Context-Aware Architecture. Artificial Intelligence in Mobile System 2003, 33–40 (2003)
3. Forstadius, J., Lassila, O., Seppanen, T.: RDF-based model for context-aware reasoning in rich service environment. In: PerCom 2005 Workshops, pp. 15–19 (2005)
4. Patkos, T., Bikakis, A., Antoniou, G., Plexousakis, D., Papadopouli, M.: A Semantics-based Framework for Context-Aware Services: Lessons Learned and Challenges. In: Indulska, J., Ma, J., Yang, L.T., Ungerer, T., Cao, J. (eds.) UIC 2007. LNCS, vol. 4611, pp. 839–848. Springer, Heidelberg (2007)
5. Gu, T., Pung, H.K., Zhang, D.Q.: A Middleware for Building Context-Aware Mobile Services. In: Proceedings of the IEEE Vehicular Technology Conference (VTC 2004), Milan, Italy (2004)
6. Wang, X.H., Dong, J.S., Chin, C.Y., Hettiarachchi, S.R., Zhang, D.: Semantic Space: an infrastructure for smart spaces. IEEE Pervasive Computing 3(3), 32–39 (2004)
7. Ranganathan, A., Campbell, R.H.: An infrastructure for context-awareness based on first order logic. Personal Ubiquitous Comput. 7(6), 353–364 (2003)
8. Gandon, F.L., Sadeh, N.M.: Semantic web technologies to reconcile privacy and context awareness. Journal of Web Semantics 1, 241–260 (2004)
9. Toninelli, A., Montanari, R., Kagal, L., Lassila, O.: A Semantic Context-Aware Access Control Framework for Secure Collaborations in Pervasive Computing Environments. In: Proc. of 5th International Semantic Web Conference, pp. 5–9 (2006)
10. Kofod-Petersen, A., Mikalsen, M.: Representing and Reasoning about Context in a Mobile Environment. Revue d'Intelligence Artificielle 19(3), 479–498 (2005)
11. Hatala, M., Wakkary, R., Kalantari, L.: Ontologies and rules in support of real-time ubiquitous application. Journal of Web Semantics, Special Issue on Rules and ontologies for Semantic Web 3(1), 5–22 (2005)
12. Khushraj, D., Lassila, O., Finin, T.: sTuples: Semantic Tuple Spaces. In: First Annual International Conference on Mobile and Ubiquitous Systems: Networking and Services (MobiQuitous 2004), pp. 267–277 (2004)

13. Krummenacher, R., Kopecký, J., Strang, T.: Sharing Context Information in Semantic Spaces. In: OTM Workshops, pp. 229–232 (2005)
14. Korpipaa, P., Mantyjarvi, J., Kela, J., Keranen, H., Malm, E.J.: Managing Context Information in Mobile Devices. IEEE Pervasive Computing 02(3), 42–51 (2003)
15. Benerecetti, M., Bouquet, P., Ghidini, C.: Contextual reasoning distilled. JE-TAI 12(3), 279–305 (2000)
16. McCarthy, J.: Generality in Artificial Intelligence. Communications of the ACM 30(12), 1030–1035 (1987)
17. Buvac, S., Mason, I.A.: Propositional Logic of Context. In: AAAI, pp. 412–419 (1993)
18. McCarthy, J., Buvač, S.: Formalizing Context (Expanded Notes). In: Aliseda, A., van Glabbeek, R., Westerståhl, D. (eds.) Computing Natural Language, pp. 13–50. CSLI Publications, Stanford (1998)
19. Giunchiglia, F., Serafini, L.: Multilanguage hierarchical logics, or: how we can do without modal logics. Artificial Intelligence 65(1) (1994)
20. Ghidini, C., Giunchiglia, F.: Local Models Semantics, or contextual reasoning=locality+compatibility. Artificial Intelligence 127(2), 221–259 (2001)
21. Roelofsen, F., Serafini, L.: Minimal and Absent Information in Contexts. In: IJCAI, pp. 558–563 (2005)
22. Brewka, G., Roelofsen, F., Serafini, L.: Contextual Default Reasoning. In: IJCAI, pp. 268–273 (2007)
23. Bernstein, P.A., Giunchiglia, F., Kementsietsidis, A., Mylopoulos, J., Serafini, L., Zaihrayeu, I.: Data Management for Peer-to-Peer Computing: A Vision. In: WebDB, pp. 89–94 (2002)
24. Halevy, A.Y., Ives, Z.G., Suciu, D., Tatarinov, I.: Schema Mediation in Peer Data Management Systems. In: ICDE, p. 505 (2003)
25. Calvanese, D., De Giacomo, G., Lenzerini, M., Rosati, R.: Logical Foundations of Peer-To-Peer Data Integration, pp. 241–251. ACM, New York (2004)
26. Franconi, E., Kuper, G.M., Lopatenko, A., Serafini, L.: A Robust Logical and Computational Characterisation of Peer-to-Peer Database Systems. In: DBISP2P, pp. 64–76 (2003)
27. Calvanese, D., De Giacomo, G., Lembo, D., Lenzerini, M., Rosati, R.: Inconsistency Tolerance in P2P Data Integration: an Epistemic Logic Approach. In: Bierman, G., Koch, C. (eds.) DBPL 2005. LNCS, vol. 3774, pp. 90–105. Springer, Heidelberg (2005)
28. Chatalic, P., Nguyen, G.H., Rousset, M.C.: Reasoning with Inconsistencies in Propositional Peer-to-Peer Inference Systems. In: ECAI, pp. 352–356 (2006)
29. Adjiman, P., Chatalic, P., Goasdoue, F., Rousset, M.C., Simon, L.: Distributed Reasoning in a Peer-to-Peer Setting: Application to the Semantic Web. Journal of Artificial Intelligence Research 25, 269–314 (2006)
30. Antoniou, G., Billington, D., Governatori, G., Maher, M.J.: Representation results for defeasible logic. ACM Transactions on Computational Logic 2(2), 255–287 (2001)
31. Governatori, G., Maher, M.J., Billington, D., Antoniou, G.: Argumentation Semantics for Defeasible Logics. Journal of Logic and Computation 14(5), 675–702 (2004)
32. Maher, M.J.: A Model-Theoretic Semantics for Defeasible Logic. In: Paraconsistent Computational Logic, pp. 67–80 (2002)
33. Antoniou, G., Billington, D., Governatori, G., Maher, M.J.: Embedding defeasible logic into logic programming. Theory Pract. Log. Program. 6(6), 703–735 (2006)

Analysis of Heart Stress Response for a Public Talk Assistant System

Martin Kusserow, Oliver Amft, and Gerhard Tröster

Wearable Computing Lab., ETH Zurich, Switzerland
{kusserow,amft,troester}@ife.ee.ethz.ch
http://www.wearable.ethz.ch

Abstract. Conference presentations are stressful communication tasks for many speakers. This mental stress inhibits the speaker's ability to recall information and perceive the audience. Moreover, stress deteriorates linguistic and paralinguistic capabilities of the speaker. This paper proposes a wearable talk assistant to monitor mental stress and provide relaxation feedback during public speaking. The assistant senses the speaker's body stress by means of heart activity. With this data the system recognises stressful talk phases. We evaluate the approach in authentic conference talks. The talk assistant was worn by 5 speakers before, during, and after giving a 20 minute talk. Our results demonstrate that it is feasible to distinguish the talk period from the surrounding periods and detect talk phases. These findings show that heart activity provides vital information to estimate the speaker's body stress. Moreover, we outline ways to proactively support a speaker non-disruptively while talking in order to maximise the presentation performance.

Keywords: Speaker monitoring, mental stress, heart rate variability.

1 Introduction

Giving a public talk is generally considered as a challenging task. It requires a cognitive performance to communicate expert knowledge of a particular domain. Moreover, public talking is a stressful social situation that stimulates the autonomous nervous system (ANS). In turn, most unexperienced speakers observe symptoms, such as cold hands, sweat, and increased heart rate. Nevertheless, even professional speakers may perceive such body stress, for example when talking in front of an unknown audience.

While ANS activation over a resting level may positively stimulate cognitive capabilities of a speaker [1], elevated levels of stress and anxiety restrain cognitive and communicative capabilities. Consequently the presentation may become unclear, the speaker may be unable to interact with the audience and the talk will miss its goal to transfer vital content. Hence it is desirable to control stress level during public talks.

We believe that a talk assistant system could be deployed that provides relaxation feedback stimuli and automatically adapts feedback during a talk. Several

E. Aarts et al. (Eds.): AmI 2008, LNCS 5355, pp. 326–342, 2008.

feedback strategies, applicable even during a talk were discussed in the literature, see Section 1.3. Technically, however, a talk assistant requires an appropriate stress monitoring solution in order to adapt and personalise the feedback.

In order to adapt feedback, a first vital information is to identify stressful talk phases. A talk assistant could fade in a relaxation stimulus during a stressful talk phase and remain quite otherwise. Moreover, the talk assistant feedback may incorporate the stress level during the stressful phase to fine-tune feedback.

1.1   Stress Phases in Public Talks

Body stress is a natural response of the ANS to manage critical situations, due to physical or mental load. Historically, ANS response supported the fight or flight reaction needed when facing an enemy. However physical activity, movement in particular, is not relevant during public speaking. The ANS response for presentations is primarily related to mental effort [1] and anxiety [2] and is reflected in physiological patterns. These sources of ANS response cannot be differentiated [1] and are referred to as body stress in this paper.

Behnke and Sawyer [2] analysed speaker reports after a talk and found that anxiety due to public speaking follows a temporal stimulation sequence. In an anticipatory phase before the talk, anxiety increases, e.g. during preparation and imagination of the performance. At the time being called upon and during the first minute of speaking, anxiety peaks (confrontation phase) and decays thereafter (adaptation phase). However the exact phase timing remains unclear, since a post-hoc analysis based on the speaker's memory was used. Moreover, magnitude and timing of the body reaction depends on speaker and particular situation, e.g. stress symptoms may recur even in a later stage of the talk. Coping strategies to manage these stressful talk situations require long and laborious training.

1.2   Paper Contributions

Our goals in this paper were to (1) develop a stress monitoring solution for public talks and (2) evaluate physiological responses as indicators for stressful talk phases.

Regarding the first goal, the challenge of talk stress evaluation is to non-invasively monitor the speaker. In particular, the speaker should not be hindered or influenced by the monitoring approach during a presentation. Hence, classical stress assessments, such as taking saliva samples, are not feasible during a talk. Neither the speaker could be asked during the talk, to rate momentary body stress level.

While public speaking is a general stress stimulus [1], identification of robust physiological indicators applicable for a talk assistant is an open research field. Towards this second goal, we monitored speakers during actual conference talks

In this setting, this paper makes the following contributions:

1. We utilise a commercial heart monitoring chest-belt to analyse seven physiological features from time and frequency-domain. The physiological features

included heart period, variables of heart rate variability (HRV) and respiration, extracted from the R-wave signal. Most of these features were reported to indicate body stress when recorded from Electrocardiogram recorders in laboratory settings [3]. We evaluate their capability to distinguish the talk situation from anticipation and post-talk relaxation using the chest-belt device.

2. We analyse actual talks to identify confrontation and subsequent adaptation phases using heart period. We then evaluate a phasing for all physiological features by pattern classification. To this end, our evaluation is a first attempt to confirm the sequence of anxiety reporting provided by speakers after a talk [2]. Finally, we compare the physiological response to talk anxiety self-ratings of the speakers.

Our analysis is based on 7 hours of data recorded from real conference talks of five different speakers. On each occasion, we additionally recorded at least 30 min before and after the talk to monitor anticipation and relaxation.

Vital aspects of our system are simplicity and comfort: the chest-belt is unobtrusive, easy to use, and does not interfere with the speaker's performance. We used a commercial off-the-shelf device to permit quick deployment and repeatability. Comparable systems typically require electrode attachments, such as for Holter monitors (see Section 1.4).

Below, we present our talk assistant concept. In Section 1.4 we review related works on stress analysis during public speaking. Section 2 presents the recording procedure utilised during the real talk situations and Section 3 outlines the applied data analysis procedures. The results of our work are detailed in Section 4 for the talk situation and Section 5 for the phases within the talk. A discussion of the results is given in Section 6. Section 7 concludes the findings of this work.

1.3   Talk Assistant Concept

Eventually the talk assistant shall support speakers in their performance, reducing the need for long and laborious training by the speaker. Even during a talk, such feedback can be deployed to support relaxation.

More than 35 years ago researchers first thought of using technical devices to reduce public speaking anxiety and to improve public speaking experience [4,2]. Therefore, veridical feedback was found to be essential to change physiological responses into the desired direction [5]. Talk stress feedback is related to Biofeedback that is considered a particular useful technique to reduce heart rate due to mental stressors [6,7]. Nevertheless, feedback during talks must occur without attracting attention of the audience. Examples include dedicated messages to the speaker and relaxation screens in the back of the audience [2]. In addition, particular ways of breathing [8] or speaking [9] can promote parasympathetic activation and reduce stress during talks.

Figure 1 shows our concept for the basic operation of a talk assistant. The ANS can respond with body stress symptoms to a talk situation (stressor). These symptoms include changes in physiological signals and heart activity in

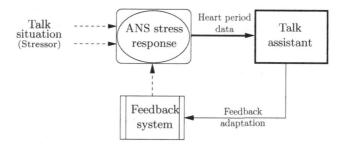

Fig. 1. Basic schematic of the talk assistant operation. This paper focuses on the recording of heart period data and analysis of heart-related physiological stress indications during actual public talks.

particular. The talk assistant records heart period data and adapts feedback systems embedded in the environment. In an initial implementation, feedback could be related to the identified confrontation phase.

1.4 Related Work

Dickens and Parker [10] first assessed stage fright in 100 male and female college students. Blood pressure and pulse rate samples were taken directly before and after classroom presentations. Significant increase in pulse rate and blood pressure between pre-talk and post-talk period was observed for over 90% of the speakers. However, no measurement was taken during the talk period. Behnke [4] reported 4 stable characteristic events in cardiac patterns of 24 male college students during public speaking: anticipation, confrontation, adaptation, and release. Confrontation and adaptation were assigned the highest levels of physiological arousal. Later Behnke [2] established two general patterns of public speaking anxiety, habituation and sensitation. They differ in the level of anxiety during the anticipation phase. The degree of anxiety reflected in the pattern of sensitation was further supported by the work of Booth-Butterfield [11] and Pörhölä [1] who categorized heart rate patterns of college students during public speaking.

Different methodologies exist in monitoring physiological signals during public speaking. The duration of the public speaking task varied from 2 minutes [11] up to 7 minutes [1]. Typically, the talk situation was manually partitioned into anticipation, confrontation, adaptation, and release phase each lasting from 30 seconds [11] up to 2 minutes [12].

Audience size and composition varied from 15 classmates [13] to 150 college students [10].

Topics of the speech were hobby or favorite activity [2], topic of own choice [1] or any other informative topic [4] rather than a scientific topic. Investigations were solely done in university classroom environments and not in front of a scientific conference audience. A comprehensive summary of these methodologies can be found in the work of Pörhölä [1].

Recording of heart rate during public speaking was done by hand [10], paper-based physiograph [4], heart rate monitors attached to the index finger [11], ear-worn device [1], and an ECG system [14].

Compared to blood pressure and skin conductance level (SCL) only heart rate yielded significant effects related to the talk situation itself [5]. Cardiac response was found to clearly differentiate between anticipation, confrontation and release phase in comparison to SCL [14].

While heart activity was confirmed to be a primary stress measure during talks, cardiac features were not analysed in detail. Most related works assumed a static phase or moment to determine stress levels of anticipation, confrontation and release. Moreover, it remains open, whether HRV or respiration features provide a robust indication for the talk situation and the talk phase timing. Moreover, a chest-belt measurement towards a talk assistant system was not investigated.

2   Conference Talk Recording

A scientific talk of five PhD and Masters students (aged 23 to 30 years, 1 female) was included in our investigation. The talks were given at three research conferences (ISWC 2007, IOT 2008, and an ETH Electronics institute colloquium). In all situations, the speakers presented their research results to an audience of 30–50 experts. The experts were of mostly unknown identity to the speakers. The speaker's performance was neither recorded on audio or video nor rated by members of the audience. All speakers have had public speaking experience with comparable audiences. None of the speakers had known clinical anxiety disorders or cardiovascular diseases.

Figure 2 illustrates the talk recording procedure. At start of the conference session speakers sat amongst the audience and followed the presentation of preceding talks (pre-talk period). Subsequently, speakers delivered their talk (talk period). A question and answer (Q&A) period followed the talk. Finally, speakers returned to their seat in the audience to listen to remaining talks of the conference session (post-talk period).

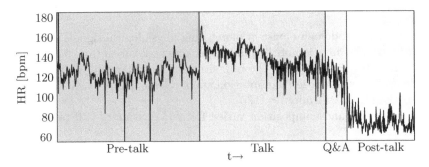

Fig. 2. Heart rate (HR) signal during the conference talk of a representative speaker. Pre-talk, talk, question and answer (Q&A), and post-talk period. Notice that peak HR is at ∼170 bpm at beginning of the talk.

For each speaker, a pre-talk period of at least 30 min before begin of the actual talk was recorded. After the talk and Q&A period, recording was continued for another 30 min (post-talk period). The average talk duration was 21±7 min, without Q&A period. After attaching the monitoring system, speakers were asked to follow their normal talk preparations. An observer followed the speaker's activities and annotated the recordings.

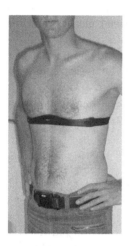 

Fig. 3. Wearable system used for the recording of heart period data during the conference session. Left: Heart monitor belt attached to the thorax and QBIC belt computer for data storage. Right: Speaker wearing the system during the conference talk.

The wearable recording system consisted of a commercially available Suunto heart rate monitor chest-belt[1] and the Q-Belt Integrated Computer (QBIC) [15]. Figure 3 depicts the wearable sensor system. The heart monitor chest-belt provides heart period data (RR intervals) by measuring the time between consecutive QRS complexes. Data was wirelessly transmitted to the QBIC using the ANT communication protocol[2]. For data recording on QBIC the Context Recognition Toolbox (CRNT) [16] was used.

For our research work, QBIC offered the flexibility to replace chest-belts and add further sensors without redesigning the recording and analysis procedure.

For the speakers, this procedure did not require interaction with the recording system, except to put it on and off. In addition all speakers answered the personal report of confidence as a speaker questionnaire (PRCS) [17]. PRCS measures general anxiety, subjectively perceived by the speaker during public speaking. Scores range from 0 (not anxious) to 30 (highly anxious).

---

[1] http://www.suunto.com

[2] http://www.thisisant.com

3   Analysis Methods

HRV analysis attempts to separate the types of ANS activation using features of the time and frequency domain. In particular, two frequency bands are associated with ANS activation: low-frequency (LF) band (0.04–0.15 Hz), reflecting parasympathetic and sympathetic activation, as well as high-frequency (HF) band (0.15–0.4 Hz) reflecting parasympathetic activation [18]. As there is no consensus on the optimal approach to extract HRV frequency domain features from RR intervals, we used a non-parametric FFT-based method according to guidelines established in [19].

Heart activity features were derived for the analysis and comparison of (1) all recording periods (pre-talk, talk, post-talk) and (2) the analysis of phases within the talk period. The first analysis shows the relation of heart activity to the entire talk situation. In the second analysis, we investigated whether the confrontation phase can be identified and discriminated from the remaining talk.

3.1   Heart Period Signal Preprocessing

The signal processing procedure was adapted to RR interval data provided by the chest-belt. In particular, signal preprocessing needed to compensate for errors in the RR interval detection.

Heart period was recorded as timestamped RR interval. Non-parametric analysis of heart period data requires an evenly sampled signal and stable first and second order moments across time [19]. Thus, to compute HRV features the raw RR intervals were filtered, interpolated, and detrended. Figure 4 summarises the signal processing flow.

In a first step, spurious RR intervals caused by added or missed R-peaks during QRS detection were filtered from the irregularly sampled time series. Spurious RR intervals that differed by more than 20% compared to their predecessor were removed [20].

Subsequent cubic interpolation was applied to obtain an evenly sampled time series at 8 Hz sampling frequency that permits the analysis of high heart rate levels [21].

After interpolation, detrending was applied to obtain a weakly stationary time series. As detrending method we used a modified smoothness priors approach [22], where the cut-off frequency can be adjusted by a single parameter λ

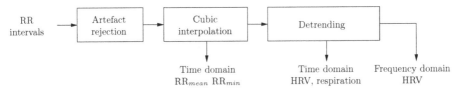

Fig. 4. Feature extraction process. Irregularly sampled RR intervals were filtered, interpolated and detrended.

and data end-point distortion is avoided. With our modification using a sliding window approach, detrending can be performed online.

The smoothing parameter λ was set to 1600 which equals a cut-off frequency of $\sim$0.04 Hz at a sampling frequency of 8 Hz. This prevents attenuation of the relevant LF frequency band, starting at 0.04 Hz.

Spectral power in LF and HF was computed from the estimation of the power spectral density (PSD), for which Welch's method was used [23]. A common sliding window size of 1024 samples (128 s, Hanning window) and a step size of 512 samples (64 s) was used. These settings provide a frequency resolution of $\sim$0.0078 Hz and satisfy the recommended length of at least 2 min for analysis of the LF frequency band [19].

3.2   Heart Activity Feature Extraction

Features of HRV in time and frequency domain were selected according to the recommendations made in [24]. In the frequency domain, the following HRV features were computed: low-frequency spectral power (LF), high-frequency spectral power (HF), and LF/HF ratio. The following time domain features were computed using the same sliding window configuration: standard deviation of all RR intervals (SDNN)[3], and standard deviation of differences between adjacent RR intervals (SDSD).

In addition to the HRV features the minimum RR interval (RR_{min}), time of occurrence of RR_{min} (τ_{min}), and respiration frequency (f_{resp}), calculated from respiratory sinus arrhythmia (RSA), were computed. For calculation of f_{resp} the advanced counting method [25] was used. For that method, performance was found to be superior compared to other RSA techniques.

4   Talk Situation Analysis

In the talk situation analysis we investigated the relation of heart activity features between anticipation (pre-talk), relaxation (post-talk) and the talk period. With this approach we identified features that change significantly during the talk period.

We computed features (see Section 3) for the following time segments: last 10 min before talk begin (pre-talk period), first 10 min after talk begin (talk period), and first 10 min after end of the Q&A period (post-talk period). These segment durations were chosen to provide an acceptable number of observations for analysis and compare features across the three periods. The Q&A period was not included in the talk period as the direct interaction of speaker and audience may raise different physiological responses.

Figure 5 shows four selected time and frequency domain features (mean RR interval, mean SDNN, mean LF power, and mean HF power) for all subjects across the three periods.

---

[3] RR intervals are also referred to as NN (normal-to-normal) intervals [24].

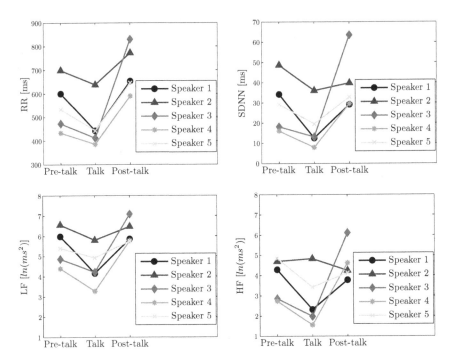

Fig. 5. Mean RR interval (top left), mean SDNN (top right), mean LF power (bottom left), and mean HF power (bottom right) of the pre-talk, talk, and post-talk period for all five speakers

Mean RR interval decreases from pre-talk to talk period by 50 to 150 ms and significantly increases by 200 to 400 ms from talk to post-talk period. For all speakers, this result confirms the strong variations in heart rate shown in the example heart rate plot in Figure 2. Lowest mean RR interval occurs in the talk period, highest mean RR interval in the post-talk period. This pattern conforms to previous findings [2].

Mean SDNN shows a similar pattern however, in contrast to mean RR interval, pre-talk and post-talk levels were similar. Mean LF power is higher than mean HF power across all periods and speakers. Mean LF power drops during the talk period and recovers to pre-talk level in the post-talk period. Except for speaker 2, mean HF power follows a similar pattern.

Speaker 2, in contrast to the other speakers, shows a slight increase in mean HF power during the talk and a decrease in the post-talk period. Only speakers 3 and 4 exceed their pre-talk level in mean LF and mean HF power during the post-talk period.

Paired t-tests were used to analyse the differences in feature means of the talk period with both surrounding periods. The analysis was made for a hypothesis that two matched samples come from distributions with equal means at a significance level of 5%. Table 1 details the speaker-specific p-values and

Table 1. Paired t-test for talk vs. pre-talk and talk vs. post-talk periods at the 5% significance level for all features; (n.s. = not significant).

Talk vs. pre-talk p-values							
	RR	**LF**	**HF**	**LF/HF**	**f_{resp}**	**SDSD**	**SDNN**
Speaker 1	< 0.001	0.009	0.002	n.s.	0.027	< 0.001	< 0.001
Speaker 2	< 0.001	0.012	n.s.	0.002	n.s.	n.s.	0.004
Speaker 3	0.002	n.s.	n.s.	n.s.	n.s.	n.s.	0.021
Speaker 4	0.001	0.036	n.s.	n.s.	n.s.	0.033	0.002
Speaker 5	< 0.001	0.035	0.037	n.s.	0.037	0.037	0.015
# **sig. results**	5	4	2	1	2	3	5

Talk vs. post-talk p-values							
	RR	**LF**	**HF**	**LF/HF**	**f_{resp}**	**SDSD**	**SDNN**
Speaker 1	< 0.001	0.004	0.007	n.s.	n.s.	< 0.001	< 0.001
Speaker 2	< 0.001	0.018	n.s.	0.035	n.s.	0.041	n.s.
Speaker 3	< 0.001	0.001	< 0.001	0.005	0.036	< 0.001	< 0.001
Speaker 4	< 0.001	0.004	< 0.001	0.011	n.s.	< 0.001	< 0.001
Speaker 5	< 0.001	0.011	0.048	n.s.	n.s.	0.005	0.001
# **sig. results**	5	5	4	3	1	5	4

number of significant results per feature for talk vs. pre-talk and talk vs. post-talk periods.

For all speakers RR intervals were significantly different between pre-talk, talk, and post-talk periods. Analysis of pre-talk and talk periods showed significant differences across all speakers in SDNN. For talk and post-talk periods, features LF and SDSD showed a significant difference in addition to RR for all speakers. Speaker 3 showed a significant difference for talk and post-talk periods across all features. All other features showed sparse significance for individual speakers only.

Lilliefors' goodness-of-fit test of composite normality was applied to prove normal distribution of the features prior to the t-test. Nevertheless it must be noted that the eight observations available per feature in each period restricts the result interpretation. We assume it here as a preliminary indication of informative features that distinguish the talk period from the surrounding periods.

Table 2. Talk characteristics analysis: speaker-specific minimum RR interval RR_{min} and time of occurrence τ_{min}, time τ_{ant} until recovery to mean RR interval of anticipation phase, and PRCS score. τ_{min}, τ_{ant} are relative to talk start time.

	$\mathbf{RR_{min}}$ [ms]	$\tau_{\mathbf{min}}$ [s]	$\tau_{\mathbf{ant}}$ [s]	**PRCS Score**
Speaker 1	404.7	218.9	n.a.	8
Speaker 2	500.1	12.6	262	3
Speaker 3	348.8	18.1	629	11
Speaker 4	349.9	81.8	580	20
Speaker 5	397.0	38.5	n.a.	2

5   Talk Phases Analysis

We investigated whether the confrontation and adaptation phases within a talk can be identified and separated.

Without considering a static partitioning of the talk period into confrontation and adaptation phase, we determined three distinct points in time with respect to talk start time: (1) time τ_{min} until minimum RR interval RR_{min} occurs, (2) time τ_{ant} until the RR interval first reaches mean RR interval RR_{ant} of the anticipation phase (pre-talk), and (3) time τ_{rel} until the RR interval first reaches the mean RR interval RR_{rel} of the release phase (post-talk). Table 2 details the speaker-specific results.

Except for speaker 2, RR_{min} ranged from 348 ms (172 bpm) to 404 ms (146 bpm). Speaker 2, similar to the talk situation analysis, showed a higher RR_{min} of 500 ms (120 bpm). The minimum RR interval occurs within the first 12 to 82 s for all five speakers[4].

Except for speaker 1 and 5, τ_{ant} is within 262 to 629 s. For speakers 2 to 4 this indicates that lower RR_{min} is related to longer τ_{ant}. Although in range of the other speaker's, RR_{min} of speaker 1 and 5 did not recover to RR_{ant}. None of the five speakers recovered to RR_{rel} within the talk period.

Moreover, table 2 shows the PRCS scores of all speakers. We used PRCS as an indicator of how the measured physiological response related to generally self-perceived stress during a talk. We observed that lower RR_{min} is reflected by higher PRCS scores (more anxious). However, speaker 5 reported the lowest PRCS score that does not correspond to the RR_{min} result. It would rather corresponds to RR_{min} of speaker 1 having a PRCS score of 8.

In order to analyse the hypothesis of two talk phases (interpreted here as confrontation and adaptation) for all features, we computed features (according

---

[4] In fact, speaker 1 also showed a local minimum RR interval of 406 ms at 37 s after talk begin. Due to a failing technical demonstration during the talk, the global minimum RR interval was found 219 s after talk begin.

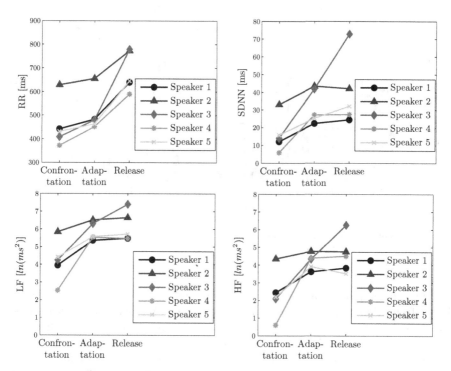

Fig. 6. Mean RR interval (top left), mean SDNN (top right), mean LF power (bottom left), and mean HF power (bottom right) of the confrontation, adaptation, and release phase for all speakers

to Section 3) for the first 5 min and last 5 min of the talk period. Similar to the talk situation analysis, we excluded the Q&A period in this investigation. Ideally, the talk assistant should require measurement data from the talk period only in order to adapt feedback. Moreover, the durations represent a tradeoff between number of observations and assumed stationarity of the physiological state. For comparison to the relaxation effect after the talk period we additionally derived features for the first 5 min of the post-talk period (release phase).

Figure 6 visualises the speaker-specific results for confrontation, adaptation, and release phases. Results are represented for mean RR interval, mean SDNN, mean LF power, and mean HF power.

Mean RR interval, mean SDNN, mean LF power, and mean HF power showed an increase from confrontation to adaptation phase. Increase in mean RR interval is even larger from adaptation to release phase. Except for speaker 3, whose features continue to increase in the release phase, mean SDNN, mean LF power, and mean HF power remain similar between adaptation and release phases. These results indicate an adaptation trend during the talk.

In order to determine whether the two talk phases could be discriminated, we applied a Naïve Bayes classifier. Moreover, we estimated in this analysis those features that are particular informative to indicate a phase structure.

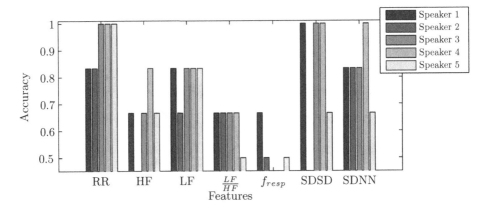

Fig. 7. Speaker-specific leave-one-out discrimination test of confrontation and adaptation talk phases for all features

From the computed feature set of each speaker we included 3 observations of the confrontation and adaptation phase respectively. We performed a leave-one-out cross-validation to determine training and testing set for the classification. For classifier training 2 observations were used, 1 observation was used for testing. Figure 7 shows the speaker-specific classification performance for all features.

Among the features mean RR interval showed the best classification performance along with mean SDSD, mean LF power and mean SDNN. Mean HF power, mean LF/HF ratio, and mean respiratory frequency f_{resp} performed less well. Except for mean RR interval, features showed high variations between speakers.

6 Discussion

6.1 Talk Situation Analysis

Both, the visual analysis and the t-test of heart activity features showed that the talk period was best identified from time-domain features. In particular, the mean RR interval showed significant differences when compared to pre-talk and post-talk periods. In contrast, the averages for LF/HF and respiration frequency f_{resp} did not change in a similar way. This is an interesting observation, since the LF/HF ratio is frequently cited as stress indicator in laboratory studies [3]. Nevertheless, public speaking is a clear cue for mental stress and hence is reflected in the body stress response.

In our analysis, we found that in particular the HF feature is less stable. We assume that these results are related to the talk scenario: speaking can influence the LF and HF power since irregular breathing can affect both frequency bands [26]. Moreover, using the chest-belt device may deteriorate frequency-domain features due to deviation in RR interval measurement compared to a wet electrode ECG devices. However, a classic wet electrode ECG device would have been more cumbersome for a speaker and is less acceptable for a talk assistant system. We plan to investigate this effect in the future.

Nevertheless, these results do indicate that the chest-belt device provides relevant information in temporal features under real conference talk situations. These findings were confirmed by our subsequent analysis of talk phases.

We observed that one speaker (speaker 2) had larger values for the RR interval in all periods while maintaining the same overall pattern, compared to others. These results were attributed to the high level of physical fitness of that speaker.

6.2   Talk Phases Analysis

The talk phases analysis confirmed a confrontation phase including τ_{min} for all speakers during the first minutes of the talk. After this distinct time, RR interval increased differently for each speaker. Two speakers did not reach the anticipation level, all speakers missed the average post-talk level. Hence the talk was activating for all speakers, while some could not recover from the confrontation level heart activity.

To this end, our analysis procedure can be directly applied for a talk assistant system. We considered the time from talk begin to τ_{ant}, including τ_{min} as most challenging moment during the talk. Whereas, when assuming a steady process, the two remaining points τ_{ant}, τ_{rel} are indicators of a recovery activity from this particular activation state of the body. Thus, assuming two phases during a talk period, the goal of a talk assistant system should be to minimise τ_{ant}. The reference measure RR_{ant} is available to the system when the assistant is switched on before the talk. This procedure requires no further calibration to RR_{rel} or mean resting RR interval. Nevertheless, the speaker should have the option to adjust the feedback online. This can be achieved by adapting confrontation phase identification threshold incorporating individual heart activity limits [1] corresponding to either favourable arousal or unfavourable stress.

The visual feature analysis showed a most consistent relation between assumed talk phases for the RR interval. This observation was confirmed by the classification test. It is important to note that the two phases classification is an inappropriate relaxation feedback to the speaker. Rather it should trigger relaxation cues incorporating the temporal trend of the features.

The PRCS scores of speaker anxiety confirmed the estimated RR_{min} result, with one exceptional speaker. We attributed this observation to an inaccurate questionnaire response.

Monitoring of behaviour and physiological response in a conference environment is clearly limited in data size and constant conditions: talk length is fixed by the conference session constraints. Artificial extension under laboratory condition may not elicit the same physiological responses as the field study since social implications and talk conditions change.

A limitation for this investigation was the low number of observations available for each talk phase, constrained by the tradeoff between resolution of the frequency-domain features and assumed stationarity in physiological responses.

For the spectral features, a time window of 2 min was needed to analyse the spectral LF band, while a duration of 5 min was assumed as upper limit for a stable physiological state. Physiological response in this particular scenario, however, may contain a number of short time phenomena, too short for sufficient frequency resolution using FFT-based PSD estimation [27]. We plan to investigate this issue in the future.

7   Conclusion

In this paper we analysed heart stress response during actual conference presentations using a body-worn monitoring system. We expect that this system can be used in a talk assistant system that supports a speaker during stressful talk situations with automatic relaxation feedback. Different options for such feedback have been proposed in the literature.

Towards the talk assistant system we addressed two most critical challenges. Firstly, a comfortable speaker monitoring system is needed to measure body stress of the speaker. For this purpose, we deployed a commercial heart monitor chest-belt that can transfer readings wirelessly to an on-body or room-installed base system. Secondly, relevant physiological information must be obtained from the speaker in order to adapt and personalise assistant feedback. To this end we investigated seven features of heart activity from time- and frequency-domain that were reported to indicate body stress in laboratory investigations [3].

Our investigations showed that time-domain features, in particular heart period, can provide robust information for the talk situation. Moreover, these features help to discriminate the talk phases. Using this phasing information a talk assistant system could adapt feedback during the confrontation phase. Minimising the duration that the speaker stays in this phase is the primary goal of the talk assistant.

Classical HRV stress indicators did not respond as expected in our analysis. This finding requires further investigation and validation of a chest-belt device, in particular for public talk situations. Currently, we investigate the use of complementary sensor modalities to include additional information in the speaker's body stress estimation. To this end, we like to investigate whether a simple notification or reminder is an acceptable and effective speaker feedback solution.

Acknowledgements

We would like to thank the conference speakers for participating in the talk recordings.

References

1. Pörhölä, M.: Arousal styles during public speaking. Communication Education 51(4), 420–438 (2002)
2. Behnke, R.R., Sawyer, C.R.: Public speaking anxiety as a function of sensitization and habituation processes. Communication Education 53(2), 1164–1173 (2004)

3. Pagani, M., Lucini, D., Rimoldi, O., Furlan, R., Piazza, S., Biancardi, L.: 20. In: Heart Rate Variability, pp. 245–266. Futura Publishing Company, Inc. (1995)
4. Behnke, R.R., Carlile, L.W.: Heart rate as an index of speech anxiety. Speech Monographs 38, 65–69 (1971)
5. Rohrmann, S., Hennig, J., Netter, P.: Changing psychobiological stress reactions by manipulating cognitive processes. International Journal of Psychophysiology 33, 149–161 (1999)
6. Sharpley, C.F.: Biofeedback training versus simple instructions to reduce heart rate reactivity to a psychological stressor. Journal of Behavioral Medicine 12(5), 435–447 (1989)
7. McKinney, M.E., Gatchel, R.J.: The comparative effectiveness of heart rate biofeedback, speech skills training, and a combination of both in treating public-speaking anxiety. Biofeedback and Self-Regulation 7(1), 71–87 (1982)
8. Sakakibara, M., Takeuchi, S., Hayano, J.: Effect of relaxation training on cardiac parasympathetic tone. Psychophysiology 31, 223–228 (1994)
9. von Bonin, D., Frühwirth, M., Heuser, P., Moser, M.: Effects of speech therapy with poetry on heart rate variability and well-being (in German). Research in Complementary Medicine 8(3), 144–160 (2001)
10. Dickens, M., Parker, W.R.: An experimental study of certain physiological introspective and rating-scale techniques for the measurement of stage fright. Speech Monographs 18(4), 251–259 (1951)
11. Booth-Butterfield, S.: Action assembly theory and communication apprehension - a psychophysiological study. Human Communication Research 13(3), 386–398 (1987)
12. Behnke, R.R., Beatty, M.J.: A cognitive-physiological model of speech anxiety. Communication Monographs 48, 158–163 (1981)
13. Beatty, M.J., Behnke, R.R.: Effects of public speaking trait anxiety and intensity of speaking task on heart rate during performance. Human Communication Research in Complementary Medicine 18(2), 147–176 (1991)
14. Croft, R.J., Gonsalveza, C.J., Gandera, J., Lechema, L., Barry, R.J.: Differential relations between heart rate and skin conductance, and public speaking anxiety. Journal of Behavior Therapy and Experimental Psychiatry 35(3), 259–271 (2004)
15. Amft, O., Lauffer, M., Ossevoort, S., Macaluso, F., Lukowicz, P., Tröster, G.: Design of the QBIC wearable computing platform. In: ASAP 2004: Proceedings of the 15th IEEE International Conference on Application-specific Systems, Architectures and Processors, pp. 398–410 (2004)
16. Bannach, D., Amft, O., Lukowicz, P.: Rapid prototyping of activity recognition applications. IEEE Pervasive Computing 7(2), 22–31 (2008)
17. Paul, G.L.: Insight versus desensitization in psychotherapy: An experiment in anxiety reduction. PhD thesis, Stanford University, Palo Alto, CA (1966)
18. Malik, M.: Task Force of The European Society of Cardiology and The North American Society of Pacing and Electrophysiology: Heart rate variability - standards of measurement, physiological interpretation, and clinical use. European Heart Journal 17, 354–381 (1996)
19. Berntson, G., Thomas Bigger Jr., J., Eckberg, D.L., Grossman, P., Kaufmann, P.G., Malik, M., Nagaraja, H.N., Porges, S.W., Saul, J.P., Stone, P.H., van der Molen, M.W.: Heart rate variability: Origins, methods, and interpretive caveats. Psychophysiology 34, 623–648 (1997)
20. Kleiger, R.E., Miller, J.P., Thomas Bigger Jr., J., Moss, A.J.: Decreased heart rate variability and its association with increased mortality after acute myocardial infarction. The American Journal of Cardiology 59, 258–262 (1987)

21. Singh, D., Vinod, K., Saxena, S.: Sampling frequency of the RR interval time series for spectral analysis. Journal of Medical Engineering and Technolgy 28(6), 263–272 (2004)
22. Tarvainen, M.P., Ranta-aho, P.O., Karjalainen, P.A.: An advanced detrending method with application to HRV analysis. IEEE Transactions on Biomedical Engineering 49(2), 172–175 (2002)
23. Welch, P.D.: The use of fast Fourier transform for the estimation of power spectra: A method based on time averaging over short, modified periodograms. IEEE Transactions on Audio and Electroacoustics AU-15(2), 70–73 (1967)
24. Malik, M., Camm, A.J.: Heart Rate Variability. Futura Publishing Company, Inc. (1995)
25. Schäfer, A., Kratky, K.W.: Estimation of breathing rate from respiratory sinus arrhythmia. Annals of Biomedical Engineering 36, 476–485 (2008)
26. Beda, A., Jandre, F.C.: Heart-rate and blood-pressure variability during psychophysiological tasks involving speech: Influence of respiration. Psychophysiology 44(5), 767–778 (2007)
27. Cerutti, S., Bianchi, A.M., Mainardi, L.T.: 5. In: Heart Rate Variability, pp. 63–74. Futura Publishing Company, Inc. (1995)

Stone-Type Physiological Sensing Device for Daily Monitoring in an Ambient Intelligence Environment

Ahyoung Choi[1], Yoosoo Oh[1], Goeun Park[2], and Woontack Woo[1,2]

[1] GIST U-VR Lab.,Gwangju 500-712, S. Korea
[2] GIST CTI, Gwangju 500-712, S. Korea
{achoi,yoh}@gist.ac.kr, ge9156@hotmail.com, wwoo@gist.ac.kr

Abstract. Recently there has been increasing research into mobile physiological sensing devices to explore the benefits in the areas of monitoring health and well-being. However, previous works have mainly focused on functionality, and less so on affective shape, comfort use, and stable sensing. In this work, we propose a stone-type physiological sensing device for general users, rather than professional experts. We found that our device was comfortable, stable and had aesthetic appeal for users during monitoring. To develop an affective shape, and to increase comfort, we applied a user-centered design process. We also used context-based physiological signal analysis to obtain stable analysis results according to individual users. As an application, we developed a rainbow ambient display to give visual feedback to users. We expect that this product can be applied in various healthcare applications.

Keywords: Physiological sensing device, Real-time physiological signal analysis, Context awareness, Daily health monitoring.

1 Introduction

Currently there has been increased research interest in physiological sensing devices for use in daily life [1-3]. For developing sensing devices in Ambient Intelligence (AmI) environments, AmI technology is of interest because people normally do not carry their belongings and any portable devices. The following issues need to be considered: unobtrusive monitoring of physiological status with embedded sensors, intelligent analysis methods for health monitoring, and appropriate altering of the ambient display [4-5]. With the advent of wireless communication technology, light-weight Micro-electromechanical Systems (MEMS) technology, and greater computing power on mobile computing devices, various kinds of physiological sensing devices have been developed [6-7]. These include glove-type, wrist-type, armband-type, ring-type and embedded unconstrained-type sensing devices, all of which can be equipped in beds or bathrooms [8-11]. Glove-type sensing devices can conceal sensing lines and therefore have better aesthetics compared to the wrist-type and band-type sensing devices. In the case of wrist-type sensing devices, uncorrupted signals can be reliably detected in the static condition. In addition, this type of device does not interfere with the user's work. In the case of band-type sensing devices,

E. Aarts et al. (Eds.): AmI 2008, LNCS 5355, pp. 343–359, 2008.

these can resolve the problem of movement in the sensing positions, because they can be more firmly attached to the body of the user.

However, most previous work developed sensing devices and analysis which supported light-weight wireless communication, multiple signals sensing and processing. Sensing devices in the AmI environment need to be comfortable to handle and need to capture the variations in sensing signals. In addition, most mobile devices are sensitive to environmental noise and motion. Therefore, a monitoring system that is both comfortable and stable is required. Some users of glove-type sensing devices report discomfort from increased weight and perspiration over a period of time. In the case of wrist-type sensing devices, in situations where there is a significant amount of movement by the user, signals can be corrupted because of changes in the sensing position [12]. In addition, band pressure and weight often mean that the user may become tired or uncomfortable during long term monitoring [13]. In terms of signal analysis, previous devices provided wireless and stable analysis results under experimental conditions. Employing these devices in daily life, some researchers proposed a pattern classification method for collecting activity information [14]. Activity information from the inference engine is used for ECG sensor activation, with a Bayesian classifier to remove activity noise.

To address these issues, we propose a stone-type mobile physiological sensing device, BioPebble. It provides an effective gripping sensation, aesthetic appeal and stable analysis of multiple context information. To maximize the aesthetic appeal of BioPebble, our research utilized a two axes positioning map with cool-warm and soft-hard axes. In order to develop the most effective gripping sensation, we applied a user-centered design process, which is a stepwise design process. In addition, BioPebble supports real-time wireless and multiple signal processing and adaptive analysis with context awareness technology. Context information is obtained from heterogeneous sensory inputs from multiple sensors and services.

As a result of these improvements, we have been able to derive significant benefits for users of the BioPebble, stone-type sensing devices and its analysis. These advantages include stable sensing, repeatability, and reproducibility of measurements in daily monitoring. In addition, BioPebble is comfortable to use and maximizes the aesthetic appreciation applicable to the AmI environment. From the usability test, BioPebble shows an example of appropriate physiological sensing devices in the future AmI environments. Some level of intention from users to monitor their physiological status, is beneficial not only usability but also stable sensing. It means that semi-automatic method combining cognitive aspect is more appropriate to check rough health status.

The outline of this paper is as follows. In Section 2, we explain the details of BioPebble with respect to three characteristics: aesthetic appeal, comfort, and stable sensing. Section 3 describes the implementation details. The experimental setup and analyses are discussed in Section 4. Section 5 illustrates the ambient display of BioPebble in future AmI environments. We conclude in Section 6, and suggest possible directions for future work.

2 BioPebble: Stone-Type Physiological Sensor

It is necessary for sensing devices to meet users' requirements during monitoring with particular attention to such aspects as design, usability, as well as the essential sensor functions. The concept of physiological sensors for use in daily life should therefore be concerned about comfort, aesthetic shape and stable sensing in order to provide better health monitoring and prevention services. In this section, we describe BioPebble, a stone-type grippable physiological sensing device which has been designed with three key words in mind: "Human, Well-being, and Simple User Interface."

2.1 User-Centric Physiological Sensor Design

In order to construct the shape of the first prototype of BioPebble, we observed commonly used mobile apparatus such as cellular phones, MP3 players, the computer mouse and so on. These commercial products were categorized according to two criteria: the sense of touch and the degree of warmth. Based on these axes, we constructed a sample BioPebble with a positioning map. The commercial products were divided into 4 groups, Groups A, B, C and D according to their place on the positioning map as described in Table 1.

Table 1. Description of Positioning Map

Group	Features	Key words
Group A	Soft-Warm	Soft, Simple, Feminine, Comfortable
Group B	Soft-Cool	Sweet, Fun, Clean, Cheerful
Group C	Hard-Warm	Dynamic, Strong, Intensive, Bold
Group D	Hard-Cool	Masterful, Gentle, Solid, Heavy

We designed BioPebble by reference to Group A's device because users felt most comfortable while using this particular device. The form of Group A is preferable because it is streamlined, and its size is designed to be fully covered by the hand. These two features mean that the area which is directly in contact the user's hand is larger than that of the other groups' designs. We analyzed Group A's common features with respect to the whole form, including the left and right side view, decorations, materials, color, and accessories. In BioPebble, in order to maximize the area which is covered by the hand, we designed a bulged center. Accessories such as wheels, displays, buttons and so on, are also made in a similar smooth circular shape. In addition, we designed our sensor based on the metaphor of a stone, because in the healthcare industry, natural stone has conceptual accordance with health and well-being.

After building the basic form of BioPebble, we designed BioPebble in greater detail with the user-centered design (UCD) process for comfort and usable physiological sensor development [15]. UCD is a repetitive and stepwise process. Users first work with a prototype, and from this, developers and designers obtain necessary feedback. During the initial development of BioPebble we collected feedback from the subjects and concretize the details in each step as shown in Fig. 1.

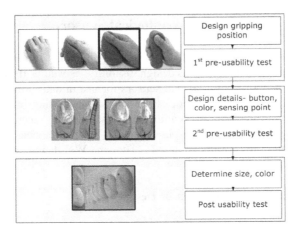

Fig. 1. BioPebble design process

After selecting the shape of our sensor, we sketched details using a 3D modeling program and made prototypes. For the 2nd usability test, we observed the users over a period of about ten to fifteen minutes in order to collect subjective data, as described in Table 2.

Table 2. Requirement for Mobile Physiological Sensor Design

Problem	Requirement
Increased weight over time	Use light weight materials
Increased perspiration during long-term monitoring	Use anti-sweat materials
Sensor positions (especially, temperature sensors) can cause discomfort or pain	Minimize the projection of sensors
Difficulty in maintaining finger attachment during long term monitoring	Attach to the palm for greater stability
Difficulty in establishing common standards for sensor lines and length	Sensor position should avoid individual body characteristic and should be general
Ability to easily change batteries	Place the battery cover on reverse side of sensor
Users are unaware if the device is activated	Simple displays such as LEDs should be able to provide this information
Inconvenience in activating the sensor	Power begins automatically when users hold the sensor
Learning to use the device	The sensing interface and method should be intuitive and easy to understand
Difficulty in maintaining static sensing conditions	Sensors should support wireless technology to allow the user more freedom to measure
Should be pleasant	Gentle curves and lines should be used

From this, we were able to collect feedback from multiple users for further design modifications to the BioPebble design referenced by the previous work [16].

2.2 Real-Time Physiological Signal Processing

BioPebble is equipped with three kinds of sensors, photoplethysmography (PPG) sensor, galvanic skin response (GSR) sensor and skin temperature (SKT) sensor. These three sensory inputs are delivered by Bluetooth communication from BioPebble to a mobile device. In this way, BioPebble can give real time and multiple physiological sensing. In addition, we carefully selected the sensing methods and points. The essential features of any sensing device are the individual sensor points. The position of these separate sensor points on BioPebble is determined according to the range of corrupted signal. For example, a PPG sensor point is located at the thumb position because that position minimizes the problem of differences in finger length among people. In addition, we can obtain the PPG signal clearly on the peripheral. A skin conductance sensor point and a skin temperature sensor point are located under the palm because this type of bio-data is most accurately collected through the palm. Of these sensors, it was decided that the PPG sensor should be located on the periphery but the other sensors (GSR, SKT) do not need to be limited in terms of their sensing position. Based on this theory, we selected the sensing points for stable analysis.

For physiological signal analysis, we apply the following processing steps, as shown in Fig.3. First, three kinds of signal are retrieved from the sensor, and then we remove the baseline of the sensed signal with a band-pass filter. Signal tendency information is gathered after low-pass filtering, and high frequency noise is also removed. For regulating the size of sensed data, down-sampling is then processed. In addition, calibrating the sensory information is done in a modification step. If the sensory data is not sufficient, an interpolation is activated. Second, a feature extraction step is processed. In this step, we utilize the features from the time-domain and frequency-domain. In the case of pulse signals, frequency domain analysis is required. From this step, we compute the basic feature values such as peak to peak intervals, intensity, differences and slopes, and frequency.

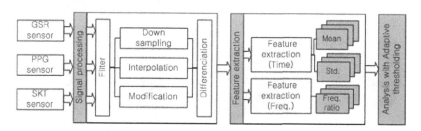

Fig. 3. Steps for Physiological signal processing of BioPebble

In the physiological signal analysis step, finally, we proposed the adaptive physiological signal analysis method. Physiological signals obtained from devices such as mobile phones can have significant variations according to prevailing environmental conditions and any movement of the user. Therefore, if the measurements are taken within a certain time period, they may provide unstable results due to these variations. Also the heart can be sensitive to other conditions, such as outdoor temperatures, the weather, caffeine, and even the mood of the user.

In previous work, it has been reported that thermal stress is influenced by personality, and that gender has an effect on the heart rate [17-18]. Therefore, an integrated analysis considering the user`s condition and context is crucial in physiological signal analysis.

In this section, we applied context awareness technology on a framework for decision making, which provided seamless communication between sensors and services [19]. This framework includes the functions of context integration, inference and decision making, and therefore can easily obtain multiple sensory contexts from sensors in the framework. This multiple contextual information is utilized in the decision making step. In order to get the distribution of data, we collected the data for a week and modeled it using a non-parametric method. The modeled physiological signal was then interpreted by the weighted values which describe the amount of excessive range. We divided the user's condition into two cases: normal and abnormal, and then computed the distribution of each status. The outliers were eliminated from the measurement set.

3   Implementation

In this section, we explain the implementation of BioPebble.   We developed BioPebble in several steps of modeling, pre-usability test and pro-usability test. In the first step, we devised several different gripping shapes: a computer mouse, a joystick, a stone and a bar. These are shown in Fig. 4.

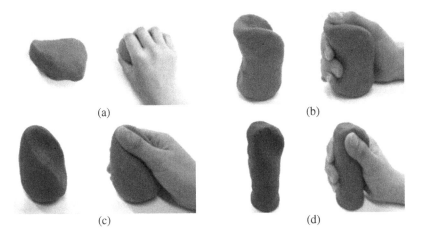

(a)   (b)

(c)   (d)

Fig. 4. Grip design: (a) mouse-type (b) joystick-type (c) stone-type (d) bar-type

From this usability test, we eliminated the designs which did not meet our themes of design, aesthetics, comfort, and stable sensing. The mouse-type prototype met the criteria for comfort to be covered by the hand. However its shape was a little unfamiliar to users. In the case of the joystick sensing device, most users also felt comfortable while gripping it. However, the overall shape did not adequately satisfy the criteria of warmth and softness. The bar-type sensing device was also somewhat comfortable, but there was some space between the user's palm and the device's body. Therefore, this type was not appropriate for measuring signals in a stable manner. From among the four types, we concluded that the stone-type sensing device was the most effective with respect to size, shape and sensation when measuring physiological signals. At the same time, the stone-type sensor was found to be aesthetically pleasing for users. For the pretest, we constructed a prototype of BioPebble, as illustrated in Fig. 5.

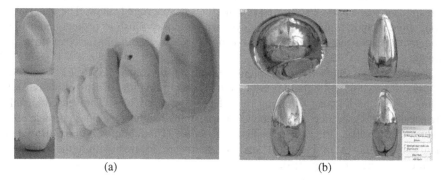

(a)   (b)

Fig. 5. BioPebble prototype (a) mock-up (b) 3D model

We built a 3D model of BioPebble according to the measurement of a mock-up using a CAD program. This modeling data was then used to make the prototype. We obtained the final application with rapid prototyping equipment. From the user survey and data analysis of BioPebble, we obtained the final design given in Fig. 6, which illustrates the front, back, side and top views.

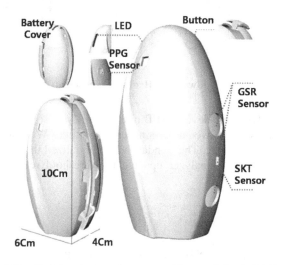

Fig. 6. Detailed description of sensor positions and size in BioPebble

A detailed description of BioPebble is provided in Fig. 6. BioPebble is 6 centimeters long, 4 centimeters wide and 10 centimeters high. It is divided into two pieces: an upper section and a lower section. The battery cover is located on the lower section, and the on/off button is on the top. A PPG sensor is located at the thumb position. GSR and SKT sensors are placed at the side of the sensor, in the palm. For the on/off button, we use a tag switch, which activates only if the tag button is pushed by the index finger. Two LEDs show the status of power and wireless Bluetooth network connection. The final design of our stone-type sensing device has a streamlined shape and all sensor points and lines have a round shape. The materials of BioPebble include a plastic coating cover with a glossy finish to protect against heat and sweat. For a more light-weight sensing device we use a plastic cover to reduce weight.

BioPebble has three kinds of physiological sensor points: GSR, PPG and SKT sensors. It transmits its signal via Bluetooth. The sampling rate of BioPebble is 100Hz which meets the Nyquist sampling rate of heart rate variables. The sensed signal is transferred with a header. The sequence of transmitted signals includes carriage return value, GSR value, PPG value and SKT value. The composition of BioPebble hardware is shown in Fig. 7(a), and the hardware located within the BioPebble prototype is shown in Fig. 7(b).

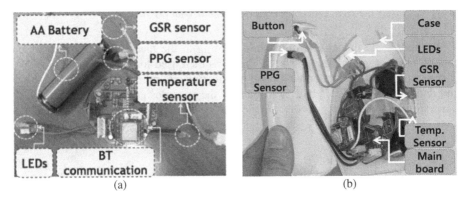

Fig. 7. BioPebble hardware: (a) Hardware component (b) Inside view

For adaptive analysis, we developed BioPebble analysis software which captures, stores and analyzes signals over a certain period of time. We constructed the user model from the stored data set. The standard value initialized the threshold at the first step, and then an adaptive analyzer updated the threshold referenced by the user model.

4   Experimental Analysis

We believe our proposed BioPebble can provide users with a measurably better affect, a more comfortable grip, and stable signal analysis with adaptive threshold. In order to verify this, we conducted three experiments. For the aesthetic appreciation

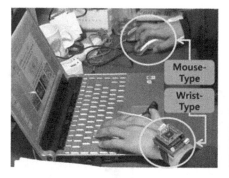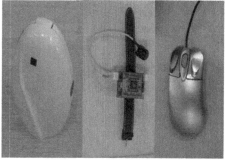

Fig. 8. Usability test with several types of physiological sensing devices (Left: BioPebble, Center: wrist-type device, Right: mouse-type device)

evaluation and satisfaction with sensor positions, we undertook a usability test with 12 subjects, as shown in Fig. 8, and took subjective measures, such as questionnaires, while the subjects were using BioPebble.

The independent variables of this experiment were the type of physiological sensing device: a wrist-type, a mouse-type, or a stone-type device. We chose these devices for evaluating the appropriateness of monitoring devices in the AmI environment. A mouse-type device can monitor the physiological signal while users are working. A wrist-type device can unobtrusively measure changes in physiological status. In this experiment, we used for comparison with BioPebble has been in use since 2004. Dependent variables were error rate, sensing accuracy. We kept the dependent variables constant. Of the 12 subjects, 5 of them were female and 7 were male. 6 of the subjects had engineering backgrounds, 3 were majors in art, and the remainder had no academic background. The average age of participants was 34.5 years old. First we surveyed user profiles, looking at such things as age, gender, occupation and basic background, all of which can have an effect on physiological signal sensing. Basic background information included the length of time on computers, whether subjects normally wear wrist watches, and the usage time of cellular phones. After this basic survey, we allowed the participants to make use of each device sequentially over both long term (over 15 minutes) and short term (within 5 minutes). Finally, we conducted usability test for feedback. In this experiment, we also recorded the degree of the satisfaction about the questionnaire.

4.1 Aesthetic Shape

For aesthetic appreciation, we asked the participants to grade the various devices in terms of attractiveness. The grading rate was from 1 for least attractive, to 5 for most attractive. Fig. 9 shows the results of the aesthetic satisfaction of BioPebble.

Compared to other sensing devices, BioPebble gave the best satisfaction. The average degree of satisfaction was 3.9, while the wrist-type sensing device and the mouse-type sensing device had 3.4 and 2.9 on aesthetic satisfaction, respectively. For

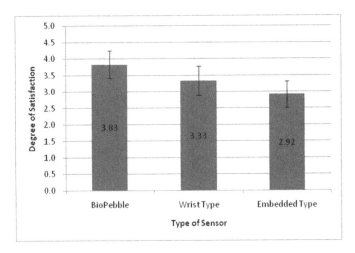

Fig. 9. Aesthetic satisfaction according to the type of sensing device (Degree of satisfaction)

statistical analysis, we used the ANOVA and Tukey's post analysis. There are significant differences among the different types of sensing devices (p=0.039<0.05), in terms of aesthetic satisfaction.

4.2 Comfort Grip

In the second experiment, we surveyed satisfaction in terms of the position of the three sensor points by varying the measurement time. In this investigation, we questioned the participants about their satisfaction degree on these sensor positions and handling comfort.

In the case of sensor position intervention, BioPebble and the mouse-type device were more satisfactory than the wrist-type device. However, the satisfaction decreased in long term monitoring. Normally, the wrist-type device rated better in long term measuring even if the absolute grade record was the lowest among the tested devices. Therefore we concluded that BioPebble had little intervention in long term and short term monitoring compared to the other types of sensors. In the second survey, we observed that BioPebble was the most comfortable for short term monitoring. However the degree of satisfaction also largely diminished when data collection occurred over a longer period of time, for example, 15 minutes. We also did statistical analysis using post analysis method such as ANOVA tests and Tukey tests. In the case of sensor point position comfort, we observed that there were significant differences among the different devices (p=0.026<0.05). In the test for handling comfort, there were significant differences (p=0.0<0.05). BioPebble and the mouse-type device showed the most significant differences. Participants informally provided the following information. BioPebble is designed to be used by just one hand, but participants suggested a sensor that could be used with both hands. Also participants noticed that BioPebble interferes with normal work. Also, in long term monitoring, participants noted increased discomfort in two areas: on the finger tips which measure heart beat, and from slippery surfaces caused by hand perspiration.

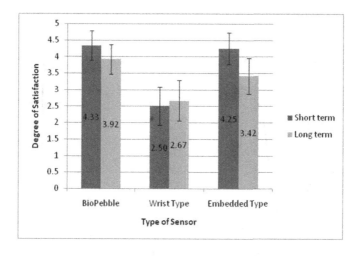

(a)

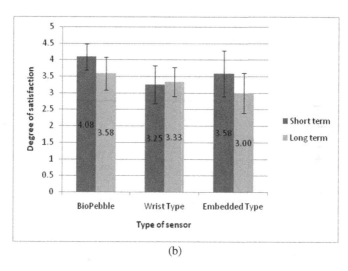

(b)

Fig. 10. Satisfaction in long term and short term monitoring (a) about sensor position (b) about gripping comfort

4.3 Stable Sensing

In this section, we evaluated the performance of the sensors. To do this, we collected signals from the three sensors, GSR, PPG, and SKT over a period of one minute using BioPebble. We analyzed 100 measurements and measured the average response time and response intensity. All results were processed through a normalization function, shown in Fig. 11.

In this experiment, we observed how BioPebble reacts to stimuli. We gave the subjects certain stimulus such as striking, a fright, noisy music and so on. According

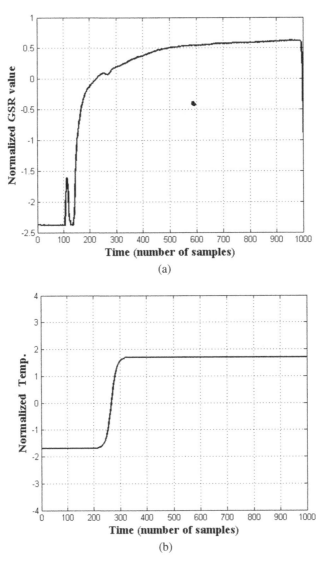

Fig. 11. Distribution of measurements of BioPebble: (a) Normalized GSR (b) Normalized hand temperature

to the type of stimuli, the response time and response intensity can be quite different. However, we selected the average value, excluding the outliers. The responses of BioPebble are summarized in Table 3.

In order to evaluate the stability of BioPebble in sensing capability, we compared the analysis results in the situation where a subject moves during monitoring. Using BioPebble, we collected data when the subject was in the normal body condition.

Table 3. Responses of BioPebble

Sensor type	Response Time (Second)	Response Magnitude (Norm. Value)
GSR	2.35	3
Temp.	2.10	4

From this experiment, we observed that BioPebble gave better stability and more stable results compared to commercial equipment. Analysis results of commercial equipment showed them to be more greatly influenced by the motion artifact.

In addition, we observed the stable sensing had an effect on cognitive aspects of users, such as the intention to measure the physiological status, and agreement to monitor their physiological status. BioPebble reflects some level of cognitive intentions of users because most users agree to measure and monitor the physiological signal before gripping the BioPebble. Comparing to the other devices, BioPebble showed stable sensing results because it supported explicit measures of physiological status. Even though the mouse-type and the wrist-type devices sense signals in a seamless manner, a mouse-type device is sensitive to movement, and a wrist-type device is harder to fix in the sensing position. From this observation, we conclude that for better stable sensing, users need to follow instructions.

5   Ambient Display with Rainbow Shape

Ambient displays use the physical environment as an interface to obtain digital information, engage human senses, and present information by using an object which can be processed in the background of awareness [21]. In an ambient intelligence environment, ambient displays are more useful than conventional displays such as monitors for the engagement of our senses. In previous works, intelligent furniture had been devised in order to display daily information [22]. However, there is no research about physiological information visualization. We developed the physiological signal display taking into account that the end user would be a non-specialist, i.e., one who has no specialized academic background in human physiology. In order to make this signal more understandable for these users, we visualized information through every-day objects such as pots, tangible bars and so on, as in Fig. 12. Some of these objects were used as display tools.

The simple scenario in an AmI environment is as follows. The user holds the BioPebble with one hand, and data is transferred to a mobile PC and LEDs in smart pots and objects. The user can see the information from both the mobile PC and the LEDs of the smart pots and trees. This information enables the user to understand their entire body condition from the ambient display embedded in the background. In one of the applications, we implemented a pot with a display of a rainbow shape, as seen in Fig.13. The mapping of the processed physiological signals from BioPebble to this ambient display in a rainbow shape is suitable for showing the steps of digital information through different colors and levels.

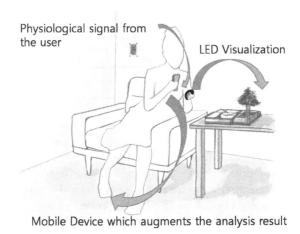

Physiological signal from the user

LED Visualization

Mobile Device which augments the analysis result

Fig. 12. Application scenario in a smart home environment with BioPebble and ambient display

Fig. 13. Implementation of rainbow/stripe visualization with a pot

Each line of the rainbow represents a measured signal. A red line indicates the pulse signal of the heart and the orange line shows skin conductance. The green line indicates hand temperature. Each sensing signal is mapped in each line of the rainbow. The mapping from BioPebble to rainbow display linearly represents the step of sensed values by referencing the threshold value. The stripe display also represents data linearly. The sensed values are divided into abnormal and normal condition. Table 4 shows how normal and abnormal conditions are identified. Each level is decided by the size of LEDs in the rainbow display. The division of conditions is referenced by each value of the sensed signals. If the user's sensed values are abnormal, the rainbow display will show an irregular shape, as shown in Fig.14 (b).

This application was demonstrated at the Korean HCI conference (Feb. 13~15, 2008). During the exhibition in the KHCI conference, we had the opportunity to do field tests of BioPebble. Most users showed interest in the system of BioPebble and the rainbow display. According to individual interests and academic background,

Table 4. The identification of normal/abnormal conditions

Conditions	Body Temperature		Skin Conductance		Heart rate	
	Level(8)	Values	Level(14)	Values	Level(16)	Values
Abnormal	1-4,6-8	otherwise	1-9, 11-14	otherwise	1-11,13-16	otherwise
Normal	5	29-31	10	1700 ~ 1800	12	80~90

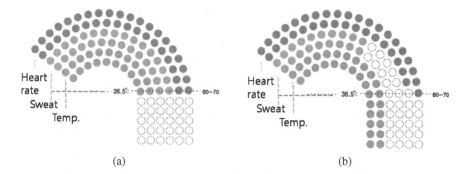

(a)   (b)

Fig. 14. Physiological information visualization with Rainbow Display (a) normal condition (b) abnormal condition

responses were quite different. Participants who have interests in sensor development expressed curiosity about the sensing positions and sensing methods. They agreed that BioPebble is satisfactory in terms of stable and comfortable sensing. Participants used increased movement, such as running and jumping in order to check and evaluate analysis results. Most of them felt that the measurements and analysis results seemed accurate. Participants from design backgrounds focused on the meaning of the stone-type sensor and well-being care applications. They said that the pot with the rainbow display and BioPebble was consistent with the concept of well-being. In addition, after simple observation, they were quickly able to understand how to grip BioPebble, thus confirming our claim that BioPebble is intuitively usable. From these field tests, we believe that BioPebble can be readily used as a physiological sensing device applicable in a daily life.

6   Conclusion

In this work, we propose a stone-type physiological sensing device, BioPebble, which maximizes the gripping sensation from the user and increases the aesthetic appreciation in short and long term monitoring. We compared BioPebble's performance in these areas with wrist-type and mouse-type sensing devices. BioPebble supports real-time, wireless and multiple signal sensing and provides adaptive analysis based on contextual information. In future work, we will evaluate the BioPebble focusing on hedonic and ergonomic qualities [23], and elaborate the design to allow users greater comfort in long term monitoring situations. We will also develop a computational model for context based physiological signal analysis. We will apply this model with a basic standard data set and evaluate the user model with scientific theory. The proposed sensing and analysis method could be applied to hand phones or mobile PCs. Our goal would be to reduce user awareness of the health monitoring process.

References

1. Ilkka, K., Juha, P., Mark, V.G.: Health monitoring in the home of the future. IEEE Eng. Med. Biol. Mag. 22, 66–73 (2003)
2. WenChung, K., WeiHsin, C., ChunKuo, Y., ChinMing, H., ShengYuan, L.: Portable Real-Time Homecare System Design with Digital Camera Platform. IEEE Trans. Consumer Electron. 51, 1035–1041 (2005)
3. Marketta, N., Rafael, G.F., Eija, K., Jorge, L.G.: Supporting Independent Living of the Elderly with Mobile-Centric Ambient Intelligence: User Evaluation of Three Scenarios. In: Schiele, B., Dey, A.K., Gellersen, H., de Ruyter, B., Tscheligi, M., Wichert, R., Aarts, E., Buchmann, A. (eds.) AmI 2007. LNCS, vol. 4794, pp. 91–107. Springer, Heidelberg (2007)
4. Emmanuel, M.T., Stephen, I., Kent, L.: Portable Wireless Sensors for Object Usage Sensing in the Home: Challenges and Practicalities. In: Schiele, B., Dey, A.K., Gellersen, H., de Ruyter, B., Tscheligi, M., Wichert, R., Aarts, E., Buchmann, A. (eds.) AmI 2007. LNCS, vol. 4794, pp. 19–37. Springer, Heidelberg (2007)
5. Erik, G., Luca, P., Alessandro, P., Alessia, R., Giuseppe, A.: Assemblies of Heterogeneous Technologies at the Neonatal Intensive Care Unit. In: Schiele, B., Dey, A.K., Gellersen, H., de Ruyter, B., Tscheligi, M., Wichert, R., Aarts, E., Buchmann, A. (eds.) AmI 2007. LNCS, vol. 4794, pp. 340–357. Springer, Heidelberg (2007)
6. DongWan, R., Changseok, B.: Design of The Wearable Gadgets for Life-Log Services based on UTC. IEEE Trans. Consumer Electron. 53, 1477–1482 (2007)
7. Robert, M., Neil, J.M., Paul, H., Peter, J.T., Martin, A.S.: A Wearable Physiological Sensor Suite for Unobtrusive Monitoring of Physiological and Cognitive State. In: 29th Annual International Conference of the IEEE EMBS, pp. 5276–5281. IEEE Press, New York (2007)
8. Rosalind, W.P., Jocelyn, S.: The Galvactivator: a glove that senses and communicates skin conductivity. In: 9th International Conference on Human-Computer Interaction (2001)
9. Sokwoo, R., BooHo, Y., Haruhiko, H.A.: Artifact-Resistant Power-Efficient Design of Finger-Ring Plethysmographic Sensors. IEEE Trans. Biomed. Eng. 48, 795–805 (2001)
10. Urs, A., Jamie, A.W., Paul, L., Gerhard, T., François, D., Michel, B., Fatou, K., Eran, B.S., Fabrizio, C., Luca, C., Andrea, B., Dror, S., Menachem, A., Etienne, H., Rolf, S., Milica, V.: AMON: A Wearable Multi parameter Medical Monitoring and Alert System. IEEE T. Inf. Technol. Biomed. 8, 415–427 (2004)
11. Toshiyo, T., Tatsuo, T., Mitsuhiro, O., Mikiko, Y.: Fully automated health monitoring system in the home. Med. Eng. Phys. 20, 573–579 (1998)
12. Matthew, J.H., Peter, R.S.: Artifact reduction in photoplethysmography. Appl. Optics 37, 7437–7446 (1998)
13. Michael, S., Carl, M., Alex, P.: Wearable feedback systems for rehabilitation. Journal of NeuroEngineering and Rehabilitation 2, 17 (2005)
14. Winston, H., Wu, M.A., Batalin, L.K., Au, A.A., Bui, T., William, J.K.: Context-aware Sensing of Physiological Signals. In: 29th Annual International Conference of the IEEE EMBS, pp. 5271–5275. IEEE Press, New York (2007)

15. Donald, A.N., Stephen, W.D.: User Centered System Design. Lawrence Erlbaum Associates, Mahwah (1986)
16. Francine, G., Chris, K., John, S., Malcolm, B., Richard, M.: Design for Wearability. In: 2nd International Symposium of Wearable Computers, pp. 116–122. IEEE CS Press, Los Alamitos (1998)
17. LeBlanc, J., Ducharme, M.B., Pasto, L., Thompson, M.: Response to thermal stress and personality. Physiol. Behav. 80, 69–74 (2003)
18. Rod, K.D., Yoshio, N., Melissa, E.G., Ray, W.T., Andrea, L.D., Steven, N.B.: Heart rate variability, trait anxiety, and perceived stress among physically fit men and women. International Journal of Psychophysiology 37, 121–133 (2000)
19. Dongpyo, H., Youngjung, S., Ahyoung, C., Umar, R., Woontack, W.: wear-UCAM: A Toolkit for Mobile User Interactions in Smart Environments. In: Sha, E., Han, S.-K., Xu, C.-Z., Kim, M.-H., Yang, L.T., Xiao, B. (eds.) EUC 2006. LNCS, vol. 4096, pp. 1047–1057. Springer, Heidelberg (2006)
20. Yoosoo, O., Woontack, W.: A Unified Application Service Model for ubiHome by Exploiting Intelligent Context-Awareness. In: Murakami, H., Nakashima, H., Tokuda, H., Yasumura, M. (eds.) UCS 2004. LNCS, vol. 3598, pp. 192–202. Springer, Heidelberg (2005)
21. Wisneski, C., Ishii, H., Dahley, A., Gorbet, M., Brave, S., Ullmer, B., Yarin, P.: Ambient Displays: Turning Architectual Space into an Interface between People and Digital Information. In: Streitz, N.A., Konomi, S., Burkhardt, H.-J. (eds.) CoBuild 1998. LNCS, vol. 1370, pp. 22–32. Springer, Heidelberg (1998)
22. Hiroko, S., Youichi, H., Yukinobu, M., Takeshi, H.: Information-Accessing Furniture to Make Our Everyday Lives More Comfortable. IEEE Trans. Consumer Electron. 52, 173–178 (2006)
23. Hassenzahl, M., Platz, A., Burmester, M., Lehner, K.: Hedonic and Ergonomic Quality Aspects Determine a Software's Appeal. In: CHI Letters 2, 1, pp. 201–208. ACM Press, New York (2000)

Author Index